HISTORICAL DICTIONARIES OF U.S. DIPLOMACY
Jon Woronoff, Series Editor

Historical Dictionary of U.S. Diplomacy since the Cold War

Tom Lansford

Historical Dictionaries of
U.S. Diplomacy, No. 6

The Scarecrow Press, Inc.
Lanham, Maryland • Toronto • Plymouth, UK
2007

08 April 14
B+T
75.- (75.-)

SCARECROW PRESS, INC.

Published in the United States of America
by Scarecrow Press, Inc.
A wholly owned subsidary of
The Rowman & Littlefield Publishing Group, Inc.
4501 Forbes Boulevard, Suite 200, Lanham, Maryland 20706
www.scarecrowpress.com

Estover Road
Plymouth PL6 7PY
United Kingdom

Copyright © 2007 by Tom Lansford

British Library Cataloguing in Publication Information Available

Library of Congress Cataloging-in-Publication Data

Lansford, Tom.
  Historical dictionary of U.S. diplomacy since the Cold War / Tom Lansford.
    p. cm. — (Historical dictionaries of U.S. diplomacy ; no. 6)
  Includes bibliographical references.
  ISBN-13: 978-0-8108-5635-6 (hardcover : alk. paper)
  ISBN-10: 0-8108-5635-2 (hardcover : alk. paper)
  1. United States—Foreign relations—1989—Dictionaries. I. Title. II. Title:
Historical dictionary of US diplomacy since the Cold War.

E840.L355 2007
973.928003—dc22

                                                        2007016182

Contents

Editor's Foreword

Few periods in American diplomacy were ushered in with such hope and optimism as that following the end of the Cold War and also the demise of the Soviet Union. Gone were the constant, terrifying threats of mutual nuclear destruction and even the nasty local wars that dangerously if indirectly pitted the great powers against one another. Moreover, the United States had won, or so it seemed, and had become the only superpower in the world. It could not really be said that everything changed with the terrorist attacks of 11 September 2001, but certainly much did. Obviously, the United States had to defend itself from terrorism and even launch a war on terror. It did seem plausible that America should sort things out in Afghanistan, where the center of Islamic terrorism was then located. But that it should then go to war against the regime of Saddam Hussein of Iraq, getting bogged down in the deadliest and most frustrating war since Vietnam, was less obvious and was bitterly contested at the time, within the country and among its allies. This, combined with such problems as nuclear proliferation, drug trafficking, unpleasant side effects of globalization, and still many local wars, has given the new era a decidedly negative twist.

This is the broad background to *Historical Dictionary of U.S. Diplomacy since the Cold War*, and it is described in general terms in the introduction and charted, step by step, in the chronology. The details are then examined more closely in the dictionary section. Naturally, there are entries on the most noteworthy figures, starting with Ronald Reagan, the last of the cold warriors but also the first to make policy for the new era, and including not only American but numerous foreign leaders and decision makers. There are also entries on the major crises, including Afghanistan, Iraq, Somalia, and North Korea, and crucial issues such as arms control, drug trafficking, and trade relations. Other entries deal with the major institutions and organizations and some of the new concepts and terminology. This period, more so than some earlier ones, has already generated a considerable literature—one that is constantly growing but in which it is still hard to find in-depth, long-term, and especially objective analysis, thus making the bibliography a particularly important component.

This new addition to the series of Historical Dictionaries of U.S. Diplomacy is most welcome, since it is the period we are living through today, and the more we know about it, the better. The author, Tom Lansford, is an associate professor of political science at the University of Southern Mississippi, where he teaches international relations and American foreign policy, among other things. He has already written extensively on these subjects, including a book he authored on U.S. foreign policy on Afghanistan and others he coedited on transatlantic security, America's war on terror, and the George W. Bush administration. He is associated with several learned journals in the area, among them, *White House Studies*, *Horizons*, and *Politics and Ethics Review*. This varied and relevant experience has stood him in good stead in this very useful and handy guide to American foreign policy in—as ever—troubled times.

Jon Woronoff
Series Editor

Acronyms and Abbreviations

ABM	antiballistic missile
ACI	Andean Counterdrug Initiative
AGOA	African Growth and Opportunity Act
AIDS	Acquired Immune Deficiency Syndrome
AMIS	African Union Mission in Sudan
ANC	African National Congress
ANZUS	Australia–New Zealand–United States [alliance]
AP	Alianza Popular (Spain)
APEC	Asia-Pacific Economic Cooperation [forum]
ASEAN	Association of Southeast Asian Nations
BJP	Bharatiya Janata Party (India)
BMD	ballistic missile defense
BWC	Biological Weapons Convention
CAFTA	Central American Free Trade Agreement
CBD	Convention on Biological Diversity
CDU	Christian Democratic Union (Germany/West Germany)
CFE	Conventional Forces in Europe [Treaty]
CFR	Council on Foreign Relations (U.S.)
CFSP	Common Foreign and Security Program (Europe)
CIA	Central Intelligence Agency (U.S.)
CIS	Commonwealth of Independent States
CITES	Convention on International Trade in Endangered Species of Wildlife Fauna and Flora
CJTF	Combined and Joint Task Force [System] (NATO)
CPA	Coalition Provisional Authority (Iraq)
CSCE	Conference on Security and Cooperation in Europe
CTBT	Comprehensive Test Ban Treaty
CWC	Chemical Weapons Convention

DHS	Department of Homeland Security (U.S.)
DNI	director of national intelligence
DRC	Democratic Republic of the Congo
DR-CAFTA	Dominican Republic–Central American Free Trade Agreement
DTSI	Defense Trade Security Initiative (U.S.)
EC	European Community
ECB	European Central Bank
ECOWAS	Economic Community of West African States
EEZ	exclusive economic zone
EMI	European Monetary Institute
EMU	European Monetary Union
EPC	European Political Cooperation
ERRF	European Rapid Reaction Force
ESDI	European Security and Defense Identity
ESDP	European Security and Defense Policy
EU	European Union
FARC	Revolutionary Armed Forces of Colombia
FBI	Federal Bureau of Investigation (U.S.)
FDP	Free Democratic Party (West Germany)
FMF	Foreign Military Financing [program] (U.S.)
FNLA	National Front for the Liberation of Angola
FRG	Federal Republic of Germany
FTA	free trade agreement
FTAA	Free Trade Area of the Americas
G-7	Group of Seven [Industrialized Nations]
G-8	Group of Eight [Industrialized Nations]
GATT	General Agreement on Tariffs and Trade
GDP	gross domestic product
GDR	German Democratic Republic
HIV	Human Immunodeficiency Virus
ICC	International Criminal Court
ICCPR	International Covenant on Civil and Political Rights
ICTY	International Criminal Tribunal for the Former Yugoslavia
IFOR	Implementation Force, Bosnia (UN)
IMF	International Monetary Fund
INTERFET	International Force East Timor (UN)

ISA	International Seabed Authority
ISAF	International Security Assistance Force (UN/NATO)
IWC	International Whaling Commission
KEDO	Korean Peninsula Energy Development Organization
LDP	Liberal Democratic Party (Japan)
LURD	Liberians United for Reconciliation and Democracy
MEADS	Medium Extended Air Defense System
MPLA	Movement for the Liberation of Angola
MVR	Movimiento V República [Fifth Republic Movement] (Venezuela)
NAAEC	North American Agreement for Environmental Cooperation
NAALC	North American Agreement on Labor Competition
NAFTA	North American Free Trade Agreement
NATO	North Atlantic Treaty Organization
NCS	National Security Council (U.S.)
NGO	nongovernmental organization
NPT	[Nuclear] Nonproliferation Treaty
OAS	Organization of American States
OAU	Organization of African Unity
ONDCP	Office of National Drug Control Policy (U.S.)
OPCW	Organization for the Prohibition of Chemical Weapons
OPEC	Organization of Petroleum Exporting Countries
OSCE	Organization for Security and Cooperation in Europe
PDF	Panamanian Defense Forces
PfP	Partnership for Peace
PLO	Palestine Liberation Organization
PNA	Palestinian National Authority
POW	prisoner of war
PP	Partido Popular (Spain)
PRC	People's Republic of China
PSC	Political and Security Committee (EU)
PTBT	Partial Test Ban Treaty
QDR	Quadrennial Defense Review (U.S.)
RPF	Rwandan Patriotic Front
SACEUR	Supreme Allied Commander, Europe (NATO)
SACO	Special Action Committee on Okinawa (U.S.–Japan)

SDF	Self-Defense Force (Japan)
SDI	Strategic Defense Initiative (U.S.)
SFOR	Stabilization Force, Bosnia (NATO)
SII	Structural Impediments Initiative (U.S.–Japan)
SORT	Strategic Offensive Reductions Treaty (U.S.–Russia)
SPD	Social Democratic Party (Germany/West Germany)
START	Strategic Arms Reduction Treaty (U.S.–USSR)
TIFA	Trade and Investment Framework Agreement
UK	United Kingdom
UN	United Nations
UNAMIR	United Nations Assistance Mission for Rwanda
UNFCCC	United Nations Framework Convention on Climate Change
UNITAF	United Task Force (Somalia)
UNOSOM	United Nations Operation in Somalia
UNSCR	United Nations Security Council Resolution
UNTAET	United Nations Transitional Administration in East Timor
USSR	Union of Soviet Socialist Republics
WEAG	Western European Armaments Group
WEU	Western European Union
WMD	weapon(s) of mass destruction
WTC	World Trade Center (New York City)
WTO	World Trade Organization

Chronology

1989 February–December: Eastern European countries that were part of the Soviet bloc adopt democratic governments in mostly peaceful regime changes. Washington supports the democratic transitions, but avoids direct involvement in the overthrow of the Communist regimes. **15 February:** The last Soviet troops withdraw from Afghanistan. **April–June:** Prodemocracy demonstrations in Tiananmen Square in Beijing lead to widespread suppression and repression by the government. **4 November:** An estimated 500,000 gather in East Berlin to protest Communist rule. Similar protests across the country undermine the Communist government. **9 November:** The Berlin Wall falls. Crowds demolish portions of the barrier after the German Democratic Republic opens border crossings and removes travel restrictions to the West. **2–3 December:** U.S. president George H. W. Bush and Soviet premier Mikhail Gorbachev meet at the Malta Summit and agree to develop a treaty to reduce conventional forces in Europe. **20 December:** Following increasing tensions between the United States and Panama, U.S. forces invade the country to depose dictator Manuel Noriega, whose regime is accused by the Bush administration of drug trafficking and political repression.

1990 3 January: Noriega surrenders to American troops in Panama. American troops continue to provide security while an interim government replaces the dictatorship. **15 January:** The American embassy in Lima, Peru, is bombed by the Tupac Amaru insurgency group. **30 May:** Reformist politician Boris Yeltsin is elected president of the Russian Federation. **2 August:** Iraq invades Kuwait. The United Nations (UN) Security Council adopts Resolution 660, condemning the Iraqi invasion and calling on the regime of Saddam Hussein to immediately withdraw its forces. **8 August:** Bush delivers a major address on the Iraqi invasion and articulates a series of American goals, including the withdrawal of the

Iraqi forces and the restoration of the Kuwaiti government. **12 September:** The Two-Plus-Four Treaty is signed by the German Democratic Republic, Federal Republic of Germany, Soviet Union, United Kingdom, United States, and France. The agreement allows the two Germanys to be unified. **3 October:** Germany is reunified as a member of the European Community and the North Atlantic Treaty Organization (NATO). **5 November:** The United States imposes a range of economic and other sanctions on Iraq. **17 November:** The Conventional Forces in Europe Treaty is signed by members of NATO and the Warsaw Pact. **29 November:** The UN Security Council adopts Resolution 678, which authorizes the use of force to compel Iraq to withdraw from Kuwait. The resolution prompts countries to join the American-led "coalition of the willing," which opposes the Iraqi regime.

1991 12 January: Congress grants Bush the authority to use military force to liberate Kuwait. **17 January:** U.S.-led coalition forces launch an air campaign against Iraq, thereby starting the Persian Gulf War. **18–19 January:** Iraqi agents attempt bombings of the U.S. ambassador's residence in Jakarta, Indonesia, and an American library in Manila, Philippines. **1 February:** Bush and Yeltsin declare the Cold War officially ended during a summit at Camp David. **23 February:** The United Nations (UN) Security Council enacts Resolution 687, which requires Baghdad to allow UN inspectors to search for and destroy weapons of mass destruction in Iraq. **24–28 February:** The coalition ground offensive drives Iraqi forces out of Kuwait. **3 April:** Allied air units begin to enforce a "no-fly" zone over northern Iraq to protect ethnic Kurds. **5 April:** Resolution 688 is adopted by the UN Security Council, authorizing international humanitarian aid for the Iraqi Kurds. **6 April:** A UN-sponsored cease-fire agreement is signed by Iraq. **1 July:** The Warsaw Pact is dissolved by mutual consent of its members. **31 July:** Strategic Arms Reduction Treaty (START I) is signed by the United States and Soviet Union. The accord reduces the number of nuclear warheads in each country by one-third. **19–21 August:** Communist hard-liners in Moscow launch a failed coup against Gorbachev. Yeltsin becomes the dominant political figure in Russia. **29 August:** The Communist Party is banned in Russia. **7–8 November:** North Atlantic Treaty Organization (NATO) leaders create a new strategic plan for the alliance designed to maintain the relevancy of the organization in the post–Cold War world. NATO also creates new bodies to increase security and political cooperation with the states of the former Warsaw Pact. **8 December:** The Commonwealth of Independent States is created by former socialist republics of the Soviet Union. **10 December:** The United States supports a UN Security Council resolution that creates a register of conventional arms and weapons of individual states.

1992 1 January: The Union of Soviet Socialist Republics is dissolved. **1 January:** Boutros Boutros-Ghali of Egypt begins terms as secretary-general of the United Nations (UN). **7 February:** The Treaty of European Union (Maastricht Treaty) is signed by members of the European Community (EC). It transitions the EC into the European Union and initiates the drive for a single currency, the euro. **March:** Fighting breaks out in Kabul between supporters of the pro-Russian government and the Afghan resistance. **24 March:** An Open Skies Treaty is signed by members of the Conference on Security and Cooperation in Europe. The agreement calls on states to open their airspace to unarmed reconnaissance flights by other states, with all signatories to have access to any information gathered. **April:** Civil war between Serbs, Bosnians, and Croats begins in the former Yugoslav republic of Bosnia-Herzegovina. **7 April:** The United States offers diplomatic recognition to the states of the former Yugoslavia. **21 May:** North Atlantic Treaty Organization (NATO) and the Western European Union (WEU) begin regular meetings. **3–14 June:** An Earth Summit is held in Rio de Janeiro, Brazil. Agreement on the UN Framework Convention on Climate Change, forerunner to the Kyoto Protocol, is finalized. **8 June:** The Senate ratifies the International Covenant on Civil and Political Rights (ICCPR). The ICCPR was drafted in 1976, but the Senate approved the agreement only after adding exclusions that prevented provisions of the accord from being incorporated into domestic law. **13 August:** James A. Baker III resigns as secretary of state to manage the reelection campaign of George H. W. Bush. **27 August:** Allied aircraft commence enforcement of a no-fly zone over southern Iraq to protect Shiites. **2 September:** NATO agrees to provide support for the UN and other multilateral bodies in the former Yugoslavia. **16 September:** Noriega is convicted of money laundering and drug trafficking and sentenced to 40 years in prison. **2 October:** NATO creates a rapid reaction force to respond to crises and undertake humanitarian missions. **23 October:** The Cuban Democracy Act becomes law, tightening the economic embargo on the island. **3 November:** William J. "Bill" Clinton is elected president of the United States. **22 November:** NATO and WEU naval forces begin operations in the Adriatic in support of the UN arms embargo on the former Yugoslavia. **2 December:** Bush authorizes the deployment of U.S. forces to Somalia as part of an international humanitarian mission. Seven days later, the first of 25,000 American troops arrive in Somalia. **8 December:** Lawrence S. Eagleburger is appointed secretary of state. **17 December:** The North American Free Trade Agreement is signed by the leaders of Canada, Mexico, and the United States. **28 December:** Somali warlords agree to U.S.-brokered cease-fire.

1993   3 January: Strategic Arms Reduction Treaty (START II) is signed by the United States and the Commonwealth of Independent States. It attempts to cut the nuclear arsenals of the two former superpowers by almost 50 percent. **13 January:** The United States signs the Chemical Weapons Convention. **13 January:** Bush orders military strikes against 100 Iraqi air defense and radar facilities in retaliation for repeated violations of the northern and southern no-fly zones. **20 January:** Warren M. Christopher becomes secretary of state upon Clinton's inauguration. **21 January:** North Atlantic Treaty Organization (NATO) approves guidelines to integrate the Eurocorps. **21 January:** Leslie Aspin Jr. is sworn in as secretary of defense. **26 January:** Clinton orders cruise missile attacks on Iraqi intelligence facilities. **5 February:** R. James Woolsey is sworn in as director of the Central Intelligence Agency. **26 February:** A terrorist car-bombing of Tower One of the World Trade Center in New York leaves six dead and more than 1,000 wounded. Ten suspects will subsequently be tried and convicted of the attack. **27 March:** Jiang Zemin becomes president of the People's Republic of China. **12 April:** NATO takes on no-fly zone enforcement operations over Bosnia as part of the broader United Nations (UN) peacekeeping mission. **14 April:** Iraqi intelligence agents try to assassinate former president Bush during a visit to Kuwait. **May:** Samuel P. Huntington publishes his influential essay, "Clash of Civilizations," in the journal *Foreign Affairs*. **4 May:** The United States turns over command of the Somali peacekeeping mission to the UN. **5 June:** Somali militias massacre 24 Pakistani peacekeepers. The UN subsequently launches a series of unsuccessful missions to capture warlord Mohamed Farrah Aidid. **26 June:** The United States launches missile strikes against Iraq in retaliation for the plot to assassinate Bush. **13 September:** The Oslo Accords are signed between Israel and the Palestinians, calling for mutual recognition and the withdrawal of Israeli forces from occupied territories. A transitional government, the Palestinian National Authority, is created. **3–4 October:** The Battle of Mogadishu leaves 18 American soldiers dead and one captured. **7 October:** Clinton announces a withdrawal of U.S. forces by March. **14 October:** Captured American helicopter pilot Michael Durant is freed by Somali militias.

1994 1 January: North American Free Trade Agreement takes effect. **10–12 January:** At North Atlantic Treaty Organization's (NATO) Brussels Summit, the alliance creates the Partnership for Peace program for former Soviet bloc countries and endorses the creation of a European Security and Defense Identity. **14 January:** The Kremlin Accords, a series of arms control agreements, are signed by Clinton and Yeltsin in Moscow. Among other measures, the accords require the two countries to stop targeting each other with nuclear weapons and provide a strategy to dismantle the remaining Soviet-era nuclear weapons in the states of the former Soviet Union. **3 February:** Clinton announces the lifting of the trade embargo on Vietnam. **3 February:** William J. Perry is appointed secretary of defense. **24 February:** Baruch Goldstein, a U.S. citizen and right-wing Israeli extremist, attacks Muslim worshippers at a mosque in Hebron, Israel, killing 29 and causing renewed conflict between Arabs and Israelis. **10 April:** NATO launches air strikes against Serb positions following attacks on ethnic Bosnians and Croats by ethnic Serbs and soldiers of the Serb-controlled former Yugoslavian army. **8–10 July:** The Group of Seven industrialized nations invites Russia to participate in its meetings at the Naples Summit. **13 August:** NATO secretary-general Manfred Wörner dies in office. **31 August:** The last Russian troops withdraw from Germany. **3 September:** A NATO study recommends enlarging the alliance to include states from the former Soviet bloc. **8 September:** The final Allied troops withdraw from Berlin following a ceremony in honor of their presence through the Cold War. **17 October:** Willy Claes of Belgium is chosen to be secretary-general of NATO. **21 October:** The Framework Agreement with North Korea is signed in an unsuccessful effort to halt Pyongyang's nuclear weapons program. **26 October:** Under U.S. auspices, Israel and Jordan sign a peace treaty. **6 November:** The United Nations Convention on the Law of the Sea comes into force. The Senate refused to ratify it because of objections to its prohibition on seabed mining (despite amendments to the convention in 1994 to address these American concerns). **8 November:** In a historic election, Republicans regain control of Congress for the first time since 1956, winning 54 formerly Democratic seats in the House of Representatives and nine seats in the Senate. **5–6 December:** At the Budapest Summit of the Conference on Security and Cooperation in Europe, the organization decides to change its name to the Organization for Security and Cooperation in Europe and seek a greater role in transatlantic security. **11 December:** At the Miami Summit, representatives of the countries of the Western Hemisphere meet to launch discussions on a potential Free Trade Area of the Americas.

1995   1 January: The World Trade Organization is created. **1 January:** A four-month cease-fire is signed by factions involved in the Bosnian civil war. During the armistice, the parties agree to negotiate a settlement to the conflict. **1 January:** The General Agreement on Trade and Services (GATS) enters into force. The GATS extends to the services sector free-trade measures that already existed for merchandise and products. **10 May:** John M. Deutch becomes director of the Central Intelligence Agency. **2 June:** A U.S. fighter aircraft is downed by Serb antiaircraft missiles. The pilot is rescued five days later. **11 July:** Clinton announces the resumption of diplomatic relations with Vietnam. **30 August:** North Atlantic Treaty Organization (NATO) launches air strikes following Serb attacks on Sarajevo. **4–15 September:** The United Nations (UN) Fourth World Conference on Women is held in Beijing. First Lady Hillary Clinton leads the U.S. delegation to the event. **13 September:** A grenade is fired at the U.S. embassy in Moscow by unknown assailants, ostensibly in response to NATO air strikes against the Serbs. **28 September:** The interim agreement on implementing the Oslo Accords is signed. **1–21 November:** Negotiations in Ohio result in the Dayton Accords, which divide Bosnia into a Serb republic and a joint Bosnian-Croat federation. The agreement also allows the deployment of a NATO-led peacekeeping mission. **13 November:** Terrorists bomb an American military facility in Riyadh, Saudi Arabia, killing more than 40. **1 December:** Javier Solana of Spain becomes the secretary-general of NATO after his predecessor Claes is forced to resign because of ethical questions over his involvement in illicit arms procurement. **14 December:** The Dayton Accords are formally signed in Paris.

1996   13 January: Russia deploys troops as part of the North Atlantic Treaty Organization–led peacekeeping mission in Bosnia. **March:** A Taiwan Strait crisis occurs following People's Republic of China military exercises and the subsequent deployment of American naval forces to protect Taiwan. **March:** Amman allows Allied aircraft to fly through Jordanian airspace to enforce the no-fly zones over Iraq. **25 June:** Terrorists explode a car bomb outside the Khobar Towers American military housing facility in Saudi Arabia, killing 20 and wounding 372. **3 September:** The United States expands the northern and southern no-fly zones so that they cover 60 percent of Iraq. **10 September:** The Comprehensive Test Ban Treaty is approved by the United Nations (UN) General Assembly. **5 November:** Clinton is reelected president. **17 December:** Kofi Annan is elected secretary-general of the UN by the General Assembly.

1997   18 January: Israel and the Palestinians finalize an agreement on the withdrawal of troops from Hebron. **23 January:** Madeleine K. Albright is sworn in as secretary of state. **24 January:** William S. Cohen becomes secretary of defense. **12 April:** The United States signs the World Intellectual Property Organization Copyright Treaty. The agreement extends protections on intellectual property, including artistic productions and even computer programs. **May–July:** The East Asian Financial Crisis results in a dramatic downturn in the economies of Hong Kong, Indonesia, Malaysia, the Philippines, South Korea, and Thailand. **19 May:** The first Quadrennial Defense Review is published. **27 May:** The Founding Act is signed by the North Atlantic Treaty Organization (NATO) and Russia. The measure increases cooperation between the former Cold War enemies and opens the way for NATO expansion among the former states of the Soviet bloc. **8 July:** At the Madrid Summit, NATO invites the Czech Republic, Hungary, and Poland to join the alliance. **9 July:** NATO signs the Charter on Distinctive Partnership with Ukraine to enhance security cooperation and collaboration. **11 July:** George Tenet becomes director of the Central Intelligence Agency. **24 October:** The NATO-Russia Permanent Joint Council is created to provide Moscow with a permanent, though nonvoting, seat to discuss alliance issues. **3–4 December:** An international convention in Ottawa, Canada, finalizes the Land Mine Treaty (Ottawa Treaty). The agreement bans antipersonnel land mines. The Clinton administration refuses to sign the accord, a stance continued by the subsequent George W. Bush administration.

1998   19 January: The United States and the People's Republic of China sign the Agreement on Establishing a Consultation Mechanism to Strengthen Military Maritime Safety, which creates a range of measures to reduce tensions and prevent military escalations between the two countries. **29 January:** The United States and Russia sign the International Space Station Agreement. **30 April:** The Senate approves North Atlantic Treaty Organization enlargement to include the Czech Republic, Hungary, and Poland. **11–13 May:** India conducts a series of five nuclear tests at its Pokhran facility. These tests are followed by reciprocal nuclear explosions by Pakistan. **15–17 May:** Russia becomes part of the Group of Seven, which is renamed the Group of Eight at the Birmingham United Kingdom (United Kingdom [UK]) Summit. **21 May:** The Agreement on the International Dolphin Conservation Program is signed in Washington by the United States, the European Union (EU), and 12 other nations. **17 June:** The Rome Statute on the International Criminal Court is signed. The United States refuses to sign the treaty. **7 August:** Simultaneous Al Qaeda terrorist attacks on the U.S. embassies in Nairobi, Kenya, and Dar-es-Salaam, Tanzania, kill 257 and injure more than 4,000. **14 August:** Congress enacts the Iraqi Breach of International Obligations Act, which authorizes the president to take all appropriate action to force Iraq to comply with its international obligations. **20 August:** American forces launch cruise-missile attacks on suspected terrorist facilities in Afghanistan and Sudan. **23 October:** The Wye River Agreement calls for Israel to withdraw from 13 percent of the territory it was currently occupying in exchange for Palestinian suppression of terrorism and the elimination of illicit arms stockpiles. Israel also undertakes the release of Palestinian prisoners. **31 October:** Clinton signs the Iraq Liberation Act, which makes regime change a foreign policy goal of the United States. **15 December:** United Nations (UN) inspectors leave Iraq because of continued interference and harassment by the Saddam regime. **16 December:** The United States and the UK launch air strikes and cruise-missile attacks on Iraq in Operation

Desert Fox in response to continued Iraqi interference with UN weapons inspections. **19 December:** The House of Representatives votes to impeach Clinton for obstruction of justice and perjury.

1999 1 January: The euro becomes the official currency of the European Union (EU). **12 February:** The Senate acquits Clinton on the impeachment charges. **12 March:** The Czech Republic, Hungary, and Poland formally join the North Atlantic Treaty Organization (NATO). **24 March–10 June:** NATO conducts an air campaign in Kosovo in response to a Serb ethnic-cleansing campaign against Albanians. The conflict is resolved by a settlement between the alliance and Belgrade that authorizes the deployment of a NATO-led peacekeeping force in the province. **17 April:** The capital of Germany is changed from Bonn to Berlin. **25 July:** The United States and Vietnam finalize negotiations on the first trade agreement between the two states since the Vietnam War. **30 August:** A referendum in East Timor results in independence of the province from Indonesia. **15 September:** The United Nations Security Council adopts Resolution 1264, which authorizes the deployment of a peacekeeping mission in East Timor. **13 October:** The Senate rejects the Comprehensive Test Ban Treaty. **14 October:** Lord Robertson of the United Kingdom becomes the secretary-general of NATO following the resignation of Javier Solana, who becomes the foreign policy chief of the EU. **15 November:** The United States and the People's Republic of China sign far-ranging trade agreement. **30 November–3 December:** The third World Trade Organization Summit, in Seattle, ends in failure, highlighted by widespread protests and riots. **12 December:** Jordanian security forces arrest more than 20 terrorists who planned to carry out attacks on religious and cultural sites in Jordan as part of the Millennium Bombing Plot. **14 December:** U.S. customs officials arrest Ahmed Ressam, who planned to bomb Los Angeles International Airport in another facet of the Millennium Bombing Plot. **31 December:** Vladimir Putin becomes president of Russia after the resignation of Yeltsin.

2000 January–March: Israeli-Syrian peace negotiations fail to resolve major differences between the two states or achieve a final peace. **May:** Israel finalizes the withdrawal of its forces from southern Lebanon. **19 June:** The Clinton administration provides $1.7 million to Vietnam to destroy or disarm mines and other unexploded ordinance left over from the Vietnam War. **11–25 July:** A Camp David summit fails to achieve any breakthrough in the Arab-Israeli conflict. **13 July:** The United States and Vietnam sign a trade agreement. **28 September:** Renewed violence in the Middle East follows a visit to the Temple Mount, a holy site, by future Israeli prime minister Ariel Sharon. **12 October:** Al Qaeda–linked terrorists use a boat bomb to attack the USS *Cole* in the Yemeni port of Aden, killing 17 sailors and wounding 30 others. **7 November:** George W. Bush is elected president of the United States. The election was marked by a bitter ballot recount in Florida and ultimately Supreme Court intervention. Bush lost the popular vote, but won the majority of the electoral votes.

2001   16 January: Laurent Kabila is assassinated, resulting in a new civil war in the Democratic Republic of Congo. **20 January:** On Bush's inauguration day, Colin Powell becomes the first African American appointed secretary of state, and Donald Rumsfeld is sworn in as secretary of defense. **21–27 January:** At the Taba Summit, Clinton fails to achieve a diplomatic breakthrough on the Arab-Israeli conflict. **27 May:** Abu Sayyaf, an Al Qaeda–linked Philippine terrorist group, kidnaps 16 tourists and staff members from a resort, including three Americans. Two are eventually killed, while the final captive is held until June 2002. **11 September 2001:** Al Qaeda terrorists hijack four airliners and fly two into the Twin Towers of the World Trade Center, destroying both buildings. A third crashes into the Pentagon, while the fourth is brought down in Pennsylvania when passengers attempt to regain control of the aircraft. More than 3,000 people are killed in the strikes, which result in the American-led war on terror. **20 September:** The Office of Homeland Security is established. Former governor Thomas Ridge is appointed the first director of the office. **25 September:** More than 7,000 National Guard troops are deployed at airports throughout the United States to bolster security. **2 October:** The North Atlantic Treaty Organization invokes its collective defense clause for the first time in history in response to the terrorist strikes on the United States. The alliance deploys airborne early warning craft to the United States and stations naval vessels to support Operation Enduring Freedom. **7 October:** The U.S.-led coalition launches attacks on the Taliban regime in Afghanistan in Operation Enduring Freedom. **7 October:** Anthrax spores are sent through the mail to a news magazine in Florida and later to television networks in New York and Senate offices in Washington, D.C. The case remains unsolved. **26 October:** The Patriot Act is signed into law. The measure curtails certain civil liberties and enhances the ability of law enforcement to track and detain suspected terrorists. Most provisions of the Act are set to expire after five years unless renewed by Congress. **23 November:** The United States signs the Convention on Cybercrime. **5 December:** Washington and Moscow announce that all of the terms of the Strategic Arms Reduction Treaty (START I) agreement have been fulfilled. **9 December:** The Taliban government is deposed by coalition forces and the anti-Taliban Northern Alliance. A transitional Afghan government, led by Hamid Karzai, is created. **11 December:** The People's Republic of China joins the World Trade Organization, gaining expanded access to American markets. **12 December:** U.S.-led coalition forces undertake an unsuccessful campaign in Afghanistan's Tora Bora area to capture Osama bin Laden and other senior Al Qaeda figures. **12 December:** The United States and Canada sign a new agreement that increases security measures along the world's longest undefended border.

2002   23 January: U.S. journalist Daniel Pearl is kidnapped, and later killed, by Islamic terrorists in Karachi, Pakistan. **29 January:** In his annual State of the Union address, Bush identifies Iran, Iraq, and North Korea as members of an "axis of evil" and asserts that the United States will undertake preemptive strikes to forestall attacks by weapons of mass destruction. **25 February:** The National Guard is deployed along the borders with Canada and Mexico to bolster security. **12 March:** A national advisory system, based on a color code, is implemented to ensure that citizens, businesses, and various government agencies are aware of the threat level. **22 March:** The United States and Mexico sign the Smart Border initiative to increase border security and reduce illegal immigration. **29 March:** In response to concerns over bioterrorism, the Department of Health and Human Services inaugurates a plan to stockpile 75 million doses of the smallpox vaccine. **8 April:** The Immigration and Naturalization Service begins to implement changes in the nation's visa program, including new restrictions on the ability of students and tourists to come to the United States, along with new limitations on their length of stay. **20 May:** East Timor becomes independent. **21 May:** The U.S. military begins to train and equip a new Afghan national army. **24 May:** The Treaty on Strategic Offensive Reductions (SORT), also known as the Moscow Treaty, is signed. **29 May:** The

Federal Bureau of Investigation announces new reforms and restructuring that elevates the importance of counterterrorism and bolsters the ability of the agency to share information with other intelligence and law enforcement bodies. **24 June:** In a major policy speech, Bush calls for the creation of a Palestinian state if the Palestinian National Authority (PNA) adopts democratic reforms and more stringent security measures. **15 July:** Four suspects in the Pearl kidnapping are convicted and given sentences ranging from death to life imprisonment. **16 September:** The Office of Homeland Security releases the *National Homeland Security Strategy*, which emphasizes domestic counterterrorism, the protection of critical infrastructure, and improvements to border and port security. **17 September:** The Bush administration issues the *National Security Strategy of the United States of America*, which endorses the use of preemptive war to forestall attacks on the United States by weapons of mass destruction. **12 October:** Al Qaeda–linked terrorists bomb a tourist area on the island of Bali, Indonesia, killing 202 and injuring more than 200. **16 October:** Congress enacts a measure authorizing the president to use military force against Iraq. **3 November:** The Central Intelligence Agency uses an unmanned drone to conduct an air strike in Yemen on the suspected planner of the 2000 *Cole* bombing. **8 November:** The United Nations Security Council unanimously adopts Resolution 1441, which requires Iraq to submit to new weapons inspections and threatens action if Iraq is found to be in breach of the conditions of the resolution. **25 November:** The Department of Homeland Security is created. **23 December:** To supplement the *National Homeland Security Strategy*, the Coast Guard publishes the *Maritime Strategy for Homeland Security* to define the agency's new mission as a part of the Department of Homeland Security.

2003 January–February: The United States undertakes a broad diplomatic effort to gain support for a United Nations (UN) resolution that specifically authorizes the use of military forces against Iraq. **10 January:** North Korea withdraws from the Nuclear Nonproliferation Treaty. **28 January:** In his State of the Union address, Bush makes an argument for military strikes against the Saddam regime. **5 February:** Powell addresses the UN in an effort to garner support for military action against Iraq. He presents the Bush administration's case against Iraq and charges the regime with continuing programs to develop and stockpile weapons of mass destruction and repeated failures to comply with past UN resolutions. **19 February:** Turkey requests aid from its North Atlantic Treaty Organization (NATO) allies on the eve of the invasion of Iraq, creating a contentious debate among the alliance states that oppose the war and those that support the invasion. A compromise is reached, in which individual states provide assistance to Ankara on a bilateral basis. **1 March:** The Turkish parliament votes not to allow U.S. forces to launch an invasion of Iraq from its territory. **15 March:** Hu Jintao becomes president of the People's Republic of China. **20 March:** U.S. and coalition forces launch an invasion of Iraq to depose the regime of Saddam Hussein. **29 April:** Baghdad is captured by coalition forces. Organized resistance in Iraq ceases, and an insurgency commences. **1 May:** Bush declares an end to "major combat operations" in Iraq, despite the growing insurgency. **6 June:** A bilateral free trade agreement is signed by the United States and Chile. **28 June:** Washington transfers sovereignty of Iraq to an interim government. **11 August:** NATO assumes command of the Afghan peacekeeping mission from the UN. **13 October:** The UN Security Council, in Resolution 1510, authorizes NATO to expand its peacekeeping and reconstruction mission in Afghanistan beyond the region of Kabul. **6 November:** Bush signs into law an $87.5 billion aid package for Afghanistan and Iraq. **13 December:** Saddam is captured by American troops. **17 December:** Negotiations finalize the Central American Free Trade Agreement between the United States and the countries of El Salvador, Guatemala, Honduras, and Nicaragua.

2004   6 January: The North Atlantic Treaty Organization (NATO) takes command of regional reconstruction teams in Afghanistan and expands the program to rebuild and repair the country's infrastructure. **25 January:** Costa Rica and the Dominican Republic agree to join Central American Free Trade Agreement (CAFTA). Since the Dominican Republic is outside of the geographic area of Central America, the accord is renamed the Dominican Republic–CAFTA (DR-CAFTA). **8 March:** An interim Iraqi constitution is promulgated. **11 March:** Terrorist attacks on the Madrid train system kill 191. The attacks cause the conservative government to lose the imminent national elections, and the new socialist government quickly moves to withdraw Spanish troops from the U.S.-led coalition in Iraq. **29 March:** Bulgaria, Estonia, Latvia, Lithuania, Romania, Slovakia, and Slovenia join NATO in the largest round of enlargement in alliance history. **28 May:** The DR-CAFTA is signed in Washington. **24 June:** At the Istanbul Summit, NATO leaders agree to increase the number of alliance troops in Afghanistan from 6,500 to 10,000. NATO also agrees to launch a training program for Iraqi security forces. **28 June:** The coalition provisional authority transfers power to the interim Iraqi government. **9 July:** The International Court of Justice rules that Israel's new security fence along the occupied territories is illegal. **3 August:** The U.S.-Australia Free Trade Agreement is signed into law by Bush. **10 September:** Washington declares the ethnic conflict in the Darfur region of Sudan to be genocide. **24 September:** Porter J. Goss is appointed director of the Central Intelligence Agency. **4 October:** The first free presidential elections in Afghan history are won by Karzai. **2 November:** Bush is reelected president. **11 November:** Longtime Palestinian leader Yasser Arafat dies. **2 December:** NATO turns command of its peacekeeping mission in Bosnia over to the European Union. **14 December:** Egypt, Israel, and the United States sign an economic agreement that allows the first two countries to export certain products to America without tariffs. **26 December:** An earthquake off the coast of Indonesia creates a series of tsunamis that strikes the coast of countries in the Indian Ocean. More than 200,000 people are killed. **29 December:** Washington forms a coalition to coordinate tsunami relief. After initial criticism over the amount of American aid, the United States provides more than $950 million in official recovery assistance and another $1 billion in private contributions.

2005   3 January: Former presidents Bush and Clinton are named to lead the Asian tsunami relief effort. **12 January:** The Bush administration announces that the search for weapons of mass destruction in Iraq is officially over, with no significant stockpiles having been found. **26 January:** Condoleezza Rice becomes the first female, and the second African-American, secretary of state. **30 January:** Iraq conducts the first free and open parliamentary elections in the country's history. An interim legislature is elected and charged to draft a permanent constitution for the nation. **10 February:** North Korea announces it possesses nuclear weapons. **14–28 February:** Following the assassination of former prime minister Rafik Hariri, the Cedar Revolution begins in Lebanon, leading to the election of an anti-Syrian government and the subsequent withdrawal of Syrian forces after 30 years of occupation. **15 February:** Michael Chertoff is sworn in as secretary of homeland security. **23 March:** The United Nations approves the deployment of a 10,000-member peacekeeping force for Darfur. **26 May:** Bush declares support for a Middle East peace initiative that would be based on the borders of the 1949 cease-fire between Israel and the neighboring Arab states. He also pledges increased aid for the Palestine National Authority (PNA). **21 June:** Rice is unable to achieve a settlement agreement between Israel and the PNA during a Middle East summit. **7 July:** Terrorists conduct attacks on two subways and a bus in London, killing 52 and wounding more than 700. **2 August:** Bush signs the Dominican Republic–Central American Free Trade Agreement legislation into law. **18 September:** Afghan parliamentary elections are held with security support from U.S. and North Atlantic Treaty Organization forces. The balloting is the first open legislative elections in Afghanistan in 33 years. **15 October:** Iraqi voters approve new, democratic constitution. **15 December:** Balloting is conducted in Iraq for the 275-member Council of Representatives, created by the October constitution. **20 December:** Coalition forces turn over the first Iraqi province to national security forces.

2006   26 January: Hamas wins a majority of seats in Palestinian National Authority (PNA) parliamentary elections. The organization refuses to recognize Israel. In response, the United States and other donor states withhold economic aid from the PNA. **15 March:** Congress creates the Iraq Study Group, cochaired by former secretary of state Baker and former Democratic congressman Lee Hamilton, to prepare recommendations on the administration's Iraq policy. **22 April:** Shiite politician Nuri al-Maliki becomes prime minister of Iraq, ending a four-month standoff over who would lead the Iraqi government. **31 May:** Washington and Hanoi sign a bilateral agreement that allows Vietnam to join the World Trade Organization. **7 June:** The leader of Al Qaeda in Iraq, Abu Musab al-Zarqawi, is killed during a U.S. air strike. **12 July:** Israel invades southern Lebanon in response to Hezbollah attacks and the seizure of two Israeli soldiers. The Bush administration supports the deployment of a United Nations (UN) peacekeeping operation and the disarmament of the Hezbollah fighters in southern Lebanon. **31 August:** The UN Security Council adopts Resolution 1706, authorizing the deployment of a peacekeeping force in Darfur of 22,500 troops. **5 October:** North Atlantic Treaty Organization forces assume control of coalition military operations throughout the whole of Afghanistan. **9 October:** North Korea conducts a nuclear weapons test. **26 October:**

Bush signs into law the Secure Fence Act, which authorizes the construction of several hundred miles of additional fencing along the border with Mexico, along with additional border checkpoints and the use of advanced technology to identify illegal aliens. **3 November:** North Korea announces it will resume negotiations on nuclear disarmament. **5 November:** Saddam is sentenced to death for crimes against humanity by an Iraqi court. **7 November:** In midterm elections, Democrats regain control of both houses of Congress for the first time since 1994. **8 November:** Rumsfeld resigns as secretary of defense over his management of the Iraq insurgency. Former secretary of defense Robert Gates is nominated to replace him. **6 December:** The Iraq Study Group issues its final report, which calls for increased regional diplomacy, linkage of Iraq policy and U.S. diplomacy in the Arab-Israeli conflict, and the withdrawal of American forces beginning in 2008. **30 December:** Saddam is executed by Iraqi officials. **31 December:** The death toll of U.S. service personnel in Iraq reaches 3,000.

2007   5 January: Nancy Pelosi becomes the first female Speaker of the House of Representatives. **8 January:** U.S. forces launch strikes on Somali Islamic Courts Union militias as they retreat before Ethiopian and interim government troops. **10 January:** Bush announces plans for a surge of troops, up to 21,000, in Iraq to quell the ongoing insurgency. **13 February:** North Korea agrees to dismantle its nuclear program in exchange for renewed economic and fuel aid from the United States, South Korea, and Japan.

Introduction

The post–Cold War diplomacy of the United States has evolved in stages that reflect changes in the international system. Through the 1990s, the nation's foreign affairs were marked by an evolution away from the post–World War II focus on security and superpower competition to a more multifaceted and nuanced series of policies that included economic concerns, social and cultural issues, and environmental matters. However, an escalating series of terrorist attacks that culminated in the 11 September 2001 strikes on New York and Washington, D.C., led to the reemergence of security as the main foreign policy issue for the United States. The subsequent American-led war on terror mirrored the Cold War in its goals, and the administration of President George W. Bush endeavored to build a multinational counterterrorism coalition that paralleled the Western alliance of the bipolar era.

Until the advent of the war on terror, the nation's post–Cold War diplomacy lacked the overarching coherence that had marked American foreign affairs since the 1940s. Successive administrations also faced a more divided Congress and public. By the 1990s, the Cold War consensus on foreign policy, which was manifested in legislative bipartisanship, had dissipated. Both political parties utilized foreign policy issues as a means to seek short-term political advantages. The dominance of the American president in foreign and security affairs continued, but the presidents of the post–Cold War period increasingly faced constraints on their management of the nation's diplomacy. Furthermore, until 2001, domestic issues tended to overshadow foreign affairs. The 1990s comprised a neoisolationist era, in which the United States only reluctantly engaged with the global community.

The era was marked by American ascendancy as the world's sole superpower. U.S. military might was unequaled and to a large extent unparalleled in world history. A series of military conflicts, including the

1991 Persian Gulf War, the 1999 Kosovo War, the 2001 invasion of Afghanistan in Operation Enduring Freedom, and the 2003 Iraq War, confirmed the superiority of U.S. weapons, troops, and systems capabilities. The credibility and prowess of U.S. forces were instrumental in prompting conflict resolution in the Balkans and other areas. In addition, the administration of President William J. Clinton deployed forces in more operations than any previous presidency since the 1960s. Even so, the United States avoided participation in several major humanitarian crises, including the Rwandan genocide and the Darfur conflict. American military supremacy eventually began to be undermined by the inability of Washington to overcome the insurgency in Iraq following the overthrow of the regime of Saddam Hussein in 2003.

In addition, American economic power eroded with the rise of other nations and the increasing commercial and trade capabilities of the European Union (EU). The EU's common currency, the euro, challenged the dollar as the global unit of exchange after its introduction in 1999 and fast-developing economies such as the People's Republic of China (PRC), Brazil, and India increasingly competed with the United States for access to new markets and raw materials. In addition, the "soft power" of the United States—the attractiveness of the nation's political principles, economic system, and social and cultural norms—declined through the 1990s. Whereas America had been perceived as the global leader in the promotion of democracy, human rights, and environmental issues, Washington's headship on these issues was weakened as both domestic and international political and critics questioned the commitment of American leaders to the ideals they espoused. Globalization—the spread of economic, social, and cultural norms—sparked a global opposition movement, although an alternative global ideological rival failed to emerge. Instead, opposition to American soft power was mainly expressed through the rise of extremist groups in the United States and abroad. Meanwhile, the country failed to join a range of global environmental efforts. Washington's rejection of the 1997 Kyoto Protocol on Global Warming in particular undermined America's image as a leader in ecological matters.

The 2001 terrorist attacks seemed to dramatically change U.S. diplomacy. More than 100 countries and 50 international organizations offered support or assistance to the Bush administration. Even countries that had terse relationships with the United States endorsed Washington's counterterrorist initiatives. The United States also had widespread support for the invasion of Afghanistan and the overthrow of the Taliban regime. The concurrent global war on terror met with more mixed responses, as few countries were willing or able to undertake an open-ended, Cold War–style competition against international terrorism. American efforts to promote democracy in the Middle East had minimal international support.

Much of the goodwill that resulted from the 2001 attacks evaporated during the contentious debate over military action against Iraq in 2003. The conflict divided traditional American allies such as Great Britain, France, Italy, and Germany. Although the Bush administration had substantial diplomatic support for military action, the failure of the United States to gain a United Nations (UN) resolution specifically authorizing the use of force led to charges of unilateralism. Bush's second term was marked by a return to more traditional American diplomacy, which emphasized multilateral forums and cost-benefit analysis based on national interests.

POLITICAL DEVELOPMENTS

President George H. W. Bush was a staunch internationalist. A former director of the Central Intelligence Agency (CIA) and vice president, Bush established a foreign and security policy team that included some of the best statesmen of his era, including Secretary of State James A. Baker, Joint Chiefs Chairman Colin Powell, and National Security Advisor Brent Scowcroft. The Bush administration skillfully managed the end of the Cold War, including the reunification of Germany, the transition from communism to democracy among many of the former Soviet satellite states, and the transition of Russia from superpower nemesis to lukewarm ally. Washington and Moscow undertook a series of arms control agreements and consolidated the nuclear arsenal of the former Soviet Union under Russian control. The administration was able to maintain the centrality of the North Atlantic Treaty Organization (NATO) to transatlantic security and initiate new economic ties through the negotiations over the North American Free Trade Agreement (NAFTA).

Bush also conducted a series of successful military operations, culminating in the U.S.-led coalition victory in the Persian Gulf War. By the end of the conflict with Saddam, Bush's approval ratings were at or above 90 percent, the highest recorded up to that time. However, his management of the country's diplomacy proved to be his undoing when the United States sank into a recession in 1991. Many Americans came to believe that Bush overemphasized foreign policy at the expense of domestic needs. The rising federal budget deficit and tax increases (following a highly publicized pledge not to raise taxes) drew millionaire Ross Perot into the 1992 presidential campaign. Perot attracted many fiscal conservative voters, while Clinton, the Democratic nominee, ran a highly successful centrist campaign in which he promised to focus on domestic issues, especially the economy. Clinton won the election with 43 percent of the vote, followed by Bush with 37.4 percent and Perot with 18.9 percent. Clinton became the first Democratic president in 12 years.

Clinton adopted a moderate foreign policy. He endorsed free trade and supported ratification of NAFTA. The president endeavored to accelerate cuts in defense spending and to reinvest the fiscal "peace dividend" occasioned by the end of the Cold War into domestic programs. However, his administration faced a series of foreign policy crises, including Somalia and the Balkan civil wars. The failure of the Somalia mission then led the administration to avoid future humanitarian operations in Rwanda and Sudan. Clinton continued his predecessor's emphasis on the centrality of NATO and endorsed NATO expansion to states of the former Soviet bloc. Islamic terrorists detonated a truck bomb at the World Trade Center in New York City, and the United States faced a series of other terrorist strikes, launched by both domestic and international groups. Nonetheless, the Clinton administration failed to develop an effective counterterrorism policy.

Republicans gained control of both houses of Congress in 1994. The president was forced to repeatedly compromise his domestic agenda and, especially in his second term, he devoted more attention to foreign affairs. Clinton was forced to rely on the opposition party to support several of his foreign policy actions, including his trade initiatives and military interventions, because of opposition from Democrats. However, Republicans blocked other measures, including arms control agreements such as the Comprehensive Test Ban Treaty. In 1996, Clinton was reelected and reshuffled most of his senior advisors. Madeleine Albright was appointed secretary of state and former Republican senator William Cohen became secretary of defense. From 1998 onward, his impeachment further complicated the administration's policy initiatives. In the final year of his presidency, Clinton endeavored unsuccessfully to achieve a breakthrough in the Arab-Israeli conflict.

The 2000 presidential election was the most contentious in modern American history. Democratic candidate and former vice president Albert Gore won the plurality of the popular vote with 48.4 percent to Republican George W. Bush's 47.9 percent. However, Bush won the majority of the electoral votes with 271 to Gore's 266, following a bitterly contested recount in Florida. Like his predecessor, Bush initially sought to concentrate on domestic policy. However, the 2001 terrorist attacks transformed Bush's presidency and forced the chief executive to concentrate on national security and diplomacy. He benefited from an experienced foreign policy team that included Powell as secretary of state, former defense secretary Richard "Dick" Cheney as vice president, and former defense secretary Donald Rumsfeld in another stint as defense secretary.

Bush initially enjoyed widespread domestic support for the war on terror and the invasion of Afghanistan. In 2002, the Republicans even overcame historic trends in which the party in power normally loses seats in midterm elections, actually gaining seats in both houses of Congress. Following their losses in these elections, the Democrats adopted a strategy whereby they became more critical of the administration's handling of the war on terror and homeland security. This essentially ended the brief, post–11 September 2001 period of bipartisanship in foreign and security policy.

Meanwhile, the administration undertook significant changes in national defense and created the Department of Homeland Security in the most sweeping reorganization of the federal bureaucracy since World War II. The administration's use of expanded law enforcement powers under the 2001 Patriot Act eroded support for the war on terror among civil libertarians and conservatives. At the same time, Bush's decision to expand the war on terror to include military action against Iraq in 2003 alienated some American allies.

Bush was reelected in 2004 and replaced Powell with his national security advisor, Condoleezza Rice. Continued American losses in Iraq and the sustained insurgency led Bush's approval ratings to decline dramatically. In the 2006 midterm elections, the Republicans lost control of both houses of Congress after 12 years in the majority. In response, Bush reshuffled his senior defense officials, including replacing Rumsfeld with former secretary of defense Robert Gates.

THE END OF THE COLD WAR AND
THE PERSIAN GULF WAR

Although superpower tensions had been steadily reduced during the final years of the administration of Ronald W. Reagan, the rapidity of the end of the Cold War took many U.S. officials by surprise. George H. W. Bush pursued a cautious approach to the Soviet Union in its final years. He supported reforms and increased freedom in the Soviet bloc, but American diplomacy emphasized stability. For instance, Bush opposed the breakup of Yugoslavia. Although Washington supported European efforts to bring peace to the region, Bush would not authorize the deployment of American forces as part of a UN-led peacekeeping mission.

In 1989, the United States condemned the suppression of prodemocracy demonstrators in Beijing by the Chinese Communist government. With congressional support, Bush enacted a series of sanctions on the PRC.

In November, the Berlin Wall fell, and the Federal Republic of Germany and the German Democratic Republic began the process of reunification. Bush supported a united Germany and signed the Two-Plus-Four Treaty in September 1990, which allowed reunification in October.

Bush and Soviet leader Mikhail Gorbachev agreed to dramatically reduce troop levels in Europe during a summit in December 1989. In November 1990, the two leaders and other European heads of state signed the Conventional Forces in Europe Treaty that set limits on military deployments on the continent. Bush supported Gorbachev during the August 1991 Communist coup, but then developed a close relationship with Russian president Boris Yeltsin following the demise of the Union of Soviet Socialist Republics and the formation of the Commonwealth of Independent States. Bush nevertheless rebuffed calls from Yeltsin for the United States to provide a Marshall Plan–style package of financial aid and technical assistance to rebuild the decrepit Russian economy.

Meanwhile, a series of crises forced the administration to undertake military action. In December 1989, the United States invaded Panama and overthrew the regime of Manuel Noriega because of the dictator's involvement in drug trafficking and his efforts to prevent democratic reforms. In August of the following year, Iraq invaded Kuwait, presenting Bush with his greatest foreign policy challenge. The UN condemned the invasion and called on the Saddam regime to withdraw. Bush articulated American goals in the conflict in August and launched a highly successful diplomatic offensive to build an anti-Saddam coalition. In November, the UN adopted a resolution authorizing the use of force against Iraq if the regime did not withdraw by January 1990. Coalition forces attacked Iraqi positions on 17 January, starting the Persian Gulf War. U.S.-led forces quickly overwhelmed the Iraqis. A cease-fire was signed in April, which authorized the creation of a no-fly zone over northern Iraq to protect the Kurdish minority (a southern no-fly was also subsequently created).

The success of the coalition led Bush to seek an expanded role for the UN in resolving ethnic conflicts, and he authorized the deployment of American forces as part of a humanitarian mission in Somalia as one of his last acts in office. In addition, on 17 December 1992, Bush signed the NAFTA accord, and on 3 January 1993, he signed the Strategic Arms Reduction Treaty (START II) agreement with Yeltsin.

FOREIGN AFFAIRS OF THE 1990s

Clinton entered office with a goal of concentrating on domestic affairs. Although he had criticized Bush's foreign policy, particularly the administration's failure to engage in the peacekeeping efforts in the Balkans, Clinton initially continued the main elements of his predecessor's diplomacy. He declined to significantly increase U.S. financial assistance to Moscow, but continued efforts at arms control. In January 1994, Clinton and Yeltsin signed the Kremlin Accords, which ended the reciprocal targeting of the United States and Russia by the other country's nuclear arsenals. Russia was also invited to participate in the Group of Seven meetings (and eventually joined the heads-of-state summit, which was renamed the Group of Eight). At first, Clinton declined to become directly involved in the UN mission in the Balkans, but did support NATO enforcement of the UN-mandated no-fly zones over Bosnia. He continued American participation in the Somalia operation. On 26 February 1993, terrorists attacked the World Trade Center in New York in the first of a series of strikes against the United States during Clinton's tenure. The Federal Bureau of Investigation was designated the nation's lead counterterrorism agency.

In April 1993, Iraqi agents attempted to assassinate former president Bush. Clinton ordered air strikes on Iraq in response. On 3–4 October, the Battle of Mogadishu left 18 American soldiers dead and one captured in a failed effort to capture Somali warlord Mohamed Farrah Aidid. The battle was the first major foreign policy crisis of the Clinton administration. The president ordered the withdrawal of American forces, effectively ending the UN mission. He subsequently avoided UN missions or other humanitarian operations that were not directly related to American interests, including participation in efforts to prevent the Rwandan genocide in 1994 or the Congo civil wars of the late 1990s.

In 1994, the administration threatened military action against North Korea if Pyongyang did not terminate its nuclear weapons program. The standoff was resolved by the Framework Agreement, in which Pyongyang agreed to cease its weapons program in exchange for the construction of two light-water nuclear reactors and food and energy aid from the United States and South Korea.

The president attempted to make trade one of his foreign policy priorities. In 1994, Clinton developed a $50 billion package in grants and loans to aid Mexico during a severe economic crisis brought on by the devaluation of the peso. The intervention worked very well; the country's economy began to recover by year's end, and Mexico was able to repay its American loans in 1997. In 1994, Clinton also lifted the economic embargo on Vietnam that had been in place since the 1970s, and full diplomatic relations with Hanoi were restored in 1995. He later decoupled American trade relations with the PRC from that country's human rights record, and in 1999, the United States and the PRC signed a historic trade agreement. Washington sought unsuccessfully to develop a Free Trade Area of the Americas (FTAA) to expand NAFTA. While there was general support for FTAA, Latin American countries sought reductions in farm subsidies and other protectionist measures that the Clinton administration was unwilling to end.

In 1995, the World Trade Organization (WTO) was created to expand free trade and build on the accomplishments of the General Agreement on Tariffs and Trade. American support for global free trade came under criticism by nongovernmental groups in the late 1990s, with the emergence of a widespread antiglobalization movement. Protests and demonstrations became common at WTO meetings and other economic summits.

Following the 1994 midterm elections in which the Republicans took control of Congress, Clinton endeavored to concentrate more on foreign policy. The first significant manifestation of this trend was American sponsorship of negotiations among the Serbs, Croats, and Bosnians that resulted in the Dayton Accords. The agreement divided Bosnia into a Croat-Bosnian federation and a Serb republic and paved the way for the deployment of a NATO-led peacekeeping mission. By putting the mission under NATO control, Clinton and his senior advisors believed the operation could avoid the mistakes of previous multilateral efforts in the region and end a source of instability in Europe.

Clinton's more assertive foreign policy also resulted in the deployment of naval forces to the Taiwan Strait in response to PRC military exercises and diplomatic pressure on Taiwan. Sino-American relations were subsequently repaired during a state visit by PRC leader Jiang Zemin the following year.

On 25 June 1996, radical Islamic terrorists detonated a truck bomb outside an American military housing facility, the Khobar Towers, in Saudi Arabia, killing 20 and injuring more than 300. Counterterrorism funding was dramatically increased in the United States, and new security programs were developed for overseas facilities, including embassies and military establishments. The security improvements were phased in over a multiyear period, but proved to be inadequate to stop terrorist strikes in 1998 and 2000.

At the beginning of Clinton's second term, his attention remained focused on Asia. Between May and July 1997, the East Asian Financial Crisis resulted in Hong Kong, Indonesia, Laos, Malaysia, the Philippines, South Korea, and Thailand suffering severe economic contractions as the result of currency depreciations. Washington worked mainly with international bodies such as the International Monetary Fund to support regional currencies through monetary intervention and debt relief.

Meanwhile, NATO leaders agreed to invite the Czech Republic, Hungary, and Poland to join the alliance and signed the NATO-Russia Founding Act to assuage Moscow's concerns over expansion. The NATO-Russia Permanent Joint Council was created in October to enhance cooperation between the Cold War adversaries. In December 1997, the Clinton administration refused to sign the Ottawa Treaty, which banned the use of antipersonnel land mines.

In 1998, Clinton faced the most significant foreign policy challenges of his administration. His management of a succession of crises was complicated by his impeachment. In May, India and Pakistan conducted reciprocal nuclear tests. The tests were an embarrassment to the United States, since American intelligence agencies failed to predict them and the administration could undertake only reactive measures, including sanctions on both countries.

In June, Clinton refused to sign the treaty that created the International Criminal Court, a body mandated to try cases involving crimes against humanity and genocide. The U.S. rejection of the treaty led to global criticism over Washington's commitment to human rights and international war. The United States argued that the treaty would expose American peacekeepers to potential political prosecutions.

On 7 August, Al Qaeda–linked terrorists conducted twin attacks on the U.S. embassies in Nairobi, Kenya, and Dar-es-Salaam, Tanzania, killing 257 and wounding more than 4,000. In retaliation, the United States launched cruise missile strikes on Al Qaeda facilities in Afghanistan and a suspected chemical weapons plant in Sudan. The attacks failed to kill Osama bin Laden or any other senior Al Qaeda figures. The failure of the American attacks made Clinton more cautious, and he subsequently denied repeated requests by the CIA and Defense Department to attack bin Laden or other Al Qaeda leaders.

In October, over opposition from his own party, Congress enacted and Clinton signed the Iraq Liberation Act, which made regime change in Iraq a foreign policy goal of the United States and gave the president the authority to fund antiregime groups. On 15 December, UN weapons inspectors left Iraq and Clinton ordered air strikes against the regime. The attacks were criticized at the UN by France, Russia, and Secretary-General Kofi Annan.

In February 1999, Clinton gave a major policy speech in which he formally enunciated the foreign policy goals that had been loosely termed the Clinton Doctrine, including the need for the United States to undertake humanitarian and military operations to promote global stability and the need to refine American military capabilities to respond to small and medium-size conflicts. In March, the Czech Republic, Hungary, and Poland joined NATO. The new allies participated in the 77-day air campaign against Serbia during the Kosovo War, in which NATO endeavored to stop ethnic cleansing in the separatist province of Serbia. The alliance subsequently undertook a peacekeeping mission in Kosovo. In December 1999, customs agents arrested participants in a plot to bomb the Los Angeles airport as part of a broader series of planned attacks known collectively as the Millennium Bombing Plots.

In the final year of his presidency, Clinton launched an extensive effort to achieve a major breakthrough in the Arab-Israeli conflict. The 2000 Camp David Summit failed to result in a significant agreement, as did the later Taba Summit. On 12 October 2000, terrorists detonated a boat bomb against the USS *Cole*, killing 17 sailors and injuring 30 others. With presidential elections in November, Clinton deferred any action on the *Cole* strike for the next administration.

THE WAR ON TERROR

George W. Bush was critical of Clinton's foreign policy during the presidential campaign and charged that U.S. diplomacy lacked focus and was reactive. Once in office, Bush endeavored to revive efforts to create the FTAA and announced his support for the establishment of a missile defense system, in spite of objections from Russia. Bush also ordered reviews of the nation's defense and counterterrorism policies. However, the September 2001 Al Qaeda terrorist attacks prompted an immediate recalculation of American foreign and security policy. The short-term goal of American policy was to destroy Al Qaeda and the Taliban regime, which harbored the terrorist group. The Bush administration developed a "coalition of the willing" that included participation by foreign states and international organizations at varying levels. Some allies contributed troops to the invasion of Afghanistan, Operation Enduring Freedom, while other countries offered intelligence and law enforcement cooperation.

Military strikes on the Taliban began on 7 October, and by December, the regime had been overthrown by a combination of anti-Taliban Northern Alliance Afghan troops and coalition special operations forces, supported by air power and missile strikes. The coalition failed to kill or capture the senior leadership of Al Qaeda or the Taliban, but their ability to undertake major combat operations was destroyed. The remnants of Al Qaeda and the Taliban continued to undertake terrorist and insurgency attacks from Pakistan. A UN peacekeeping mission was deployed in Afghanistan. The operation was later placed under NATO command, and the alliance became responsible for security throughout the country in 2005. In October 2004, pro-American Hamid Karzai was elected president of Afghanistan after serving as interim leader of the country since the fall of the Taliban.

Bush also proceeded with ballistic missile defense (BMD) as a means to defend the American homeland. In December 2001, he announced that the United States would withdraw from the 1972 Antiballistic Missile Treaty. From 2002 onward, the country spent about $9 billion annually on BMD. A number of other countries, including the United Kingdom, Australia, and Japan, participated in its development. In 2005, America began the first of three planned phases in the deployment of the system.

In May 2004, Bush and Russian president Vladimir Putin signed the Treaty on Strategic Offensive Reductions, also known as the Moscow Treaty, which superseded the START II accord and called for the two countries to reduce their nuclear arsenals by two-thirds.

In 2002, Washington vigorously supported a large round of NATO expansion to include states from central and eastern Europe. The countries of the region were highly supportive of NATO and the United States, and Washington perceived that they would help maintain the importance of the alliance to transatlantic security, as well as being good allies in the war on terror. Bulgaria, Estonia, Latvia, Lithuania, Romania, Slovakia, and Slovenia were invited to join the Alliance and became formal members in March 2004 in the largest round of enlargement in NATO history.

The long-term goal of the administration was the suppression of global terrorism. Bush launched the war on terror in an attempt to garner international support to defeat terrorist groups around the world.

Bush and his advisors perceived the new conflict as being analogous to the Cold War. The United States employed a strategy that included continuing direct attacks against suspected Taliban and Al Qaeda positions in Afghanistan and conducting covert operations against terrorists around the world. In addition, Washington increased military aid to countries confronted by terrorist insurgencies such as the Philippines, Colombia, and Uzbekistan. This aid included the deployment of American military advisors and special operations forces. The United States had significant success in increasing counterterrorist intelligence cooperation and with efforts to suppress the financing of terrorist groups, although states such as Iran and Syria continued to support specific terrorist organizations such as Hamas and Hezbollah.

Bush also articulated support for democratization as a means to counter support for terrorism. However, as was the case during the Cold War, Washington continued to provide aid and assistance to undemocratic regimes in key countries such as Pakistan, Egypt, and the Gulf states in return for their support in the war on terror. In June 2002, Bush called for the creation of Palestinian state if the leadership adopted government reforms and suppressed anti-Israeli terrorism. The administration also endorsed the 2004 democracy movement in Ukraine, known as the Orange Revolution, and the 2005 Cedar Revolution in Lebanon that resulted in the withdrawal of Syrian forces.

In order to prevent future terrorist attacks on the United States, a new office, and later department, of homeland security was created to improve coordination among federal, state, and local law enforcement organizations, as well as the nation's intelligence and defense agencies. In addition, domestic law police powers were bolstered through the 2001 Patriot Act, which provided expanded surveillance and detention abilities. The Patriot Act and the administration's policy of indefinitely detaining unlawful enemy combatants led to significant domestic and international criticism by human rights groups. The administration also tightened immigration policy, including implementing new restrictions on entry visas and requiring new documentation for entry into the United States.

America's goals and strategy in the war on terror were formally promulgated in the Bush Doctrine. The doctrine was annunciated during Bush's 2002 State of the Union address and formally codified in that year's *National Security Strategy of the United States.* The Bush strategy emphasized preemption. The administration declared that it would use preventive military force to forestall potential terrorist attacks on the United States.

On 12 October 2002, Al Qaeda–linked terrorists exploded bombs in a tourist area of Bali, Indonesia, killing 202 and wounding more than 200. The attacks confirmed the continuing global reach of Al Qaeda.

Meanwhile, the Bush administration identified the regime of Saddam Hussein as the next target in the war on terror. Washington accused Iraq of pursuing weapons of mass destruction and supporting terrorism. On 16 October, Congress authorized the use of force against Iraq. On 8 November, the UN Security Council unanimously adopted Resolution 1441, which ordered Iraq to submit to weapons inspections or face consequences (although the consequences were not explicitly detailed). Efforts to gain international support for military action against Iraq were mixed. Some traditional American allies offered varying degrees of support for a U.S.-led invasion, while other countries such as France, Germany, and Russia blocked Anglo-American attempts to gain a second resolution authorizing the use of force (the Bush administration subsequently argued that a second resolution was unnecessary).

THE IRAQ WAR AND CONCURRENT CRISES

On 20 March 2002, coalition forces launched the invasion of Iraq. The initial military phase of the invasion went very well for the United States. By the end of April, coalition forces had captured Baghdad and defeated the main Iraqi formations. However, an insurgency began and grew steadily among Sunnis and a growing number of foreign fighters. On 1 May, Bush declared an end to major combat operations. On 28 June, sovereignty was transferred to an interim Iraqi government. To support the American military efforts in Afghanistan and Iraq, Congress authorized an emergency appropriation of $87.5 billion (through 2006, the cost of the Iraq war was $500 billion). In December, Saddam was captured by American forces. He was subsequently turned over to the Iraqi civil government for trial on charges of crimes against humanity and genocide. He was tried and convicted, and then executed on 30 December 2006.

While conducting the war on terror and the Iraq conflict, the Bush administration endeavored to make progress on FTAA. In December 2003, negotiations were finalized between the United States and Latin American countries for the Central American Free Trade Agreement (CAFTA). CAFTA initially included El Salvador, Guatemala, Honduras, and Nicaragua, but Costa Rica and the Dominican Republic joined talks in January 2004 and the accord was signed on 28 May. CAFTA was seen as a step toward FTAA. In addition to the broad effort for a hemispheric trade accord, the United States initiated a series of bilateral trade agreements with countries in the Western Hemisphere and elsewhere around the world, including Australia and Chile. Negotiations over FTAA failed to result in an agreement, however, especially after Venezuela launched an effort in 2005 to prevent the accord.

On 11 March 2004, terrorists detonated a series of bombs on trains in Madrid. The attacks killed 191 and led to the conservative government's defeat in subsequent elections. The new Socialist government withdrew Spanish troops from the coalition in Iraq in 2005. In Afghanistan, the NATO-led force was steadily increased, which allowed more American troops to be shifted to Iraq. Meanwhile, the NATO-led peacekeeping mission in Bosnia was turned over to the EU, allowing more alliance forces to be transferred to Afghanistan.

In March 2004, a new interim Iraqi constitution was developed. Meanwhile, the insurgency in Iraq shifted from attacks on coalition military forces to the targeting of civilians, infrastructure, and government sites. This led to a dramatic increase in civilian casualties. Sunni attacks on Shiite religious sites and leaders prompted retaliatory attacks. The increase in sectarian violence in Baghdad and several provinces (known collectively as the "Sunni Triangle") was linked to Al Qaeda, which adopted a strategy to incite civil war as a means to undermine the pro-American government. The Kurdish areas of the north and the mainly Shiite southern regions faced minimal violence.

In January 2005, at the beginning of Bush's second term, the administration announced that the search for weapons of mass destruction in Iraq had ended and no significant stockpiles had been discovered. On 30 January, Iraqis elected an interim legislature to draft a constitution. This was followed by elections in October to approve a new constitution and by balloting in December to decide the composition of a new legislative body, the Council of Representatives. The elections were a significant success for the Bush administration and underscored American efforts to transition Iraq to a democracy. Nevertheless, internal disagreements among the nation's political parties caused a four-month delay after the polling before a prime minister, Nuri al-Maliki, and cabinet were appointed. U.S. forces also began to turn over control of Iraqi provinces to the nation's security forces. In June, Al Qaeda's commander in Iraq, Abu Musab al-Zarqawi, was killed by an American air attack.

American public support for the Iraq War declined through 2005 and 2006 as the conflict did not appear to have an end. Comparisons were drawn to the quagmire of the Vietnam War. On 15 March 2006, Congress created the Iraq Study Group to review U.S. strategy and offer suggestions to improve Washington's policy. The bipartisan panel drew up a list of 72 recommendations that revolved around increased regional diplomacy, including with Iran and Syria, and beginning U.S. troop withdrawals in 2008. In the November midterm elections, the Democrats regained the majority in both houses of Congress for the first time since 1994, which further complicated Bush's Iraq strategy. In January 2007, Bush reshuffled his senior Iraq team and replaced Rumsfeld with former defense secretary Robert Gates, in addition to other replacements.

While the focus of the Bush administration remained on Iraq, a number of other foreign policy crises emerged. In 2002, the United States disclosed that North Korea had an active nuclear weapons program in contravention of the 1994 Framework Agreement. Washington threatened to stop its shipments of fuel and food supplies unless North Korea ended its program and opened all facilities to UN inspections. North Korea refused and instead demanded further concessions, including a nonaggression pact with the United States. The Bush administration participated in new multilateral negotiations with Pyongyang. The six-party talks that began in August 2003 included the United States, North Korea, South Korea, Japan, the PRC, and Russia. Washington sought unsuccessfully to convince the PRC to use its influence with North Korea to end the standoff. The discussions failed to resolve the crisis, which was exacerbated when Pyongyang conducted a nuclear test in October 2006. The UN and individual states imposed a range of sanctions on North Korea. However, the six-party talks were resumed in February 2007 following an offer by Pyongyang to dismantle its nuclear program in exchange for the resumption of economic assistance.

The United States also faced a nuclear confrontation with Iran. In August 2002, U.S. officials revealed evidence that Tehran had constructed a uranium enrichment facility and a heavy-water production plant in violation of the Nuclear Nonproliferation Treaty. During the summer of 2003, UN inspections revealed weapons-grade uranium at Iranian nuclear sites. Iran subsequently informally agreed to end its program, but continued production. In April 2005, Tehran announced its plan to resume wide-scale uranium conversion to weapons-grade material. The United States deferred to the EU in negotiations with Iran, but pressed for a timeline for Tehran to cease its weapons program. The EU, United States, and Russia agreed to set August 2006 as a deadline for the cessation of its nuclear weapons efforts. However, when Iran ignored the date, American and European diplomats were unable to persuade Moscow and Beijing to agree on sanctions on Tehran.

The Bush administration supported the creation of a Palestinian state, but only after the Palestinian government suppressed terrorist groups and enhanced security against suicide bombings. Following attacks by Hezbollah, Israel invaded southern Lebanon in an effort to suppress the group. The Bush administration supported the UN armistice plan that called for the deployment of a peacekeeping force and the disarmament of nongovernment forces in southern Lebanon in exchange for the withdrawal of Israeli forces. Efforts to establish a lasting cease-fire between the Israelis and Palestinians were complicated by conflict between Hamas and the Fatah movement of the Palestine Liberation Organization. Both groups sought to control the Palestinian National Authority (PNA). In 2006 elections, Hamas gained a majority in the Parliament and subsequent control of the government. Hamas sought the ouster of PNA president Mahmud Abbas. The Bush administration supported Abbas and sought to isolate the Hamas government. Fighting between Hamas and Fatah left more than 200 dead at the end of 2006. More than 50 people were killed in January 2007, before an armistice was negotiated under the auspices of Egypt. Concurrently, a cease-fire between the PNA and Israel was negotiated in November 2006 and lasted until January 2007, when new fighting broke out.

In Somalia, militias allied to a radical Islamic group, the Islamic Courts Union, gained control of Mogadishu and most of the countryside. The Bush administration accused the Union of having ties to Al Qaeda and supported the interim Somali government. Washington endorsed a

UN resolution to deploy peacekeepers to end fighting between the Union and the interim government. In December, Ethiopia launched an incursion against the Union and its allies, and on 28 December, Ethiopian and government forces recaptured Mogadishu. In January 2007, the United States launched a series of military strikes on the retreating Union militias after intelligence revealed the presence of Al Qaeda figures among the forces. The attacks were conducted with the permission of the interim government.

THE DICTIONARY

– A –

AFGHANISTAN INTERVENTION. Afghanistan was a military quagmire for the Soviet Union, and Moscow's withdrawal of forces in 1988 led to a period of instability that resulted in the rise of the Islamic fundamentalist Taliban regime and the eventual U.S.-led invasion of the country in 2001. Following the 1991 **Soviet coup** against **Mikhail Gorbachev**, an agreement was reached between Moscow, Washington, and the main mujahideen groups that called for the cessation of external military assistance and the concurrent creation of an interim government, along with plans for future elections. However, various factions immediately commenced a civil war, which lasted until 1996 when the predominately Pashtun Taliban took control of 90 percent of the country. The remaining 10 percent, mainly in the northeast of the country, was under the control of the anti-Taliban Northern Alliance, composed mainly of ethnic Tajiks and Uzbeks. In 1997, the Taliban renamed the country the Islamic Emirate of Afghanistan. Only Pakistan, Saudi Arabia, and the United Arab Emirates granted diplomatic recognition to the Taliban.

The Taliban was led by the reclusive Mullah Mohammed Omar (1959–). It initiated a strict theocratic regime based on Sharia (Islamic law). Women's rights were limited. For instance, they could not appear in public without a veil or burqa. In addition, there were harsh penalties, including execution, for crimes, and music and films were banned. The Taliban also welcomed the **Al Qaeda** terrorist group, led by **Osama bin Laden**, into Afghanistan. Al Qaeda established a network of training camps throughout the country. In 1998, the United States conducted strikes with cruise missiles on suspected Al Qaeda sites in retaliation for the **embassy bombings** on American sites in Kenya and Tanzania. The

United States endeavored to pressure the Taliban to turn over bin Laden, but Washington also granted the regime more than $200 million per year in aid from 2000 to 2001 to help eradicate poppy production. Afghanistan was the world's largest producer of heroin until the Taliban launched a program to stop cultivation in 1999.

After the **September 11 terrorist attacks**, the **George W. Bush** administration demanded that bin Laden and his terrorist network be disbanded and handed over to the United States for prosecution. The Taliban refused, and America led a multinational military coalition in an invasion of Afghanistan, designated **Operation Enduring Freedom**. The allies also supplied weapons and equipment to the Northern Alliance and carried out air and missile strikes against the Taliban. The regime was overthrown, and the senior Taliban and Al Qaeda leaders were killed, captured, or fled the country (Mullah Omar and bin Laden reportedly escaped to Pakistan).

A transitional government was created under moderate Pashtun leader **Hamid Karzai**, who was subsequently appointed interim president in 2002 by a Loya Jirga (a traditional council of ethnic and religious leaders). A **United Nations** peacekeeping mission was deployed alongside U.S. and coalition forces. However, regional leaders retained significant political and economic power that limited the authority of Kabul. By 2003, Afghanistan was again the world's leading poppy producer. In 2004, Karzai was elected president in the country's first free and democratic balloting. In 2006, in response to increased terrorist attacks and Taliban insurgent attacks, the **North Atlantic Treaty Organization** took command of an expanded peacekeeping mission.

AL QAEDA. An international Islamic terrorist group. Al Qaeda (in Arabic, "the base" or "the foundation") had its roots among the Sunni mujahideen who opposed the Soviet occupation of **Afghanistan** during the 1980s. Al Qaeda was formed in 1988 by **Osama bin Laden**. The group sought to use the military training and weaponry from the anti-Soviet struggle to aid other Islamic groups involved in insurgency movements. In addition, bin Laden had developed an elaborate financial network to funnel donations from wealthy supporters of the mujahideen in states such as Saudi Arabia and Kuwait to armed Islamic groups. Throughout its history, Al Qaeda remained a loosely affiliated group whose core leadership provided some funding, training, and coordination for terrorist activities, but whose primary operations were carried by autonomous cells. The organization was estimated to include some 20,000 terrorists at its height in 2001.

In 1991, Al Qaeda opened a number of operations in Sudan, including businesses such as a construction firm and an export group. These firms further expanded the group's financial network. However, under pressure from the United States, the Sudanese government forced Al Qaeda to leave in 1996. Bin Laden and 200 members of Al Qaeda subsequently set up headquarters in Afghanistan and established training and operations bases with the support of the Taliban regime. To oversee the group, four major bodies were created: a military planning and operations executive, a financial committee, an advisory group on Islamic law and tradition, and a media group tasked to influence opinion among Muslims.

Through the 1990s, Al Qaeda operatives conducted a series of terrorist attacks against Western targets, including the 1993 **World Trade Center bombing** and the 1998 **embassy bombings** on the American missions in Tanzania and Kenya. The group also provided arms and financing for anti-Western, Islamic militia groups in Somalia. Senior Al Qaeda figure Muhammad Atef led a group of terrorists to Somalia to train fighters and create a network within the country. The defeat of American special operations forces and Army Rangers in the Battle of **Mogadishu** (1993) was seen by Al Qaeda's leaders as a potential model for future direct military engagements with Western militaries. Washington's withdrawal from the **Somalia intervention** was regarded by bin Laden as the beginning of the decline of U.S. global power. In 1996, bin Laden began to concentrate Al Qaeda resources in operations against the United States. In 1998, he issued a religious decree, or *fatwa*, against the United States and urged his followers to attack American and pro-Western targets. In response to the embassy attacks, Washington launched a series of cruise missile attacks on Al Qaeda sites in Afghanistan. That same year, Ayman al-Zawahiri, a leader of the Egyptian Islamic Jihad terrorist group, began working closely with bin Laden. Al-Zawahiri eventually became the number two leader for Al Qaeda and its chief operations planner. In 2000, Al Qaeda conducted a suicide bombing against the **USS Cole** in Yemen.

On 11 September 2001, Al Qaeda delivered its most devastating strike to date against the United States when 19 terrorists took control of four passenger airliners and flew one into the Pentagon and two others into the World Trade Center, destroying the Twin Towers and inflicting more than 3,000 casualties (the fourth plane crashed in Pennsylvania when passengers attempted to retake control of the aircraft from the hijackers). In response to the **September 11 terrorist attacks**, Washington and its allies invaded Afghanistan and overthrew the Taliban with the assistance of the anti-Taliban Northern Alliance. The United States also initiated a worldwide antiterrorism campaign, targeting Al Qaeda–linked groups in areas such the Philippines and Yemen. Bin Laden and al-Zawahiri escaped U.S. forces in Afghanistan and continued operations, although the majority of Al Qaeda fighters in Afghanistan were killed or captured. By 2004, many senior Al Qaeda leaders, including Khalid Sheikh Mohammed, the lead planner for the 2001 strikes, had been either captured or killed.

One result of the global counterterrorism campaign was a diffusion of leadership and command, so that individual cells gained greater autonomy and operational freedom (although access to funding was constrained). By 2003, Al Qaeda was estimated to spend about $30 million per year in operations, including training, weapons acquisitions, and covert activities such as the production of false identity paperwork. Operations around the globe began to be conducted by regional groups, while Al Qaeda served as a loose network to raise or transfer funds. Regional groups connected with Al Qaeda carried out a number of operations in the early 2000s, including the **Bali bombings** in 2002 and strikes in Istanbul in 2003. Attacks in Muslim countries, including Saudi Arabia, Morocco, and Jordan, undermined the group's popularity and led Arab governments to initiate steps to disrupt recruiting and fundraising within their borders.

Following the 2003 invasion of Iraq, Al Qaeda emerged as one of the more capable insurgency groups. The Al Qaeda leadership perceived that the U.S. invasion of Iraq would be a replication of the Soviet invasion of Afghanistan. Resources and fighters were concentrated in Iraq following the overthrow of the **Saddam Hussein** regime. Meanwhile, Abu Musab al-Zarqawi (1966–2005) merged his terrorist group with Al Qaeda in 2004 and emerged as the leader of

Al Qaeda in Iraq. Al-Zarqawi oversaw a dramatic increase in the use of suicide attacks on Iraqi civilian and governmental targets as a means to undermine the nascent pro-U.S. regime. His sanction of attacks on Muslims led to differences with al-Zawahiri, who preferred that Al Qaeda concentrate on U.S. targets. Al-Zarqawi was killed during an American attack on 7 June 2006, but was quickly replaced, and Al Qaeda continued operations in Iraq. *See also* NATIONAL COMMISSION ON TERRORIST ATTACKS UPON THE UNITED STATES (9/11 COMMISSION); INTERNATIONAL TERRORISM; IRAQ WAR; WAR ON TERROR.

ALBRIGHT, MADELEINE (1937–). U.S. secretary of state. Albright was born in Prague in 1937 to a Czechoslovakian diplomat who fled in 1949 to escape the Communists. The family eventually settled in the United States, and Albright graduated in 1959 from Wellesley College, before she earned a doctorate from Columbia University in 1976. She served on the National Security Council from 1979 to 1981 in the administration of **James E. Carter**. In 1993, she was appointed ambassador to the **United Nations (UN)** by President **William J. Clinton**.

In 1996, Albright became the second secretary of state in the Clinton administration and the first woman appointed to the position. She implemented reforms at the State Department in the face of significant budget cuts and streamlined the agency's bureaucracy. She generally enjoyed good relations with Congress, but was unable to convince the legislature to pay U.S. arrears to the UN or to expand funding for family planning and other social programs of the State Department. In addition, during her tenure, the Senate rejected the **Comprehensive Test Ban Treaty**.

One of Albright's priorities was **North Atlantic Treaty Organization (NATO)** expansion, and she secured both domestic and international support for the **NATO enlargement** to include the Czech Republic, Hungary, and Poland. Russian acquiescence for expansion was secured through the creation of new, joint structures within the alliance. Albright also maintained support for the continuation of economic sanctions against the regime of **Saddam Hussein** and was one of the leading advocates for air strikes on the Iraqi regime following the 1998 forced removal of UN weapons inspectors. Albright opposed early admission of the People's Republic of China into the **World Trade Organization**, but endorsed decoupling **human rights and trade policy** in order to maintain most-favored-nation trade status for Beijing.

Albright quickly emerged as a leading hawk within the administration on hard-line policies toward Serbia over the treatment of ethnic minorities in the former Yugoslavia. She ensured continued congressional support for the deployment of a NATO-led peacekeeping force in **Bosnia**. Following Serb atrocities against ethnic Albanians in **Kosovo**, Albright garnered support within NATO for military action, even though she was unable to secure a UN resolution that specifically authorized the use of force because of Russian opposition. NATO forces conducted a 77-day air campaign to compel a settlement. She was eventually able to negotiate an agreement for Russian participation in the subsequent peace mission in Kosovo.

Albright was criticized when the United States did not take a more active role in ending the **Rwandan genocide**. Efforts to promote a settlement of the **Arab-Israeli conflict** languished until the personal intervention of Clinton in a series of summits. Although Albright advocated military action against **international terrorist** groups such as **Al Qaeda** following attacks against American interests, she was unable to convince the president to undertake a systematic campaign against the groups. After leaving office, Albright remained active in public affairs and has been a vocal critic of the **George W. Bush** administration's launch of the **Iraq War** in 2003. *See also* BALKAN WARS.

ANDEAN COUNTERDRUG INITIATIVE (ACI). In 2001, the administration of President **George W. Bush** expanded an existing counternarcotics initiative, **Plan Colombia**, to provide greater economic and security assistance to Latin American countries trying to suppress **drug trafficking** and trade through the Andean Counterdrug Initiative. Between 2001 and 2005, funding for ACI expanded from $676 million to $725 million. Funds, equipment, and training were provided to Bolivia, Brazil, Colombia, Ecuador, Panama, Peru, and Venezuela. ACI provided money and equipment for countries to eradicate drug crops and support increases in non-narcotic agriculture. Several countries initiated or expanded aerial spraying programs with the American assistance. Coca production was the main target in most countries. ACI programs included security training and assistance in Colombia and Ecuador, as well as funding for judicial reforms and improvements in Brazil, Panama, and Venezuela. All countries received support to improve border security in order to suppress narcotrafficking. Security aid dominates ACI. In 2005, $462.6 million in U.S. aid was related to security and law enforcement, while $262.4 went to economic development and restructuring. Under ACI, the United States deployed 800 American military advisors and 600 civilian security contractors in Colombia, which remains the main beneficiary of ACI. In 2005, Colombia received $462.7 million in assistance, while Peru, the second largest recipient of ACI support, got $115.4 million. Meanwhile, Venezuela received just $2.97 million. In spite of ACI, coca cultivation has continued to increase throughout the region, growing by 8 percent between 2001 and 2005. Meanwhile, there has also been an increase in poppy production in the region.

ANGOLAN CONFLICT. Africa's longest civil war, and one of the many proxy struggles conducted during the **Cold War** by the United States and the Soviet Union. An estimated one million Angolans died during the four-decade-long struggle. In 1956, a Marxist group, the Popular Movement for the Liberation of Angola (Movimento Popular de Libertação de Angola, MPLA), was formed to fight for independence from Portugal. Through the 1960s, the MPLA conducted a guerrilla war against the colonial administration and a rival group, the National Front for the Liberation of Angola (Frente Nacional de Libertação de Angola, FNLA). A third group, the National Union for the Total Independence of Angola (União Nacional para a Independência Total de Angola, UNITA), emerged in 1966 under the leadership of Jonas Savimbi. The MPLA was supported by the Soviet Union and Cuba, while the FNLA received aid and assistance from the United States and UNITA was backed by South Africa. Cuban troops and military advisors helped the MPLA gain control of most of Angola, including the rich oil-exporting coastal regions.

When Angola became independent in 1975, the MPLA seized control of the government. Antiapartheid rebels used Angola to launch attacks on the South African–controlled province of Namibia, prompting Pretoria to launch military incursions into Angola. The FNLA and UNITA conducted an armed insurgency against the MPLA regime. Successive peace agreements through the 1970s failed. UNITA emerged as the main opposition, as the FNLA became increasingly marginalized. As a result, Washington began to provide aid to Savimbi and UNITA, although a 1980 law prevented the deployment of military advisors or U.S. forces in Angola. Meanwhile, Cuba maintained 50,000 troops in Angola throughout the 1980s.

In 1989, a peace agreement brokered by Washington and Moscow called for the withdrawal of Cuban and South African forces and pledged an end to foreign military aid. Although the cease-fire arrangement paved the way for an end to outside intervention, fighting continued between the government and UNITA. A second major peace agreement was signed in 1991 and allowed elections in 1992. In the balloting, the MPLA won 53 percent of the vote, UNITA 34 percent, and the FNLA 2.4 percent. In concurrent presidential elections, Jose Eduardo dos Santos, the leader of the MPLA, won the polling with 49 percent of the vote to 40 percent for Savimbi. UNITA rejected the election results and resumed fighting. However, the United States stopped all military aid and recognized the MPLA-led government. The administration of President **William J. Clinton** supported the deployment of **United Nations (UN)** peacekeepers following another cease-fire accord in 1994. Through the 1990s, illicit diamonds funded UNITA's continuing guerrilla campaign. In 1999, the United States sponsored a UN resolution to ban the export of gems, commonly called conflict or blood diamonds, from the region.

Savimbi was killed during fighting in 2002, and UNITA finally agreed to disarm and renounce violence. Beginning in August 2002, some 350,000 UNITA fighters and their families were demobilized and reintegrated into society.

ANNAN, KOFI (1938–). Seventh secretary-general of the **United Nations (UN)**. Annan was elected to lead the world body with strong support from the administration of **William J. Clinton**, which viewed him as a reformer who would cut corruption and inefficiency at the UN. Annan was born in Kumasi, Ghana, to a prominent and influential family. He earned a degree from Macalester College in St. Paul, Minnesota, in 1961. The following year, he began work for the World Health Organization. In 1972, Annan earned a master's degree from the Massachusetts Institute of Technology. He returned to Ghana to serve in a government post, before returning to work at the UN as an assistant secretary-general in 1987.

In 1990, Annan negotiated the withdrawal of 900 Westerners and UN workers following the invasion of Kuwait. After the **Persian Gulf War**, he arranged the **Oil-for-Food Program**, which allowed Iraq to sell energy resources in exchange for humanitarian supplies, including food and medicine. Annan was in charge of peacekeeping operations during the **Rwandan genocide** and was criticized by the Clinton administration for the UN's slow response to the Tutsi massacres. However, he served as a special representative to the former Yugoslavia from 1995 to 1996, where he worked with U.S. and European officials to facilitate the **Dayton Accords** and the subsequent deployment of the **North Atlantic Treaty Organization**–led peacekeeping force.

In 1996, the Clinton administration opposed the reelection of **Boutros Boutros-Ghali** as secretary-general of the UN. Washington even threatened to veto Boutros-Ghali's nomination. U.S. officials argued that Boutros-Ghali was unsuited to conduct needed reforms at the world body. Instead, the United States promoted the candidacy of Annan, who was subsequently nominated by the Security Council on 13 December and confirmed by the General Assembly four days later. The Clinton administration hoped Annan would carry out a range of reforms. In 1997, Annan released his plan to restructure the UN, "Renewing the United Nations." Annan consolidated some agencies and improved record-keeping and auditing. He also negotiated a reduction of UN dues for the United States in exchange for payment of arrears by Washington in an effort to end the **United Nations Dues Controversy**.

Annan criticized the Clinton administration's military strikes in Afghanistan and Sudan in response to the **embassy bombings** in Kenya and Tanzania in 1998. The following year, he helped negotiate an agreement among Libya, the United States, and Great Britain to resolve compensation over the 1988 **Pan Am Flight 103 bombing**. Also in 1999, Annan worked with the Clinton administration to facilitate an end to the ethnic conflict in **East Timor** and the subsequent deployment of a UN-sponsored peace mission.

In 2000, the secretary-general issued a report that served as the basis for the Millennium Summit. He called for greater involvement by wealthy states in efforts to increase economic development in poorer states, including debt relief and the reduction of trade barriers. He further called for technological investments to overcome the "digital divide" between developed and developing countries. In 2001, Annan launched an HIV/AIDS initiative designed to slow the spread of the disease in developing countries. The administration of **George W. Bush** later pledged $15 billion to support HIV/AIDS prevention and treatment in Africa. Following the **September 11 terrorist attacks**, Annan worked with the Bush administration to formulate a series of antiterrorism measures and to foster intelligence and law enforcement cooperation among member states.

In December 2001, Annan and the UN were jointly awarded the Nobel Peace Prize. The next year, Annan was reelected for a second term with broad support. From 2003 onward, Annan endorsed efforts by the United States to convince the UN Security Council to deploy a peacekeeping force in response to the **Darfur Crisis**.

Annan opposed U.S. military action in the 2003 **Iraq War** and repeatedly urged the United States and Great Britain to not attack the regime of **Saddam Hussein** without the backing of the UN Security Council. Annan later labeled the invasion as illegal. Nonetheless, a UN mission was deployed in Iraq until August 2003, when a suicide bombing killed 22 people. UN personnel were then withdrawn, and Annan rejected a 2005 internal report that recommended the return of UN operations to Iraq. An investigation revealed a range of problems and mistakes in the 2003 UN Iraq mission, and the secretary-general fired several staffers and demoted others.

Following the Iraq War, relations between Annan and the Bush administration deteriorated significantly. Annan opposed U.S. efforts to keep American military personnel exempt from prosecution by the **International Criminal Court**. Meanwhile, the Bush administration criticized the secretary-general's management of the world body. Annan was criticized for his role in the $64 billion Oil-for-Food Program. A 2005 investigation led by former chairman of the U.S. Federal Reserve Paul Volcker found numerous instances of fraud and bribery in the program and faulted the secretary-general for lack of oversight, although it did not find evidence of illegal activity by the secretary-general himself. Annan rejected calls for his resignation following the revelations.

In 2005, Annan proposed sweeping reforms to the UN, including changes in the secretariat and an expansion of the Security Council. He also called for the relocation of UN offices from New York and Geneva to less expensive areas as a cost-saving measure. In 2006, Annan's tenure was further tainted by the revelation of widespread sexual misconduct by UN peacekeepers during a 2003 mission in the Democratic Republic of the Congo. Meanwhile, an investigation discovered more than 200 instances of fraud in equipment purchasing for UN peacekeeping operations. Eight senior UN officials were suspended. Annan's term ended on 31 December 2006.

APARTHEID. A notorious system of racial segregation in South Africa that was dismantled under intense domestic and international pressure in 1991. Apartheid's roots were in laws enacted in South Africa in 1910, stripping blacks of most political rights, and subsequent legislation that limited black land ownership to 7.3 percent of the total area of the country. In the 1950s, a series of laws formalized apartheid, including measures that classified the population into one of three categories (whites, colored or mixed, and native), segregated public facilities, and required all South Africans to carry identification paperwork. Domestic resistance to apartheid was led by the African National Congress (ANC). The **United Nations (UN)** and individual countries protested the measures through various diplomatic channels. In 1962, the UN created a special committee to foster a peaceful end to apartheid.

Because the minority-led South African regime was staunchly anticommunist, successive U.S. administrations supported the government. Washington imposed an arms embargo in 1964, but it refused to sever economic ties with Pretoria until the 1980s. Until the end of apartheid, the United States was South Africa's second largest trading partner with an average trade of more than $4 billion in imports and exports. The administration of President **James E. Carter** increased diplomatic pressure on Pretoria to repeal apartheid legislation. Carter also refused to recognize the four newly created black homelands in 1976. In 1983 Congress enacted a measure that banned the **International Monetary Fund (IMF)** from providing funds to Pretoria, and in 1985, further restrictions were placed on the export of police and security equipment to the regime.

Within the United States, a broad antiapartheid campaign spread among domestic groups and the general public. Stockholders pressured firms to divest from South Africa, leading more than 200 U.S. corporations to end their economic involvement in the country. Other countries followed suit; for instance, by 1988, 92 British, 21 Canadian, and 17 Australian companies had also divested from South Africa. Worldwide, more than 400 corporations left or withdrew investments from the apartheid regime. The boycott movement was particularly strong in the United States among college students, leading to a series of protests and other tactics to force divestiture. By 1987, more than 155 colleges and universities had withdrawn funds from ventures in the country. American foreign investment in South Africa declined from $4 billion in 1986 to less than $1 billion in 1988.

In 1986, Congress enacted the Comprehensive Antiapartheid Act. The measure forbade U.S. firms from making new investments in South Africa. It also called for those companies that remained engaged in the South African economy to employ practices that mitigated the economic impact of apartheid by hiring or promoting blacks and investing in segregated areas. The Act also required the president to issue an annual report on apartheid and to make recommendations on additional sanctions. President **Ronald W. Reagan** vetoed the legislation, arguing that the economic sanctions would harm blacks, but Congress overrode the veto. The following year, Congress forbade intelligence-sharing between Washington and Pretoria. State and local governments also adopted economic restrictions on trade and investment with the apartheid regime. By 1990, 27 states, 24 counties, and more than 90 individual cities and towns had enacted some form of sanctions against South Africa.

In the late 1980s, the Reagan administration undertook a diplomatic offensive to resolve regional conflicts and therefore remove the security imperatives to support Pretoria. The most significant strife involved the **Angolan Conflict** and the related insurgency in Namibia. In Angola, a pro-Soviet regime was supported by Cuban troops in an ongoing civil war against pro-American rebels with South African support. Anti–South African rebels also used Angola to conduct a guerrilla campaign in Namibia. In 1988, Washington initiated peace negotiations, which led to the withdrawal of Cuban forces from Angola and the concurrent withdrawal of South African troops from Namibia. In 1989, Namibia conducted its first free and open elections, and the country gained full independence the following year.

In 1991, South African president F. W. de Klerk ended the apartheid regime and ordered that a new constitution be drafted. Two years later, a transitional, multiracial body was inaugurated to oversee open elections and the installation of a permanent, constitutional government. Washington lifted the sanctions imposed on South Africa, including constraints in IMF lending. The administration of President **William J. Clinton** provided $10 million for the elections and dispatched U.S. observers as part of the international observation team that monitored the balloting. ANC leader **Nelson R. Mandela** was elected as the country's first post-apartheid president, and the ANC dominated the legislature. The Clinton administration provided Pretoria with a three-year, $600 million package of trade and economic assistance. Mandela criticized the amount of American aid and called for dramatic increases to allow the restructuring of the South African economy. Tensions also emerged between Pretoria and Washington over the increasingly close ties between South Africa and states such as Cuba, Libya, and Iran. Meanwhile, by 1998, U.S. investments in South Africa had increased to more than $5 billion, while annual trade returned to its previous, presanctions levels.

ARAB-ISRAELI CONFLICT. The end of the **Cold War** seemed to usher in an era of progress in resolving the Arab-Israeli conflict; however, tensions and strife continued into the new century. Palestinian Liberation Organization (PLO) support for the regime of **Saddam Hussein** during the **Persian Gulf War** undermined the organization's credibility among many Arab states and led to renewed pressure on PLO leader **Yasser Arafat** to reach a political settlement with Israel. In 1991, President **George H. W. Bush** threatened to withhold $10 billion in loan guarantees to Israel unless the country stopped new settlements in the Occupied Territories (construction was halted in 1992). Meanwhile, Israel and the PLO conducted a series of secret negotiations, which resulted in the 1993 Oslo Accords. Under that agreement, Israel and the PLO recognized each other, and Arafat was allowed to return to Gaza. In addition, Israel pledged to turn over land for an eventual Palestinian state, and the PLO promised to renounce violence. Many contentious issues, such as the status of Jerusalem, were left for future agreements. To oversee the Palestinian areas, a transitional government, the Palestinian National Authority (PNA), was created. Arafat was elected president of the PNA in 1996. However, further progress was halted by a series of suicide bombings by the radical Islamist group Hamas and the subsequent Israeli retaliations.

In 1997, the two sides reached an accord on the withdrawal of Israeli force from Hebron, and the following year, under the sponsorship of President **William J. Clinton**, Arafat and Israeli prime minister Benjamin Netanyahu signed the Wye River Agreement. The pact called for Israel to withdraw from additional territory in exchange for Palestinian security measures, including a renunciation of terrorism, bans on certain types of weapons, and prohibitions on incitement to violence by PNA leaders. The outbreak of renewed violence in 2000 (the Second Intifada) and subsequent Israeli military attacks led to the failure of the Wye River principles. Meanwhile, U.S.-sponsored talks to negotiate a settlement between Israel and Syria also collapsed in 2000. Nevertheless, in May, Israel withdrew its forces from southern Lebanon after almost 20 years of occupation.

Clinton hoped to secure a major Middle East peace agreement before he left office, and so he invited Arafat and Israeli prime minister **Ehud Barak** to renewed discussions that culminated in the 2000 **Camp David Summit**. Barak offered Arafat a comprehensive package that included all of the Gaza Strip and 90 percent of the West Bank to become a Palestinian state. Against the advice of the Americans and even most of his own close advisors, Arafat rejected the offer. Realizing that he had made a mistake, Arafat offered to accept Barak's proposal with some additional concessions at the 2001 **Taba Summit**. However, Barak was engaged in an election campaign and was unwilling to make a deal until after the balloting. Barak lost the election and Likud leader **Ariel Sharon** became prime minister in February 2001.

In the aftermath of the **September 11 terrorist attacks**, Israel and the Palestinians agreed to a cease-fire, but fighting continued. In 2002, Israel began construction of a wall to prevent Palestinian incursions and suicide attacks. The wall became the demarcation line between Israel and the PNA. President **George W. Bush** called for Israeli withdrawal from occupied areas and the creation of a Palestinian state in a June 2002 speech. In 2004, the International Court of Justice ruled that the wall violated international law. Also, in 2004, Arafat died. Moderate Palestinian leader Mahmoud Abbas was elected president of the PNA. Strife escalated after the election of Abbas, as Hamas battled the president's Fatah Party for control of the PNA, especially after Hamas won a majority in the parliament in January 2006. The 2005 **Cedar Revolution** in Beirut and the subsequent removal of Syrian troops from Lebanon was seen by the Bush administration as a diplomatic opening. However, in June 2006, Hezbollah guerrillas attacked an Israeli patrol, killing several soldiers and capturing two. In response, Israel launched an invasion of Lebanon. The **United Nations (UN)** Security Council passed resolutions that called for an Israeli withdrawal, the disarmament of Hezbollah forces in southern Lebanon, and the deployment of a UN peacekeeping force. *See also* INTERNATIONAL TERRORISM.

ARAFAT, YASSER (1929–2004). Leader of the Palestinian Liberation Organization (PLO) and the first president of the Palestinian National Authority (PNA). Arafat was born in Cairo to Palestinian exiles, but moved to Jerusalem when he was five. He became a Palestinian nationalist and briefly served in the Egyptian Army. In 1959, he formed the Fatah Movement, which came to dominate the PLO. Arafat became the leader of the PLO in 1969. The following year, after the PLO was forced out of Jordan, Arafat located the organization in Lebanon and became involved in that country's civil war, while continuing to wage a terrorist campaign against Israel. In 1982, the United States and other Western powers negotiated safe passage for Arafat to Tunis during the Israeli invasion. Throughout the 1980s, Arafat survived repeated Israeli efforts to kill him. In 1988, he proclaimed an independent Palestinian state and began to transition the official PLO stance from the destruction of Israel to a two-state solution.

Arafat supported the regime of **Saddam Hussein** during the **Persian Gulf War**. His stance led many moderate Arab states to withdraw assistance from the PLO. After the U.S-led coalition victory, Arafat engaged in a new series of negotiations. The 1993 Oslo Accords endorsed the creation of a Palestinian state in return for a renunciation of violence by the PLO and recognition of Israel. For his part in the talks, Arafat shared the Nobel Peace Prize in 1994.

In 1996, Arafat was elected president of the PNA, which had been formed as a transitional government under the terms of the Oslo Accords. He had difficulty in constraining the more militant groups such as Hamas that carried on a struggle with Fatah over control of the Palestinian Authority and a terrorist campaign against Israel, which led to repeated Israeli incursions into the PNA. Through the 1990s, terrorist attacks led to Israeli retaliatory strikes and escalating violence. The pattern undermined Arafat's authority among the Palestinians and his legitimacy before Israeli leaders.

In 1998, President **William J. Clinton** convinced Arafat to restart talks to finalize a long-term peace agreement with Israel. The resultant Wye River Agreement led to the release of Palestinian prisoners and Israeli redeployments in exchange for new security measures by the PNA. Clinton continued to pressure both Arafat and Israeli leaders to reach a settlement. At the 2000 **Camp David Summit**, Arafat was offered a Palestinian state consisting of the Gaza Strip and 90 percent of the West Bank. Arafat made a tactical mistake in the negotiations and attempted to gain more territory. He rejected the Israeli offer, but, later seeing his mistake, Arafat endeavored at the 2001 **Taba Summit** to gain a settlement based on the terms from the Camp David sessions. Elections in Israel brought the nationalist Likud Party to power and led to the collapse of peace talks, along with a new round of violence. His leadership among the Palestinians was undermined by rampant corruption among the Fatah-dominated PNA government. During the final years of his life, the struggle for control of the PNA between Fatah and Hamas intensified. Arafat died in 2004. *See also* ARAB-ISRAELI CONFLICT; INTERNATIONAL TERRORISM.

ARMS CONTROL. One of the foreign policy priorities of successive post–**Cold War** administrations. Washington sought to expand agreements developed during the bipolar conflict in order to gain a **peace dividend** in reduced domestic defense expenditures and lessen global tensions. U.S. arms control efforts included attempts to reduce both strategic and conventional weapons.

In 1991, U.S. president **George H. W. Bush** and Soviet premier **Mikhail Gorbachev** signed the first **Strategic Arms Reduction Treaty (START I)**, which reduced the nuclear arsenal to 6,000 total warheads for each superpower. START I was the culmination of negotiations that began in 1982. Talks immediately began on START II, which would further reduce nuclear stockpiles. Bush and Russian president **Boris Yeltsin** signed START II in January 1993. The U.S. Senate ratified the accord in 1996, but the Russian Duma delayed approval until 2000 in protest over U.S. military strikes against Iraq and the 1999 **Kosovo War**. Negotiations over START III never came to fruition, as the new **Strategic Offensive Reductions Treaty (SORT)** superseded START II. SORT was agreed upon by presidents **George W. Bush** and **Vladimir Putin** in 2001 and signed the following year. It limited the nuclear arsenal of each country to 2,200 warheads. Although the United States had signed the 1996 **Comprehensive Test Ban Treaty (CTBT)**, the Senate declined to ratify the prohibition on nuclear tests, based on concerns that the accord's verification procedures would compromise American security.

Central to U.S. counterproliferation efforts was the Nuclear Nonproliferation Treaty (NPT), signed in 1968. Under its terms, only the People's Republic of China, France, the Soviet Union (and later Russia), the United Kingdom, and the United States were permitted to possess nuclear weapons. The NPT suffered a setback in 1998 when India and Pakistan conducted reciprocal nuclear tests. In addition, the United States has been frequently criticized for tolerating Israel's undeclared nuclear program. India, Pakistan, and Israel are not signatories to the NPT. U.S. efforts to curtail North Korea's nuclear program were unsuccessful through the 1990s and early 2000s. Pyongyang withdrew from the NPT in 2006 following nuclear tests in October 2006. Washington was also unsuccessful in attempts through 2007 to stop Iran's nuclear program. In 1993, the United States, along with other countries, signed the Chemical Weapons Convention. By 2004, more than 80 percent of the American chemical weapons had been destroyed.

U.S. conventional arms control policy emphasized reductions in overall weapons numbers. In 1990, members of the **North Atlantic Treaty Organization** and the Warsaw Pact signed the **Conventional Forces in Europe Treaty (CFE)**. The CFE dramatically reduced the number of troops, tanks, artillery pieces, and other conventional forces. After the demise of the Soviet Union, the successor states agreed to abide by the CFE. In 1996, the CFE was expanded through the Flank Agreement, which further lessened conventional troops and weapons. Washington also participated in the Wassenaar Arrangement to control the proliferation of missile technology. Both the **William J. Clinton** and **George W. Bush** administrations refused to sign the **Ottawa Treaty**, which banned the use of land mines, citing the need to use the weapons as a deterrent in areas such as South Korea. The United States also declined to sign the **United Nations** convention on small arms (the Firearms Protocol), which is designed to reduce the illicit trafficking in small arms and weapons transfers. *See also* FRAMEWORK AGREEMENT WITH NORTH KOREA; HADLEY, STEPHEN J.; INDIAN AND PAKISTANI NUCLEAR TESTS; NORTH KOREAN NUCLEAR CRISES; SIX-PARTY TALKS.

ARMS SALES AND WEAPONS TRANSFERS. An important component of United States foreign and security policy during the Cold War, arms sales and weapons transfers were elevated to become one of the nation's key goals during the administration of **William J. Clinton**. Weapons sales were seen as a way to promote the domestic American arms industry and to ensure interoperability among the country's key allies. Defense sales were also a tool to gain or maintain influence with regional allies.

During the **Cold War**, the Soviet Union was the main competitor to the United States in the global arms market. However, the end of the superpower conflict and the superiority of U.S. arms during the 1991 **Persian Gulf War** led America to become the world's leading exporter of weapons. For instance, from 1986 to 1989, the United States exported $34.5 billion in weapons, but that figure more than doubled in the 1991–1994 period to $81.3 billion. In order to promote arms sales and weapons transfers, Clinton issued Presidential Decision Directive 34 (PDD-34) in 1997, which asserted that arms exports were an important component of the nation's foreign policy. PDD-34 also directed government agencies to implement policies to support and bolster military exports. For instance, the Department of Commerce developed marketing strategies that were employed by American embassy staff to assist U.S. defense companies. In addition, the Clinton administration provided more than $20 billion in direct assistance to defense firms between 1993 and 2001. Furthermore, Clinton removed restrictions on sales to certain geographic regions with a history of instability. In 1997, Clinton overturned a ban put in place by President **James E. Carter** on the sale of high-technology weaponry to Latin America. Within a year, U.S. arms sales to the region doubled from $600 million to $1.2 billion.

Support for defense firms was designed to bolster an industry that was experiencing dramatic declines. Between 1987 and 1997, the American defense sector lost 1.2 million jobs. Some of the employment losses were due to a wave of mergers. The Clinton administration supported the consolidation of the large defense corporations in order to ensure a more robust and vibrant sector. Several large firms received subsidies when they joined together. For instance, the merger between Lockheed and Martin-Marietta was supported by a $1.8 billion subsidy. From 1993 to 2001, there were 21 major mergers, as 14 large companies were consolidated into four.

The Clinton administration launched a new proposal in 2000, the Defense Trade Security Initiative (DTSI). The program made U.S. technology and arms transfers to America's closest allies easier and quicker through export licensing systems, expedited review for exports, and increased export exemptions for qualified nations, including **North Atlantic Treaty Organization** partners, Japan, and Australia. The program also benefited European firms with U.S. subsidiaries by streamlining the licensing process and allowing for increased joint projects between defense firms on both sides of the Atlantic.

The strategies worked and the United States dominated the global arms trade through the 1990s. In 1999, arms sales under the Clinton administration peaked at $20.78 billion. The administration of President **George W. Bush** continued the main arms sales policies of its predecessor and expanded sales and weapons transfers as part of the broader **war on terror**. By 2005, the United States supplied almost half (48.5 percent) of all arms and weapons sold to the developing world. That year, Washington had total global sales of $21 billion. In comparison, Russia provided 15 percent and third-place Great Britain accounted for 13 percent. Through 2006, Saudi Arabia, Israel, Taiwan, Egypt, and Japan were the largest buyers of American weaponry. The Bush administration also expanded the Foreign Military Financing (FMF) program, which provides funds for countries to purchase American weaponry. Between 2001 and 2005, FMF funding increased from $3.5 billion to $4.5 billion. Among the 71 recipients of FMF were Afghanistan, Colombia, Jordan, Pakistan, and the Philippines. Israel remains the largest beneficiary of FMF and receives approximately $1 billion per year to purchase U.S. weapons.

ASIA-PACIFIC ECONOMIC COOPERATION (APEC). The APEC forum is a regional organization that promotes economic and political collaboration among countries in the Pacific Ocean or along its rim. APEC was formed in 1989 by 12 countries: Australia, Brunei, Canada, Indonesia, Japan, Malaysia, New Zealand, the Philippines, Singapore, South Korea, Thailand, and the United States. Membership grew to 21 states with the addition in the 1990s of Chile, Hong Kong, Mexico, Papua New Guinea, the People's Republic of China, Peru, Russia, Taiwan, and Vietnam. The administration of **George W. Bush** has supported India's admission to APEC. The organization has sponsored a range of agreements that reduced tariffs and other impediments to trade.

APEC was initially proposed by Australia. **George H. W. Bush** enthusiastically supported the creation of the organization as a way to improve American trade relations with Asia and as a means to maintain American influence in the region. APEC was also an important part of the foreign policies of subsequent administrations. In 1993, following stalled economic negotiations through the **World Trade Organization (WTO)**, the administration of President **William J. Clinton** began to emphasize the strengthening of regional trade groups such as APEC and the **North American Free Trade Agreement** as the nation's main foreign economic policy goal. That year, Clinton invited the heads of government of the APEC nations to an economic summit at Blake Island, Washington. The meeting was the first of the annual APEC Leaders' Meetings, which subsequently provided a forum for national leaders to negotiate major issues. In 1997, APEC leaders developed an action plan to assist countries harmed by the **East Asian Financial Crisis**, including the temporary reductions in tariffs and the extension of credits to countries affected by the financial downturn. In 1998, the United States and Japan cosponsored an agreement to provide $10 billion in debt relief to countries in the region. The following year, APEC leaders endorsed the creation of a **United Nations** peacekeeping force for **East Timor**. At the 2006 gathering, Washington and Moscow signed an agreement to allow Russia to enter the WTO.

ASPIN, LESLIE, JR. ("LES"; 1938–1995). Longtime member of the U.S. House of Representatives and the first secretary of defense for President **William J. Clinton**. Aspin was born in Milwaukee, Wisconsin. He attended Yale University, was a Rhodes Scholar, and eventually received a doctorate in economics from the Massachusetts Institute of Technology in 1966. He was elected to the House of Representatives as a Democrat from Wisconsin in 1970 and served until 1993, when he was appointed secretary of defense. Aspin's tenure at the Department of Defense was marked by controversy. He was beset by health problems and angered many conservatives by his embrace of deep cuts in defense expenditures and personnel. In addition, in December 1993, Aspin endeavored to craft a new policy toward homosexuals in the military. The resultant policy, known as "Don't Ask, Don't Tell," mandated that personnel would not be asked about their sexual orientation, but could be dismissed from the service for homosexual acts. The policy was criticized by gay rights groups for not going far enough and condemned by conservative groups for going too far. Aspin also angered conservatives by allowing women to fly combat aircraft and serve on combat ships in the navy. One result was that Aspin alienated military supporters in Congress.

Aspin was also criticized for the planning and operations during the 1993 **Somalia intervention**, especially after he refused a request by **Colin Powell**, the chairman of the Joint Chiefs of Staff, for helicopter gunships and tanks to support the U.S. operation in **Mogadishu**. The defeat of U.S special operations forces during the Battle of Mogadishu was a low point in post–Cold War U.S. military history and constrained American participation in future humanitarian missions.

In 1993, Aspin opposed Clinton's decision to dispatch an American military force to Haiti to pressure the nation's military junta. When it confronted an angry mob in Port-au-Prince, the force withdrew before it even landed. The episode further undermined the credibility of the American military. The secretary also opposed U.S. intervention in the **Balkan Wars**, including the disbursement of humanitarian aid through airdrops. Aspin oversaw the military strikes against the regime of **Saddam Hussein** following revelations of a plot to assassinate former president **George H. W. Bush** by the Iraqis. In addition, Aspin managed successful rounds of base closures, which eliminated or consolidated more than 130 military facilities, including 30 large bases. The realignment resulted in savings of more than $2 billion per year.

As a result of ongoing differences with Clinton, Aspin resigned in 1994. He died of a stroke the following year.

ASSOCIATION OF SOUTHEAST ASIAN NATIONS (ASEAN).
ASEAN was formed in 1967 as a regional organization to prevent Communist expansion during the **Cold War**. It evolved into a trade organization and welcomed former Communist countries as members in the 1990s. ASEAN members include Brunei, Cambodia, Indonesia, Laos, Malaysia, Myanmar (Burma), the Philippines, Singapore, Thailand, and Vietnam. In 2006, the trade bloc consisted of more than 554 million people with a combined economy worth more than $2.17 trillion. In 2005, the ASEAN region was the fourth largest trade partner with the United States. In 1994, the ASEAN members began meeting with other countries and organizations through what became known as the ASEAN Regional Forum. The forum grew to include 26 countries, including the United States, the **European Union**, Australia, Japan, and Russia. ASEAN helped coordinate the national reactions to the 1997 **East Asian Financial Crisis** and endorsed the response of the **International Monetary Fund (IMF)** to the regional crisis. Individual ASEAN states provided funding and credits to the IMF recovery program. In 1999, some ASEAN members endeavored to have the organization lead the **United Nations**–sponsored peacekeeping mission during the **East Timor** crisis. The body decided in-

stead to endorse Australia's leadership of the mission, and ASEAN members Malaysia, the Philippines, Singapore, and Thailand contributed forces to the operation.

The ASEAN members regularly meet with American diplomats in what are known as the "10+1 sessions." Annual meetings provide a means for the United States to harmonize **trade policy** with the ASEAN states and to address economic issues. In 2002, ASEAN endorsed American involvement in regional counterterrorism efforts, including the deployment of forces in the Philippines. In addition, that year, Washington proposed the creation of the Enterprise for ASEAN Initiative (EAI), which allowed individual ASEAN states to negotiate bilateral free trade agreements with the United States. The first step in the bilateral agreements was a Trade and Investment Framework Agreement (TIFA). By 2003, Washington had TIFAs with Indonesia, the Philippines, and Singapore. In 2006, the administration of **George W. Bush** signed a TIFA with ASEAN that would pave the way for a comprehensive free trade accord between the United States and the organization. An exception to the TIFA was the continuation of American trade sanctions on Myanmar because of that country's **human rights** record. Meanwhile in 2006, the United States and the ASEAN nations also signed a separate agreement to improve security cooperation in counterterrorism and anti-**drug trafficking** efforts.

AXIS OF EVIL. In his State of the Union speech on 29 January 2002, President **George W. Bush** declared that Iran, Iraq, and North Korea were part of an "axis of evil" that supported **international terrorism** and sought to develop and proliferate weapons of mass destruction (WMD). The president's speech came in the aftermath of the **September 11 terrorist attacks** and the resultant **war on terror**. Bush's address harkened back to World War II and the Axis powers of Germany, Italy, and Japan. The phrase and the speech also had roots in the foreign policy beliefs of **neoconservatives**. In the initial drafts of the speech, only Iran and Iraq were mentioned; North Korea was added by speechwriters to ensure that the address did not appear to be anti-Muslim. Bush also asserted that the United States had a right to use preemptive force to prevent a strike against it. The Axis of Evil Speech was seen as the beginning of the diplomatic efforts to lay the groundwork for the invasion of Iraq. The 2003 **Iraq War** removed Baghdad from the axis, but both North Korea and Iran expanded their WMD programs. The phrase was used by the regime in Tehran and leaders such as **Hugo Chávez** of Venezuela to criticize the Bush administration, which also faced domestic criticism over the perceived expansion of the global antiterrorism campaign. *See also* FRAMEWORK AGREEMENT WITH NORTH KOREA; NORTH KOREAN NUCLEAR CRISES; SIX-PARTY TALKS.

AZNAR, JOSÉ MARIA ALFREDO (1953–). Prime minister of Spain from 1996 to 2004. Aznar's fiscal conservatism allowed Spain to qualify for the single currency of the **European Union (EU)**, the **euro**. He was also staunchly pro-American and supported the United States in the 2003 **Iraq War**.

Aznar was born in Madrid. He earned a law degree from Complutense University in 1975. After graduation, he worked as a tax inspector. Aznar became the local head of the conservative People's Alliance (Alianza Popular, AP) in 1979 and was then appointed to the party's national board. In 1982, he was elected to the Spanish parliament. Three years later, he was chosen as assistant secretary-general of the AP. In 1989, he led the party in its transformation to the People's Party (Partido Popular, PP) and became the first national leader of the new grouping. In 1995, he survived an assassination attempt by Basque separatists. The PP won the largest percentage of votes in the 1996 elections, but not an absolute majority. Aznar formed a coalition government with two conservative parties and became prime minister.

Aznar implemented a range of fiscal reforms to ensure that Spain remained on track to join the EU's single currency. The 1997 austerity budget lowered Spain's deficit to less than 3 percent of gross domestic product for the first time in the 1990s. He also launched a series of privatizations, reversing the nationalization campaign of the former socialist government. In 1999, Spain joined other members of the EU in adopting the euro. His economic reforms lowered unemployment, from 18 percent to 10 percent by 2003, but Spain continued to have one of the highest jobless rates in the EU. Nonetheless, Spain had one of the fastest-growing economies in the EU. The reforms also resulted in the first budget surplus in Spain in more than a decade.

In the late 1990s, Aznar proposed an expansion of the **North Atlantic Treaty Organization** to include countries outside of Europe, including Japan and Israel. In 2000, Aznar and the PP secured an outright majority in the parliament in national elections. He continued his reform platform, including a controversial plan for changes to the nation's university system and a failed effort to revise the nation's unemployment policies.

Following the **September 11 terrorist attacks** on the United States, Aznar emerged as a supporter of the U.S.-led global **war on terror**. He offered assistance to the United States in the **Afghanistan intervention** and endorsed increased intelligence and law enforcement cooperation against terrorism. The prime minister sought new global emphasis on the counterterrorism against Basque terrorist groups in Spain. In 2003, Aznar backed the **Iraq War**, even though it was domestically unpopular. After the fall of the regime of **Saddam Hussein**, Aznar dispatched Spanish troops to support the American-led coalition.

Ahead of elections in 2004, Aznar announced he would adhere to a campaign pledge and not seek a third term. He handpicked his successor, and the PP seemed to enjoy a comfortable lead in preelection polls. However, on 11 March 2004, an **Al Qaeda**–linked terrorist group carried out a series of strikes on the Madrid train system. The attacks took place three days before the national elections and killed 191. Aznar's government initially blamed Basque terrorists. The attacks swung public opinion against the PP, and the socialists won the polling with 43.3 percent to the PP's 38.3 percent. Aznar's successor, José Luis Rodriguez Zapatero of the Socialist Party, then withdrew Spanish troops from Iraq. After leaving office, Aznar accepted a teaching position at Georgetown University in the United States.

– B –

BAKER, JAMES A., III (1930–). U.S. secretary of state, secretary of the treasury, and White House chief of staff. Born in Houston, Texas,

James Addison Baker III graduated from Princeton University in 1952 and then joined the Marine Corps. After his discharge, he entered the law school at the University of Texas in Austin, where he earned a doctorate in 1957. Baker entered politics as a close friend of **George H. W. Bush** and later managed Bush's campaign for the Senate, Gerald R. Ford's bid for the presidency, and in 1980, Bush's presidential campaign. When **Ronald W. Reagan** became president in 1981, Baker was named chief of staff at the White House, where he oversaw the 1981 legislation that reformed the U.S. tax code. In 1985, he was named to the cabinet as secretary of the treasury. He was instrumental in initiating a policy of fair trade designed to level the economic playing field by punishing unfair trade practices. After the election of Bush in 1988, Baker was named secretary of state, a post he held until 1992.

As secretary of state, Baker worked with Bush to develop a degree of cohesion seldom matched in U.S. foreign policy. Bush and Baker worked to rebuild a bipartisan consensus on foreign policy in the aftermath of the Iran-Contra scandal. In addition, the two sought to enhance trade and diplomatic relations with Canada and Mexico (a strategy they referred to as "securing our base"). Improving economic relations with Asian states was also a priority of the administration and was manifested in the role of the United States in the creation of the **Asia-Pacific Economic Cooperation** forum in November 1989. Baker helped Bush manage U.S. policy in the waning days of the **Cold War**, including seeking reforms of **North Atlantic Treaty Organization** in an effort to counter proposals for a pan-European security structure and providing support for the domestic economic and political reforms of Soviet leader **Michael Gorbachev**.

Baker's tenure witnessed the end of the Cold War and the transition of Russia from enemy to ally. He negotiated a series of **arms control** agreements, including the 1990 **Conventional Forces in Europe Treaty** and the 1991 **Strategic Arms Reduction Treaty (START I)**. Baker opposed a large, Marshall Plan–style aid program to assist the former Communist states of Eastern and Central Europe.

One of Baker's greatest achievements was the formation of the international coalition that defeated **Saddam Hussein** in the 1991 **Persian Gulf War**. Baker engaged in extensive shuttle diplomacy to secure

Arab support for the coalition and garnered successive **United Nations** resolutions, which ultimately authorized the use of military force.

In the Western Hemisphere, Baker negotiated an end to Soviet aid for the Sandinistas in Nicaragua and subsequent elections that removed the pro-Soviet regime from power. He coordinated the diplomatic response that surrounded the successful invasion of Panama in 1990 and resulted in the overthrow of **Manuel Noriega**. Baker oversaw the negotiations with Mexico and Canada that led to the signing of the **North American Free Trade Agreement**. His foreign policy was less successful in dealing with such issues as the onset of civil war in Yugoslavia, where Baker opposed the breakup of the former Communist state. Baker's efforts to repair Sino-American relations after the **Tiananmen Square protests** were less than successful, but helped to prevent a wider breach with the People's Republic of China.

In 1992, Baker resigned as secretary of state in order to manage Bush's unsuccessful reelection campaign. In the 2000 presidential election, Baker was asked to represent **George W. Bush** in the Florida recount. Baker was a cochair for the 2006 commission that recommended increased regional diplomacy and a U.S. military withdrawal as a means to end the country's intervention in Iraq. *See also* BALKAN WARS; IRAQ WAR.

BALI BOMBINGS (2002). Three coordinated terrorist attacks against Western targets on the Indonesian tourist island of Bali on 12 October 2002. The attacks were undertaken by Jemaah Islamiyah, an Islamic terrorist group with links to **Al Qaeda**. The first attack occurred at Paddy's Bar and involved a suicide bomber with a backpack loaded with explosives. The second explosion occurred across the street at the Sari Club, a large nightclub. A van packed with ammonium nitrate, a commercial fertilizer, was detonated by remote control. These two bombings left 202 dead and 209 injured. The majority of the dead were foreign tourists, including 89 Australians, 25 Britons, and 7 Americans. The third attack was against the U.S. consulate in Denpasar. A small bomb exploded outside the consulate. It caused only minor damage and injured one person.

The attacks undermined Indonesia's lucrative tourist trade. Western governments also questioned Jakarta's willingness and ability to suppress Islamic terrorist groups. In response, the government launched a series of investigations and raids against Islamic organizations. In 2003, Amrozi bin Haji Nurhasyim was sentenced to death for buying the van and explosives used in the Sari Club attack. Two other figures were also convicted and given death sentences. A fourth defendant was given life in prison after he publicly expressed regret for his role in the bombings. The radical Islamic cleric leader of Jemaah Islamiyah, Abu Bakar Bashir, was accused of involvement in the attacks. He was sentenced on conspiracy charges to two and a half years in prison in 2005. Twenty-four others were arrested in 2005 for suspected participation in the Bali bombings or a subsequent attack on the Marriott Hotel in Jakarta in 2003 in which 14 people were killed. In 2006, many of those convicted, although none of those sentenced to death, were released in an amnesty by the Indonesian government. *See also* WAR ON TERROR.

BALKAN WARS. A series of conflicts that broke out in the Balkans as areas of the former Yugoslavia sought independence. The strife was marked by **ethnic cleansing** and was ultimately resolved through international intervention. During the **Cold War**, the six republics of Yugoslavia were kept under control of the central government through a mixture of concessions and suppression. The death of Yugoslav leader Tito in 1980 led to the ascension of **Slobodan Milošević** as leader of the federation. Milošević endeavored to enhance Serbian power at the expense of the other republics. This strengthened his political control within Serbia, but fueled separatist sentiments in Croatia and Slovenia.

With the end of the Cold War, in 1990 open elections were held throughout Yugoslavia, bringing nationalist parties to power in Slovenia, Croatia and Serbia. Serbs in Croatia launched an insurrection against the newly elected Croat leader Franjo Tuđman, but the rebellion only fueled support for Croatian independence, since the rebels sought closer ties with Serbia. In 1991, both Slovenia and Croatia declared independence. Yugoslav Army troops and Serbian paramilitaries were quickly defeated by the Slovenes in what became known as the "Ten-Day War." However, the federal units made a concentrated effort to defeat the Croats. Former U.S. secretary of state Cyrus Vance negotiated an armistice that ended the major fighting between Serbia and Croatia by creating safe zones for ethnic Serbs and paving the way for the deployment of a **United Nations (UN)** peace-keeping force, the United Nations Protection Force (UNPROFOR). With the deployment of UNPROFOR, the Yugoslav Army units withdrew from Croatia.

In 1992, Bosnia-Herzegovina and Macedonia declared independence. The remaining republics, Serbia and Montenegro, formed the Federal Republic of Yugoslavia, while Bosnia, Croatia, and Slovenia were granted international recognition (including seats at the UN). Recognition of Macedonia was blocked by Greece because the country's name was the same as a Greek province, and Athens had concerns over potential efforts to create a Greater Macedonia.

Ethnic Serbs launched an ethnic cleansing campaign against Muslims in an attempt to create an autonomous republic from Bosnian territory. Civil war also commenced between ethnic Bosnians and Croats in 1993. The following year, the United States helped formalize a peace agreement in the **Bosnian Conflict**. The Serb ethnic cleansing campaign in Bosnia resulted in the deaths and displacement of tens of thousands of Bosnians and Croats. In 1995, Croatia commenced an offensive that drove most of the remaining Serbs from the country. The fighting marked the end of the Serb-Croat War. The inability of UNPROFOR to end the conflict led the **North Atlantic Treaty Organization (NATO)** to assume command of the peace-keeping mission under the terms of the U.S.-brokered **Dayton Accords**. NATO involvement ended the Bosnian Conflict.

In 1998, new fighting broke out between ethnic Albanians and Serbs in what became the **Kosovo War**. Once again, Serb paramilitaries, supported by the Yugoslav Army, initiated an ethnic cleansing campaign. Serb oppression prompted a NATO-led, 77-day air campaign against Belgrade. Milošević was forced to grant autonomy to Kosovo and allow the deployment of a NATO-led peacekeeping force.

Milošević lost the elections in 2000 and was forced from office. He and other officials were arrested and tried by the International Criminal Tribunal for Yugoslavia (Milošević died in 2006 during his trial). In 2006, Montenegro became independent. The following year, the UN proposed a settlement in Kosovo that would grant the province a significant degree of autonomy. *See also* BUSH, GEORGE H. W.;

CHRISTOPHER, WARREN; CLINTON, WILLIAM J.; WESTERN EUROPEAN UNION.

BALLISTIC MISSILE DEFENSE (BMD). Also known as National Missile Defense, BMD is a planned system to protect all 50 U.S. states from incoming missile attack. Throughout the **Cold War**, the United States relied on deterrence instead of missile defense to counter potential threats. This policy preference was codified by the 1972 Antiballistic Missile (ABM) Treaty between the United States and the Soviet Union. Nonetheless, there were repeated efforts to develop a missile defense system. The Strategic Defense Initiative (SDI) of the administration of **Ronald W. Reagan** was the most significant manifestation of the drive to develop a BMD system. In its efforts to develop SDI, the Reagan administration unilaterally reinterpreted the ABM Treaty and argued that the development—though not deployment—of space-based antimissile systems were acceptable under the agreement.

Iraq fired 90 Scud missiles during the **Persian Gulf War**, and these attacks accelerated interest in missile defense systems, as did the **North Korean nuclear crises**. In 1991, **North Atlantic Treaty Organization (NATO)** endorsed the development of tactical missile defense systems. The United States, France, Germany, and Italy subsequently launched a multilateral initiative to replace the Patriot Antimissile System under the Medium Extended Air Defense System (MEADS). France withdrew from MEADS in 1996 to develop a unilateral system. In 1997, Washington and Ottawa signed an accord to cooperate on space-based BMD.

At the 1999 NATO Summit in Washington, D.C., the administration of **William J. Clinton** launched a twin initiative to enhance BMD cooperation and bolster counterproliferation efforts. However, the BMD proposals were opposed by many alliance members because of the costs. In addition, Russia opposed the effort, and some NATO states were unwilling to risk alienating their former Cold War enemy after years of improving relations. The Senate rejection of the **Comprehensive Test Ban Treaty** undermined confidence in American efforts to lead on counterproliferation. Nevertheless, BMD remained popular with congressional Republicans. In 1999, Congress passed, and Clinton signed into law, the National

Missile Defense Act. The Act required that the United States develop and deploy a BMD system. In 2000, the United States conducted an unsuccessful BMD test (an interceptor drone failed to destroy a simulated incoming ballistic missile). Russian opposition to BMD prompted Clinton to suspend work on missile defense after the failed test.

After his inauguration in 2001, **George W. Bush** publicly declared his intent to proceed with BMD, even if it meant unilaterally abrogating the ABM Treaty. Even close American allies questioned Bush's decision. There was concern that the Bush administration would increase tensions with Russia. Allies also feared that if America were successful in deploying BMD, the nation would return to an isolationist foreign policy. In order to reassure allies and build support, Washington offered to extend any BMD system to include key states such as the NATO states, Japan, and Australia. Bush also tried to negotiate a compromise with Russian president **Vladimir Putin** over the ABM Treaty.

In the aftermath of the **September 11 terrorist attacks**, Putin dropped his objections to U.S. BMD in an act of support for the Bush administration. Without formal Russian opposition, Bush announced the American withdrawal from the ABM Treaty on 13 December 2001 to take effect after the required six-month notification period. Russia even began to work with the United States and its allies on missile defense. Moscow was invited to participate with NATO on tactical missile defense and, in 2004, NATO and Russia conduct their first joint BMD exercises. Meanwhile, the alliance affirmed its interest in BMD with the creation of the NATO Missile Defense Project Group, which was tasked to develop agreements on missile defense and ensure interoperability. In 2003, Australia announced that it would collaborate with the United States on BMD.

In 2002, the U.S. Ballistic Missile Defense Organization, the agency with primary responsibility for BMD, was transformed into the Missile Defense Agency. From that year onward, America spent about $9 billion per year on BMD. In 2005, the United States began initial deployment of the BMD system. The first phase included 20 ground-based (10 in Alaska and 10 in California) and 20 ship-based interceptor missiles and an air-launched Patriot missile system. In addition, there were upgrades to missile tracking facilities in the United

States (in Alaska) and in Great Britain and Denmark. A new class of ballistic missile sensors was deployed on naval vessels.

Both domestic and international critics of BMD questioned the costs of the program and argued that the funds could be better spent on **homeland security** programs such as border protection and cargo inspection. They also argued that BMD could give the United States a false sense of security and encourage enemies to attempt to attack America by smuggling a nuclear device into the country. Meanwhile, no system envisioned would be able to destroy the 2,400 ballistic missiles of Russia. Finally, opponents asserted that potential enemy states such as North Korea or Iran did not possess ballistic missiles with the range to hit the United States.

BARAK, EHUD (1942–). Prime minister of Israel from 1999 to 2001. Barak was born Ehud Brog in the then British colony of Palestine. He joined the Israeli military in 1959 and became one of the most decorated soldiers in Israeli history. Barak rose through the ranks to become the chief of the general staff and the highest-ranking Israeli soldier. Barak's political career began in 1995, when he was appointed minister of the interior. He subsequently served as foreign minister and was elected to the Knesset in 1996. That year he also became leader of the Labor Party. On 17 May 1999, Barak was elected prime minister.

Barak initiated a range of efforts to resolve the **Arab-Israeli conflict**. He ordered the withdrawal of Israeli forces from southern Lebanon and launched peace negotiations with Syria. At the 2000 **Camp David Summit**, Barak put forward the most far-reaching peace proposal made to date by an Israeli leader, offering to turn over the entire Gaza Strip to the Palestinians, along with 90 percent of the West Bank and 3 percent of the Negev Desert. Palestinian leader **Yasser Arafat** rejected the proposal. A new *intifada*, or uprising, was initiated by the Palestinians, leading to widespread loss of life among both Palestinians and Israelis. In 2000, the Barak government agreed to start construction of a multilayered security fence to separate Jewish and Palestinian areas and to provide better security against terrorist attacks after a study reported that 75 percent of suicide bombers crossed illegally into Israel through areas where the border was undefended. The fence was condemned by international organizations, including the **United Nations**, but it reduced suicide bombings in the areas where it was constructed by 90 percent, leading successive governments to expand the barrier. At the 2001 **Taba Summit**, Barak and Arafat were again unable to reach a lasting agreement following the prime minister's loss in Israeli elections. In 2001, Barak left office and was succeeded by **Ariel Sharon**. In 2005, Barak unsuccessfully campaigned for the leadership of the Labor Party.

BATTLE OF MOGADISHU. *See* MOGADISHU, BATTLE OF.

BERGER, SAMUEL R. ("SANDY"; 1945–). National security advisor for President **William J. Clinton** from 1997 to 2001. Berger was born in Sharon, Connecticut. He graduated from Cornell University in 1967 and then earned a law degree from Harvard University in 1971. He worked on the presidential campaign of George McGovern in 1972, where he met and became lifelong friends with Clinton. Berger joined a prestigious Washington law firm in 1973, served as the deputy director for policy planning from 1977 to 1980, and then returned to private practice.

Berger was instrumental in convincing Clinton to run for the presidency in 1992 and served as a foreign policy advisor during the campaign and then as a member of the transition team. Clinton appointed Berger the deputy national security advisor in 1993. He worked closely with National Security Advisor **Anthony Lake** to formulate and implement policy, but was frustrated by the administration's initial focus on domestic policy and urged greater U.S. involvement in the **Bosnian Conflict**. Berger aided in the development of the 1995 **Dayton Accords** and the subsequent deployment of **North Atlantic Treaty Organization**–led force to monitor the peace agreement.

In 1997, Clinton appointed Berger as national security advisor to replace Lake, who had resigned. Berger formulated the administration's diplomatic and military response to the 1998 **embassy bombings** in Kenya and Tanzania. He also worked with the departments of State and Defense to coordinate the 1998 air strikes on Iraq during Operation Desert Fox following interference with **United Nations** weapons inspections. Berger helped convince Clinton to make regime change a component of U.S. policy toward Iraq. He also helped prepare the guidelines for the failed 2000 **Camp David Summit**, one of the last major efforts to resolve the **Arab-Israeli conflict** during the Clinton administration.

Berger left office in 2001. In 2004, the justice department launched an investigation into Berger's theft of classified documents from the National Archives. The documents were about the Clinton administration's management of the **Millennium Bombing Plots**. Berger pleaded guilty to misdemeanor charges and was sentenced to 100 hours of community service, a $50,000 fine, and probation. *See also* IRAQ WAR.

BERLIN WALL. The Berlin Wall was constructed in 1961 to separate the Communist and non-Communist areas of Berlin, and it became a potent symbol of the **Cold War**. At the end of World War II, Berlin was divided into two areas, East and West. The eastern area was under the control of the Soviets, while the West was divided between the United States, France, and Great Britain. Through the 1950s, large numbers of Germans fled the eastern zone for the freedom and economic opportunity of the West. To stop the exodus, the Soviets constructed a fortified wall, with minefields and surveillance equipment. More than 900 people subsequently died while trying to escape to West Berlin (at least 270 were shot by Communist border guards). Meanwhile, more than 5,000 managed to successfully escape to freedom between 1961 and 1989. In November 1989, border crossings through the wall were opened, and crowds spontaneously began to dismantle the barrier. Reunification of the two Germanys followed in 1990. The fall of the Berlin Wall was one of the most vivid events of the end of the Cold War.

BERLUSCONI, SILVIO (1936–). Two-time prime minister of Italy, including a term from 2001 to 2005 that made him the longest-serving Italian leader since World War II. Berlusconi's tenure was marked by close relations with the United States, including support for **Operation Enduring Freedom** and the U.S.-led military action during the **Iraq War**.

Berlusconi was born in Milan and received a law degree from Statale University in Milan in 1961. He had a highly successful business career and earned a fortune through the media corporation Fininvest, which operated Italy's first private television station. Fininvest eventually controlled more than 150 media firms, including the country's largest publishing company and main daily newspaper.

Berlusconi also became well known throughout Italy as the owner of the football team AC Milan. He was the wealthiest man in Italy with a worth of $12 billion by 2005.

In 1993, Berlusconi formed his own political party, Forza Italia ("Go Italy"). Forza Italia did very well in the 1994 elections and gained 113 seats in the 630-member Chamber of Deputies (the second most of any of the conservative parties). Berlusconi formed a coalition government with the National Alliance and the Northern League, but the government lasted only seven months before the coalition broke apart and new elections were called. Berlusconi became prime minister in 2001 as the leader of a coalition government. During his second term, Berlusconi was a staunch supporter of the U.S.-led **war on terror**. The prime minister dispatched Italian forces to participate in **Operation Enduring Freedom** and ordered enhanced intelligence and law enforcement cooperation with the United States. He also emerged as one of the foremost European backers of military action against the regime of **Saddam Hussein**. Following the 2003 **Iraq War**, Italy deployed troops as part of the multilateral coalition in Iraq even though there was widespread domestic opposition to the U.S.-led invasion.

Meanwhile, Berlusconi faced a range of charges on corruption and antitrust violations. He maintained that efforts to indict him were politically motivated, while prosecutors argued that the prime minister used his office to evade charges. Parliament enacted a controversial immunity law to protect Berlusconi, who was able to avoid indictment. He was defeated in elections in April 2006, but remained active in politics. *See also* COMMON FOREIGN AND SECURITY POLICY; EUROPEAN SECURITY AND DEFENSE IDENTITY.

BIN LADEN, OSAMA (1957–). Osama Muhammad Awad bin Laden was one of the founders and leaders of the **Al Qaeda** terrorist organization. He was born in Riyadh to a wealthy Saudi Arabian family, the 17th of more than 50 children. Bin Laden studied economics and business administration at King Abdulaziz University, but failed to obtain a degree. He became attracted to fundamentalist Islam and, meanwhile, inherited millions following his father's death in 1968.

Following the Soviet invasion of Afghanistan in 1979, bin Laden traveled to Pakistan to join the anti-Soviet mujahideen. During the

1980s, bin Laden worked to raise money for the mujahideen. In 1988, he helped found Al Qaeda. Bin Laden and Al Qaeda embraced an extremist interpretation of the Quran that emphasized the role of *jihad*, or holy war, in liberating Muslim areas from domination by foreign powers, Western culture, and pro-Western regimes. He asserted that any means were justified in the jihad against the enemies of Islam, including attacks on civilians. During the **Persian Gulf War**, bin Laden offered to raise troops to defend Saudi Arabia from a possible Iraqi invasion, but the Saudi government rebuffed his proposal. As the conflict progressed, bin Laden grew increasingly hostile to the presence of American troops in the country. His criticisms of the royal family led the Saudis to seek his arrest, but bin Laden went into exile. His Saudi citizenship was revoked in 1994. Nonetheless, many prominent Saudis continued to provide bin Laden and Al Qaeda with funds. Bin Laden then attempted to set up operations in Sudan, but was forced to leave under American and Saudi pressure in 1996.

Bin Laden traveled to Afghanistan and became involved in the ongoing civil war. He provided monetary support to the Taliban, and Al Qaeda members fought alongside the Islamic extremist movement. When the Taliban gained control of Afghanistan, they allowed bin Laden to establish a series of training camps. Meanwhile, he issued a *fatwa* or religious decree in 1998 calling upon Muslims to attack and kill Jews, Americans, and other Westerners. Al Qaeda was subsequently involved in the 1998 **embassy bombings**. The administration of President **William J. Clinton** conducted a series of retaliatory missile strikes on Al Qaeda camps in Afghanistan and a suspected terrorist site in Sudan. The raids failed to kill bin Laden, who intensified his campaign against the United States.

Bin Laden and the senior Al Qaeda leadership generally did not plan specific operations, but provided funding and coordination for attacks, including the failed 1999 **Millennium Bombing Plots**, the 2000 **USS *Cole* bombing**, and the **September 11 terrorist attacks**. Bin Laden was indicted on a variety of charges related to these attacks, and the administration of President **George W. Bush** placed a bounty of $25 million on bin Laden after the 2001 strikes. The Taliban was overthrown during **Operation Enduring Freedom**, but U.S.-led coalition forces failed to kill or capture bin Laden and the senior Al Qaeda and Taliban leaders. Bin Laden and his allies fled to a remote area of Pakistan, where he issued a series of video and audio tapes condemning the United States and its allies in the **war on terror**. After 2001, Al Qaeda became even more diffuse, and individual terrorist cells became increasingly autonomous. Nonetheless, bin Laden remained the spiritual leader of the movement. *See also* AFGHANISTAN INTERVENTION; INTERNATIONAL TERRORISM; NATIONAL COMMISSION ON TERRORIST ATTACKS UPON THE UNITED STATES (9/11 COMMISSION).

BLAIR, TONY (1953–). British prime minister. A staunch ally of successive American presidents, Blair ensured the continuation of the "special relationship" between the United States and Great Britain. Blair won his first parliamentary seat as a Labour candidate in 1983 and then became leader of the party in 1994. Three years later, Blair led the Labour Party to victory in its first electoral win in nearly two decades and became the youngest prime minister of the 20th century. Blair's foreign policy rested on efforts to both improve relations with the **European Union (EU)** and maintain Britain's strong ties with the United States. He endorsed the creation of a stronger **European Security and Defense Identity** and deeper economic integration with the EU. Blair was also a strong supporter of EU expansion. He worked closely with President **William J. Clinton** to maintain sanctions on Iraq, and the British continued to supply forces to enforce the no-fly zones in the country. The two leaders also cooperated over the **North Atlantic Treaty Organization**–led air campaign in **Kosovo**, although Blair unsuccessfully advocated for the early use of ground forces.

Following the **September 11 terrorist attacks**, Blair offered the United States a range of military support. British forces participated in **Operation Enduring Freedom** in **Afghanistan** and generally supported the administration of **George W. Bush** in its global **war on terror**. In spite of domestic opposition, Blair also supported the 2003 **Iraq War**. He endeavored in vain to secure a **United Nations** resolution specifically authorizing the use of force in Iraq. Nevertheless, British troops participated in the invasion even without the resolution and although the deployment created tensions with Britain's main European allies, Germany and France. Although Blair won reelection in 2001 and 2005, his popularity was undermined by allegations that the decision to go to war was based on faulty intelligence and concerns about the continuing deployment of forces in Iraq. Nonetheless, the Anglo-American alliance remained the cornerstone of Blair's foreign policy.

BOLTON, JOHN R. (1948–). Undersecretary of state and then U.S. ambassador to the **United Nations (UN)** in the administration of **George W. Bush**. John Robert Bolton was born in Baltimore, Maryland, and earned a law degree from Yale University in 1974. During the 1980s and 1990s, Bolton served in the departments of Justice and State in the administrations of **Ronald W. Reagan** and **George H. W. Bush**. Bolton also served as a member of the Republican Party National Committee. Following the election of 2000, Bolton worked with **James A. Baker III** to represent the Republicans during the Florida recount. George W. Bush subsequently appointed Bolton undersecretary of state for arms control and international security. In this position, he was in charge of the country's counterproliferation efforts. Bolton also led the administration's opposition to the **International Criminal Court**. The hawkish Bolton clashed repeatedly with Secretary of State **Colin Powell** over the administration's Iraq policy. In 2005, Bolton was nominated to be UN ambassador, but his confirmation was blocked by a Democratic-led filibuster in the Senate. Bush subsequently kept Bolton in place through a recess appointment. In 2006, the outspoken Bolton led efforts for UN reform and oversaw the administration's response in the UN to the **North Korean nuclear crisis**, the Sudan Crisis, and the Iranian Nuclear Crisis. In December 2006, Bolton resigned when it became apparent that he would not be able to win confirmation in the Senate.

BOSNIAN CONFLICT. Ethnic strife in Bosnia provided one of the first tests of the post–Cold War security order. Although the **European Union (EU)** and the **United Nations (UN)** initially took the lead in trying to diffuse the conflict, stability was restored only with the deployment of U.S.-led **North Atlantic Treaty Organization (NATO)** forces.

Following a declaration of independence from Yugoslavia, Bosnia was engulfed in a bitter civil war. Estimates were that some 250,000 people were killed and more than 1.3 million were displaced. The European Community (EU after 1993) sought to manage the conflict without U.S. involvement. The administration of **George H. W. Bush** supported the maintenance of Yugoslavia as a consolidated state and, in light of other security commitments, was very willing to allow the EU and UN to lead. However, a coordinated EU/UN effort failed to stop the violence—labeled "**ethnic cleansing**" because of the effort to remove populations—despite the deployment of a UN peacekeeping mission, the United Nations Protection Force (UNPROFOR). In 1992, NATO agreed to support the international effort. NATO and **Western European Union (WEU)** forces were deployed around the states of the former Yugoslavia to enforce an arms embargo. During the 1992 U.S. presidential campaign, then-candidate **William J. Clinton** had been very critical of inaction by the Bush administration; however, once in office, Clinton continued Bush's policies until 1995.

In 1993, NATO and WEU air assets began to monitor a "no-fly" zone (Operation Deny Flight) as mandated by the UN. On 28 February 1994, NATO aircraft downed four Serb aircraft that were violating the no-fly zone. This was the first instance in NATO's history in which alliance forces engaged in combat. On 2 June 1995, a U.S. F-16 participating in Operation Sharp Guard was downed by a surface-to-air missile. The pilot ejected, survived for five days in Bosnian Serb territory and was rescued by U.S.-led NATO special operations forces.

Serb attacks on Sarajevo prompted NATO to launch air strikes beginning on 30 August 1995. The strikes finally compelled the Serbs to accept the U.S.-sponsored **Dayton Accords** in November 1995. Under the terms of the accords, a NATO-led peace enforcement force, Implementation Force (IFOR), was deployed, including American ground troops. IFOR numbered 60,000 troops, with forces from NATO and 18 other states. IFOR was succeeded by the Stabilization Force (SFOR) with some 32,000 troops, subsequently reduced to 18,000. During the combined IFOR/SFOR operations, 723,000 refugees were returned and resettled. SFOR also oversaw open elections in Bosnia and conducted a range of infrastructure repair and reconstruction efforts.

Although not initially a formal part of the SFOR mission, NATO and allied forces also apprehended more than 30 indicted war criminals for prosecution by the UN Special Tribunal for the Former Yugoslavia at The Hague. Nonetheless, NATO was significantly criticized for failing to undertake more aggressive efforts to capture war criminals, especially after several incidents in which NATO personnel identified indicted persons but were unable or unwilling to take action. On 2 December 2004, NATO turned command of the peace mission in Bosnia over to the EU, and SFOR was succeeded by European Union Force (EUFOR), consisting of 7,000 troops.

BOUTROS-GHALI, BOUTROS (1922–). United Nations (UN) secretary-general from 1992 to 1996. Boutros-Ghali was born in Cairo and earned a Ph.D. in international law from the University of Paris in 1949. He held a variety of academic posts and was Egypt's foreign minister from 1977 to 1991. He played an important part in the negotiations that culminated in the 1978 Camp David Accords between Israel and Egypt.

Boutros-Ghali became secretary-general of the UN in 1992. He was criticized by the administration of President **William J. Clinton** for the inability of the world body to take strong action in a range of ethnic conflicts. Boutros-Ghali was unable to garner international support to force a settlement in the **Balkan Wars** or to intervene in the 1994 **Rwandan genocide**. Washington also accused Boutros-Ghali of not taking strong action to prompt the regime of **Saddam Hussein** into greater compliance with UN sanctions in the early 1990s. The United States unsuccessfully attempted to pressure the secretary-general into a range of reforms and restructurings at the world body, including reducing the share of UN dues paid by America.

In 1996, Boutros-Ghali was nominated for a second term, but his candidacy was blocked by the United States, which threatened to veto the nomination. Boutros-Ghali became the first UN secretary-general not elected to a second term. Instead, **Kofi Annan**, an American-backed candidate, was chosen to lead the UN into the new century. *See also* BOSNIAN CONFLICT; SOMALIA INTERVENTION.

BRUSSELS SUMMIT (1994). One of the most significant meetings in **North Atlantic Treaty Organization (NATO)** history, the Brussels Summit initiated three U.S.-sponsored efforts to address the changing international security environment in the wake of the end of the **Cold War**. At the meeting, three major initiatives were endorsed: the **Partnership for Peace (PfP)**, the Combined and Joint Task Force (CJTF) system, and a **European Security and Defense Identity (ESDI)**. The PfP program created a means for security cooperation between NATO and non-NATO states, including potential new members. The CJTF established a system to allow NATO resources to be used in non-NATO missions. This laid the groundwork for the subsequent NATO-led peacekeeping missions in the Balkans. NATO partners also agreed on the utility of a greater European role in transatlantic security through the further development of the ESDI. NATO leaders ordered a comprehensive study on enlargement, which later paved the way for the 1999 **NATO enlargement** to include the Czech Republic, Hungary, and Poland. Finally, the summit also saw agreement on the need for closer cooperation between NATO and its former Cold War enemies. *See also* BALKAN WARS; ORGANIZATION FOR SECURITY AND COOPERATION IN EUROPE.

BUCHANAN, PATRICK J. (1938–). Conservative American commentator and political candidate who advocated renewed isolationism after the end of the **Cold War**. Patrick Joseph Buchanan was born in Washington, D.C. He graduated from Georgetown University in 1961 and earned a master's degree from Columbia University the following year. He became a journalist, but in 1969 was appointed as an advisor to President Richard M. Nixon. Buchanan also served as an aide and speechwriter to presidents Gerald R. Ford and **Ronald W. Reagan**. In the 1980s, he gained national fame as a conservative columnist and commentator, with regular appearances on various television programs.

Buchanan unsuccessfully campaigned for the presidency in 1992, 1996, and 2000. In his first two campaigns, he sought the Republican nomination, but in the 2000 campaign he was the Reform Party's candidate and placed fourth in the general election with 0.4 percent of the vote. Buchanan advocated a traditional, isolationist form of conservatism that appealed to working-class Americans. He was an opponent of contemporary **immigration policies** and interventionist foreign policy. Buchanan also opposed free trade agreements and called for the repeal of the **North American Free Trade Agreement**.

Instead, he advocated the selective use of tariffs and duties to protect American industries and jobs.

BUSH, GEORGE H. W. (1924–). Forty-first president of the United States. George Herbert Walker Bush was born in Milton, Massachusetts, on 12 June 1924, to a prominent family. His father was a wealthy investment banker who served two terms as a U.S. senator. On his 18th birthday, during World War II, the younger Bush joined the U.S. Navy as an aviator and subsequently fought in the Pacific Campaign. He was awarded several decorations, including the Distinguished Flying Cross, and was honorably discharged in 1945.

Bush received a degree from Yale University in 1948 and went on to earn a fortune in the burgeoning Texas oil industry. He lost a 1964 Senate bid in Texas, but was elected to the U.S. House of Representatives in 1966. He served until 1971, when he was appointed U.S. ambassador to the **United Nations (UN)**, serving until 1973. That year, Bush was named chairman of the Republican National Committee. In 1974, the future president was sent to the People's Republic of China as a special envoy. Bush then served as the director of the Central Intelligence Agency from 1976 until 1977. After unsuccessfully pursuing the 1980 Republican Party nomination for president, Bush was selected by **Ronald W. Reagan** for the position of vice president. He served as the 43rd vice president from 1981 until 1989. Bush was Reagan's handpicked successor and was elected president in 1988, serving from 1989 until 1993.

The Bush presidency was a period of rapid change in the international community. The fall of the **Berlin Wall** and the demise of the Soviet bloc marked a time of promise for what Bush termed a "new world order" based on democracy and free-market capitalism. Several arms control treaties were signed between the United States and the Union of Soviet Socialist Republics, including the 1991 **Strategic Arms Reduction Treaty (START I)**. Bush also developed a warm relationship with Soviet leader **Mikhail Gorbachev** and implemented a cautious approach to the end of the **Cold War**. The two leaders negotiated the withdrawal of Soviet forces from Afghanistan and the management of nuclear weapons during the breakup of the Soviet Union. The United States provided funding for the consolidation of the Soviet nuclear arsenal and the destruction of warheads through the Nunn-Lugar Cooperative Threat Reduction program. Bush supported Gorbachev in the aftermath of the **Soviet coup** of 1991. In July 1991, the two leaders declared the Cold War over.

The Bush administration initiated a renewed focus on limiting economic barriers as the centerpiece of his **trade policy**. During Bush's term, the controversial **North American Free Trade Agreement** and the Enterprise for the Americas were initiated. The Bush administration also unilaterally cut U.S. nuclear forces by eliminating ground-launched tactical nuclear missiles and removing nuclear cruise missiles from naval vessels. Throughout his presidency, Bush worked closely with Secretary of State **James A. Baker III** (who resigned in 1992 to manage Bush's reelection campaign). Bush and Baker sought to manage the end of the Cold War so as to minimize international conflict. Consequently, the United States opposed the breakup of states such as Yugoslavia and Czechoslovakia for fear of ethnic strife.

Meanwhile, **German reunification** led to considerable turmoil within the **North Atlantic Treaty Organization (NATO)**. Great Britain and France were particularly wary of a reunified German state because of the world wars. The Bush administration showed considerable skill and patience in alleviating the worries of NATO while not dampening the emerging democracies in the former Soviet bloc. The end of the Cold War made many question the relevancy of NATO in the new global security environment, and Bush and Baker helped maintain the centrality of NATO to transatlantic security by arguing for new missions for the alliance and an expanded scope of operations.

In December 1989, Bush ordered the invasion of Panama to depose the dictator Gen. **Manuel Noriega** in **Operation Just Cause**. Although Noriega had been viewed as an important ally during the Cold War, his deep involvement in **drug trafficking** and suppression of democracy in Panama led to estrangement with Washington. U.S. forces quickly defeated Noriega's supporters, and the general was captured. He was later tried and convicted in the United States for cocaine trafficking and money laundering.

Following the 1990 invasion of Kuwait by Iraq, the Bush administration built a broad anti-Iraq **coalition of willing** partners, including NATO allies, Arab states, and the Soviet Union. Bush and Baker used personal diplomacy to garner support for military action to remove

Iraqi forces from Kuwait, and some 34 nations provided troops to the coalition, which eventually numbered 540,000. The UN Security Council passed a series of resolutions to prompt an Iraqi withdrawal, including Resolution 678, which authorized the use of force if Iraq did not withdraw by 15 January 1991. On 12 January 1991, Congress authorized the use of force, and the **Persian Gulf War** began five days later. Coalition forces quickly overwhelmed the Iraqis and a UN-sponsored cease-fire ended the fighting after the liberation of Kuwait. Success in the conflict led the Bush administration to seek to use international cooperation to end disputes elsewhere in the world, including the **Somalia intervention**.

With pressures to rapidly downsize the military and continue the withdrawal of U.S. forces from around the world, Bush worked to redefine the United States and NATO. In his 1992 reelection campaign, Bush was accused of devoting too much attention to foreign affairs and diplomacy at a time when the United States was in the grips of a recession. He lost the election, but became an elder statesman and was involved in a number of humanitarian causes, including the 2004 Asian tsunami relief effort and the 2005 Hurricane Katrina recovery.

BUSH, GEORGE W. (1946–). Forty-third president of the United States. Elected in 2000, and reelected in 2004, Bush's presidency was defined by the **September 11 terrorist attacks** and the subsequent U.S.-led global **war on terror**.

George Walker Bush was the son of future president **George H. W. Bush** and, although born in Connecticut, he grew up in Midland, Texas. The younger Bush earned a degree in history from Yale University and a master's in business administration from Harvard in 1975. He worked in the oil industry until 1989, when he and fellow investors purchased a baseball team, the Texas Rangers. Bush ran unsuccessfully for Congress in 1978 and did not reenter politics until the 1994 gubernatorial race in Texas. Bush won that election and served as governor from 1995 to 2001. He was elected president in 2000 in balloting in which he lost the popular vote to his Democratic opponent, former vice president **Albert A. Gore**, but won the majority of votes in the Electoral College.

After his inauguration as president, Bush had some domestic successes, including more than $1.3 billion in tax cuts and the No

Child Left Behind educational initiative. During his first year in office, Bush rejected the **Kyoto Protocol** and opposed efforts to establish an international war crimes tribunal. His decision to unilaterally withdraw from the 1972 Antiballistic Missile Treaty and pursue a **ballistic missile defense** system led to tensions in diplomatic relations with Russia, China, and European allies such as France and Germany.

International differences were quickly put aside following the 11 September 2001 terrorist attacks. The Bush administration endeavored to build a **coalition of the willing**, allowing different countries to participate in the U.S.-led war on terror to varying degrees, ranging from military cooperation to joint counterterrorism initiatives and intelligence or law enforcement collaboration. The **North Atlantic Treaty Organization (NATO)**, **Organization of American States**, and Australia–New Zealand–United States (ANZUS) alliance all invoked their collective defense clauses to support the United States. Meanwhile, more than 100 nations offered some type of support for Washington (27 countries provided some military assistance). The **United Nations (UN)** Security Council adopted Resolution 1373, which required states to take action against the terrorists and their financial networks. During the crisis, Bush developed a very close relationship with British prime minister **Tony Blair**, who remained an important ally for the remainder of his term.

Bush's foreign policy team included former general **Colin Powell** as secretary of state, **Condoleezza Rice** as national security advisor, and **Donald Rumsfeld** as defense secretary. Rice, Rumsfeld, and Vice President **Richard B. Cheney** emerged as the foremost hawks in the administration, while Powell was the most cautious senior figure. After the 2004 election, Rice replaced Powell as secretary of state. Rumsfeld resigned in December 2006.

On 7 October 2001, Bush authorized U.S. and coalition forces to begin operations against the Taliban and **Al Qaeda** in **Operation Enduring Freedom**. U.S.-led forces aided the anti-Taliban Northern Alliance, which conducted a ground offensive, supported by coalition air power and special operations troops. By December, the Northern Alliance and coalition forces had captured Kabul and the other major Afghan cities during the **Afghanistan intervention**. The senior leadership of the Taliban and Al Qaeda were killed or captured or went into hiding. **Hamid Karzai** was appointed the interim leader of Afghanistan and the United States initiated an effort to secure international aid and economic reconstruction. The Bush administration continued to station approximately 20,000 American troops in Afghanistan, although in 2006 NATO took command of coalition security operations.

Bush supported **NATO expansion** to the central and eastern European countries of the former Soviet Union. The 2004 expansion was the largest in the alliance's history and included seven new members. Bush also supported the 2004 **European Union** expansion and promoted membership for Turkey in the regional body. U.S. support for Israel remained strong during the Bush presidency. The centerpiece of U.S. policy toward the **Arab-Israeli conflict** was the "roadmap for peace," which called for Israeli withdrawal from occupied areas and the creation of a Palestinian state in exchange for the recognition of Israel and democratic elections in the Palestinian National Authority. Bush endorsed Israeli military strikes into Lebanon in 2006.

President Bush initially had widespread domestic popularity. He was able to secure congressional approval for a number of initiatives, including the creation of the Department of **Homeland Security** and the **Patriot Act**. The Patriot Act highlighted tensions over civil liberties that continued throughout Bush's presidency. The administration endeavored to create a legal definition for terrorists and other fighters captured during the war on terror. It sought the authority to detain suspected terrorists and to interrogate with the use of extrajudicial techniques. Bush wanted suspected terrorists tried before military tribunals, and he authorized the use of interrogation centers outside of the United States. These facilities, operated by the Central Intelligence Agency, led to both domestic and international criticism. In 2005 and 2006, Bush agreed to a series of compromises with Congress that limited interrogations and detention of suspected terrorists, but stopped short of granting the detainees the full legal rights of prisoners under the Geneva Convention. The detention of suspected terrorists at Guantanamo Bay was a constant source of tension between the United States and the international community.

In 2002, Bush promulgated a doctrine of preemption in the *National Security Strategy of the United States.* Commonly known as the **Bush Doctrine**, the policy authorizes first strikes by U.S. forces in order to forestall terrorist strikes or attacks using weapons of mass destruction (WMD). The doctrine served as the basis for the U.S.-led invasion of Iraq in March 2003. Bush accused the Iraqi regime of **Saddam Hussein** of possessing WMD, supporting terrorism, and failing to comply with UN resolutions.

Congress passed a resolution in October 2002 that authorized the president to use force against Iraq. Bush attempted to gather international support for an invasion. However, the invasion created rifts in the antiterrorism coalition. While countries such as Great Britain, Australia, and Italy supported the United States, other allies such as France, Germany, Turkey, and Russia opposed military action. During the **Iraq War**, the American-led coalition quickly defeated the Iraqi military, but an insurgency movement emerged and constantly challenged coalition and Iraqi security forces. The insurgents included members of the former regime, Sunnis, and foreign terrorists, including Al Qaeda. The administration's Iraq policy was bolstered by the 2003 capture of **Saddam Hussein** and a succession of successful democratic elections, the first in the country's history.

The Bush administration tried to build on the success of elections in Afghanistan and Iraq to promote democracy. Pressure was exerted on states such as Saudi Arabia, Kuwait, and Syria to enact democratic reforms. The administration also supported the **Orange Revolution** in Ukraine. However, by 2004, elections in Latin America and Europe brought leftist and center-left parties to power that opposed much of Bush's foreign policy, especially in Iraq.

As part of the broader war on terror, Bush increased military and economic aid to countries fighting Islamic terrorists, including the Philippines, the Central Asian states, and a range of countries in Africa. In addition, U.S. special operations forces were deployed to train and assist security forces battling terrorists. Bush also embarked on other foreign policy initiatives. In 2003, he announced that the United States would provide $15 billion in aid to African states to support programs to treat and contain the spread of HIV/AIDS. The administration also endeavored to prompt international action to address the **Darfur Crisis**. Furthermore, Bush sought to develop a multilateral approach to the **North Korean nuclear crises** and its nuclear weapon program. U.S. strategy toward North Korea remained one of containment after that nation's 2006 nuclear tests.

Bush did not face a Republican challenger in his 2004 presidential primaries, but his opponent in the general election, **John F. Kerry**, presented an unexpectedly difficult challenge in light of the president's previously high approval ratings. The insurgency in Iraq undermined public support for the war on terror, and the administration lost credibility following a series of scandals over the treatment of prisoners at the Abu Ghraib prison in Iraq. Both presidential campaigns argued that the election was a referendum on the Bush presidency and especially the president's foreign policy. Bush won the election 51 percent to 48 percent, becoming the first presidential candidate since his father in 1988 to receive more than 50 percent of the popular vote.

The insurgency in Iraq continued to be the central issue for Bush's foreign policy in his second term, but the president also launched an ambitious domestic agenda. He proposed broad reforms to Social Security and sought to cut the federal deficit—which had ballooned because of the war on terror—in half by the end of his second term. In 2005, Bush tried several strategies, including a speaking tour of the country, to increase support for his Social Security reform package, but he was unable to stir the public, and Congress failed to enact his reform agenda. Throughout his presidency, Bush attempted to develop and implement the **Free Trade Area of the Americas (FTAA)** as the cornerstone of his **trade policy**. While bilateral trade agreements were signed between the United States and countries such as Chile, opposition to the FTAA by other states, including Brazil and Venezuela, prevented hemispheric agreement on the trade accord.

In 2006, Bush's domestic priority shifted to **immigration**. He ordered additional Border Patrol and National Guard forces to be deployed along the border with Mexico and asked Congress for changes to the nation's immigration laws. The emphasis on immigration reform led to increased tensions with Mexico. *See also* BERLUSCONI, SILVIO; CHIRAC, JACQUES; NATIONAL COMMISSION ON TERRORIST ATTACKS UPON THE UNITED STATES (9/11 COMMISSION); NEOCONSERVATIVES.

BUSH DOCTRINE (2002). The Bush Doctrine was the first significant recodification of U.S. foreign and security policy since the end of the **Cold War**. Promulgated in 2002, the Bush Doctrine emphasizes preemptive military action, unilateralism, increased military capabilities, and a renewed emphasis on the promotion of democracy. In the aftermath of the **September 11 terrorist attacks**, the administration of **George W. Bush** sought to develop a comprehensive, overarching strategy for U.S. foreign and security policy.

During the Cold War, American policy had revolved around four priorities: containment of communism, promotion of free trade, expansion of democracy, and multilateralism. The demise of the other superpower then brought new challenges for the United States, and the 1990s were a decade of transition as the former Cold War goals were reshaped or reprioritized. The administration of **William J. Clinton** endeavored to develop an overarching set of principles for U.S. foreign and security policy, but what came to be known as the **Clinton Doctrine** was never formalized as policy; it was merely a set of principles to guide decisions by policy makers.

There was considerable debate within the administration over post-9/11 diplomacy. The more hawkish officials, including Vice President **Richard B. Cheney** and Secretary of Defense **Donald Rumsfeld**, wanted a new, assertive security policy that broke with the past and endorsed proactive military action to counter national threats. They wanted to use guidelines written by Deputy Secretary of Defense **Paul Wolfowitz** when he was an undersecretary of defense under Cheney in the administration of **George H. W. Bush**. Wolfowitz codified many of the themes of what would become the Bush Doctrine in the controversial 1992 *Defense Planning Guidance*, but his initial proposal was rejected by the elder Bush. Wolfowitz's ideas were based on what came to be known as **neoconservatism**, a view of foreign policy that asserts that the United States should use its military and economic power to promote such American principles as democracy, free trade, and individual rights. Conversely, Secretary of State **Colin Powell** and National Security Advisor **Condoleezza Rice** wanted to refine existing foreign and security policy to take into account the new threat of terrorism. For instance, Powell proposed an expansion of the principles of containment to states that supported terrorism, combined with increased support for countries fighting domestic or **international terrorism**. The expanded containment doctrine would be modeled after the multilateral coalition developed against the Soviet Union during the Cold War.

Bush ultimately accepted the school of thought led by Cheney and Rumsfeld, although he ordered that some points raised by Powell and Rice be incorporated into the nation's new policy statement. Within the new framework, the administration sought to accomplish three objectives. First, Bush wanted a new security strategy to counter terrorism. The president and his advisors believed that the 11 September 2001 terrorist attacks demonstrated that terrorism could not be fought through the Cold War containment doctrine. With the **Afghanistan intervention** as a prime example, the Bush team argued that antiterrorist strategy could not be reactive—it had to be proactive, and America had to interdict threats before harm was inflicted on the United States, even if that meant undertaking unilateral preemptive action (and thereby abandoning the Cold War principle of multilateralism). Second, officials in the Bush administration, especially Cheney and Rumsfeld, contended that the United States needed to dramatically reevaluate its military doctrine and force capabilities. They argued that defense expenditures should be increased and the military reorganized to better counter post–Cold War threats such as terrorism. Third and finally, administration members such as Powell and Rice asserted that the United States needed to address some of the root causes of terrorism by expanding democracy. These officials asserted that democratic regimes were also more likely to cooperate with the United States on other broad foreign policy goals.

The president first outlined the principles of the Bush Doctrine in a speech at the U.S. Military Academy at West Point on 1 June 2002. The formal enunciation of the Bush Doctrine occurred with the issuance of the *National Security Strategy of the United States* on 20 September. The document was drafted by the National Security Council staff, under the oversight of Rice and her deputy, **Stephen J. Hadley**.

The Bush Doctrine embraced a policy of preventative war to forestall terrorism or to thwart attacks on the United States by enemies utilizing weapons of mass destruction. Preemptive strikes would be used to stop rogue states from attacking America as a manifestation of the right of self-defense enshrined in Article 51 of the **United Nations** Charter. The doctrine also announced that the United States would use unilateral military force if multilateralism failed. This principle was included to cover situations where swift action was required. It was also a manifestation of the notion that the administration reserved the right to undertake strikes when efforts to form multilateral coalitions were unsuccessful. The *National Security Strategy* declared that the "United States has, and intends to keep, military strength beyond challenge." In other words, the country would maintain the ability to militarily defeat any other nation or combination of states. In addition to the endorsement of continued military primacy, the document pledged that the administration would adopt policies to ensure that America retained the necessary capabilities to engage in multiple conflicts while securing the defense of the homeland. The influence of Rice and Powell was manifested in the final component of the Bush Doctrine, an emphasis on the promotion of democracy. Democracy was seen as the most effective long-term tool to combat terrorism, as it was seen as the means to alleviate many of the root causes that prompted people to become terrorists.

The Bush Doctrine was very controversial. In Congress, it received support from Republicans and some conservative Democrats. The doctrine was criticized by **John F. Kerry**, Bush's opponent in the 2004 presidential election, and other leading Democrats. The emphasis on preventative war created considerable debate. While international law and customs allow preemptive strikes under certain conditions, including the threat of imminent attack, critics argued that the doctrine could be used to justify a range of military strikes. In addition, the emphasis on unilateralism was seen as a revocation of the past century of U.S. foreign policy principles as exemplified in institutions such as the **Organization of American States** and the **North Atlantic Treaty Organization**. Unilateralism was also perceived as a rejection of a key goal that had worked very well in the past in situations such as the 1991 **Persian Gulf War**.

The first manifestation of the Bush Doctrine was the 2003 **Iraq War**. Proponents of the doctrine contended that the regime of **Saddam Hussein** was actively seeking weapons of mass destruction for potential use against the United States or its allies. They also asserted that the removal of Saddam could promote democracy, pointing to the series of successful elections in the post-Saddam era. Critics argued that the invasion of Iraq was based on misinformation about the regime's pursuit of weapons and support for terrorism. Opponents also questioned the apparent lack of a long-range strategy for the occupation of Iraq. Meanwhile, the continued insurgency in Iraq undermined the capability of the administration to apply the Bush Doctrine to other situations and reduced congressional support for the policy. *See also* McCAIN, JOHN S.; PELOSI, NANCY P.; PERLE, RICHARD N.

– C –

CAMP DAVID SUMMIT (2000). One of the last significant efforts by the administration of **William J. Clinton** to negotiate a settlement to the **Arab-Israeli conflict**. The 2000 Camp David Summit included Clinton, Israeli prime minister **Ehud Barak**, and Palestinian leader **Yasser Arafat**. On 5 July 2000, Clinton invited Barak and Arafat to meet at Camp David in an effort to replicate the success of the 1978 accords between Israel and Egypt. The summit lasted from 11 July to 25 July. During the discussions, Barak offered to accept the formation of a Palestinian state comprising 100 percent of the territory of the Gaza Strip; 73 percent of the West Bank (later improving the offer to 90 percent); and 3 percent of the Negev Desert. Israel would maintain a road that bisected the West Bank and reserve the right to close the road during national emergencies. In exchange, Israel sought formal recognition from the Palestinian National Authority (PNA) and the suppression of all terrorist organizations.

Arafat countered with a demand that Israel return to the 1967 borders, which would mean the return of 100 percent of the West Bank and Gaza. He further called for the right of return, which would allow Palestinians who had been displaced since the 1948 war to reclaim territory or be granted compensation for their losses. Arafat also rejected the Israeli proposal for joint oversight of the Temple Mount.

Barak rejected Arafat's demands and argued that the Israeli parliament would never endorse a complete withdrawal from the West Bank. Clinton endeavored to convince the Palestinians that the Israeli offer was the best they would receive now or in future negotiations. Clinton and Barak later asserted that Arafat rejected the proposal for two reasons. First, Arafat knew that the PNA would not be able to suppress terrorist groups such as Hamas. Second, he believed that continued resistance to Israel bolstered popularity among his people and the wider Arab community.

While no lasting agreement was reached, the parties did agree on the text of a document to guide future negotiations. The resultant Trilateral Statement asserted that both Israel and Palestine sought a lasting settlement within the framework of existing **United Nations** Security Council resolutions. Both parties pledged not to undertake unilateral actions that would jeopardize future discussions. They also affirmed the importance of the United States in any potential settlement. After Camp David, Clinton launched one final initiative to produce a settlement at the January 2001 **Taba Summit**.

CARTER, JAMES E. ("JIMMY"; 1924–). Thirty-ninth president of the United States (1977–1981), who subsequently emerged as an international diplomat promoting democracy and a range of charitable causes. James Earl "Jimmy" Carter Jr. was born in Plains, Georgia, and graduated from the U.S. Naval Academy in 1946. Carter, a Democrat, served in the Georgia legislature before being elected governor of the state in 1970. He was elected president in 1976.

Carter's tenure was marked by economic malaise and renewed tensions during the **Cold War**, especially after the 1979 Soviet invasion of Afghanistan. Carter sponsored the 1978 Camp David Peace Accords between Egypt and Israel. However, his domestic support was seriously undermined by his management of the Iranian hostage crisis, in which 52 Americans were held by the Iranians for 444 days. Carter was defeated by **Ronald W. Reagan** in the 1980 presidential election.

After leaving the White House, Carter emerged as an elder statesman and advocate for democracy. In 1982, the former president created the Carter Center, which subsequently helped organize and monitor elections in a range of countries in Latin America, Africa, and Asia. In 1994, President **William J. Clinton** asked Carter to lead the American negotiating efforts that resulted in the **Framework Agreement with North Korea**. That year, Carter also conducted talks with Haiti's military regime in an effort to avoid American intervention. Through the 1990s, he engaged in a range of private diplomatic efforts (often called "freelance diplomacy" by his critics). While many of his initiatives were praised, the Clinton and **George W. Bush** administrations criticized the former president on several occasions for interference with formal diplomacy and foreign policy. In 2002, Carter received the Nobel Peace Prize in recognition of his humanitarian contributions and efforts to promote global peace. He was a staunch opponent and critic of the 2003 **Iraq War**. *See also* HUMAN RIGHTS.

CASTRO, FIDEL (1926–). Leader of Cuba from 1959 until 2006, when he transferred power to his brother Raul. Fidel Alejandro Castro Ruz was born in the Oriente Province, Cuba. He became involved in revolutionary politics as a student at the University of Havana in the 1940s. Castro formed an underground organization and attempted to overthrow Cuban dictator Gen. Fulgencio Batista. He was briefly imprisoned in 1953–1955 and then went into exile in Mexico.

Castro returned to lead a successful revolution to overthrow Batista in January 1959. Washington recognized the new regime, but tensions emerged over Castro's expropriation of land and repression of wealthy Cubans and opponents of the government. Meanwhile, Castro opened relations with the Soviet Union. Successive American efforts to remove the Cuban leader during the **Cold War** failed. Economic and political sanctions were placed on Cuba following the 1962 Cuban Missile Crisis, in which the United States and the Soviet Union almost went to war over the deployment of Soviet nuclear weapons on the island.

Throughout the Cold War, Cuba received large subsidies from the Soviet Union, including shipments of food and fuel. With the end of the Cold War, however, Moscow ended support for the regime, resulting in a massive economic downturn in the Cuban economy. The administration of **William J. Clinton** expanded enforcement of the embargo in 1993 in an effort to force Castro from power. In 1996, Cuban forces downed two civilian aircraft piloted by a Miami-based exile group. In response, Congress enacted new legislation that made aspects of the embargo permanent and repealable only by legislation instead of executive action. Nonetheless, in 1998, restrictions on remittances to Cuba were eased and, in 2000, Congress authorized the sale of U.S. food products to Cuba in the aftermath of Hurricane Michelle. Meanwhile, in 1999, U.S. authorities rescued six-year-old Elian Gonzalez off the coast of Florida after his mother and other relatives died while trying to flee to the United States. Gonzalez became the center of a significant controversy when his birth father, who was still in Cuba, requested his return from relatives in Miami. The Clinton administration raided the home where the child was staying and forcibly returned him to Cuba, provoking significant domestic criticism. In October 2003, the administration of **George W. Bush** launched a new anti-Castro campaign, which included more rigorous enforcement of travel restrictions and new funding for antiregime propaganda.

Castro sought to allow limited economic reforms, including the legalization of some private enterprises and joint ventures with foreign firms. The Cuban leader also developed a close relationship with Venezuelan president **Hugo Chávez**, who subsequently provided energy and economic aid to the island. In 2006, Castro became ill and transferred power to his younger brother. The transfer was initially temporary, but Castro's declining health precluded a return to power.

CEDAR REVOLUTION. A series of demonstrations and political actions in Lebanon that resulted in the withdrawal of Syrian forces and the demise of the pro-Damascus regime. On 14 February 2005, former prime minister Rafik Hariri, a vocal opponent of the Syrian intervention in Lebanon, was assassinated in an attack that also killed 20 others and injured more than 100. Many blamed his assassination on Syrian intelligence agents and demanded an international inquiry. However, the pro-Syrian government resisted calls for an investigation, sparking massive demonstrations. Protests were held on an almost daily basis throughout the country. In addition, international leaders condemned the attack. Presidents **George W. Bush** of the United States and **Jacques Chirac** of France issued a joint statement calling for the withdrawal of Syrian forces in compliance with existing **United Nations** resolutions.

On 28 February, the pro-Syrian government resigned. Under growing international pressure, Syria withdrew its forces in April, ending the 30-year occupation of Lebanon. In parliamentary elections, an anti-Syrian bloc won 72 of the 128 seats in the assembly. Officials in the Bush administration hoped the Cedar Revolution was part of a broader trend toward democracy in the Middle East. However, in the summer of 2006, guerrillas from the Islamic group Hezbollah attacked an Israeli patrol, prompting Tel Aviv to launch an incursion into southern Lebanon that developed into large-scale hostilities. The conflict undermined domestic support for the anti-Syrian government, and in December 2006, Hezbollah organized massive demonstrations in an unsuccessful effort to drive the pro-Western prime minister Fouad Siniora from power and prevent the establishment of an international tribunal to investigate the assassinations that had sparked the revolution.

CHÁVEZ, HUGO (1954–). President of Venezuela since 1998, based on a populist campaign, and subsequently as a leading global critic of U.S. foreign policy. Hugo Rafael Chávez was the son of school teachers. He graduated from Venezuela's Academy of Military Sciences in 1975 and was commissioned a lieutenant in the national army. Chávez served in counterinsurgency units and as an instructor at the Academy of Military Sciences. He also became an ardent devotee of "Bolivarianism," a blend of the liberation philosophy of Simón Bolívar (1783–1830) with contemporary Marxism. In 1983, Chávez founded the Revolutionary Bolivarian Movement 200 (*Movimiento Bolivariano Revolucionario 200*, MBR-200), a political group whose name commemorated the 200th anniversary of the birth of Bolívar. MBR-200's goals were centered on the implementation of Bolivarianism. The group attracted followers in the Venezuelan military.

On 4 February 1992, Chávez and members of MBR-200 launched a coup attempt. They unsuccessfully tried to capture the Venezuelan president, but the majority of the military remained loyal to the government. Fourteen soldiers were killed, 50 were injured, and 80 civilians were wounded. Chávez surrendered, but gained broad appeal during his trial, when on national television he claimed that his coup was on behalf of the poor and downtrodden. In Venezuela, the president's supports came to be known as *chavistas*.

Chávez served two years in prison, but was pardoned in 1994. Upon his release, he revived the MBR-200 as the Fifth Republic Movement (*Movimiento V República*, MVR). The new political grouping attacked the country's traditional two-party system and foreign ownership of banks and industry. Chávez won the presidential elections in 1998 and initiated constitutional reforms that strengthened the power of the presidency and weakened the legislature and judiciary. In 1999, Chávez won approval for a new constitution, which lengthened the president's terms from five to six years and replaced the one-term limit with a two-term restriction. The bicameral legislature was converted into a unicameral body and lost much of its power, including the ability to appoint judges. The constitution also called for new elections, and Chávez was reelected president. In 2000, a referendum was passed that allowed Chávez to rule by presidential decree for a year (the decrees could not be challenged by the legislature or the courts).

Chávez sought to use the military to expand his personal power and implement antipoverty programs. The centerpiece of Chávez's effort was Plan Bolívar 2000, which used the military in an attempt to improve the quality of life for the poor. The plan called upon the military to build roads, schools, and other infrastructure projects, as well as to deliver health care to the poor. Revelations of corruption and mismanagement in 2001 led to the end of the initiative, and several senior officers and government officials were arrested or sacked.

In 2002, the military launched an abortive coup against Chávez (who subsequently accused the United States of sponsoring the coup). Chávez's anti-American rhetoric played well among Venezuela's lower classes, and the president increasingly blamed the United States for global problems. Chávez reversed the previously close ties between Venezuela and the United States and ended military relations between the two countries. Among other actions designed to demonstrate Venezuela's new anti-American foreign policy, in 2000 Chávez traveled to Iraq to become the first head of state to meet with **Saddam Hussein** since the 1991 **Persian Gulf War**.

Chávez ended privatization efforts and increased corporate taxes in order to fund social programs. A universal health care program was created, and education was expanded. Chávez also launched a broad land-transfer program. He tried to use price controls to lower inflation, but despite some initial success, inflation climbed above 25 percent in 2003 and 2004. Opposition to Chávez was strong among the middle and business classes, but he was able to retain his popularity among the poor by blaming economic problems on the bourgeoisie and foreign powers, mainly the United States. Chávez won a 2004 recall with 59 percent of the vote (some outside observers criticized the vote as fraudulent). New press restrictions were enacted in 2005.

Chávez limited oil production in Venezuela as a means to drive international energy prices higher, thereby increasing profits. During meetings of the **Organization of Petroleum Exporting Countries**, Chávez consistently argued for production cuts. The spike in energy prices in 2005 and 2006 allowed for increased social spending. Chávez bolstered health care though an agreement with **Fidel Castro**'s government in which Cuban doctors served in Venezuela in exchange for oil transfers from Caracas. In 2004 and 2005, he led opposition to the U.S.-backed **Free Trade Area of the Americas (FTAA)** and managed to prevent progress on economic discussions over the proposed economic union. Chávez proposed the creation of a new regional trade bloc that would not include the United States nor the expansion of existing Latin American trade groups to counter perceived U.S. economic hegemony in the region (and to block American **trade policy**). He adopted a strategy of using oil as an incentive to gain support for diplomatic initiatives. For instance, in its bid for a nonpermanent seat on the **United Nations** Security Council, Venezuela offered oil in exchange for support of its effort. Chávez also emerged as leader of anti-American states and reached out to states such as Cuba, Iran, and Syria in an attempt to develop a broad-based balancing group to U.S. global primacy.

Chávez's relations with regional countries have been mixed. He offered to fund social programs in other Latin American states and agreed to create a medical center to train Cuban physicians to work in the region. He also supplied low-cost heating oil to communities in the United States in 2005. However, his consistent hostility to the United States marginalized his ability to forge bridges with regional partners. In addition, Venezuela–Mexico relations have been strained due to Chávez's opposition to the FTAA and Mexico's economic policies. Meanwhile, a series of political incidents with Colombia and Peru led to constant tensions between Venezuela and those countries.

CHEMICAL WEAPONS CONVENTION (CWC; 1993). The Convention on the Prohibition of the Development, Production, Stockpiling, and Use of Chemical Weapons and on Their Destruction—commonly known as the Chemical Weapons Convention—bans the use, production, and stockpiling of chemical weapons. Signed in

1993, the convention bolstered existing international law against the use of chemical weapons and the 1925 Geneva Convention Protocol for the Prohibition of the Use in War of Asphyxiating, Poisonous or Other Gases, and of Bacteriological Methods of Warfare.

The roots of the CWC were in the November 1969 unilateral decision by the administration of President Richard M. Nixon to ban the use of chemical and biological weapons. The following year, the United States and Western European states began negotiations with the Soviet Union on potential treaties against both biological and chemical weapons. Moscow proposed a single treaty to ban both categories of weapons, but the United States wanted to negotiate one treaty at a time in order to establish clear verification systems—and Washington was more interested in a Biological Weapons Convention (BWC). After the BWC was signed in 1971, periodic negotiations on the CWC began. It was not until the end of the **Cold War**, however, that significant progress was made on the CWC. Verification was the main sticking point. The BWC lacked adequate verification mechanisms, and Washington refused to enter into a new treaty without the means to ensure compliance. Moscow consistently rebuffed American proposals until 1991.

By late 1992, the main tenets of the CWC had been agreed upon. On 13 January 1993, the CWC was signed in Paris. It came into force on 29 April 1997 after the 50th country ratified the agreement; by 2006, there were 180 signatories to the CWC. The accord created the Organization for the Prohibition of Chemical Weapons (OPCW). Headquartered in The Hague, the OPCW was tasked to oversee verification and conduct inspections. By 2006, the OPCW had performed more than 1,500 inspections. In addition, 47 of the 64 known facilities in the world capable of producing chemical weapons had been shut down or converted to civilian usage. All 64 had ceased production of weapons. The OPCW had identified more than 71,000 tons of chemical weapons, of which by 2006, 17 percent had been destroyed.

As of 2006, only six nations acknowledged that they had chemical weapons stockpiles: Albania, India, Libya, Russia, South Korea, and the United States. Albania, India, and South Korea were on schedule to destroy their stockpiles by the end of 2007. More than 80 percent of the U.S. stockpiles were destroyed by 2004, and all were scheduled to be eliminated by 2012. Russia received more than $2 billion from donor countries to assist its destruction program, but delays have extended Moscow's completion date to as late as 2025.

Critics of the CWC charge that several signatories to the convention, including the People's Republic of China and Sudan, have covert stockpiles of weapons that have not been disclosed. Without disclosure, the OPCW lacks the authority to monitor compliance with the CWC. Moreover, two states with extensive chemical programs, Syria and North Korea, have not signed the convention.

CHENEY, RICHARD B. ("DICK"; 1941–). After a long career in public service, Cheney became one of the most influential vice presidents in American history and exerted a significant influence on U.S. foreign policy in the administration of **George W. Bush**. Richard Bruce "Dick" Cheney was born in Lincoln, Nebraska. He earned bachelor's (1965) and master's (1969) degrees in political science from the University of Wyoming. He legally avoided service in the Vietnam War through a series of draft deferments. In 1969, Cheney was hired as a special assistant to **Donald Rumsfeld** in the Office of Economic Opportunity. In 1974, he was appointed to President Gerald R. Ford's transition team after the resignation of Richard M. Nixon. A year later, Cheney became the youngest White House chief of staff.

After Ford's loss in the 1976 election, Cheney briefly left public service. However, in 1978, he successfully ran for the U.S. House of Representatives. The future vice president remained a member of the House until 1989. In 1981, he was elected chair of the House Republican Conference and in 1988, he was chosen as the House minority whip. During his House service, Cheney was best known for his staunch support for domestic energy exploration and development.

In March 1989, Cheney was appointed secretary of defense in the administration of **George H. W. Bush**. Cheney oversaw the initial transition of the military from its **Cold War** posture to a more lean and flexible force structure. He preferred to concentrate on broad policy issues and to delegate basic management to his subordinates, including Undersecretary of Defense for Policy **Paul Wolfowitz**. Cheney recommended Gen. **Colin Powell** to be chairman of the Joint Chiefs of Staff (Powell assumed office in October 1989). Meanwhile,

Cheney's experience in Congress and his extensive personal relationships with individual members made him a highly effective lobbyist for the Bush administration's foreign and security policies.

The United States had supported Panamanian dictator general **Manuel Noriega** during the height of the Cold War. However, tensions between the United States and Panama escalated over Noriega's involvement in the drug trade and his annulment of democratic elections. In December 1988, Panamanian security forces shot and killed an American sailor. Bush ordered U.S. forces to invade Panama and depose Noriega. Cheney oversaw the planning and attack. An American force of 24,000 troops invaded Panama on 20 December 1989. The Americans quickly overran Panama, and Noriega was captured (he was subsequently sent to the United States and tried and convicted for **drug trafficking**). The invasion underscored the need for rapid reaction capabilities.

On 1 August 1990, Iraq invaded Kuwait, triggering the **Persian Gulf War**. Cheney had to first develop and implement a defensive strategy to protect Saudi Arabia and the other Gulf states from a possible attack from Iraq. Concurrently, he and the senior defense and military officials were tasked to plan the liberation of Kuwait. Their mission was complicated by the multilateral coalition developed by Bush and Secretary of State **James A. Baker III**. Cheney and his staff had to plan and coordinate their operation among the disparate militaries. Operation Desert Storm, the liberation of Kuwait, began on 17 January 1991, and coalition forces overran the Iraqi defenses. A cease-fire was signed on 3 March.

Following the Gulf War, Cheney unsuccessfully advocated U.S. military and diplomatic support for the breakaway republics of the former Yugoslavia. He also oversaw the deployment of 26,000 American troops in the **Somalia intervention** in 1992 as part of a **United Nations**–sponsored peacekeeping mission. When Bush lost the 1992 election, Cheney left office. In 1994, he was appointed the chief executive officer of the Halliburton Corporation.

George W. Bush chose Cheney to be his running mate in the 2000 presidential election. He managed Bush's transition team, including the choice of senior cabinet and staff personnel. Cheney was influential in the selection of Powell as secretary of state and Rumsfeld as defense secretary. In addition, Wolfowitz was appointed a deputy secretary of defense, while another colleague, **Stephen J. Hadley**, was chosen as the deputy national security advisor. Cheney developed a close relationship with Bush and even integrated the vice presidential staff with the presidential staff to bolster coordination. The vice president's constitutional duties as president of the Senate were especially important during the 107th Congress following the defection of Republican senator Jim Jeffords of Vermont, who in 2001 declared himself an independent and caucused with the Democrats, leaving the Senate with a 50–50 tie between parties. Cheney cast seven tie-breaking votes. The vice president also served as a major lobbyist for the administration in Congress. Cheney asked for and was given an office in the House building (as president of the Senate, he already had offices in the upper chamber).

Throughout his political career, there were concerns over Cheney's health. He had four heart attacks before he became vice president. Once in office, he suffered three heart-related episodes and had to have a device similar to a pacemaker installed. Cheney's ties to the energy sector also created controversy, especially after he was appointed to chair the National Energy Policy Development Group. Environmental and media groups sued the administration for the records of the group's meetings, but the administration refused, citing executive privilege (in 2002, a federal court ordered the records released, but the administration appealed the decision).

The president came to rely on Cheney for advice and counsel in the aftermath of the **September 11 terrorist attacks**. In the period immediately following the strikes, Cheney and his staff were moved away from Washington, D.C., as a means of protecting the succession in case of future attacks. Although physically separated, Cheney was in constant contact with Bush through telecommunications systems. He participated in all major strategy meetings, including sessions on **Operation Enduring Freedom**, the military response to the terrorist attacks. Cheney was also influential in developing the Office, later Department, of **Homeland Security**. The vice president urged Bush to appoint former Pennsylvania governor **Thomas J. Ridge** as its first director.

Cheney had more influence in foreign and security policy than any of his predecessors. In addition to his informal role as an advisor, Cheney was granted a range of formal powers. For instance, he was given the authority to chair sessions of the National Security Council (NSC) if Bush was not in attendance; Cheney's staff also regularly attended NSC sessions. In addition, in 2003 Bush granted Cheney the power to classify national security documents. He was dispatched on diplomatic missions, including a March 2002 mission to the Middle East to reduce Israeli-Palestinian strife on the eve of the invasion of Iraq. Foreign dignitaries also regularly met with Cheney along with their sessions with Bush.

Cheney was the leader of the hawkish wing of the administration. He argued for an expansion of the **war on terror** and backed U.S. aid and assistance for countries facing terrorist threats. The vice president was the foremost advocate for the doctrine of preemption to forestall potential terrorist strikes (the **Bush Doctrine**). Cheney was also one of the strongest backers of the invasion of Iraq. He embarked on a two-level campaign to win support for military action. Cheney personally lobbied members of Congress and political leaders in the United States. Meanwhile, he conducted a series of speeches and public interviews to win approval for the use of force. The vice president regularly charged that Iraq possessed weapons of mass destruction and was supporting terrorism. Cheney urged Bush to undertake military action with or without the support of a **United Nations** resolution and in spite of opposition by traditional American allies such as Germany and France.

While defense secretary, Cheney had supported the expansion of the **North Atlantic Treaty Organization (NATO)** to the former countries of the Soviet bloc. As vice president, he endorsed the extension of the alliance to seven central and eastern countries in the **NATO expansion** of 2004. He also supported the **Free Trade Area of the Americas** as a way to remove trade barriers and counter the growing economic power and influence of the **European Union**.

During the 2004 presidential election, Bush rejected pressure to replace Cheney with a more popular political figure. During the campaign, Cheney emerged as the most vocal critic of the Democratic candidate, **John F. Kerry**. The vice president specifically challenged Kerry's foreign and security policies. Cheney was also a popular campaigner for individual Republican candidates and an important fundraiser for the party.

The vice president's relationship with Halliburton created ethical questions after the company was granted a wide range of contracts for the supply of the U.S. military in Iraq, as well as reconstruction efforts. Cheney's public reputation was further damaged in 2005 following allegations that the vice president's office had leaked the identity of Central Intelligence Agency operative Valerie Wilson in retaliation for her husband's criticism of the **Iraq War**. The accusations were discounted in 2006 when former assistant secretary of state Richard Armitage announced that he had revealed the name of Wilson during a private media interview. In 2006, the vice president was involved in a hunting incident in which he accidentally shot a fellow hunter, Harry Whittington. Prior to the 2006 midterm elections, in which the Republican Party lost its majority in both houses of Congress, Cheney's popularity was at an all-time low. *See also* TRADE POLICY.

CHERTOFF, MICHAEL (1953–). Second secretary of **homeland security**. Chertoff was born in Elizabeth, New Jersey, and gained a law degree from Harvard University in 1978. After service as a federal prosecutor, he was an advisor to **George W. Bush** during the 2000 presidential campaign. From 2001 to 2003, Chertoff worked for the Department of Justice prosecuting terrorists, including Zacarias Moussaoui. In 2001, Chertoff was one of the coauthors of the **Patriot Act**. He was made a federal judge in 2003. Following the resignation of **Thomas J. Ridge**, Chertoff was appointed to succeed him as secretary of homeland security. He endeavored to improve the department's border security programs and supported the deployment of National Guard troops to bolster Border Patrol agents along the boundary with Mexico. Initially praised for his leadership, Chertoff was criticized for his oversight of the rescue and recovery efforts following Hurricane Katrina in New Orleans in 2005.

CHIRAC, JACQUES (1932–). President of France, 1995–2007. During his first term, Chirac was regarded as the most pro-American president in modern French history, but his second term was marked by transatlantic tensions.

Jacques René Chirac was born in Paris in 1932. In 1959, he completed an advanced degree at the prestigious École Nationale d'Administration, which educates France's top civil servants. In 1962, Chirac was appointed to the staff of Prime Minister Georges Pompidou (1911–1974). In 1965, Chirac left his staff position after he was elected to the municipal council for Sainte-Fereole. Two years later, Pompidou convinced Chirac to seek a seat in the National Assembly. He was elected and subsequently appointed state secretary for economy and finance. Chirac continued to serve in the cabinet of Valery Giscard d'Estaing (1926–) after Pompidou became president. In 1973, he was appointed minister of agriculture and rural development. When Pompidou died in office in 1974, Giscard d'Estaing became president and appointed Chirac prime minister. Chirac served until 1976, when differences over the scope of the prime minister's authority led to his resignation.

In 1976, Chirac was elected president of the Union of Democrats for the Republic (Union de Démocrates pour la République, UDR), the main Gaullist grouping. The party subsequently changed its name to the Rally for the Republic (Rassemblement pour la République, RPR). The election confirmed Chirac as the leader of French conservatives. In 1977, Chirac was elected mayor of Paris on a platform that emphasized moderate social policies with probusiness measures, including incentives to attract companies to the city. In 1979, Chirac launched a public campaign against the pro-Europeanist policies of Giscard d'Estaing and warned that deeper integration into the European Common Market would undermine France's social and political autonomy. Chirac ran for the presidency in 1981 against Giscard d'Estaing and Socialist **Francois Mitterrand**, but finished third in the balloting. He was nevertheless reelected to the National Assembly, a position he maintained until 1995. Chirac also continued to serve as mayor of Paris until 1995.

When the Gaullists gained a majority in the Assembly in 1986, Chirac was appointed prime minister by Mitterrand. Tensions were high between the two figures, however, and Chirac endeavored to use his post as a foundation for a presidential bid in 1988. He lost the election to Mitterrand. Despite his earlier opposition to European integration, Chirac supported the Maastricht Treaties and campaigned in favor of the **European Union (EU)** in the 1992 national referendum.

In 1995, Chirac was elected president. He improved relations with the United States and deepened France's role in the **North Atlantic**

Treaty Organization (NATO). He also continued Mitterrand's policy of close cooperation with Germany. Chirac endorsed NATO's peacekeeping role in the Balkans and argued for a greater European role in resolving the **Arab-Israeli conflict**. He tried to negotiate a peaceful settlement in the 1999 **Kosovo War**, but then supported NATO air strikes when the talks failed to resolve the conflict. Chirac faced international criticism for French nuclear tests in Polynesia in 1996, but later announced an end to all French atomic testing and signed the **Comprehensive Test Ban Treaty**. The president endeavored to refocus NATO and European security policies toward the Mediterranean and Middle East, but did support NATO's 1999 expansion. In 1999, in response to charges of corruption, a court decision declared that Chirac had immunity from prosecution as the current president of France.

Chirac offered diplomatic and military support to the United States in the aftermath of the **September 11 terrorist attacks**. France increased intelligence and law enforcement cooperation with the United States. In addition, France provided troops and military support for **Operation Enduring Freedom**. However, he opposed the U.S.-led invasion of Iraq and was instrumental in ensuring that the United States did not gain a **United Nations** resolution authorizing military force against Iraq. Chirac even threatened to use France's veto on the Security Council to prevent a resolution on the use of force. Chirac's opposition to Iraq increased his popularity in France. In an effort to unify the Gaullist parties and other conservative groupings, Chirac launched a new political party in 2002, the Union for a Popular Movement (Union pour un Mouvement Populaire, UMP). In the 2002 presidential election, Chirac faced far-right extremist candidate Jean-Marie Le Pen (1928–) in a runoff election. Chirac easily defeated his opponent as moderates, Gaullists, and Socialists joined together to beat Le Pen.

Chirac consistently sought to maintain French influence in its traditional spheres of influence. He proposed the creation of an EU rapid reaction force to be used in humanitarian crises in Africa. He also deployed troops to the Côte d'Ivoire (Ivory Coast) in 2002 in response to a civil war and to protect French citizens and interests. Conversely, he was opposed to intervention in other instances, including the **Darfur Crisis**.

Chirac reluctantly endorsed the EU and **NATO expansion** in 2004. He was afraid that the new members, most of whom supported the U.S. invasion of Iraq, would dilute French influence in both organizations. In negotiations in 2005 over the EU Constitution, Chirac opposed a federative structure with significant supranational powers. He campaigned in support of the compromise constitution ahead of a national referendum on the document. However, voters rejected the EU Constitution by a 55 percent majority. Since the document required approval by all member states, the no vote effectively derailed the proposed basic law.

Chirac's popularity declined significantly during his second term. In October and November 2005, there were widespread riots in Paris and other urban areas by North African immigrants who charged widespread discrimination by police and complained about government inaction on chronic high levels of unemployment. An unpopular unemployment law led to renewed rioting in 2006, this time by students, and he ultimately withdrew the measure. Chirac supported the multilateral effort to negotiate a resolution to the 2006 Iranian nuclear crisis. *See also* BALKAN WARS; BUSH, GEORGE W.; COMMON FOREIGN AND SECURITY POLICY; EUROPEAN SECURITY AND DEFENSE IDENTITY; IRAQ WAR.

CHOMSKY, NOAM (1928–). A brilliant linguist who became known for his leftist politics and critiques of U.S. foreign policy. Chomsky was born in Philadelphia and earned a Ph.D. in linguistics from the University of Pennsylvania in 1955. He joined the faculty at the Massachusetts Institute of Technology and gained academic fame as a grammar theorist. However, Chomsky rose to national prominence for his opposition to the Vietnam War. The conflict led Chomsky to pen a number of antiwar essays. Throughout the **Cold War**, Chomsky criticized successive administrations for their support of regimes that violated **human rights**. He has also asserted that the modern mass media merely reinforce the existing class system in the United States, dominated by elites. After the end of the bipolar conflict, Chomsky roundly condemned **neoliberalism** as an economic philosophy, and his work highlighted flaws in free-market capitalism and **globalization**. He was especially critical of U.S. **trade policy**. Chomsky opposed the 1991 **Persian Gulf War**, **Operation Enduring Freedom** in 2001, and the 2003 **Iraq War**. On the other hand, critics of Chomsky contend that the professor failed to acknowledge the repression and totalitarian nature of leftist regimes. *See also* BUSH DOCTRINE; CASTRO, FIDEL; CHÁVEZ, HUGO; CLINTON DOCTRINE.

CHRISTOPHER, WARREN (1925–). Secretary of state in the first administration of President **William J. Clinton.** Christopher graduated from the University of Southern California in 1945 and was then commissioned as a naval officer. He earned a law degree from Stanford University in 1949. Christopher held in a variety of government posts, including deputy attorney general in the administration of President Lyndon B. Johnson. He was also deputy secretary of state under **James E. Carter.** Following the 1992 elections, Christopher led the transition team of Clinton before his appointment as secretary of state.

Christopher identified three main goals during his tenure. First, he sought to reorganize the nation's security arrangements to take advantage of the "**peace dividend**" occasioned by the end of the **Cold War.** Second, he wanted to promote economic liberalization through expanded international agreements as the cornerstone of the administration's **trade policy.** Finally, Christopher endeavored to reorient American foreign policy to emphasize **human rights** and democracy. His goals were constrained by a series of crises. The United States withdrew from the **Somalia intervention** in 1994 following the deaths of 18 American troops in a 1993 battle. The administration failed to take strong action in the former Yugoslavia, preferring to allow the **European Union** to take the lead in the crisis. This prolonged the civil war until eventual U.S. involvement began through the 1995 **Dayton Accords.** The United States participated in the subsequent **North Atlantic Treaty Organization (NATO)** peacekeeping mission during the **Bosnian Conflict.** Internal strife in **Haiti** also led to the deployment of U.S. forces following negotiations that resulted in the removal of a military dictatorship. The United States avoided participation in efforts to prevent the 1994 **Rwandan genocide** and was unable to achieve a breakthrough in the **Arab-Israeli conflict.**

Christopher opposed the decoupling of trade and human rights issues toward the People's Republic of China and emerged as the administration's most vocal critic of Beijing's internal policies. He did support a negotiated settlement over the **North Korean nuclear crisis**. The 1994 **Framework Agreement with North Korea** was supposed to end the country's nuclear weapons program in exchange for American economic aid; however, North Korea continued its program and developed nuclear weapons.

Christopher's major success in security policy involved a series of initiatives at the 1994 **Brussels Summit**. These efforts were designed to maintain a U.S. role, through NATO, in European security through the **Partnership for Peace** program and eventual **NATO enlargement**. Christopher's greatest trade success was ensuring domestic support for the ratification of the **North American Free Trade Agreement** despite considerable opposition from his own party. *See also* ALBRIGHT, MADELEINE; BALKAN WARS.

CLARK, WESLEY (1944–). Clark became the supreme Allied commander, Europe (SACEUR), and commander-in-chief, United States European Command in 1997. As the senior **North Atlantic Treaty Organization (NATO)** military commander, Clark commanded NATO forces during the **Kosovo War**. For 77 days, beginning on 24 March 1999, NATO airpower conducted sustained bombing operations with the goal of forcing Serbian compliance with **United Nations** Security Council Resolution 1199. On 3 June 1999, President **Slobodan Milošević** accepted peace terms with NATO, allowing peacekeeping forces to deploy into Kosovo on 10 June 1999. Clark was lauded for his ability to maintain unity among the NATO partners. The longer-than-expected campaign, the bombing of the Chinese embassy in Belgrade, and the arguments over strategy led to Clark's early departure as SACEUR under pressure from President **William J. Clinton**. Clark retired from the military in May 2000, and in 2003, he campaigned unsuccessfully for the 2004 Democratic nomination for the presidency. *See also* KERRY, JOHN F.

CLARKE, RICHARD (1951–). National security official under five U.S. presidents. Richard "Dick" Clarke was born in 1951 and graduated from the University of Pennsylvania in 1972. In 1973, he began work at the Department of Defense and transferred to the State Department, where he worked in the Bureau of Politico-Military Affairs until 1985. In the administration of **Ronald W. Reagan**, Clarke was a deputy assistant secretary of state, and he became an assistant secretary of state under **George H. W. Bush**. In 1990, Clarke worked on the diplomatic efforts to develop a **coalition of the willing** prior to the 1991 **Persian Gulf War**. Bush subsequently appointed Clarke to the National Security Council (NSC). He continued to serve on the NSC under **William J. Clinton**. Clarke became the chair of the interagency committee on counterterrorism, which oversaw efforts to coordinate intelligence collaboration and antiterrorism programs among the nation's security agencies. He was also tasked to oversee American peacekeeping operations.

In the aftermath of the **Somalia intervention**, Clarke was asked to develop a set of guidelines to direct the president in future international crises. He developed a set of 16 criteria, each of which, he argued, had to be met before the United States should commit forces to humanitarian missions. The guidelines were codified in Presidential Decision Directive 25 (PDD-25), which was used by the Clinton administration to justify inaction during the **Rwandan genocide**. In 1998, Clinton appointed Clarke to a newly created position to coordinate security, infrastructure protection, and counterterrorism in the wake of **embassy bombings**. In the final years of the Clinton administration, Clarke failed to recommend a comprehensive counterterrorism policy for the nation and recommended against more strikes on **Al Qaeda** after the 1998 U.S. attacks' failure to kill **Osama bin Laden** or significantly damage the terrorist group's infrastructure.

In 2001, President **George W. Bush** named Clarke to a new position as head of the country's efforts to combat cyberterrorism. Clarke opposed the Bush administration's drive for military strikes against Iraq in the aftermath of the **September 11 terrorist attacks**. He resigned from government service in January 2003. During questioning by the **National Commission on Terrorist Attacks upon the United States** (9/11 Commission), Clarke criticized the Bush administration's management of the **war on terror**. *See also* INTERNATIONAL TERRORISM.

CLINTON, HILLARY R. (1947–). First Lady of the United States from 1993 to 2001; senator from New York since 2001. Hillary Rodham was born in Chicago and earned a law degree from Yale University in 1973. She married **William J. Clinton** in 1975. Clinton helped her husband campaign and served as a political advisor throughout his career. She was First Lady of Arkansas for 12 years and then became First Lady of the United States when her husband was inaugurated as president in 2001. As First Lady, Clinton endeavored to expand the role of the office. In 1993, she was appointed to chair the Task Force on Health Care Reform. The group developed a series of recommendations that were perceived as too extreme and far-reaching by the public. Opposition to the proposals contributed to the loss of Democratic majorities in both houses of Congress in the 1994 midterm elections. For the remainder of her husband's presidency, Clinton concentrated on women's and children's issues. Clinton represented the United States at the 1995 **World Conference on Women**. Throughout her marriage, Clinton endured a series of infidelities by her husband, but stood by his side during the 1998–1999 impeachment.

Clinton successfully ran for the Senate in 2000. Once in office, she established a reputation as a moderate on foreign and security policy. She voted in favor of the **Patriot Act**, the authorization for the use of force that resulted in **Operation Enduring Freedom**, and military action in the 2003 **Iraq War**. However, she became increasingly critical of President **George W. Bush** and his management of the Iraq insurgency. Clinton was one of the senators who called for the resignation of Secretary of Defense **Donald Rumsfeld**; however, she opposed the creation of a timetable for the withdrawal of U.S. forces from Iraq.

CLINTON, WILLIAM J. ("BILL"; 1946–). Forty-second president of the United States. The first true post–Cold War president, William Jefferson "Bill" Clinton was born in Hope, Arkansas, in 1946. He was a Rhodes Scholar and, in 1973, graduated from Yale Law School. Clinton, a Democrat, was elected attorney general of Arkansas in 1976 and governor two years later. He became president in 1992 and was reelected in 1996.

Clinton's main priorities were domestic; however, after the Republicans gained control of both chambers of Congress in 1994, he increasingly turned his attention to foreign policy. One of his first acts as president was to acknowledge the importance of economic policy to the nation's diplomacy through the creation of the office of economic policy advisor (similar to the national security advisor position) as part of the National Security Council. Clinton also sought to increase the importance of issues such as **drug trafficking** and **human rights** in American foreign policy.

The early years of his presidency were marked by a number of diplomatic missteps. U.S. forces were withdrawn from the **Somalia intervention** in 1994, creating a vacuum and resulting in a decade of anarchy. Instability in **Haiti** led to a wave of immigrants who sought asylum and were detained at American facilities in Guantanamo Bay until the United States intervened and convinced Haiti's military regime to surrender power. Clinton's relationship with his first secretary of state, **Warren Christopher**, was uneven, and the two disagreed on a range of issues, including U.S. policy toward the People's Republic of China (PRC) in light of that country's continuing human rights deficiencies. Clinton and Christopher did work closely to gain domestic support for the **North American Free Trade Agreement**, which had been signed by his predecessor but was ratified during his first term. The president consistently sought better economic relations with the PRC, including championing Chinese entry into the **World Trade Organization**, as a main component of his **trade policy**. Nonetheless, in 1996 Clinton dispatched U.S. carrier battle groups to the **Taiwan Strait** in response to Chinese missile tests. The deployment clearly signaled that the United States was prepared to use force in response to Chinese aggression toward Taiwan. Clinton endorsed a balanced approach to **North Korea** in light of that country's nuclear weapons program and threatened withdrawal from the Nuclear Nonproliferation Treaty. The result was the 1994 **Framework Agreement with North Korea**, through which the United States provided economic incentives in exchange for Korean cooperation with international arms inspectors (it was later revealed that North Korea "cheated" on the agreement and continued its weapons program). The Clinton administration was criticized for failing to take stronger action in response to nuclear tests by India and Pakistan in 1998.

Clinton sought to avoid entanglement in ongoing conflicts in Africa and the Balkans, but the failure of the **European Union** to resolve the civil war during the **Bosnian Conflict** led to U.S. diplomatic intervention through the 1995 **Dayton Accords** and the subsequent deployment of American forces to support the peace mission led by the **North Atlantic Treaty Organization (NATO)** in the region. Many of Clinton's greatest foreign policy successes were in fact in Europe. The 1994 **Brussels Summit** paved the way for NATO to remain the cornerstone of European security and for eventual expansion of the alliance. NATO also undertook its first major out-of-area operations in Bosnia and during the **Kosovo War**, where the alliance conducted a 77-day air campaign to end ethnic conflict.

Clinton had a better relationship with his second secretary of state, **Madeleine Albright**. Albright was more hawkish than Christopher, which suited Clinton as he increasingly looked to foreign policy in the wake of domestic scandals. Albright was also part of a broader cabinet restructuring that resulted in a new defense secretary, **William S. Cohen**, and a new national security advisor, **Samuel R. Berger**. In some cases, Clinton's domestic problems constrained U.S. diplomacy. For instance, the Senate delayed ratification of the **Chemical Weapons Convention** in 1998 and rejected the **Comprehensive Test Ban Treaty (CTBT)** in 1999. Congress also refused to pay U.S. dues to the **United Nations (UN)** in protest over perceived inefficiency and corruption in the world body. Clinton emerged as a strong supporter of **NATO enlargement** and worked to maintain domestic and international support for expansion. In 1999, the Czech Republic, Hungary, and Poland joined the alliance.

The 1997 election of **Tony Blair** in Great Britain provided Clinton with his most significant overseas ally, and the prime minister and the president enjoyed a close relationship. Clinton also enjoyed good relations with Russian president **Boris Yeltsin** and his successor, **Vladimir Putin**, although tensions emerged over Kosovo and Iraq. In response to the forced withdrawal of UN arms inspectors from Iraq in 1998, Clinton ordered military strikes. In October 1998, Clinton signed the **Iraq Liberation Act**, which made regime change in Baghdad a foreign policy goal of the United States and authorized covert and financial support for anti–**Saddam Hussein** groups. Following the **embassy bombings**, terrorist strikes against the American embassies in Kenya and Tanzania, Clinton authorized military action against suspected terrorist bases in Afghanistan and Sudan. In general, Clinton chose a reactive security toward **international terrorism**.

The administration initially cut funding for the nation's intelligence services and placed restrictions on human intelligence. At one point, President Clinton did not authorize a military response to the 2000 attack on the **USS** *Cole* in Yemen. Clinton diligently sought to propel the Arab-Israeli peace process through personal diplomacy. In 1993, the Oslo Peace Accords were signed by **Yasser Arafat** and **Yitzhak Rabin** at the White House. In 1994, with U.S. participation, Jordan became the second Arab state after Egypt to normalize relations with Israel. In 2000, Clinton attempted to the restart the stalled process through the **Camp David Summit**. Although the participants agreed on a statement of principles, they failed to agree on a lasting settlement because of differences over territory and the status of Jerusalem. Before leaving office, Clinton launched one final effort in January 2001, which resulted in the failed **Taba Summit**. *See also* AL QAEDA; ARAB-ISRAELI CONFLICT; CLINTON, HILLARY R.; CLINTON DOCTRINE.

CLINTON DOCTRINE. An informal set of foreign policy principles promulgated in the final years of the administration of President **William J. Clinton**. The doctrine was never formally elucidated in a policy statement. Instead, it remained a series of loose guidelines that were implemented in some cases and ignored in others.

The Clinton doctrine was based on three broad premises. First, by the mid-1990s, there was a growing recognition that the United States faced a number of security threats around the world, including regional instability and **international terrorism**. Second, as the world's most significant military and economic power, administration officials asserted that the United States had a vested interest in ensuring global stability. Consequently, it was in America's interest to intervene so as to maintain or restore order in areas that were strategically important. Third, the United States needed a military capable of undertaking multiple, simultaneous, small to medium-size deployments. Therefore, defense expenditures had to be increased to bolster U.S. capabilities.

Administration officials argued that the nebulous Clinton doctrine was a refinement of the nation's **Cold War** policies. U.S. foreign and security policy during the Cold War had been based on four interrelated principles: containment of the Soviet Union and its allies, a **trade policy** based on economic openness and free trade, promotion of democracy, and multilateralism. Secretary of State **Madeleine Albright** contended that the Clinton doctrine's emphasis on regional stability was a continuation of containment, as both policies sought to prevent economic and political discord from affecting global security and trade. Interventions were also seen as a potential means to promote free trade and democracy.

However, the Clinton doctrine had one major differentiation from stated Cold War policy: the administration embraced unilateral action where appropriate. Clinton asserted that the United States would undertake military action with or without approval from the **United Nations (UN)**. For instance, Clinton authorized air strikes against the regime of **Saddam Hussein** in 1998 without endorsement by the UN and in spite of opposition from a number of world leaders, including Russian president **Boris Yeltsin**. On 26 February 1999, Clinton gave a speech in San Francisco in which he asserted that the United States would intervene in ethnic conflicts or humanitarian crises "where our values and our interests are at stake, and where we can make a difference." Following the speech, the United States intervened in the **Kosovo War** to stop a Serb **ethnic cleansing** campaign against ethnic Albanians.

One manifestation of the Clinton doctrine was increased defense expenditures in the final years of the Clinton administration. In 1999, after defense spending fell to its lowest level since 1948 as a percentage of gross domestic product, Clinton called for $110 billion in new funding for security beginning in 2000.

Critics of the Clinton doctrine criticized its selective approach to international crises. They argued that Clinton's criteria justified intervention in conflicts in **Haiti, Bosnia**, and Kosovo, but were used to avoid action in Sudan or the **Rwandan genocide**. Opponents also condemned the doctrine's unilateralism for undermining both domestic and international support for U.S. foreign and security policy and warned of renewed U.S. imperialism.

COALITION OF THE WILLING. A diplomatic tool that gathers countries with similar policy goals into loose alliances by allowing individual states to participate at varying levels of commitment. Coalitions and alliances are a common feature of international relations. Through most of its history, the United States has preferred temporary coalitions to more formal alliances. The wartime coalitions of World War I and World War II were examples of this trend. However, during the **Cold War**, the United States developed more formal and permanent alliances, including the **North Atlantic Treaty Organization (NATO)**. The end of the Cold War and the concurrent demise of the Soviet Union reduced the main security threat to America and the need for lasting alliances.

Thus, the administration of President **George H. W. Bush** endeavored to build ad hoc coalitions when confronted by new threats to American interests, including the 1990 invasion of Kuwait by Iraq. Prior to the 1991 **Persian Gulf War**, the administration created a broad-based coalition of the willing that allowed states to participate at different levels. At the core of the coalition were countries such as the United States, France, and Great Britain that provided military forces; this inner band included 26 states. At the next level of the coalition were nations that provided material or financial support. For instance, while Germany and Japan did not provide troops, they did underwrite some of the costs of the military campaign. More than a dozen countries participated at this secondary level. Finally, there were dozens of states that gave diplomatic support to the coalition.

The use of coalitions of the willing declined during the administration of President **William J. Clinton**. During this period, the United States relied on formal alliances such as NATO or undertook unilateral action. However, in the aftermath of the **September 11 terrorist attacks**, George W. Bush created a coalition of the willing for **Operation Enduring Freedom**. Washington sought to develop an alliance that would allow states to offer military assistance, law enforcement and intelligence cooperation, or diplomatic support, depending on the interests and abilities of each participant. During the **Afghanistan intervention**, more than 30 nations offered military support to the United States, while another 50 provided intelligence-sharing and law-enforcement collaboration.

The Bush administration's efforts to build a coalition of the willing prior to the 2003 **Iraq War** were less successful. Only Australia, Poland, and Great Britain contributed troops during the initial phase of the invasion. Ultimately 27 countries provided some troops for the occupation force in Iraq, but the majority of these deployments were relatively small in number (most numbered less than 100 soldiers). Furthermore, the Bush administration fell short of its goal of $55 billion in international reconstruction assistance through 2005 (it collected pledges of $33 billion). One result was that the invasion and occupation of Iraq was perceived as a unilateral action, and the United States found it difficult to garner international economic and military support for the reconstruction of Iraq. *See also* BAKER, JAMES A., III; BERLUSCONI, SILVIO; BLAIR, TONY; CHIRAC, JACQUES; KOSOVO WAR; POWELL, COLIN; RICE, CONDOLEEZZA.

COHEN, WILLIAM S. (1940–). Republican senator from Maine who served as secretary of defense in the second term of President **William J. Clinton**. William Sebastian Cohen was born in Bangor, Maine, and earned a law degree from Boston University in 1965. Cohen served in the U.S. House of Representatives from 1973 to 1979 and then in the Senate from 1979 to 1997. Clinton chose Cohen to head the Department of Defense in an effort at bipartisanship and to utilize the senator's popularity among his Republican colleagues in the Senate to implement the administration's foreign and security policy. Cohen worked closely with Secretary of State **Madeleine Albright** and National Security Advisor **Samuel R. Berger**. He oversaw the continuing transformation of the U.S. military from its **Cold War** structure and force deployments and supported **North Atlantic Treaty Organization (NATO) enlargement** in 1999. Cohen also managed specific operations, including the deployment of American forces as peacekeepers in the Balkans and the 1999 **Kosovo War**. Cohen supported the development of a national **ballistic missile defense** system. Prior to leaving office, Cohen commissioned a major review of the nation's defense needs through the 1997 **Quadrennial Defense Review**, which called for the restructuring of forces, intelligence, and readiness capabilities, as well as the modernization of the military. *See also* BALKAN WARS; INTERNATIONAL TERRORISM.

COLD WAR. A bipolar struggle between the United States and the Soviet Union, and their allies and client states, that lasted from 1945 to 1991. On an ideological level, the conflict pitted democracy and free-market capitalism against Marxism and political communism. On a strategic level, the Cold War was a proxy struggle in which both Washington and Moscow used allies and satellite states to fight sub-state and regional battles while avoiding another world war.

The roots of the superpower conflict lay in the distrust and misinterpretation that existed among the Allies at the end of World War II. The Union of Soviet Socialist Republics (USSR) sought to create a buffer zone of satellite states around its periphery in order to prevent future invasions, while the United States endeavored to prevent another war through the spread of democracy. The result was a series of diplomatic and armed struggles over states such as Iran, Greece, and Turkey in the immediate aftermath of the World War II. By the late 1940s, the United States had adopted the strategy of *containment*, which was based on the notion that the Soviet economic and political system was untenable in the long run and would collapse if the United States and its allies could prevent Soviet expansion. However, Soviet policy was based on expansion and the export of communist revolution. Therefore, Soviet support for Marxist insurgencies in countries such as China were seen as a direct confrontation with American interests.

To contain the Soviets, the administration of President Harry S. Truman initiated a range of programs, including the 1947 Truman Doctrine that pledged U.S. economic and military aid to countries fighting communist insurgencies. The United States promoted free trade and democracy in Europe through the 1948 Marshall Plan, which provided $13 billion for the reconstruction of Western Europe. Truman also reversed long-standing American foreign policy and entered into the nation's first permanent, peacetime military alliance, the **North Atlantic Treaty Organization**, in 1949. Moscow countered with its own alliance, the Warsaw Pact, in 1955.

The Communist takeover of China in 1949 created new domestic pressure on Truman to resist Soviet expansion. The invasion of South Korea by the Communist regime of Pyongyang led to the Korean War (1950–1953) that left 48,000 Americans dead. Through the 1950s, the United States and the USSR increasingly competed through covert operations and proxy wars within individual states in the developing world. The focus of the Cold War shifted to Africa, Asia, and Latin America. Successive U.S. administrations used economic and military aid to support anti-Communist regimes, even if those governments were not democratic. American covert actions in countries such as Iran (1953), Guatemala (1954), and later in Chile (1973) toppled elected governments and replaced them with military regimes. In 1961, Moscow constructed a wall between East and West Berlin in an effort to stop the flow of refugees from Communist East Germany. The **Berlin Wall** became one of the foremost symbols of the Cold War. The Soviets also supported the rise of totalitarian regimes throughout the developing world and brutally suppressed democracy movements in Hungary (1956) and Czechoslovakia (1968).

Tensions between the superpowers almost resulted in global war in 1962. Following the takeover of Cuba by **Fidel Castro**, the Soviets secretly installed nuclear weapons and missile launchers on the island. President John F. Kennedy imposed a naval blockade around Cuba. Conflict was avoided when Soviet premier Nikita Khrushchev ordered vessels carrying military materials to return to the USSR. To avoid such crises in the future, a direct phone line (the "hotline") was installed between Washington and Moscow.

Through the 1960s, the United States steadily increased its military presence in South Vietnam in an effort to prevent that country's takeover by North Vietnam. The Vietnam conflict divided the American public and resulted in the deaths of more than 55,000 U.S. military personnel. Following the withdrawal of American forces from Vietnam, the country was conquered by the Communist North.

Meanwhile, Soviet expansionism reached its peak in the 1970s, culminating in the invasion of Afghanistan in 1979. Efforts to reduce tensions between the two adversaries led to a series of **arms control** measures in the early 1970s, including the Antiballistic Missile (ABM) Treaty (1972) and the Strategic Arms Limitation Talks (SALT I) Agreement (1972). This era was known as *détente*.

The election of **Ronald W. Reagan** in 1980 reinvigorated the Cold War. Reagan oversaw dramatic increases in defense spending and procurement. He also launched the Strategic Defense Initiative (SDI) to develop a space-based **ballistic missile defense** system. The inability of the Soviet Union to keep pace with the American defense buildup and concerns over SDI led Soviet leader **Mikhail Gorbachev** to launch a new diplomatic effort to reduce tensions with the United States in 1985. New arms control measures were initiated, including the resumption in 1985 of the **Strategic Arms Reduction**

Treaty (START I) and the 1990 **Conventional Forces in Europe Treaty**. In 1987, Reagan met with Gorbachev in Berlin and urged the Soviet leader to "tear down" the Berlin Wall. Gorbachev's efforts to reform the Soviet economic and political system failed, while his attempt to lessen control over the East European satellite states resulted in the demise of pro-Moscow regimes and the installation of pro-Western, democratic governments. The Berlin Wall was torn down in 1989, and **German reunification** occurred the following year. In 1991, the Cold War was officially declared over. *See also* AFGHANISTAN INTERVENTION; ANGOLAN CONFLICT; APARTHEID; ARMS SALES AND WEAPONS TRANSFERS; COMMON FOREIGN AND SECURITY POLICY; COMMONWEALTH OF INDEPENDENT STATES; CONGO CIVIL WARS; NATO EXPANSION; PEACE DIVIDEND; SOMALIA INTERVENTION; SUHARTO, HAJI MOHAMMAD.

COMMON FOREIGN AND SECURITY POLICY (CFSP). The effort to create a Common Foreign and Security Policy is a manifestation of the broader movement for European integration. The CFSP aims to coordinate foreign and security policy among all of the member states of the **European Union (EU)**. Pro-Europeanist states, led by France, consistently sought to increase coordination and cooperation among the continental states. On one level, CFSP and the concurrent push for a **European Security and Defense Identity (ESDI)** are designed to increase the potential military power of the EU. On another level, this drive for a foreign and security policy was originally a manifestation of autonomy and independence from the United States during the **Cold War**; however, since the end of the superpower struggle, the CFSP has emerged as a means to assert Europe's interests and influence in the global arena.

From the first steps of defense cooperation in Western Europe at the end of World War II, there have been various proposals and initiatives to coordinate foreign and security policies among the states of the region. Nonetheless, the most significant concrete steps toward integration occurred in the economic sphere. It was not until 1970 that the countries of the European Community began to officially consult on matters of foreign policy through the wider mechanism of European Political Cooperation (EPC), whose core purpose was to promote cooperation on foreign policy. The 1986 Single European Act increased the level of interaction and consultation among the members through the EPC.

In 1991, France and Germany proposed the establishment of a CFSP for the EU within the **Maastricht Treaty**. The ratification of the treaty in 1993 created the CFSP as the second of the three main "pillars," or areas, of the EU (the first was economic cooperation and integration, and the third was police and general law enforcement cooperation). Maastricht contained 11 provisions on CFSP and called for the EU member states to cooperate in international affairs and to adopt common positions on related matters, all the while pursuing multilateral action. The provisions also called for the EU to develop a "common defense" and for the **Western European Union (WEU)** to become the military arm of the EU. The WEU participated in operations including the Iran-Iraq War, the **Persian Gulf War**, and the **Balkan Wars**.

Concurrently, the WEU increased its operational capabilities and was tasked to develop ESDI. One technique to achieve this goal without dramatic increases in defense expenditures was the "double-hatting" concept, in which forces were assigned multiple roles. Under this concept, units could be assigned to both the **North Atlantic Treaty Organization (NATO)** (wearing one "hat") and the WEU (putting on a different "hat"). NATO retained its role as the main guarantor of peace and stability in Europe, but its focus was mainly on hard security threats to the national sovereignty or national interests. Meanwhile, the WEU became increasingly focused on soft security, including humanitarian operations, crisis management, and peace enforcement missions. The WEU's focus on these areas reflected the 1992 Petersburg Declaration, which designated the WEU as the body for these types of operations (the "Petersburg Tasks"). Hence the concentration of ESDI was on soft security missions and not a challenge to NATO. The WEU also oversaw the Western European Armaments Group (WEAG). By coordinating defense industries, WEAG could reduce redundancy and encourage efficiency among Europe's arms firms and thereby reduce procurement costs and increase resources for ESDI. Nevertheless, the WEU never fully reached its potential, as EU states remained constrained by budgetary and resource pressures. Instead, NATO remained the default security mechanism for the EU.

The role of a CFSP of the EU was further expanded in the Amsterdam Treaty, which came into force in 1999. It gives the EU the right to establish common strategies and provides the European Council the ability, under certain conditions, to impose decisions upon the member states through a system of qualified voting. The treaty also provided for the creation of the position of high representative for CFSP, a post to be held concurrently by the secretary-general of the EU's Council of Ministers. The EU's first high representative was former NATO secretary-general **Javier Solana**, who was appointed in October 1999. Finally, the Amsterdam accord provided for funding CFSP through the common EU budget.

The Treaty of Nice, which came into force in 2003, added additional measures for the CFSP, including an expansion of the areas under which qualified voting may enforce decisions. In addition, new powers were given to the structures of the CFSP. The treaty also accelerated the absorption of the WEU into the EU. By 2005, the main functions of the WEU, with the exception of WEAG, had been transferred to the EU.

In order to conduct the CFSP, the EU created several agencies and committees to support the high representative. Among these groups are the European Union Institute for Security Studies and the European Union Satellite Center. While these groups are primarily advisory bodies, the Political and Security Committee (PSC) is tasked with monitoring events within the transatlantic region or areas in which the EU has significant interests. In addition, the PSC provides opinions to, and monitors the enforcement of decisions of, the EU Council of Ministers. The PSC is directly responsible to the General Affairs and External Relations Council, which is composed of the foreign ministers of the EU member states.

The development of a CFSP by the EU is seen by many as a means to lessen the role of NATO and, by extension, the United States in European security. This perception is reinforced because of the ongoing fiscal constraints on defense expenditures that force states to fund their preferences in the security realm. The funding problem has also limited the ability of the EU to develop more significant security structures. In addition, many within the smaller European states perceive a CFSP as a means for more powerful states such as France and Germany to dominate the external and defense policies of Europe. Momentum for a stronger CFSP accelerated in the aftermath of the

2003 **Iraq War**, during which there were deep disagreements among the NATO allies over the propriety of the military action.

The main component of the CFSP became the implementation of ESDI through a European Security and Defense Policy (ESDP). The EU has declared that an ESDP is critical to the development of the second pillar, or CFSP, but also compatible with NATO. Steps toward an ESDP include the aforementioned transition of Petersburg Tasks and capabilities from the WEU to the EU. In addition, the European Council has created a range of bodies as a means to activate the ESDP. There is now an EU Military Staff and EU Military Committee. In order to give the EU significant operational capability, in 2004 the Council authorized the creation of a 60,000-member rapid deployment corps, the European Rapid Reaction Force (ERRF). In order to staff the ERRF, the EU relies on the earlier double-hatting arrangement so that member states can assign troops to both NATO and the ERRF.

ESDP has manifested itself in missions that either complimented ongoing NATO operations or were operations that the alliance chose not to undertake. These include EU Force (EUFOR), in which the EU has taken over the NATO-led mission in the **Bosnian Conflict**, and Operation Artemis, in which the EU deployed forces to the Democratic Republic of the **Congo** at the request of the **United Nations** Security Council.

Nevertheless, CFSP has been supported by the United States as a means of lessening America's share of the burden of European defense and promoting burden sharing. CFSP would also provide a means to allow the EU to undertake missions and operations that the United States chose not to undertake. It can be viewed as the continuation of the failed European Defense Community of the 1950s and a maturation, not diminution, of the transatlantic security relationship. Nonetheless, as with earlier efforts to develop ESDI, fiscal and political constraints continue to limit the development of the EU's CFSP. *See also* ARMS SALES AND WEAPONS TRANSFERS; BLAIR, TONY; CHIRAC, JACQUES; DEFENSE SPENDING AND ALLIANCE BURDEN SHARING.

COMMONWEALTH OF INDEPENDENT STATES (CIS). A loose political, economic, and military alliance between 11 former states of the Union of Soviet Socialist Republics (USSR). The CIS had its origins in a meeting between the leaders of Russia, Ukraine, and Belarus in December 1991. The three leaders signed the founding documents of the CIS on 8 December and invited other states to join. Soviet premier **Mikhail Gorbachev** denounced the new organization, but when 11 of the 15 republics agreed to join the CIS, he realized that the body marked the end of the USSR. He resigned on 25 December and the Soviet Union ceased to exist on 1 January 1992.

Estonia, Latvia, and Lithuania declined to join the CIS. Georgia, too, initially declined membership, but acceded to the organization in 1993. Turkmenistan was one of the initial members of the CIS, but in 2005, the country withdrew from full membership. As of 2006, the CIS included Armenia, Azerbaijan, Belarus, Georgia, Kazakhstan, Kyrgyzstan, Moldova, Russia, Tajikistan, Ukraine, and Uzbekistan. The headquarters of the CIS was established in Minsk, Belarus. The organization consists of separate councils for the heads of state, heads of government, defense ministers, and foreign ministers. There is also a council for the commanders of border guards and patrols that was created to ameliorate or prevent boundary disputes. Finally, there is an interparliamentary assembly. The CIS also has a number of bodies charged with specific tasks, including economic and political cooperation. The basis for defense cooperation was the Collective Security Treaty (signed in 1992). The treaty created a collective defense system, in which the members pledged to not attack each other and to come to the aid of member states if they were attacked. Moldova and Ukraine never signed the treaty, while Azerbaijan, Georgia, and Uzbekistan withdrew from the agreement in 1999. The CIS coordinated a series of border and law enforcement cooperation agreements in the 1990s and also served as a means to coordinate economic policy. CIS members reduced internal tariffs and other barriers to trade. The organization sought to ultimately develop a free trade area among its members. A joint customs union was announced in 2006 among Belarus, Kazakhstan, and Russia.

The CIS had less success in coordinating foreign and security policy. At various times, different states within the organization have sought to bolster their ties to the West, even at the expense of the CIS. Following the 2004 **Orange Revolution** in Ukraine, the country took steps to move closer to the West, including possible membership in the **European Union** and the **North Atlantic Treaty Organization**.

Meanwhile, diplomatic tensions between Russia and Georgia in 2006 led the latter country to withdraw from the Council of Defense Ministers and announce it would undertake a reevaluation of the benefits of CIS membership. Turkmenistan's withdrawal from permanent membership (it was granted associate status, which allowed it to participate in certain CIS bodies) was cited as a potential course of action by pro-Western states. *See also* PUTIN, VLADIMIR; SOVIET COUP; YELTSIN, BORIS.

COMPREHENSIVE TEST BAN TREATY (CTBT). A 1996 international agreement that outlawed nuclear tests. The CTBT was a follow-up to the 1963 Partial Test Ban Treaty (PTBT). The PTBT banned atomic tests in space or underwater, but its effectiveness was limited by the refusal of France and the People's Republic of China to sign the accord (France continued to conduct nuclear tests as late as 1995). With the end of the **Cold War**, momentum for a revised treaty that would completely eliminate nuclear tests was renewed. In 1991, the PTBT signatories agreed to launch a new round of negotiations on a complete ban. The **United Nations (UN)** endorsed the discussions, and talks began in 1993. Initial divergences over verification slowed progress, but in 1996, an accord was finalized. The resultant CTBT was adopted by the UN General Assembly on 10 September 1996 and was subsequently signed by 177 nations and ratified by 137.

However, before the agreement can come into force, it has to be approved by 44 countries listed in Annex 2 of the CTBT (the countries with advanced nuclear capabilities). By 2006, only 34 Annex 2 countries had ratified the accord. The United States was one of the first signatories to the CTBT. However, in 1999, the U.S. Senate rejected the CTBT on a vote of 51 opposed to 48 in favor. The vote reflected ongoing tensions between the Republican-controlled Senate and the administration of **William J. Clinton** in the aftermath of the 1998 Clinton impeachment, as well as lingering concerns over the verification procedures. Conservative Republicans charged that the CTBT verification protocols, which included the establishment of monitoring stations and on-site inspections, would undermine U.S. security. Republicans also sought to link ratification of the CTBT with development of a national **ballistic missile defense** system. The failure of the United States to adopt the CTBT undermined the nation's traditional leadership role in nonproliferation efforts. *See also* ARMS CONTROL.

CONGO CIVIL WARS (1996–2002). The First Congo Civil War (1996–1997) resulted in the overthrow of pro-American dictator Mobutu Sese Seko, while the Second Congo Civil War (1998–2003) expanded into a regional conflict that drew in eight other countries.

Mobutu came to power in 1965 and renamed the former Belgian colony Zaire. His rule was noted for its corruption and graft. Throughout the **Cold War**, the Mobutu regime received economic and military support from the United States and other Western powers in return for its staunch anticommunism. However, at the end of the superpower conflict, Western aid was curtailed. In 1990, Congress rejected a request by the administration of President **George H. W. Bush** for continued military assistance to Zaire and stipulated that $40 million in economic aid be directed through humanitarian organizations. In 1991, the Bush administration launched a tripartite initiative with Belgium and France to promote a transition to democracy and, in 1992, Washington recognized a transitional national government, although Mobutu remained head of state (and retained most of the political power). In 1993, the administration of **William J. Clinton** suspended all aid to Zaire and increased diplomatic pressure on Mobutu to allow open and free elections. However, the United States refused to support economic sanctions against the government.

Following the **Rwandan genocide**, more than one million ethnic Hutus fled into neighboring Zaire. The Clinton administration initially pledged to deploy 1,000 troops as part of an international humanitarian mission, but withdrew the offer as the security situation deteriorated. Militia groups among the Hutus undertook raids into Rwanda. In response, Rwandan soldiers and anti-Mobutu forces under the command of Laurent-Désiré Kabila launched an invasion of Zaire. The advance met little resistance and, in May 1997, Mobutu fled into exile and Kabila took control of the capital, Kinshasa, and became president. He renamed the country the Democratic Republic of the Congo (DRC).

In 1998, the Second Civil War began when Kabila attempted to force foreign troops out of the DRC. The Rwandan troops and their

Congolese allies refused, ushering in a new round of fighting. The pro-Rwandan coalition almost captured Kinshasa, but troops from Angola, Zimbabwe, and Namibia intervened. The progovernment forces drove the pro-Rwandan troops back from the capital, but the rebels retained control over large portions of the eastern areas of the DRC. Meanwhile, Uganda provided assistance for former Mobutu supporters who took control over the northern third of DRC. Efforts to establish a cease-fire were unsuccessful, partially as a result of Kabila's refusal to allow the deployment of international peace-keepers.

On 16 January 2001, Kabila was assassinated. His son, Joseph Kabila, became president. The younger Kabila launched a meditation effort and agreed to the deployment of a 16,700-member **United Nations** peacekeeping mission. In 2002, foreign troops withdrew from the country. A peace agreement, the Pretoria Accords, was ratified by all parties in 2003. A transitional government was put in place, and elections were held in July 2006. The conflicts in the Congo killed more than 3.8 million people and resulted in millions of refugees. *See also* HUMAN RIGHTS.

CONVENTIONAL FORCES IN EUROPE TREATY (CFE; 1990). A major step in **arms control** between the **North Atlantic Treaty Organization (NATO)** and the Warsaw Pact. Whereas previous arms control agreements had focused on weapons of mass destruction, including the 1972 Strategic Arms Limitation Talks and the 1972 Biological Weapons Convention, the CFE marked the most significant conventional arms control initiative between the rival superpower blocs.

The original initiative for the accord came from Soviet leader **Mikhail Gorbachev**, who proposed unilateral reductions in conventional arms and then ordered some withdrawals of forces from Eastern Europe. Gorbachev hoped that the reductions would allow Moscow to shift resources away from military spending into his efforts to restructure the Soviet economy. The NATO allies endorsed negotiations to achieve mutual conventional reductions as a way to reduce tensions and limit the offensive capabilities of the Soviet Union. Direct talks between Gorbachev and U.S. president **George H. W. Bush** at the 1989 Malta Summit facilitated the start of negotiations.

The CFE agreement was signed on 19 November 1990 by the members of NATO and the Warsaw Pact. It went into effect in 1992 and gave the member states within each military alliance four years to complete the reductions. The treaty was designed to reduce conventional weapons in Europe so that there would be parity between the Western and Eastern blocs. The agreement covered the entire transatlantic area, from the Ural Mountains to the Atlantic Ocean, but excluded the entire area of the United States and Canada.

The CFE treaty also called on both sides to issue notification prior to large-scale troop deployments or military exercises. It specifically limited weapons in five major categories: main battle tanks, artillery, armored combat vehicles, attack helicopters, and combat aircraft. The agreement limited each bloc to 20,000 main battle tanks, 20,000 artillery pieces, and 6,800 combat aircraft. By the end of the initial four-year period, the signatories had either destroyed or converted some 52,000 tanks. In addition, around 4,000 verification inspections had been conducted.

With the demise of the Soviet Union and the Warsaw Pact, the successor states, including Armenia, Azerbaijan, Belarus, Kazakhstan, Moldova, and Ukraine, agreed to abide by the terms of the treaty. The 1996 Flank Agreement adapted the limits on regional arms numbers. In 1999, the treaty was adapted to allow new states to join the CFE process and created national and territorial limitations on arms and personnel. The adapted treaty was signed on 10 November 1999, but has not been ratified by all of the parties, or their successor states, to the original CFE Treaty (a precondition for the revised treaty to go into force). *See also* BAKER, JAMES A., III.

COUNCIL ON FOREIGN RELATIONS (CFR). A prestigious non-partisan policy group that specializes in international relations and diplomacy. Founded in 1921, the CFR brings together academics, current and former policy makers, government officials, and members of the media to discuss and debate contemporary issues. The organization's primary goal is to serve as a resource for policy makers and to inform the American public about important issues in international affairs.

The CFR grew out of meetings by American delegates at the Versailles Peace Conference in 1919. A parallel organization, the Royal

Institute of International Affairs (RIIA), was created in Great Britain, and the two groups have cooperated through the years on a range of projects and topics. The CFR originally had 75 members, but that number grew to more than 4,000 by the 1980s. The group regularly conducts conferences and commissions advisory reports on international topics. There are two categories of members: life membership, and term membership that lasts for five years and is available to promising young scholars and officials between the ages of 30 and 36. Potential members must be American citizens (or in the process of gaining citizenship) and be nominated by existing CFR members. The CFR is led by a 31-member Board of Directors.

Since the 1930s, most secretaries of state and secretaries of defense have been members of the group. The CFR publishes the influential journal *Foreign Affairs*, which regularly contains articles by leading policy makers; by 2006, 11 sitting or former secretaries of state had contributed essays. Prominent past or current members of the CFR include former secretary of state **Madeleine Albright**, former news anchor Tom Brokaw, and former **United Nations** ambassador **Richard C. Holbrooke**. The group has been criticized through the years as an elitist organization that perpetuates the dominance of the wealthy and upper-class in U.S. foreign policy. It has also been criticized by fringe groups as one component of a larger worldwide **globalization** conspiracy by multinational corporations and elites to control markets and individual governments.

– D –

DARFUR CRISIS. An ethnic conflict in Sudan between militias supported by the government and local tribes. The conflict began in 2003 and has resulted in more than 400,000 dead and 2.5 million displaced as a result of **ethnic cleansing**. Sudan had already been divided by civil war through the 1970s and 1980s, with fighting between the predominately Muslim north and the Christian and animist south. A series of peace agreements failed to end the fighting until a comprehensive peace accord was signed in 2005 granting the south considerable autonomy. Even as the north-south conflict ended, a new round of ethnic strife emerged in the western region of Darfur.

Tensions in Darfur had existed for a long period of time between herders and farmers divided along tribal lines. The herders were mainly Baggara, while the farmers were members of the Fur, Zaghawa, and Massaleit tribes. Central to the conflict was control of water supplies. The Baggara were supported by the Sudanese government. In 2003, a profarmer group, the Darfur Liberation Front, overran a military post at Golu. The rebels subsequently attacked police stations and security posts. The government launched a counteroffensive in the summer. In addition to regular troops, militia forces known as the Janjaweed attacked the farmers. Both government forces and the Janjaweed committed atrocities and launched a broad ethnic cleansing campaign. By the end of the summer, there were thousands dead and more than 100,000 refugees.

The administration of **George W. Bush** endeavored to exert pressure on Khartoum to negotiate an end to the fighting. However, the Sudanese government was reluctant to grant autonomy to Darfur or to take action against the Janjaweed. U.S. secretary of state **Colin Powell** pushed the Khartoum government into initiating peace talks, which began on 16 July 2004 but broke down soon afterward when the government refused to disarm the militias. Continued fighting had by then produced more than 1 million refugees. The **United Nations (UN)** Security Council passed a resolution on 24 July that threatened sanctions unless talks were restarted. On 10 September, Powell declared that the administration viewed the ethnic cleansing in Darfur as genocide. He attempted to gain support for the deployment of a UN peacekeeping force in Darfur, but efforts to adopt strong action were blocked by the People's Republic of China and Arab states.

Following peace talks in Nigeria, Khartoum agreed to ban military flights in the region and to take action to constrain the militias. However, the Janjaweed continued their attacks. The Bush administration maintained pressure for multilateral action, and in 2004, supported by a UN resolution, the African Union deployed 7,000 troops to Darfur. The operation, known as the African Union Mission in Sudan (AMIS) consisted of troops mainly from Rwanda and Nigeria. AMIS was able to create several safe areas, but unable to contain the Janjaweed. AMIS forces were repeatedly attacked by the militias. In one instance, on 9 October 2005, 38 AMIS soldiers were taken hostage by the Janjaweed, only to be freed by rebel forces. In November 2005, in response to attacks on AMIS, the Sudanese government deployed troops and armored personnel carriers. The deployment coincided with the start of the seventh set of negotiations between the government and rebels since 2003.

On 23 March 2005, the UN Security Council unanimously endorsed the deployment of a 10,000-member force in Darfur to replace AMIS. In May, U.S. and UN negotiators sponsored discussions that resulted in an agreement whereby the Janjaweed would be disbanded and the rebel groups would be incorporated into the national army. In spite of the agreement, renewed fighting began in July and the militias cut off food aid to more than 350,000 refugees.

The planned UN force was supposed to supersede AMIS, but Khartoum refused to allow the world body to deploy its mission. Successive efforts by the Bush administration to forge an agreement failed. On 31 August 2006, the UN Security Council adopted Resolution 1706, which mandated a force of 22,500. Meanwhile, the AMIS mission was extended through 31 December 2006. *See also* ANNAN, KOFI.

DAYTON ACCORDS (1995). Officially known as the General Framework Agreement for Peace in Bosnia-Herzegovina, the Dayton Accords ended the **Bosnian Conflict**. The agreement followed a successful joint Bosnian-Croat offensive that recaptured much of the territory gained by ethnic Serbs. Air strikes by the **North Atlantic Treaty Organization (NATO)** added additional pressure on the Serbs. Negotiations were sponsored by the Contact Group, made up of France, Germany, Great Britain, Italy, Russia, and the United States. The talks began on 1 November 1995 near Dayton, Ohio, and continued until 21 November. The American representative to the talks, **Richard C. Holbrooke**, was one of the cochairs of the conference and was credited with crafting the final accords.

Under the terms of the agreement, Bosnia-Herzegovina would remain a sovereign federal state with two regional entities: the Bosnian-Croat Federation and the Bosnian Serb Republic. Each side was given approximately 50 percent of the territory of the former Bosnia-Herzegovina, with each government responsible for internal order, including security functions and defense. The two governments also committed to free and fair elections under the supervision of the **Organization for Security and Cooperation in Europe**. In addition, a central government, consisting of a president and a two-chamber legislature, was to be created. Refugees were to be allowed the right of return, although most stayed within their own ethnic communities; one of the most frequent criticisms of the Dayton Accords was that they institutionalized existing ethnic divisions. An ombudsman office was created to monitor violations of **human rights**. A key component of the accords was the deployment of a NATO-led peace enforcement command, the Implementation Force (IFOR), to monitor the agreement. Furthermore, an international police force was deployed. The formal agreement was signed in Paris on 14 December 1995. *See also* BALKAN WARS; CHRISTOPHER, WARREN; CLINTON, WILLIAM J.; ETHNIC CLEANSING.

DE HOOP SCHEFFER, JAAP (1948–). Eleventh secretary-general of the **North Atlantic Treaty Organization (NATO)** and the third Dutchman to hold the position. De Hoop Scheffer was born in Amsterdam and graduated from Leiden University in 1974. After service in the Royal Netherlands Air Force, he worked for the Foreign Ministry from 1976 to 1986 as a career diplomat. From 1986 to 1994, he served in the Dutch House of Representatives. A member of the Christian Democratic Alliance, de Hoop Scheffer had strong pro-American credentials, but was also a Francophone. As such, he was popular on both sides of the Atlantic and was a popular choice to succeed NATO secretary-general **Lord Robertson** in 2004.

Once in office, the new NATO leader endeavored to reconcile the divergences that emerged during the 2003 invasion of Iraq. He even brokered a compromise to allow NATO a role in training Iraqi security forces, without formally deploying troops in Iraq. He presided over the alliance during the aftermath of the contentious U.S.-led **Iraq War** and oversaw the **NATO expansion** of 2004, the largest in alliance history, when seven new members joined the organization.

DEFENSE SPENDING AND ALLIANCE BURDEN SHARING. With the end of the **Cold War**, the United States dramatically cut defense expenditures. This trend began in the administration of **Ronald W. Reagan** and continued through the presidencies of

George H. W. Bush and **William J. Clinton**. In spite of the decline in defense expenditures, America remained the world's foremost military power. Concurrent reductions in defense budgets by Washington's allies renewed controversies over burden sharing within the **North Atlantic Treaty Organization (NATO)** and heightened concerns over the ability of U.S. forces to operate with allied troops. By 2006, U.S. defense spending totaled more than the rest of the world combined. America's share of the NATO budget declined from almost 50 percent during the Cold War era to 26 percent by 2006 following successive waves of alliance expansion. Nonetheless, the United States spent three times as much on research and development as all of the NATO partners combined in 2006. The gap in spending on new technology highlighted concerns about the ability of U.S. and allied troops to maintain interoperability during operations. However, American weapons research bolsters the nation's defense exports. In 2006, the United States provided 65 percent of the imported weapons used by the NATO allies.

The 1990s witnessed the most significant decline in U.S. military spending since the end of World War II. The percentage of defense spending as a share of the nation's gross domestic product (GDP) fell from its 1980s peak of 6.2 percent to a low of 3 percent in 1999, before rebounding during the **war on terror** to 3.7 percent of GDP in 2006. In dollar terms, American defense expenditures at the end of the Cold War were more than $420 billion per year. Spending declined to $305 billion in 1998 and then rebounded to $470 billion in 2006. American forces were reduced by half during the 1990s to 1.4 million (by 2006 increasing slightly to 1.45 million). In addition, while military expenditures accounted for an average of 60 percent of total government discretionary spending during the 1980s, that percentage declined to 50 percent by 1995 and 47 percent in 2006.

As was the case in the aftermath of the Vietnam War, the Clinton administration oversaw a shift away from the maintenance of large standing forces to weapons development and procurement. This emphasis reinforced the administration's efforts to promote American **arms sales and weapons transfers**. The **George W. Bush** administration cut some procurement programs and refocused spending on special operations forces and information warfare. U.S. participation in international peacekeeping missions in **Haiti** and the Balkans strained the capabilities of the standing forces and resulted in the increasing use of reserve troops and National Guard units. **Operation Enduring Freedom** and the 2003 **Iraq War** accelerated this trend, with 40 percent of the troops deployed being either reserves or National Guard units. *See also* PEACE DIVIDEND; QUADRENNIAL DEFENSE REVIEW.

DEUTCH, JOHN M. (1938–). Director of the Central Intelligence Agency (CIA), 1995–1996. John Mark Deutch was born in Brussels, Belgium, and moved to the United States as a child. He earned a bachelor's degree in chemical engineering in 1961 and a doctorate in chemistry in 1966 from the Massachusetts Institute of Technology. He subsequently joined the faculty of the university as a chemistry professor. From 1977 to 1980, Deutch worked for the Department of Energy, rising to undersecretary of the department. During the administrations of **Ronald W. Reagan** and **George H. W. Bush**, Deutch was appointed to a range of government committees, including the President's Commission on Strategic Forces (1983) and the President's Intelligence Advisory Board (1990–1993).

William J. Clinton had a poor relationship with his first CIA director, **R. James Woolsey Jr.**, who left office in 1995. Deutch was recommended as a replacement by figures who wanted an outsider to undertake reforms of the agency. Deutch was initially hesitant to accept the position, arguing that he was not qualified. However, he was persuaded to accept and went on to be unanimously confirmed by the Senate and took office in May 1995. Deutch, the first Jewish director, attempted to diversify the agency to include more women and minorities. He resigned in December 1996 after 20 months in office, partly because of differences with Clinton over Iraq policy. Deutch returned to academia, again serving at MIT as a chemistry professor. In 1997, the CIA launched an investigation when it was revealed that Deutch had unauthorized classified materials on laptop computers that he had been allowed to keep after his retirement. He was stripped of his security clearance, but the Justice Department declined to prosecute Deutch. In 2001, Clinton pardoned Deutch for any crimes related to the incident.

DRUG TRAFFICKING. The drug trade and narcotrafficking have become one of America's major foreign and domestic policy problems.

To oversee the nation's counternarcotics efforts, the Office of National Drug Control Policy (ONDCP) was created in 1988 in the waning days of the **Cold War**. The director of ONDCP is popularly referred to as the U.S. drug czar. To enhance the drug czar's status and ability to gain interagency cooperation, in 1993 President **William J. Clinton** elevated the status of the office to a cabinet-level position.

Through the 1990s, a succession of domestic measures was enacted that increased penalties for drug possession or use. During the decade, drug-related arrests increased by 100 percent, to approximately one million per year, before leveling off in the 2000s. Enhanced efforts to secure the borders following the **September 11 terrorist attacks** had the additional result of forcing drug traffickers to develop new smuggling routes and methods to bring illicit drugs into the country. By 2006, the United States spent more than $12 billion annually to fight the drug trade, not including the costs of incarceration of convicted drug offenders. The emphasis on law enforcement and interdiction by successive administrations was criticized in the United States and abroad. Many have argued that treatment and prevention programs are more effective than interdiction. Furthermore, successive interdiction programs have had only moderate success in preventing the importation of illicit drugs. Official estimates in 2006 were that 30–35 percent of cocaine imported into the United States, 15–20 percent of heroin, and 10–15 percent of marijuana were interdicted.

Counterdrug efforts were manifested in a variety of actions in foreign policy. In 1989, in an effort to end Panama's role as a transshipment point for drugs, President **George H. W. Bush** launched **Operation Just Cause**. The invasion overthrew the regime of **Manuel Noriega** and forced drug traffickers to shift operations to Mexico and the Caribbean. Through the 1990s, antidrug cooperation between the United States and Mexico increased. Law enforcement agencies increased intelligence sharing and conducted joint operations. However, U.S. officials lodged complaints that endemic corruption among Mexican law enforcement agencies undermined counternarcotics efforts. A dramatic rise in violence along the U.S.-Mexico border in the early 2000s prompted the U.S. Drug Enforcement Agency to expand its presence in the region and open new offices in Mexico, growing to 11 offices and 100 agents.

Colombia remains the main source of cocaine smuggled into the United States. In 2000, the Clinton administration launched **Plan Colombia**, which provided aid and technical assistance to suppress drug production. The core of the plan was eradication of drug crops and their replacement with other agricultural products, a transition paid for with American aid. The United States also deployed military advisors to assist Colombian security forces. By 2000, Colombia had emerged as the third largest recipient of American foreign aid. The administration of President **George W. Bush** launched the **Andean Counterdrug Initiative** in 2001 in an attempt to broaden the scope of Plan Colombia into neighboring states such as Bolivia, Ecuador, and Peru.

Ironically, beginning in 2000, the Clinton and Bush administrations funded antiheroin programs by the Taliban in Afghanistan. Prior to the fall of the Taliban during **Operation Enduring Freedom** in 2001, the United States provided $125 million annually in antidrug and humanitarian assistance to the Taliban. With outside support and religious conviction, the Taliban eliminated 94 percent of the country's heroin production (Afghanistan had been the world's main supplier of the drug, providing 75 percent of all heroin in 1999). By 2002, however, the country was once again the world's main source for heroin, prompting new antidrug programs by the Bush administration. In 2006, Afghans raised more than 6,100 metric tons of heroin, a world record and 92 percent of the drug used that year.

By 2003, Pyongyang had emerged as the most significant state sponsor of narcotrafficking. Joint American and Australian law enforcement efforts were able to prevent repeated attempts by the North Korean regime to establish itself as the leading supplier of heroin to Australia and New Zealand.

DURANT, MICHAEL ("MIKE"; 1961–). American helicopter pilot who was shot down during the 1993 Battle of **Mogadishu** and held captive by Somali militias. Durant was born in Berlin, New Hampshire. He entered the army, eventually becoming a pilot with the rank of chief warrant officer. During the **Somalia intervention**, Durant's Blackhawk helicopter was hit by a rocket-propelled grenade and crashed. In order to rescue the injured crew, troops were diverted to the crash site. Two special operations forces (Delta Force) snipers volunteered to be deployed at the downed helicopter to protect the wounded crew; both were killed and posthumously received the Medal of Honor. The other crew members were also killed, but Durant was taken prisoner. He was seriously injured, with a broken back and leg (he was also beaten during his captivity). The pilot was videotaped by his captors and Durant's bloody and swollen face came to symbolize the failed American mission in Somalia. Durant was held for 11 days before his release. He was released after Somali warlord Mohamed Farrah Aidid paid his ransom in an attempt to gain favor with the Western powers. After his release, Durant continued to serve in the army and subsequently wrote a best-selling account of his ordeal. *See also* CHRISTOPHER, WARREN; CLINTON, WILLIAM J.

– E –

EARTH SUMMIT (1992). The 1992 Earth Summit was the largest formal environmental conference in history and set the stage for the **Kyoto Protocol** on **global warming**. Officially dubbed the **United Nations (UN)** Conference on Environment and Development, the conference took place in Rio de Janeiro, Brazil, from 3 to 14 June 1992. The summit was a follow-up to the first UN environmental conference held in 1972. Planning for the event began in 1989. Representatives from 172 countries attended, along with more than 2,400 delegates from nongovernmental organizations, while 108 heads of state made appearances. President **George H. W. Bush** did not attend and faced domestic and international criticism for Washington's failure to adopt a leadership position on global environmental issues. The summit was covered by more than 10,000 journalists, and the sessions were broadcast worldwide.

The Earth Summit revolved around four main issues: the scarcity of natural resources such as water, the development of alternative energy sources to replace fossil fuels, pollution, and global warming. Several major ecological agreements were signed at the summit.

The Convention on Biological Diversity (CBD) enshrined biodiversity as an important global resource and called upon national governments to engage in sustainable development and protect biodiversity. The CBD was signed by 189 counties and entered into force in 1993. The United States signed the convention, but failed to ratify it.

Work on Agenda 21, which was adopted at the summit, had begun in 1989. It was designed to provide a series of binding principles designed to promote sustainable development. Agenda 21 was approved by 179 countries at the summit and reaffirmed at the 2002 Johannesburg Earth Summit (World Summit on Sustainable Development), but was not adopted by the United States, although several of the program's goals have been incorporated into American law and environmental policies.

The Earth Summit also agreed to the Forest Principles (officially the Nonlegally Binding Authoritative Statement of Principles for a Global Consensus on the Management, Conservation, and Sustainable Development of All Types of Forests). The document was a nonbinding set of goals and guidelines for forest development that was the result of a compromise between developing states, which sought a formal treaty, and developed states led by the United States and the **European Union** countries, which wanted only a broad statement of principles.

The most significant treaty from the summit was the United Nations Framework Convention on Climate Change (UNFCCC), which was designed to reduce the emissions of greenhouse gases in order to slow or reverse global warming. The main goal was to decrease greenhouse emissions back to 1990 levels by 2000. The UNFCCC was signed by 189 countries. The United States signed the treaty, and it was approved by the Senate on 7 October 1992. The UNFCCC entered into force in 1994. According to the treaty, developed countries were listed as Annex I states, while certain developed states, including the United States, were designated as Annex II parties as well— these states were to contribute funds to cover the costs of pollution for the developing countries. The third level was comprised of developing states, including the People's Republic of China, Brazil, and India. Annex I states agreed to reduce emissions or buy credits if they fail to meet targets. Annex II states provide economic and technical aid to the developing states, which do not have restrictions on pollution. The UNFCCC did not set limits on emissions or pollution. Instead, it mandated the development of provisions that would set specific targets and create monitoring mechanisms.

In 1997, signatories to the UNFCCC met in Japan and developed the **Kyoto Protocol**. The protocol set specific climate control goals for the Annex I states. Neither the administration of President **William J. Clinton** nor that of President **George W. Bush** submitted the Kyoto Protocol to the Senate for ratification. In 2001, the Bush administration formally withdrew from the Kyoto Protocol. It asserted that the accord would have been devastating to the American economy and that the agreement needed to be renegotiated to create pollution reduction targets for the developing states. Like his father at the 1992 Earth Summit, Bush chose not to attend the 2002 Johannesburg Earth Summit.

EAST ASIAN FINANCIAL CRISIS (1997). A severe economic downturn that dramatically devalued the currencies and stock markets of countries in the East Asian region. Indonesia, South Korea, and Thailand suffered the most significant declines, but Hong Kong, Laos, Malaysia, and the Philippines were also affected. Asia's two largest economies, those of Japan and the People's Republic of China, suffered far less than other regional economies. Nonetheless, Japan went into a recession, while China was forced to spend billions to protect its currency. The roots of the economic downturn were in the dramatic growth in gross domestic product (GDP) and foreign direct investments in the region in the early 1990s. Throughout East Asia, economic growth had averaged 8–12 percent per year since the late 1980s. Significant influxes of investments had driven regional currencies to highly inflated values, especially as central banks maintained artificially high interest rates. By 1996, East Asia accounted for half of all investments among developing states. However, interest rate hikes in the United States and Europe in the early 1990s led many investors to seek these more mature and stable markets. By 1997, the flow of new funds into East Asia had begun to slow significantly. In addition, current investors began to shift funds out of the markets in the region.

The crisis began in Thailand, when the currency lost more than half its value and the country's stock market declined by 75 percent. Thailand's woes quickly spread to other countries. The value of the Filipino currency declined by more than 60 percent, and further losses were prevented only by a dramatic rise in interest rates (from 15 percent to 24 percent). Indonesia's GDP declined by 13.5 percent, while South Korea's slowed from 5 percent growth to a decline of 5.8

percent in the span of a year. Hong Kong's currency was under pressure because of the Chinese takeover of the former British colony. The new administration had to spend $1 billion in reserves to shore up the currency. The Hong Kong stock market fell by 23 percent, and interest rates rose from 8 percent to 23 percent. The main impact of the crisis was confined to East Asia, but economies throughout the world also suffered to varying degrees. Global financiers withdrew billions of dollars from investments in developing countries. Many lesser-developed states were unable to secure credit or had to pay much higher interest rates to private investors.

In the United States, the stock market declined by 7.2 percent in a single day, the third largest decline in New York Stock Exchange's history, and ultimately lost 12 percent of its value over the succeeding weeks. The crisis undermined investor and consumer confidence. However, the economy only slowed slightly, and only during that quarter. U.S. GDP growth for the year was 4.5 percent. The United States supported the **International Monetary Fund (IMF)** response to the crisis, as opposed to direct intervention. The IMF provided $35 billion in emergency support for Indonesia, South Korea, and Thailand. It required the recipient countries to undertake structural reforms of their economies, including reduction of public debt and government spending, as well as the elimination of financial support for insolvent companies and banks. The United States also provided $8 billion as part of a larger $70 billion standby credit package that was overseen by the IMF and funded by individual countries and multinational organizations such the **Asia-Pacific Economic Cooperation** and the **Association of Southeast Asian Nations**. The East Asian Financial Crisis contributed to the Russian Currency Crisis and caused a dramatic increase in the U.S. trade deficit with the region in 1998. By 1998, most of the economies of the area were in recovery, with the exception of Indonesia and Malaysia. By the 2000s, the IMF recovery programs were complete. *See also* TRADE POLICY.

EAST TIMOR. East Timor was under Indonesian control until 1999 when a **United Nations (UN)**–sponsored peace initiative began a political process that resulted in independence. In 1975, Indonesia had invaded the Portuguese colony and annexed the area (the UN and Portugal refused to recognize the takeover). The mainly Roman Catholic region underwent brutal repression that left some 100,000 East Timorese dead. In 1998, renewed violence by pro-Jakarta militias led to international efforts to mediate the conflict. The UN sponsored negotiations between Indonesia, Portugal, and Timorese independence leaders. The discussions initially deadlocked, with Jakarta offering to make the region an autonomous province while the East Timorese sought eventual independence. Meanwhile, violence escalated and created 60,000 additional internal refugees. Finally, on 5 May 1999, the parties agreed to hold a UN-sponsored referendum in August in which voters would be asked to choose between the status of an autonomous province or full independence. The polling took place on 30 August, and 78.5 percent voted in favor of independence.

The referendum sparked a new wave of violence. Militias attacked civilians, journalists, and aid workers. More than 450,000 refugees fled the fighting, and the East Timorese capital of Dili was largely destroyed. Meanwhile, Indonesian military units refused to intercede. On 15 September 1999, the UN Security Council adopted Resolution 1264, which authorized the deployment of a peacekeeping force, the International Force East Timor (INTERFET). The 8,000 troops of INTERFET deployed on 20 September, following the withdrawal of the Indonesian military. INTERFET was composed mainly of troops from Australia and New Zealand, but also included forces from Brazil, Canada, France, Germany, Great Britain, and Portugal.

In February 2000, INTERFET was superseded by the UN Transitional Administration in East Timor (UNTAET). UNTAET was tasked to oversee the transition to full independence. An interim government was created, including a 36-member legislature. In August 2001, a constituent assembly was elected. The assembly drafted a constitution, which was approved on 22 March 2002. Formal independence was achieved on 20 May. East Timor joined the UN, which continued its peace enforcement mission until 2005. The UN also authorized a special court to investigate atrocities and crimes against humanity. The court indicted 350 people, mainly Indonesian military and government officials, and by 2006, it had convicted 50 individuals. The court criticized Jakarta for not turning over indicted persons who remained in Indonesia.

EMBASSY BOMBINGS (1998). Twin terrorist attacks on the U.S. embassies in Nairobi, Kenya, and Dar-es-Salaam, Tanzania, in August 1998. These attacks demonstrated the global reach of **Al Qaeda** and resulted in military strikes against the organization's suspected facilities in Afghanistan and Sudan. The embassy bombings were part of an escalating campaign by Al Qaeda against Western targets and followed the 1996 **Khobar Towers bombing** in Saudi Arabia. Africa was seen as an opportune area to conduct operations because of the porous borders common to most countries. Kenya and Tanzania both had security forces that were less robust than their European or American counterparts, and there were significant Muslim populations in the region, especially in Tanzania. In addition, both embassies lacked modern counterterrorism protections and were easily accessible from roadways, although the Dar-es-Salaam facility did search vehicles before they entered the embassy grounds. Both facilities were warned about inefficient security procedures prior to the attacks.

Planning for the attacks began in 1997 and were coordinated by Mohammed Atef and financed through a Somali *hawala* company. U.S. intelligence estimates put the cost of the attacks at $50,000 for planning, material, and support for personnel. The attacks took place simultaneously at 10:45 A.M. on August 7. In both strikes, large vehicular bombs were driven to the outside of the embassies and detonated by the drivers. In the Kenya attack, one of the assailants threw a flash grenade, which exploded on the grounds of the embassy and brought staff to the windows of the building just prior to the detonation; 224 people were killed, including 12 Americans, and some 4,000 were injured. In the Tanzanian strike, a parked supply vehicle deflected part of the blast. In Dar-es-Salaam; 11 were killed and 85 wounded. In both attacks, the majority of those injured were civilians.

The administration of **William J. Clinton** undertook several retaliatory measures. Clinton signed executive orders that directed the Treasury Department to freeze the assets of Al Qaeda and its top leadership, when such resources were identified. U.S. firms and individuals were also prohibited from doing business with Al Qaeda and its members. On 20 August 1998, the United States conducted cruise missile attacks on suspected Al Qaeda targets in Afghanistan and Sudan. American warships fired 56 cruise missiles at Al Qaeda's training camps in the Khost Province of Afghanistan. The attack destroyed the facilities at the camps, but failed to kill any of the group's senior leadership. The strikes on the Al Shifa pharmaceutical plant in Sudan involved 20 cruise missiles and left one dead and 10 injured (a nearby candy store was also damaged). The Sudan attack created considerable controversy. The plant was believed to have been a production site for chemical weapons, but postattack analysis indicated that such usage had likely ended some time before. The incident undermined the public perception of the United States in some Muslim states.

The United States provided $60 million to Kenya and Tanzania in humanitarian and disaster relief aid. In addition, in 1999, spending on security at U.S. embassies was increased by $650 million. The costs of rebuilding the embassies in Africa, the cruise missile attacks, and new security measures totaled $1.9 billion.

U.S. and allied intelligence agencies were able to identify several of the key leaders of the plot. Four were arrested and extradited for trial, including Wadih El-Hage, the commander of Al Qaeda in East Africa. All four defendants were convicted in June 2001 and sentenced to life in prison. Other figures were arrested, tried, and convicted and sentenced to lesser terms. Thirteen additional Al Qaeda figures were indicted, including **Osama bin Laden**, but remained at large (several were captured or killed during **Operation Enduring Freedom**).

The failure of the American response to significantly damage Al Qaeda's infrastructure or its financial resources prompted future attacks on U.S. interests, including the failed **Millennium Bombing Plots** and the successful **USS *Cole* bombing**. *See also* INTERNATIONAL TERRORISM.

ETHNIC CLEANSING. The forcible displacement of peoples to allow members of a different group to create homogeneous communities. Ethnic cleansing has been practiced throughout history, but the phrase came into popular use during the **Balkan Wars** in the 1990s. The media extensively reported on the ethnic-cleansing campaigns conducted by the Serbs, and international attention prompted the administration of **William J. Clinton** to intervene in the **Bosnian Conflict** and **Kosovo War**.

Ethnic-cleansing campaigns during World War II and the early days of the **Cold War** had forced the relocation of large populations and the redrawing of national borders in Europe. However, by the end of the Cold War, most believed that the borders of both East and West Europe were relatively stable and that ethnic conflict was a thing of the past. Nevertheless, in Yugoslavia, Serbian leader **Slobodan Milošević** used ethnic divisions as a means to increase nationalism and public support for his policies. After the end of the Cold War, the Yugoslav federation broke apart, with Slovenia, Croatia, Bosnia, and Macedonia declaring independence. Slovenia quickly defeated Serb forces and became a new country. In the eastern Croatian region of Krajina from 1991 to 1995, both the Serbs and Croats endeavored to take territory from each other. More than 200,000 Croats and 300,000 Serbs were displaced during the conflict. In addition, both sides committed atrocities, including executions, torture, and rape.

The most egregious examples of ethnic cleansing occurred in Bosnia and Kosovo. In Bosnia, there were widespread atrocities, and more than 100,000 civilians were killed (mostly ethnic Bosnians). In addition, more than 1.8 million people, predominately Bosnians, were displaced. Efforts by the **United Nations (UN)** to end the conflict failed until the **North Atlantic Treaty Organization (NATO)** launched military strikes against the Bosnian Serbs. Under the threat of further NATO intervention, Serbs, Croats, and Bosnians agreed to a negotiated settlement through the **Dayton Accords** in 1995 under the auspices of the United States. The agreement divided Bosnia along ethnic lines, half going to the Serbs and half to the Bosnian-Croat federation. Critics contended that the agreement rewarded ethnic cleansing by recognizing the redrawn borders.

NATO intervened in Kosovo in 1999 to stop a Serb-sponsored ethnic-cleansing campaign. More than 3,000 ethnic Albanians were killed, and another 850,000 were forced from their homes. NATO deployed a peacekeeping force after the Serbs capitulated, but more than 200,000 Serbs became displaced as well.

Other prominent examples of ethnic cleansing in the post–Cold War era were the **Rwandan genocide** (1994), **East Timor** (1999), and the **Darfur Crisis** (2003–). The Clinton administration condemned the genocide and ethnic cleansing in Rwanda, but did not intervene. A UN force led by Australia was able to end the Indonesian-sponsored ethnic cleaning in East Timor. The administration of **George W. Bush** condemned the killing and ethnic cleansing in Darfur, and even officially labeled the crimes genocide. In addition, the UN authorized a peacekeeping mission, but the African Union force that was deployed was unable to effectively end the conflict.

In 1992, the UN condemned ethnic cleansing. Subsequently, ethnic cleansing—formally defined as the forcible removal of people—was identified as a crime against humanity by the **International Criminal Court** and the UN-sponsored International Criminal Tribunal for the Former Yugoslavia (ICTY). Various courts, including the ICTY and tribunals in Rwanda, indicted individuals for planning and involvement in ethnic cleansing. *See also* HUMAN RIGHTS.

EURO (€). The common currency of the **European Union (EU)**. The euro was introduced in 1999 as a component of the European Monetary Union (EMU), and its adoption marked the largest currency conversion in history. EMU was proposed by the 1992 **Maastricht Treaty**. Under the agreement, EMU was to be achieved in three stages. The first stage was marked by complete freedom in financial transactions and increased cooperation between national banks. In addition, the European Currency Unit or ECU, the noncurrency forerunner to the euro, was authorized for use in financial transactions. The second stage of EMU included the creation of the European Monetary Institute (EMI), which was established in 1994 as the forerunner of the European Central Bank (ECB). EMI was tasked to coordinate monetary policy among the EU's central banks. The middle stage also involved a prohibition on the extension of credit by central banks to the public sector (with that role to be absorbed by EMI and eventually the ECB). In the third and final stage, currencies were fixed to specific rates of exchange and the euro was introduced. Beginning in 1999, transactions were calculated in euros; euro banknotes and coins were introduced in 2002.

The ECB became operational in 1999, as did the Growth and Stability Pact. The ECB was granted the sole authority to print currency and mint coinage and to determine monetary policy for those states using the euro. The Growth and Stability Pact governed the fiscal policies of EU members. Specifically, it required members to keep budgetary deficits at less than 3 percent of gross domestic product (GDP) and national debts at less than 60 percent of GDP. In 2005, the Growth and Stability Pact was revised after several EU states, including France and Germany, were repeatedly unable to meet the targets (after several years with deficits above 3 percent of GDP, Germany brought its overspending down to 2.5 percent in 2006). The revisions made allowances for recessions and other economic problems that could necessitate deficit spending.

The euro is the currency of the EU members Austria, Belgium, Finland, France, Germany, Greece, Ireland, Italy, Luxembourg, the Netherlands, Portugal, and Spain. EU members Denmark, Great Britain, and Sweden chose to retain their national currencies. Voters in Denmark initially rejected the Maastricht Treaty in a national referendum and approved the document only after the country was granted the ability to opt out of the euro. Proposals to adopt the euro in Great Britain remain highly unpopular. Swedish voters rejected adoption of the euro in a 2003 referendum by a vote of 55.9 percent opposed and 42 percent in favor. The 10 countries that joined the EU in 2004 were required to adopt the euro when they meet its economic criteria.

The main goal of the euro was to ease financial transactions between EU members. A secondary purpose was to challenge the global hegemony of the U.S. dollar in international monetary transactions. Successive American administrations adopted a weak-dollar policy in order to promote U.S. exports. As a result, the conversion value averaged €1.00 to $1.25, but fell to $0.75 per euro in 2006. The high euro-to-dollar value has constrained European exports to the United States and hurt tourism markets in Europe. In successive **Group of Eight** summits in recent years, European leaders have sought unsuccessfully to convince the United States to strengthen the value of the dollar.

EUROPEAN SECURITY AND DEFENSE IDENTITY (ESDI). A broad effort to enhance the role and influence of European states in transatlantic security. ESDI reflects European efforts to gain more autonomy in security matters and U.S. preferences for increased burden sharing. At different times, ESDI has been perceived by both supporters and detractors as either competitive with or complimentary to the **North Atlantic Treaty Organization (NATO).**

Following the 1999 Washington Summit, NATO affirmed its commitment to develop ESDI within the context of the alliance. The reduction of tensions associated with the **Cold War** during the 1980s reignited the drive to meet the goals of increased autonomy and greater burden sharing as proposals were developed in the 1980s for a European pillar within NATO. Meanwhile, France and Germany moved forward with collaborative defense structures, initially outside of the auspices of NATO, through the formation of the Franco-German Brigade in 1989 and the Eurocorps in 1991. The 1991 **Maastricht Treaty** formalized the call for greater European control over **common foreign and security policy** and a higher degree of independence (fulfilling the long-standing drive by Europeanist states for greater security autonomy). Underlying the discussions was a concern that greater autonomy might lead to overlapping functions and capabilities.

The 1992 Petersburg Declaration called for the **European Union (EU)** to undertake a range of humanitarian and crisis intervention operations and made the **Western European Union (WEU)** the vehicle for such missions. These types of operations came to be known as "Petersburg Tasks," and it was envisioned that the WEU would be able to achieve an ESDI and engage in missions outside of NATO's traditional area of operations and mission type. The United States has preferred that ESDI concentrate on softer security threats associated with the Petersburg Tasks, including humanitarian missions and crisis management. The development of NATO's Combined and Joint Task Force (CJTF) system allowed alliance assets to be utilized in out-of-area operations and provided a means for some countries to participate by choice, while others could opt out of the mission.

In the 2000s, NATO and EU leaders continued to develop practical means for cooperation that eliminated redundancy. In December 2002, the parties signed the NATO-EU Declaration on European Security and Defense Policy. In the agreement, NATO pledged to make available alliance assets in prepackaged forms so that EU security forces could utilize these resources for missions that NATO endorsed but chose not to undertake. In 2003, NATO and the EU began a series of regular exercises to test cooperation in humanitarian operations. Also in 2003, they launched the NATO-EU Capability Group, which was tasked to address the military gap between U.S. and European military capabilities; it also was designated with ensuring that security goals and military priorities were consistent between NATO and the EU. *See also* ARMS SALES AND WEAPONS TRANSFERS; DEFENSE SPENDING AND ALLIANCE BURDEN SHARING.

EUROPEAN UNION (EU). The political and economic engine of Western Europe. The EU, originally the European Economic Community (EEC) and then the European Community (EC), evolved from early post–World War II efforts to improve economic cooperation in order to rebuild the battered economies of Western Europe. The EEC, and later EU, subsequently became the mechanism for integration in a broad range of areas, including most recently, foreign and security policy. Throughout its history, EU's integration has been supported by successive American administrations.

The early forerunner of the EU was the European Coal and Steel Community (ECSC), which brought together Belgium, France, the Federal Republic of Germany, Italy, Luxembourg, and the Netherlands. Parallel with the effort to develop a supranational economic body was a U.S.-supported initiative, the failed European Defense Community, which would have created an integrated European Army. The success of the ECSC in regulating coal and steel markets led the members to seek other venues of cooperation. In March 1957, the signatories of the ECSC signed two treaties, each known as the Treaty of Rome. The first created the European Economic Community (or European Community), and the second established the European Atomic Energy Community (EUROATOM). In 1973, Denmark, Great Britain, and Ireland became members of the EC, while in a national referendum, Norwegian voters rejected EC membership. Greece then joined the EC in 1981, and Spain and Portugal followed in 1986. Turkey applied for membership in the 1960s, but opposition from Greece and concern over the country's **human rights** record slowed accession talks, and it was not until 2005 that formal discussions on Turkish membership began; the United States supported Turkey's entry into the EU as a means to integrate the Muslim state more closely with the West.

Economic integration proceeded well through the EC. However, states such as France and Germany sought to increase political and security cooperation as well. In the 1980s, both countries sought to create an autonomous **European Security and Defense Identity (ESDI)** and endorsed a **Common Foreign and Security Policy (CFSP)** in order to enhance the EC's international influence. However, the military power demonstrated by the United States during the 1991 **Persian Gulf War** and the inability of the EC to contain ethnic conflict during the civil wars in the former Yugoslavia reaffirmed the centrality of the **North Atlantic Treaty Organization (NATO)** to European security (and therefore, the continuing influence of Washington).

The inability to achieve significant progress on CFSP in the 1980s led the EC to reinvigorate its drive for economic integration. French president **François Mitterrand** sought to enhance the EU as a means of preventing German economic hegemony in Europe, while Chancellor **Helmut Kohl** saw the EU as means to facilitate **German reunification**. The 1986 Single Currency Act called for a unified currency, while the 1992 **Maastricht Treaty** created monetary union and a single currency. Furthermore, the Maastricht Treaty and the subsequent Amsterdam Treaty transformed the EC into the EU. These treaties also embraced CFSP and called for the **Western European Union (WEU)** to become the defense arm of the EU. Meanwhile, Austria, Finland, and Sweden joined the EU in 1995, and Norway again rejected membership in the EU through a national referendum. In 1999, European Monetary Union (EMU) established a single currency, the **euro**, for the EU member states (Denmark, Sweden, and the UK chose not to adopt the euro).

The administration of **William J. Clinton** supported CFSP as a means to lessen the American security commitment to Europe and thereby reduce defense expenditures. In addition, U.S. trade officials generally supported deeper economic integration, arguing that it would be easier for the United States to negotiate with the EU rather than each individual member state on **trade policy** issues. Secretary of State **Madeleine Albright** argued that a strong EU also served as a balance against the potential for a resurgent Russia. However, concerns were raised that the EU might raise barriers to American trade and that the euro might emerge as a rival currency to the U.S. dollar. Washington's pursuit of regional free trade agreements reflected an attempt to counter possible trade friction with the EU.

By the late 1990s, the EU facilitated greater political cooperation and calls for a federated EU through a new constitution. In 1999, former NATO secretary-general **Javier Solana** was simultaneously appointed the secretary-general of the WEU and the high representative for CFSP of the EU. The Treaty of Nice, which came into force in 2003, further enhanced the political and security structures of the EU, while acknowledging the importance of NATO. The 2003 **Iraq War** divided the EU. Members such as Denmark, Great Britain, Italy, the Netherlands, Portugal, and Spain supported the American-led invasion, while Belgium, France, Germany, and Sweden opposed military action against Iraq.

In 2004, the EU underwent its largest expansion by incorporating 10 new members to bring the organization to 25 members. The large round of expansion was supported by the administration of **George W. Bush**. Secretary of State **Colin Powell** asserted that the new EU members would be more supportive of American security policy than long-standing EU members France, Germany, and Belgium. Furthermore, with the enlargement, NATO and EU membership became closely aligned, and the states of the former Soviet bloc were integrated into the broader institutional framework of the West. The new members were Cyprus, the Czech Republic, Estonia, Hungary, Latvia, Lithuania, Malta, Poland, Slovakia, and Slovenia. *See also* BALKAN WARS; COMMONWEALTH OF INDEPENDENT STATES; ORGANIZATION FOR SECURITY AND COOPERATION IN EUROPE; RICE, CONDOLEEZZA.

– F –

FOLEY, THOMAS S. (1929–). Speaker of the House of Representatives, 1989–1995. Thomas Stephen "Tom" Foley was born in Spokane, Washington, and gained a law degree from the University of Washington in 1957. In 1964, Foley was elected to the House. He was chosen as minority whip in 1981 and then became majority leader five years later. In 1989, he was elected Speaker. Foley opposed military action against the Iraqi regime of **Saddam Hussein**; he wanted President **George H. W. Bush** to continue sanctions instead. In October 1990, Foley and 80 other Democrats presented Bush with a letter stating their opposition to any military action and predicting that the United States would suffer between 10,000 and

50,000 American soldiers killed in action (in the **Persian Gulf War**, 147 U.S. servicemen actually died in battle). Foley was an ardent critic of term limits and led the opposition to a succession of ballot initiatives in the State of Washington to enact limitations on tenure in office. Nevertheless, in 1992, voters in Washington passed a ballot initiative on term limits and turned Foley out of office. He became the first Speaker of the House to lose a reelection bid since 1860. Foley subsequently served as ambassador to Japan from 1997 to 2001. *See also* GINGRICH, NEWTON "NEWT" L.

FOREIGN AFFAIRS. An influential American journal on international relations and foreign policy. *Foreign Affairs* is published by the **Council on Foreign Relations (CFR)**, a prominent think tank. CFR began publishing the journal in 1922. Circulation rose from 1,500 in the 1920s to 110,000 in the 1990s. The first editor was Harvard professor Cary Coolidge (1866–1928). Coolidge worked with Hamilton Fish Armstrong (1893–1973) to create the distinctive style and appearance of the journal (Armstrong became the second editor after Coolidge's death). Unlike most journals past and present, *Foreign Affairs* includes essays by both academics and policy makers. The first edition had a lead article by former secretary of State Elihu Root (1845–1937), and through the years, at least 10 other past or future secretaries of state have contributed essays. The most famous essay in the journal was written by George Kennan (1904–2005). His essay "The Sources of Soviet Conduct" (commonly known as the "X Article" since Kennan did not use his name, only "X") became the basis for the **Cold War** policy of containment. Other articles have influenced policy on issues ranging from U.S. relations with the developing world to free trade to terrorism. For instance, in 2003 former secretary of state **Madeleine Albright** used the journal to criticize the administration of President **George W. Bush** and its management of the **Iraq War**.

FRAMEWORK AGREEMENT WITH NORTH KOREA (1994). An agreement between the United States and North Korea that offered Pyong-yang food and energy assistance in exchange for the regime's cessation of its nuclear weapons program. North Korea began producing plutonium in the late 1980s, and U.S. intelligence confirmed that the country was trying to acquire enough radioactive material to produce a nuclear weapon. In 1993, Pyongyang announced that it would withdraw from the Nuclear Nonproliferation Treaty (NPT). The regime also refused to allow **United Nations** inspectors access to its nuclear facilities. By 1994, the Central Intelligence Agency estimated that North Korea had enough material to build up to 10 atomic bombs.

The administration of **William J. Clinton** employed a combination of threats and rewards to prompt North Korea to end its weapons program. The United States threatened to use air strikes to destroy North Korea's nuclear facilities if it did not enter into negotiations. During the resultant talks, North Korea agreed to stop its plutonium program in exchange for a range of incentives. The Framework Agreement was signed on 21 October 1994.

Under the terms of the accord, South Korea and Japan pledged to build two light-water nuclear reactors at a cost of $4 billion. The reactors were scheduled to be completed in 2003. Meanwhile, North Korea would shut down its existing nuclear plant and stop the construction of additional facilities. The Clinton administration agreed to provide food and energy aid, including 500,000 tons of oil per year. The energy assistance was designed to compensate for the loss of nuclear power. More than $1 billion was given to Pyongyang between 1995 and 2002, 60 percent in food assistance and the rest in oil and energy resources. The United States also gave assurances that it would not use military force against North Korea and that Washington would expand negotiations to other areas as part of a broader effort to normalize relations with Pyongyang.

In response to the U.S. and allied incentives, North Korea pledged to end its weapons program and comply with the NPT. The regime also agreed to allow inspections and monitoring of its nuclear facilities. Existing nuclear materials would be placed in storage and later disposed of under international supervision. The Korean Peninsula Energy Development Organization (KEDO) was created to implement the agreement.

In light of the fall of totalitarian regimes in Europe and the transition away from communism by Asian countries such as the People's Republic of China, Cambodia, and Vietnam, officials in the Clinton administration asserted that the North Korean regime was likely to collapse before the light-water reactors were scheduled to be completed. Consequently, the administration did not attempt to remove economic sanctions on Pyongyang or otherwise normalize relations. The Framework Agreement was not a treaty and therefore did not require Senate ratification; as a result, the administration did not endeavor to build congressional support for the measure. Republicans opposed the accord and accused the administration of rewarding North Korea for violating international norms and agreements.

Meanwhile, as early as 1997, Pyongyang launched a secret program to enrich uranium with support from Pakistan. In exchange, Islamabad was given ballistic missile technology. In 1999, North Korea warned that unless Washington removed economic sanctions and normalized trade relations, it would resume its weapons program. U.S. intelligence was aware of North Korea's covert weapons program, and the Clinton administration countered that no further progress on the agreement could be achieved until Pyongyang ceased its illicit activities. Nonetheless, in 2000 financing for the light-water reactors was secured, and construction began in 2002.

After his inauguration, **George W. Bush** ordered a review of the country's North Korean policy. In October 2002, Bush dispatched Assistant Secretary of State James Kelly to Pyongyang with evidence of that country's uranium enrichment program. When confronted by Kelly, North Korean officials asserted their right to possess nuclear weapons. In November, the United States stopped aid to North Korea, and in December, KEDO halted further construction on the light-water reactors. In his 2002 State of the Union address, Bush identified North Korea as part of an "**axis of evil**" that included Iran and Iraq. On 10 January 2003, Pyongyang withdrew from the NPT.

On 10 February 2005, the North Korean regime acknowledged that it had developed nuclear weapons as a means to defend itself from potential U.S. aggression. Throughout this period, efforts to resolve the crisis and convince North Korea to abandon its weapons program were conducted under the auspices of the **Six-Party Talks**, which included the People's Republic of China, Japan, North Korea, Russia, South Korea, and the United States. In spite of the discussions, North Korea conducted a nuclear test on 9 October 2006. *See also* ARMS CONTROL; NORTH KOREAN NUCLEAR CRISES.

FREE TRADE AREA OF THE AMERICAS (FTAA). A proposed economic agreement that would eliminate trade barriers among the 34 democratic countries of the Western Hemisphere. The FTAA was endorsed by the heads of state of the potential member states at the Summit of the Americas in Miami in 1994 and was perceived as the successor to the **North American Free Trade Agreement**. Following the summit, 12 working groups were created to establish the main principles, goals, and sequence of the proposed agreement. In 1998, the working groups presented their main findings and agreed to present a draft of the accord at the next Summit of the Americas in Quebec City in April 2001.

The leaders of the 34 states agreed on the draft proposal and set 2005 as the date for final negotiations. Meanwhile, a series of disputes emerged between the parties. The United States sought a final comprehensive agreement for the 2005 summit, while a bloc of countries led by Brazil advocated a series of bilateral trade agreements as the first step toward a final accord. In addition, Canada and the United States sought expanded access to financial sectors such as insurance and banking. Developing countries feared that firms from their northern neighbors would dominate these areas. Meanwhile, developing states wanted the United States and Canada to end farm subsidies and open their markets to agricultural imports. Washington also wanted countries to adopt strict copyright protections and prohibitions on the cross-border sale of drugs and medicines.

The 2005 Summit of the Americas in Mar del Plata, Argentina, failed to produce a final agreement on the FTAA. The differences among the various countries could not be resolved. Furthermore, Venezuela and Bolivia joined with Cuba (which had been excluded from the FTAA negotiations) to propose an alternative plan that would exclude the United States. At the 2005 meeting, only 26 of the original 34 countries agreed to hold future negotiations. *See also* CASTRO, FIDEL; CHÁVEZ, HUGO; TRADE POLICY.

FUKUYAMA, FRANCIS (1952–). American political economist who argued that the end of the **Cold War** marked the triumph of liberal democracy and free-market capitalism. Fukuyama was born in Chicago and earned a Ph.D. in political science from Harvard University in 1981. He taught at a variety of colleges, including George

Mason and Johns Hopkins universities. In 1992, Fukuyama wrote *The End of History and the Last Man*, which used the philosophy of George W. F. Hegel and contemporary Marxism to assert that history was a series of ideological struggles. The end of the bipolar conflict marked the ultimate victory of democracy and the free market over rival ideologies, since liberal democracy provided the best means to satisfy human needs for recognition and freedom. Fukuyama's work was popular among **neoconservatives** and his arguments were used to support U.S. policies that promoted democracy and **neoliberalism** in economic policies. Initially a supporter of the removal of **Saddam Hussein**, Fukuyama later opposed Washington's management of the Iraq occupation. *See also* IRAQ WAR.

– G –

GADDAFI, MUAMMAR (1942–). Muammar Abu Minyar al-Gaddafi is the longtime dictator of Libya who was a vehement opponent of the United States until the 2000s. Gaddafi became an officer in the Libyan military in 1966. He was part of a military coup that overthrew the country's monarchy in 1969. Gaddafi emerged as the leader of the country and embarked on a domestic program in which he tried to combine Arab nationalism and government control of major industries, a program he termed "Islamic socialism." His dictatorial regime brutally suppressed dissent, but used proceeds from energy exports to increase social spending. Gaddafi supported pan-Arabism and endorsed several failed initiatives to create federations of states with Libya, Egypt, Syria, and Tunisia. The Libyan leader also provided arms and funds to a range of Arab nationalist organizations. He was one of the most important backers of the Palestine Liberation Organization (PLO).

Libya's support for terrorist groups isolated the Gaddafi regime from the United States and European nations, especially after Great Britain discovered that the Libyan government was funneling weapons and cash to the Irish Republican Army. The administration of President **Ronald W. Reagan** imposed economic sanctions on the regime in 1982. Reagan also ordered air strikes against Tripoli after Libya was implicated in the bombing of a Berlin nightclub in 1986 that killed three and injured more than 200.

Libyan intelligence services were also linked to the **Pan Am Flight 103 bombing** in 1988. That attack killed 189 Americans, making it the worst terrorist strike on the United States prior to the **September 11 terrorist attacks**. The **United Nations (UN)** imposed economic and military sanctions on the Gaddafi regime for its part in the bombing. In 1993, Gaddafi survived an assassination attempt and military coup. Following mediation efforts by South African president **Nelson R. Mandela**, Gaddafi agreed to turn over two suspects indicted in the bombing. One of the two was convicted and sentenced to life imprisonment. In 2003, Libya formally accepted responsibility for the Pan Am bombing and agreed to pay $270 million to the families of the victims of the attack. In response, the UN first suspended and then repealed sanctions against Libya.

Although he supported Arab nationalism, Gaddafi opposed radical religious Islamic groups such as **Al Qaeda**. In 1999, Qaddafi pledged to combat Al Qaeda and share intelligence as part of a broader effort to improve relations with the West. He also offered to allow inspections of his chemical and nuclear programs. The Clinton administration rebuffed Gaddafi's initiatives.

Gaddafi condemned the 2001 Al Qaeda attack on the United States and offered various degrees of cooperation in the **war on terror** to the administration of President **George W. Bush**. After the overthrow of the regime of **Saddam Hussein** during the 2003 **Iraq War**, Gaddafi again offered to open his weapons programs to international oversight. Inspections documented the extent of Libya's chemical and nuclear program and started dismantling and destroying the weapons. In 2003, Washington ended its economic sanctions on Tripoli. The next year, British prime minister **Tony Blair** paid a state visit to Libya in recognition of improved relations with Gaddafi. In 2006, the Bush administration restored full diplomatic relations with Libya and removed the regime from the State Department's list of state sponsors of terrorism. *See also* ARMS CONTROL; INTERNATIONAL TERRORISM.

GERMAN REUNIFICATION. At the end of the **Cold War**, two countries—the Federal Republic of Germany (FRG), also known as West Germany, and the German Democratic Republic (GDR), or East Germany—were reunited into a single state. The division of Germany had occurred at the end of World War II when the Soviet-captured areas were incorporated into a Communist satellite state, East Germany. Meanwhile, the areas under the auspices of the Western powers—France, Great Britain, and the United States—were united as the democratic West Germany. The former German capital, Berlin, was also divided between East and West sectors. Throughout the Cold War, there seemed little likelihood that the two countries could be reunified. However, when the countries of the Soviet bloc began to enact political and economic reforms in 1989, German chancellor **Helmut Kohl** began to work to reunite the two Germanys.

Within the GDR, demonstrations and government resignations undermined the pro-Soviet regime. In October 1989, Soviet leader **Mikhail Gorbachev** visited the GDR and encouraged the government to adopt limited economic and political reforms. He also informed the regime that Moscow would not support the use of force against pro-democracy demonstrators. GDR leader Erich Honecker, who had ruled the country since 1971, was ousted by the East German Politburo on 18 October amid speculation that he planned a military crackdown against protestors and proreformists in the government. In November, crossings through the **Berlin Wall** were opened for the first time since the 1960s, and spontaneous demonstrations led to large sections of the wall being torn down. The fall of the Berlin Wall emerged as one of the most potent symbols that the Cold War was ending. By February 1990, more than 150,000 East Germans had crossed into the West seeking greater economic opportunities and political freedom.

On 28 November 1989, Kohl promulgated a plan for reunification, based on free elections in the GDR and integration of the two nation's economies. U.S. president **George H. W. Bush** and Secretary of State **James A. Baker III** urged restraint and a policy of gradual reunification. Other Western leaders, including French president **François Mitterrand** and British prime minister **Margaret Thatcher**, were even more hesitant to embrace reunification. Gorbachev proposed that a united Germany become a neutral state along the lines of Austria or Finland, but Kohl, with backing from the Bush administration, insisted that Germany remain a member of the **North Atlantic Treaty Organization (NATO)**.

In March 1990, the GDR held the country's first open elections. The new government, under Prime Minister Lothar de Maizière, began negotiations with West Germany on reunification, while Kohl launched talks with France, the Soviet Union, Britain, and the United States. The Soviets ultimately agreed to continued German NATO membership in exchange for a pledge by the alliance not to station troops or nuclear weapons on the territory of the former GDR. France and Great Britain accepted reunification on condition that the resultant Germany would be more deeply integrated with the European Community. On 18 May, the FRG and the GDR signed a treaty for immediate economic and monetary union, followed by an accord on full reunification on 31 August. On 12 September, the Treaty on the Final Settlement with Respect to Germany (commonly known as the Two-Plus-Four Treaty) was signed by the GDR, FRG, France, the Soviet Union, Britain, and the United States.

Germany was officially reunified on 3 October 1990. The six states of the former GDR were absorbed into Germany. New national elections were held in December. The balloting gave Kohl and his center-right government an expanded majority in parliament. The new government began spending what would amount to more than $1.5 trillion over the next decade to rehabilitate the economy of the former Communist state and improve the area's infrastructure and social systems, such as education and medical care. The privatization of industries in the region and the closure of noncompetitive former state-owned industries led unemployment in the region to initially rise to 25 percent. Meanwhile, Germany signed a series of treaties with neighboring states in which Berlin renounced territorial claims dating back to World War II. The new Germany continued its close alliance with the United States and became the economic powerhouse of Western Europe.

GINGRICH, NEWTON "NEWT" L. (1943–). Minority leader of the Republicans in the House of Representatives who developed the strategy that resulted in the party regaining control of the House for the first time since the administration of President Dwight D. Eisenhower and was subsequently chosen to be Speaker of the House. Newton Leroy "Newt" Gingrich was born in Dauphin, Pennsylvania, and earned a doctorate from Tulane University in 1971. He was elected to the House in 1978. Gingrich gained national fame when he led the successful effort to force the resignation of House Speaker **James C. Wright** over ethical violations. Gingrich became minority whip in 1989. In 1994, Gingrich and other Republican leaders developed the "Contract with America," a set of campaign pledges that included welfare reform, more stringent crime laws, and congressional and governmental reforms. In the November midterm balloting, the Republicans gained 54 House seats and 8 Senate seats to take control of Congress.

In recognition of his role in the election, Gingrich was elected Speaker of the House. During his tenure as Speaker, Gingrich repeatedly clashed with President **William J. Clinton** over budgetary matters and social programs. However, Gingrich supported a number of Clinton's foreign policy initiatives, including the deployment of U.S. forces as part of a peacekeeping mission in the Balkans and the **North Atlantic Treaty Organization (NATO) enlargement**. Gingrich was accused of ethical violations, but no formal charges were filed. However, he admitted that he had unintentionally provided false testimony and agreed to pay Congress $300,000 to cover the costs of investigation. In 1998, Gingrich led the effort to investigate the president that resulted in Clinton's impeachment. Following Republican losses in the 1998 midterm elections, Gingrich resigned from both his Speaker's position and his seat in Congress. He remained politically active as a media pundit and commentator. *See also* BALKAN WARS; COMPREHENSIVE TEST BAN TREATY; HASTERT, J. DENNIS; TRADE POLICY.

GLOBAL WARMING. The rise in the Earth's average temperature over time. Global warming emerged as one of the most contentious environmental issues of the late 20th century. Unlike other industrialized nations, the United States resisted international efforts to curb manmade pollutants that contribute to global warming. In the 20th century, average temperatures increased by 1.1°F (0.6°C), and the rate of increase accelerated at the end of the century. The increased temperatures have led to a range of environmental problems, including rising sea levels, changes in weather patterns (which in turn have resulted in increased droughts and storms), and damage to various ecosystems. Successive scientific studies linked the rise in temperatures to human activity, specifically deforestation and the burning of fossil fuels and their resultant pollution. Such pollutants, commonly known as "greenhouse gases," accelerate the absorption of solar radiation, thereby increasing world temperatures. International efforts to combat global warming have centered on reduction in the use of fossil fuels and attempts to prevent or limit deforestation.

The United States traditionally has led global environmental efforts. However, action on global warming created contentious debates within America. Natural phenomena such as volcanic eruptions or weather patterns also contribute to changes in the Earth's temperature, and some conservatives and probusiness groups in the United States have argued that global warming is a mainly natural occurrence that humans cannot change. Others have argued that scientific or technical advances could ameliorate the effect of greenhouse gases. These groups have combined to constrain government action on global warming. In 1992, President **George H. W. Bush** declined to attend the **Earth Summit** in Rio de Janeiro, even though government leaders from 108 other states participated.

The Earth Summit resulted in a range of environmental agreements, including the Climate Change Convention that was designed to reduce greenhouse gases and slow global warming. Under the convention, developed, industrial countries agreed to reduce their greenhouse gas emissions below 1990 levels, and certain wealthy nations, including the United States, agreed to provide funding for developing countries to help them reduce pollution. The 1997 **Kyoto Protocol** set specific targets for emissions reductions. The protocol was signed by Vice President **Albert A. Gore** on behalf of the administration of **William J. Clinton**, but it was not forwarded to the Senate for ratification. Clinton administration officials argued that the protocol would give developing states such as Brazil, India, and the People's Republic of China unfair economic advantages and generate a significant downturn in the U.S. economy. In addition, American officials argued that for any agreement to be truly effective, it had to impose limitations on pollution by developing states. In 1997, the Senate, on a vote of 95 to 0, passed a resolution that it would not approve any agreement that did not include limits on emissions for developing states.

The administration of President **George W. Bush** continued the Clinton-era policies toward global warming. The Kyoto Protocol was still not sent to the Senate for ratification. However, the administration adopted some policies to reduce emissions, while individual state and local governments have taken action on global warming. In 2006, California even enacted legislation that would put the state in line with the Kyoto recommendations. Nonetheless, the failure of the United States to take a more active role in reducing global warming led to significant international criticism and undermined the country's global standing. *See also* SCHWARZENEGGER, ARNOLD A.

GLOBALIZATION. The spread of economic, political, cultural, and social ideas throughout the world. The term was first used in the 1980s to describe the transfer of free-market capitalist principles to markets in developing countries. Initially, globalization was perceived mainly as a positive phenomenon that spread liberal democracy and fostered economic development. International economic institutions such as the **International Monetary Fund (IMF)**, the **World Bank**, and the **World Trade Organization** advocated **neoliberalist** fiscal and monetary policies among developing countries as a precondition for economic aid or membership in the organizations. Proponents of globalization argue that it raises living standards and reinforces democracy and social progress. Since the 1960s, the global economy has spurred rapid advances in income, health care, and food consumption.

Opponents of globalization, on the other hand, contend that neoliberal economic patterns elevate commerce over **human rights** and ecological concerns. They further assert that free trade does not benefit all states equally; instead, the developed, wealthy countries gain relative advantages over developing nations because of the breadth and diversity of their economies. Major economic problems, such as the 1994 **Mexican Economic Crisis** or the 1997 **East Asian Financial Crisis**, were perceived as being the result of developing states following neoliberal economic policies. Globalization is also seen as a force to spread cultural imperialism. Critics argue that the emergence of American megacorporations such as **Microsoft** or Wal-Mart promotes U.S. cultural and social norms while denigrating or degrading local customs.

A range of antiglobalization organizations frequently protest meetings of the IMF and World Bank. National leaders who have opposed globalization include **Hugo Chávez** of Venezuela and **Fidel Castro** of Cuba. In the United States, globalization has been attacked by both conservatives such as **Patrick J. Buchanan** and leftists such as **Noam Chomsky**. *See also* TRADE POLICY.

GORBACHEV, MIKHAIL (1931–). Leader of the Union of Soviet Socialist Republics (USSR) from 1985 to 1991. He instituted a range of reforms that led to the end of the **Cold War** and oversaw the transition of U.S.-Soviet relations from enemies to partners in the international system. Mikhail Sergeyevich Gorbachev was born near Stavropol and earned a degree in law from Moscow State University in 1952. As a youth, he was an active supporter of the Communist Party, and he joined the party after college. His first significant appointment was as the first secretary of the Communist Youth League in Stavropol (1955–1958). Gorbachev went on to serve in a variety of government positions. He became a member of the Central Committee in 1971 and the Politburo in 1979. In the Politburo, he attracted the attention of Soviet leader Yuri Andropov. The premier tasked Gorbachev to help reform the senior ranks of the Soviet administration. One result was that many leadership positions were filled by appointees with ties to Gorbachev. This was especially important following the death of Soviet leader Konstantin Chernenko, when Gorbachev was selected to be general secretary of the Communist Party and, consequently, premier of the Soviet Union.

Gorbachev launched a series of reforms, popularly known as *perestroika* (restructuring) and *glasnost* (openness). The Soviet leader sought to improve the superpower's economy by redirecting resources from military spending to the economy. Therefore, he proposed a series of **arms control** measures to U.S. president **Ronald W. Reagan**. Gorbachev announced the withdrawal of Soviet forces from Afghanistan in 1988 and then negotiated a settlement with the United States to end military assistance to the country. He also endeavored to decrease expenditures by ending Soviet subsidies to allies such as Cuba and redeploying forces from countries in the Warsaw Pact. Gorbachev renounced the Brezhnev Doctrine, which had promised Soviet military intervention to forestall revolutions in countries of the Warsaw Pact. Consequently, the Soviet leader accepted growing independence movements in eastern and central Europe. Nationalism also emerged in the republics that comprised the Soviet Union itself. By 1989, the Soviet bloc had collapsed, and most countries in eastern and central Europe had initiated democratic transitions. Gorbachev accepted **German reunification** in exchange for pledges of economic assistance from German chancellor **Helmut Kohl**, including the inclusion of the former German Democratic Republic within the territory of the **North Atlantic Treaty Organization**.

The erosion of Soviet power allowed the United States to reduce defense spending and prompted President **George H. W. Bush** to assert that international relations would be transformed into a "new world order," based on democracy and free trade. Gorbachev worked with Bush during the **Persian Gulf War** and in ongoing efforts to counter proliferation through the consolidation of the Soviet Union's arsenal of weapons of mass destruction.

The Soviet leader was generally popular in the West. For instance, he was named *Time* magazine's Man of the Year in 1988. In 1990, Gorbachev was awarded the Nobel Peace Prize. However, there were tensions with Washington over the Bush administration's support for independence movements in the Baltic states of Estonia, Latvia, and Lithuania, as well as Armenia, Georgia, and Moldova.

In March 1991, Gorbachev was elected as the first president of the Soviet Union, with a restructured government. However, his tenure was short-lived. **Boris Yeltsin** emerged as Gorbachev's main political opponent following the former's election as president of the Russian Federation. Yeltsin was a nationalist who advocated that the Soviet Union transition to a Russian-dominated federation. Gorbachev decided to try to reform the relationship between the republics and the central government through a new treaty of union, but before the new agreement was signed, Communist hard-liners launched a coup against Gorbachev on 19 August 1991, while the Soviet leader was on vacation in the Crimea. He was placed under house arrest, and the plotters took control of the government in Moscow. However, Yeltsin rallied the Russian people and gained the support of the army, and the **Soviet coup** was defeated on 21 August. During the coup, Armenia, Azerbaijan, Estonia, Latvia, Ukraine, Belarus, Moldavia, Georgia, Kyrgyzstan, Tajikistan, and Uzbekistan asserted their independence, precipitating the breakup of the Soviet Union. Ukraine also became independent after voters approved a 1 December referendum on leaving the Soviet Union. In addition, Yeltsin forbade the Communist Party from operating on Russian soil. He then met with the leaders of Ukraine and Belarus on 8 December, and the three agreed to form the **Commonwealth of Independent States**.

Gorbachev was forced to accept the demise of the Soviet Union on 17 December 1991. He resigned on 25 December and the Soviet Union ceased to exist on 1 January 1992. After leaving office, Gorbachev worked with a number of nonprofit organizations in Russia and the West. In 2001, he cofounded the Social Democratic Party, a coalition of several existing groupings (he resigned as party leader in 2004).

GORE, ALBERT A. (1948–). Member of both the House of Representatives and the Senate before serving as vice president from 1993 to 2001. Albert Arnold Gore Jr. was born in Washington, D.C., to a prominent political family from Tennessee (his father was a senator). He graduated from Harvard University in 1969 and served in Vietnam. He was elected to the House of Representatives in 1976 and then won a seat in the Senate in 1984. In Congress, Gore became noted for championing environmental issues.

Gore was elected vice president under President **William J. Clinton**. As vice president, Gore oversaw a major initiative, the National Performance Review, that made a series of recommendations to reduce waste and redundancy in the federal government. Gore also continued to advocate on behalf of environmental issues, including **global warming**. He was a staunch proponent of the **Kyoto Protocol**. The vice president supported military action against the regime of **Saddam Hussein** on several occasions in the 1990s, as well as the 1999 **Kosovo War**. Gore ran unsuccessfully for the presidency in 2000. He won the popular vote, but lost in the Electoral College following a bitter recount in Florida in which his opponent, **George W. Bush**, won by 537 votes.

Since leaving office, Gore has remained prominent in the environmental movement and emerged as a vocal critic of the foreign and security policy of the Bush administration. Gore declined to run for the presidency in 2004. In 2006, the former vice president launched a major environmental initiative based on his book *An Inconvenient*

Truth and the release of a documentary film by the same title. In 2007, Gore's documentary won an Academy Award. Gore also went on a nationwide speaking tour in which he condemned U.S. environmental policy and started a program to train grassroots organizations to lobby on behalf of ecological programs. *See also* BAKER, JAMES A., III; KERRY, JOHN F.

GREENSPAN, ALAN (1926–). Chairman of the Board of Governors of the Federal Reserve. Greenspan was born in New York City and earned a master's degree in economics in 1950. He had a successful career as economic consultant and served as chairman of the Council of Economic Advisors under President Gerald R. Ford. In 1987, President **George H. W. Bush** appointed Greenspan to chair the Federal Reserve. Greenspan worked to maintain low inflation and supported **neoliberalism** in **trade policy.** He was generally credited with overseeing the economic recovery from the 1987 stock market crash and the dot-com bust of the 1990s, as well as the recession following the **September 11 terrorist attacks.** Greenspan was the longest-serving head of the Federal Reserve and was reappointed for a total of five terms, retiring only in 2006.

GROUP OF EIGHT (G-8). The world's eight major industrialized countries—Canada, France, Germany, Great Britain, Italy, Japan, Russia, and the United States—which together account for more than 65 percent of the global economy. The heads of state of the G-8 meet annually for a three-day summit. The presidency of the group rotates every year and is tasked with setting the annual agenda and hosting the meeting. The G-8 began in 1975, when French president Valéry Giscard d'Estaing invited the heads of the six wealthiest industrialized democracies—France, Germany, Great Britain, Italy, Japan, and the United States—to begin regular meetings. In 1976, Canada joined the meetings, which became known as the Group of Seven (G-7). The following year, representatives of the European Community (later the **European Union**) were invited to attend the sessions and participated in all subsequent sessions. With the end of the Cold War and the Russian transition to democracy, Moscow was invited to attend the summit, although it was not involved in the main sessions (these meetings were known as the "G-7+1" or "G-7+Russia"). In 1997, Russia began full involvement and the name was changed to the G-8. Beginning in the late 1990s, the G-8 finance ministers initiated meetings with their counterparts from Brazil, India, Mexico, the People's Republic of China, and South Africa in what was dubbed the "G-8+5" sessions.

The G-8 summits provide a means to coordinate economic and political policies among the major economies. In 1994, the G-7 created a program to promote the spread of information technology throughout the world. Two years later, it conducted a special summit on nuclear proliferation. In 2005, the G-8 agreed to launch a series of antipoverty initiatives, including debt elimination. That year, the group also established a database on terrorism to enhance law enforcement and security intelligence. The G-8 has faced significant criticism from anti**globalization** groups for not doing more to curb pollution or to lessen global poverty. The summits have been targeted by large-scale protests. For instance, at the 2001 Genoa meeting, more than 300,000 demonstrators protested the summit, which was marred by violence. Nonetheless, the meetings continue to serve as an important opportunity for the leaders of the world's largest economies to coordinate activities and set priorities. *See also* NEOLIBERALISM; TRADE POLICY.

– H –

HADLEY, STEPHEN J. (1947–). National security advisor in the administration of **George W. Bush** since 2005. Stephen John Hadley was born in Toledo, Ohio. He received a bachelor's degree from Cornell University in 1969 and a law degree from Yale University in 1972. Hadley served in the office of the comptroller of the Department of Defense from 1972 to 1974 and was then appointed as a staff member of the National Security Council in the administration of President Gerald R. Ford. He was recalled to government service during the administration of **Ronald W. Reagan** as a counsel during the Iran-Contra crisis. From 1989 to 1993, Hadley served as the assistant secretary of defense for international policy, responsible for U.S. policy toward the **North Atlantic Treaty Organization** and Western Europe. Hadley also developed recommendations on **arms control** policy and advised Secretary of Defense **Richard B. Cheney** during negotiations on the first **Strategic Arms Reduction Treaty (START I)**.

After he left office in 1993, Hadley became a political consultant and a partner in the Washington, D.C., law firm of Shea & Gardner. Hadley was a security advisor to Bush during the 2000 presidential campaign, and Cheney chose him to serve on the transition team after Bush was elected. Hadley was then appointed the deputy national security advisor to **Condoleezza Rice**. He worked to coordinate intelligence during **Operation Enduring Freedom** and developed policy recommendations for Rice. Hadley helped formulate the policy of preemption known as the **Bush Doctrine** to forestall terrorist attacks using weapons of mass destruction. In 2002, Hadley was responsible for allowing questionable intelligence on Iraq's pursuit of nuclear weapons to be cited in Bush's State of the Union address. Hadley took responsibility for the mistake and later offered his resignation to Bush, who declined the offer. Bush liked and trusted Hadley and relied on his analysis of security threats and proliferation issues.

When Rice was appointed secretary of state in 2005, Hadley was chosen to replace her. Hadley differed from Rice in that he preferred to remain behind the scenes and keep a low profile. Nonetheless, his relationship with Rice and Cheney has made Hadley one of the more influential national security advisors. *See also* INTERNATIONAL TERRORISM; IRAQ WAR; WAR ON TERROR.

HAITI INTERVENTIONS. Since the 1990s, the United States has undertaken repeated diplomatic and military interventions to stabilize Haiti's government. In December 1990, democratic elections were conducted by a transitional government. Jean-Bertrand Aristide won the balloting, but was overthrown by a military coup in September 1991. He went into exile in the United States. The coup and subsequent repression by the new regime prompted a wave of Haitian immigrants to travel to Florida on boats, homemade rafts, or anything else that floated. The administration of **William J. Clinton** created a camp at the naval base at Guantanamo Bay, Cuba, to house the refugees and repatriate them. The administration argued that the majority of Haitians were economic, rather than political, refugees and therefore did not qualify for asylum.

Meanwhile, Washington pressured the Haitian military regime to resign. The junta agreed to relinquish power in 1993. The Clinton administration dispatched a force to monitor the transfer of power, but crowds forced the U.S. troops to withdraw before they ever deployed. The incident embarrassed Washington and emboldened the regime, which held onto power until American troops, as part of a 6,000 **United Nations (UN)**–sponsored peacekeeping force, were deployed in Haiti in 1994. Aristide was returned to power on 15 October 1994. He dissolved the Haitian military, and U.S. troops initiated a program to train new security forces. In 1996, Aristide was succeeded by René Préval, but the former president was elected for a second term in 2000.

UN and American troops withdrew in 2000. Almost immediately, former soldiers and Aristide opponents launched a guerrilla war. In 2004, rebels capture Haiti's second largest city, and Aristide resigned and went into exile. A new UN resolution then authorized another peacekeeping force, and troops from Canada, Chile, France, and the United States were deployed to maintain order. In addition, Washington organized an international donors conference at which $1 billion was pledged for reconstruction. In February 2006, new balloting was conducted and Préval was again elected president. *See also* ASPIN, LESLIE, JR.; CHRISTOPHER, WARREN; HUMAN RIGHTS; IMMIGRATION POLICY.

HASTERT, J. DENNIS (1942–). Speaker of the House of Representatives, 1999–2006. John Dennis Hastert was born in Aurora, Illinois, and earned a master's degree from Northern Illinois University in 1967. After serving in the Illinois legislature, Hastert was elected to the U.S. House of Representatives in 1986. Hastert rose quickly through the leadership ranks of the Republican delegation in Congress and became Speaker following the resignation of **Newton L. Gingrich.** Hastert employed a less confrontational style than his predecessor and endeavored to build bipartisan consensus on policy issues. Following his election as leader of the House, Hastert allowed Minority Leader Richard Gephardt to preside over the chamber for a short period as a signal of his bipartisanship. The Speaker worked with the administration of President **William J. Clinton** on national security issues, but opposed many of Clinton's social initiatives.

Hastert and his leadership team were able to maintain party discipline to a remarkable degree, but many of the more conservative measures enacted by the House were defeated by the more moderate Senate. Hastert collaborated with the administration of **George W. Bush** to enact the president's agenda, including tax cuts and educational reform. Following the **September 11 terrorist attacks**, Hastert managed the passage of a range of security initiatives, including the authorization to use military force in the **Afghanistan intervention** (2001); the **Patriot Act** (2001); the creation of the Office, and later Department, of Homeland Security (2002); and the bill to use military action against Iraq (2002). Hastert also managed to secure passage of campaign reform measures, in spite of opposition by some Republicans. Criticism over the Bush administration's management of the **Iraq War** and its oversight of the 2005 Hurricane Katrina relief and recovery effort combined with a series of ethical scandals in the 2006 midterm elections caused the Republicans to lose control of both chambers of Congress. Following the elections, Hastert announced he would not seek a leadership post and would retire after his term ended in 2008.

HIV/AIDS POLICY. Policy regarding the global epidemic of AIDS (Acquired Immune Deficiency Syndrome) and its causative agent HIV (Human Immunodeficiency Virus) became an increasingly important component of U.S. diplomacy in the 1990s. The pandemic disproportionately impacted developing countries, and sub-Saharan Africa was especially devastated. By 2001, more than 25 million Africans had HIV or AIDS, and more than 17 million had died from the disease. Africa accounted for more than 70 percent of the world's HIV/AIDS cases.

Through the 1990s, the United States was repeatedly accused of not providing sufficient foreign aid to combat the disease. Nonetheless, the administration of **William J. Clinton** increased funding for HIV/AIDS programs. For example, by 2000 the United States provided approximately $300 million per year for prevention and treatment programs in Africa; in 2001, funding increased to $460 million. The next year, President **George W. Bush** started a $500 million project to fund programs in the developing world designed to prevent the spread of the disease from pregnant mothers to their unborn children.

In 2003, Bush announced a major initiative to provide $15 billion to Africa for HIV/AIDS prevention and treatment over a five-year period. The United States also provided 23 percent of the total budget for the Global Fund to Fight HIV/AIDS.

Washington was also criticized for supporting the copyrights of multinational pharmaceutical companies on anti-AIDS retroviral drugs. The drugs, which were the most effective treatment to date, cost $12,000 per year, a sum well beyond the means of most people in the developing world. Countries such as India and South Africa sought permission to produce lower-cost generic versions of the drugs, but the Clinton administration opposed the potential copyright infringements and argued that such actions would reduce the incentives for further medical research. In 1997, Brazil began providing free anti-retroviral drugs to those infected with AIDS. In 2002, the Bush administration announced that it would allow countries to overturn copyright protections on some anti-HIV/AIDS drugs. Several countries, including Kenya, Tanzania, and South Africa, subsequently announced that they would produce domestic versions of the expensive drugs.

HOLBROOKE, RICHARD C. (1941–). American diplomat who helped broker the **Dayton Accords** and later served as the U.S. ambassador to the **United Nations (UN)**. Richard Charles Albert Holbrooke was born in New York. He graduated from Brown University in 1962 and joined the diplomatic service as a representative for the U.S. Agency for International Development. Holbrooke subsequently held a number of posts, including member of the U.S. delegation at the Paris Peace Talks over the Vietnam War (1967–1969), director of the Peace Corps in Morocco (1970), and assistant secretary of state for East Asian and Pacific Affairs (1977–1981).

After **William J. Clinton** became president in 1993, he appointed Holbrooke as the nation's ambassador to Germany. The following year, Holbrooke became the assistant secretary of state for European and Canadian affairs. In this new position, Clinton tasked Holbrooke with crafting an end to the **Bosnian Conflict**. Holbrooke oversaw the negotiations that resulted in the Dayton Accords in 1995, including the agreement to deploy U.S. troops as part of a peacekeeping mission led by the **North Atlantic Treaty Organization**.

Holbrooke subsequently served as Clinton's special representative to Cyprus, where he unsuccessfully attempted to forge a compromise between Greek and Turkish Cypriots. In December 1998, Holbrooke was dispatched by Clinton to Belgrade in an effort to avoid military action over Serbia's actions in Kosovo. He was unable to reach a settlement, however, and after the Russians and Europeans followed up with a new set of proposals, which also failed, the **Kosovo War** started in March 1999. He was then chosen to replace **William B. Richardson** as the nation's UN representative. Holbrooke endeavored to develop a settlement to the **United Nations Dues Controversy**, in which Congress refused to pay a portion of the country's payments to the world body. In December 2000, the ambassador arranged a deal in which U.S. dues were reduced from 25 percent to 22 percent and the American share of the UN's peacekeeping budget was cut from 31 percent to 27 percent.

Holbrooke left office in 2001 and entered private business, while also serving as the chair of the Terrorism Task Force of the **Council on Foreign Relations**. *See also* BALKAN WARS; MILOŠEVIĆ, SLOBODAN.

HOMELAND SECURITY. A new manner of coordinating domestic counterterrorism and emergency preparedness. Following the **September 11 terrorist attacks**, the administration of **George W. Bush** initiated sweeping reforms of national security policy and existing structures in an effort to bolster the nation's counterterrorism and emergency response capabilities. At the core of this effort was the creation of a new federal bureaucracy, the Department of Homeland Security (DHS). The department represents the largest restructuring of the U.S. government since World War II. Some 22 agencies and approximately 180,000 federal employees were transferred from other areas of government into four major directorates within the new department: Border and Transportation Security, Emergency Preparedness and Response, Information Analysis and Infrastructure Protection, and Science and Technology. Bush also created the National Homeland Security Council, which consisted of the president, vice president, secretary of DHS, secretary of defense, and attorney general. By 2006, the DHS had grown to 187,000 employees with an annual budget of $41.1 billion.

Opponents of the DHS argued that the department would decrease federal transparency, threaten privacy rights, and protect some corporations from liability issues. Combined with the 2001 **Patriot Act**, many civil libertarians have argued that the Homeland Security Act threatens individual rights and represents an unwarranted intrusion by the federal government into the traditional police powers of state and local governments.

The July 2002 *National Strategy for Homeland Security* articulated the main components of U.S. homeland security policy. The military was given a role in homeland security through the newly created Northern Command, responsible for military operations in the northern half of the Western Hemisphere, including domestic airway security. The military can also augment state and local personnel during domestic emergencies, most notably through federalization of the National Guard. One example of this type of federalization occurred with the deployment of the National Guard to bolster airport security following the 11 September 2001 terrorist strikes.

Thomas J. Ridge was appointed the first secretary of homeland security. Ridge resigned on 30 November 2004 to pursue a career in private industry. He was replaced by **Michael Chertoff** on 15 February 2005. The Federal Emergency Management Agency (FEMA), one of the bureaus of DHS was roundly criticized for its slow response after Hurricane Katrina devastated the Gulf Coast in August 2005. *See also* INTERNATIONAL TERRORISM; NATIONAL COMMISSION ON TERRORIST ATTACKS UPON THE UNITED STATES (9/11 COMMISSION); WAR ON TERROR.

HU JINTAO (1942–). President of the People's Republic of China (PRC) since 2003. Hu was born in Jiangyan and earned a degree in hydraulic engineering from Tsinghau University in 1964. He initially worked as an engineer, but attracted the attention of senior Communist leaders and was appointed to a minor government post in 1980. He skillfully resolved student protests in 1987 in a manner that contrasted with government actions during the 1989 **Tiananmen Square Protests**. However, the following year, Hu was appointed head of the Communist Party in Tibet and oversaw the brutal repression of a pro-democracy movement. He subsequently became a member of the Politburo and emerged as the designated successor to PRC president **Jiang Zemin**. Hu was chosen president in 2003. His foreign policy was characterized by increasingly regional assertiveness and a willingness to challenge American policies that was uncharacteristic of his predecessor, but which reflected the PRC's growing economic and political power. Hu also differed with Jiang over the PRC's One China policy toward Taiwan by adopting a more flexible approach toward relations with Taiwan.

HUMAN RIGHTS. The United States has compiled a mixed human rights record in the post–Cold War era. On the plus side, Washington signed and ratified a number of human rights measures: In 1991, the United States ratified the **International Covenant on Civil and Political Rights** and International Convention on the Elimination of All Forms of Racial Discrimination. The Convention against Torture and Other Cruel, Inhuman, or Degrading Treatment or Punishment was ratified in 1994. That same year, the **William J. Clinton** administration signed the Convention on the Rights of the Child. The Clinton administration did support the creation of international tribunals to try cases in the former Yugoslavia and Rwanda. In addition, Clinton ordered that American intelligence agencies not utilize human assets that may have been involved in human rights violations (a prohibition that was overturned following the **September 11 terrorist attacks**). In 1995, First Lady **Hillary R. Clinton** attended the **World Conference on Women** and lent diplomatic support to resolutions that called for greater human rights for women. However, the Clinton administration initially balked at participation in international efforts to end **ethnic cleansing** in the **Balkan Wars** and refused to intercede to end the **Rwandan genocide**.

Both the Clinton White House and the administration of **George W. Bush** resisted the creation of a permanent world court to try cases of genocide and human rights abuses. Clinton signed the accord that created the **International Criminal Court (ICC)**, but never submitted it for ratification; in 2001, Bush withdrew the U.S. signature to the treaty. American criticisms of the ICC centered on the potential for political prosecutions of U.S. peacekeepers, military personnel, and public officials under the court's statutes. Washington also routinely criticized the United Nations Commission on Human Rights (UNCHR) for the inclusion of totalitarian regimes in the body. In 2006, the UNCHR was replaced by a smaller Human Rights Council elected by the General Assembly.

Following **Operation Enduring Freedom** and the **Iraq War**, the Bush administration faced international criticism over its policy toward

unlawful combatants captured in the **war on terror**. In 2004, revelations emerged that American military forces had engaged in cruel and degrading treatment of Iraqi prisoners at the Abu Ghraib prison in Baghdad. Investigations resulted in demotion in rank and criminal charges against 17 U.S. soldiers and undermined the credibility of American forces and the nation's human rights record.

HUNTINGTON, SAMUEL P. (1927–). Prominent political scientist who argued that international conflict would increasingly be between civilizations in the 21st century. Samuel Phillips Huntington received his Ph.D. from Harvard in 1950 and taught there throughout his academic career. His early work was on political order and stability. In 1977–1978, he worked for the National Security Council.

In 1993, Huntington wrote "The Clash of Civilizations?" for the journal *Foreign Affairs* (the essay was expanded into a book of the same title in 1996). Huntington argued that future global strife would not be between individual states or rival ideologies. Instead, wars would be fought along cultural and societal lines (Western, Islamic, Hindu, and Sinic). Consequently, the West had to strengthen its political socialization and identity. In later works, including *Who Are We? The Challenges to America's National Identity*, Huntington contended that unchecked **immigration** into the United States undermined the nation's cohesion and threatened to create a country divided between two competing cultures. Huntington's scholarship was widely praised and criticized. Critics contend that *Clash of Civilizations* justified Western aggression and neocolonialism. His work influenced **neoconservatives**, but was denounced by leftists as divisive and xenophobic.

HUSSEIN, SADDAM. *See* SADDAM HUSSEIN.

– I –

IMMIGRATION POLICY. One of the most contentious issues in American politics. Since the 1990s, U.S. immigration policy has allowed approximately 700,000 legal immigrants per year. In addition, an estimated 500,000 to 1.5 million illegal immigrants enter the

United States each year. Into the first decade of the 21st century, the United States continued to allow more legal residents than all other countries combined. American immigration policy remains a source of contention in both domestic politics and U.S. diplomacy. Within the United States, opponents of large-scale immigration advocate for stricter border controls and increased penalties for illegal immigrants. Labor unions were the most vocal and influential anti-immigrant domestic group in the 1990s. Meanwhile, proponents have sought to ease limitations on legal immigrations and to grant amnesty to illegal immigrants currently residing in the United States (who were estimated to number between 9 million and 12 million in 2006).

In an effort to slow illegal immigration and as part of the broader enhancements in **homeland security**, in 2006 the United States began requiring additional documentation for people entering the country from Canada, the Caribbean, and Mexico. Successive Mexican governments have endeavored to convince their U.S. counterparts to increase immigration levels or to create a large-scale guest worker program. Other nations, including India, have attempted to link increases in American immigration and workers' visas to broader economic issues and U.S. **trade policy**. At the 2005 **World Trade Organization** summit, India tried unsuccessfully to force Washington to expand its issuance of professional work visas beyond the 65,000 limit after Congress required that United States Trade Representative **Robert Zoellick** not allow immigration to be linked with other economic discussions.

Following a military coup in **Haiti** in 1991, large numbers of Haitians attempted to flee violence and instability and made their way to the United States. The majority were deemed economic refugees by the administration of **William J. Clinton** and some 20,000 were repatriated. However, Cuban refugees were automatically granted political asylum. The Clinton administration refined this policy in 1994 by issuing guidelines that required Cubans interdicted at sea to be returned to Cuba, while those who physically arrived on American soil were granted resident status. The policy was derisively referred to as the "wet foot, dry foot" guidelines. As part of an agreement with Cuban leader **Fidel Castro** in 1995, Clinton allowed 30,000 Cubans who had been apprehended at sea and were detained in U.S. facilities to become American residents. In return,

Castro pledged not to retaliate against future asylum seekers or their families. In addition, as of 1995, the U.S. government began annually allowing 20,000 Cubans to immigrate legally to American through an application and lottery system.

INDIAN AND PAKISTANI NUCLEAR TESTS. In 1998, India and Pakistan conducted a series of reciprocal nuclear tests. The tests confirmed the existence of each country's nuclear program and highlighted escalating tensions between the neighboring states. The explosions also underscored deficiencies in U.S. intelligence programs, since the country's security agencies failed to predict the tests.

In Indian elections in March 1998, the nationalist Bharatiya Janata Party (BJP) won the largest number of seats and formed a coalition government. The BJP government initiated a broad review of national security policy. It also appealed to Washington to use its influence with Islamabad to resolve the ongoing conflict in the disputed region of Kashmir and to adopt sterner measures to counter the People's Republic of China's proliferation of nuclear technology (China was Pakistan's main supplier of atomic technology and expertise). In April, Pakistan conducted tests of a new intermediate-range ballistic missile. The BJP government perceived the missile tests as provocative, since the missiles dramatically expanded Pakistan's ability to deliver nuclear weapons against targets in India. In response, between 11 May and 13 May, India exploded five nuclear weapons at its Pokhran facility.

The Indian nuclear tests surprised the international community, including Washington. The administration of President **William J. Clinton** attempted to defuse the tensions between India and Pakistan. However, its relations with both countries were already strained. In April, the United States had imposed sanctions on Islamabad in response to its missile tests. Washington supported an initiative by the China to persuade Pakistan not to reciprocate by holding its own tests. Nevertheless, in May Pakistan held six nuclear tests.

The United States strongly condemned the explosions by both countries. It imposed a series of sanctions on India and Pakistan, including prohibitions on the transfer of dual-use technology and other military equipment, as well as the cessation of economic and foreign aid. The punitive measures also forbade the extension of credit by U.S. commercial entities, such as banks or other financial institutions. The Clinton administration sought to have the **Group of Eight (G-8)** agree to suspend aid to the two counties from multilateral institutions such as the **International Monetary Fund** and the **World Bank**. The G-8 was initially hesitant to endorse Washington's hard line, but in June the group agreed to block international economic assistance and called on the two countries to engage in negotiations to prevent a wider conflict. The G-8 further called on India and Pakistan to sign the **Comprehensive Test Ban Treaty** and adhere to international agreements to limit the proliferation of ballistic missiles.

In 1998, the United States initiated a series of bilateral negotiations with both India and Pakistan. The talks achieved general agreements on export controls of nuclear materials and technology and confidence-building measures to prevent military escalation and further conflict. The next year, however, U.S.-Pakistani discussions were suspended after a military coup brought **S. Pervez Musharraf** to power. In 2000, Clinton paid a state visit to India and gained additional assurances from New Delhi on its nonproliferation efforts.

In 1999, India and Pakistan completed the Lahore Agreements, which reduced tensions between the two countries by extending unilateral moratoriums on further nuclear tests and pledging advanced notice for future ballistic missile experiments. Fighting in Kashmir led to renewed strains, but Washington was able to convince Islamabad to withdraw troops from the disputed Kargil district and prevent an escalation. Beginning in 2000, Clinton began to lift some sanctions on both states. After the **September 11 terrorist attacks**, the administration of President **George W. Bush** ended the sanctions on India and Pakistan in return for cooperation in the **war on terror**. In 2006, the Bush administration signed an agreement to share civilian nuclear technology with India. *See also* ARMS CONTROL.

INTERNATIONAL COVENANT ON CIVIL AND POLITICAL RIGHTS (ICCPR). An agreement that promulgates a lengthy series of both broad and specific inherent **human rights** applicable to all people on Earth. This **United Nations** treaty was designed to promote civil liberties by allowing citizens in member states to file complaints against their respective governments. The grievances are monitored by a Human Rights Committee, elected by treaty members. A protocol of the covenant abolishes the death penalty. The ICCPR was originally signed by the United States in 1977, but congressional opposition prevented ratification through the 1980s. However, in 1992, the Senate approved the treaty with several reservations: The Senate declared that the covenant did not form part of the nation's domestic law, stipulated that the ability of U.S. citizens to petition the Human Rights Committee did not give them the right to sue in domestic courts, and rejected the prohibition on capital punishment.

INTERNATIONAL CRIMINAL COURT (ICC). A global tribunal created in 2002 to investigate and try war crimes, including genocide and crimes against humanity. The origins of the ICC were in the Nuremburg trials following World War II. Impetus to establish the ICC accelerated in the 1990s following the creation of several tribunals to try people suspected of crimes against humanity in the **Bosnian Conflict** and during the **Rwandan genocide**. International negotiations resulted in the Rome Statute in 1998, which created the ICC. The agreement to create the court was contentious, and during the conference to draft the accord, the United States, the People's Republic of China, Israel, Iraq, Libya, Qatar, and Yemen voted against the final draft. More than 140 countries ultimately signed the ICC treaty, including the United States. However, President **William J. Clinton** did not submit it for ratification by the Senate.

The ICC was designed to supplement current courts and to try only those cases that national courts were unwilling or unable to prosecute. Furthermore, the court can pursue only cases that arose after 2002, when the treaty went into force. The ICC is independent of the **United Nations (UN)**, but accepts cases referred to it by the world body. Countries that ratified the Rome accord grant the ICC jurisdiction to try citizens. By 2006, the ICC had three ongoing cases: indictments for the leaders of the Lord's Resistance Army in Uganda, other indictments for the leaders of a militia group in the Democratic Republic of the **Congo**, and an investigation into the **Darfur Crisis** (the Darfur case was referred to the ICC by the UN).

In 2001, President **George W. Bush** withdrew the U.S. signature to the ICC treaty. The Bush administration argued that the ICC usurped the authority of the UN to create special courts to deal with individual instances of genocide or crimes against humanity. American officials argued that the ICC would likely become a political tool whereby individual U.S. civilian and military leaders could be brought to trial by opponents of Washington's polices. For example, the ICC was asked to investigate the United States for its actions in the 2003 **Iraq War** and the subsequent occupation of the country (the ICC declined to investigate). In 2002, Congress, with bipartisan support, enacted a measure to protect U.S. military personnel who might be charged during the conduct of their duties. The Act authorized the administration to withhold military aid to countries that ratified the Rome agreement and even permitted the use of force to free U.S. soldiers held under the jurisdiction of the ICC. The Bush administration furthermore negotiated a number of immunity agreements with individual states in which ICC signatories agreed to exempt U.S. personnel operating in that country. In 2002, the United States declared it would veto ongoing peacekeeping operations unless its officials, servicemen, and civilians were granted immunity from prosecution. A compromise was reached under which the United States received a one-year blanket immunity, subject to renewal by the Security Council every year. *See also* HUMAN RIGHTS.

INTERNATIONAL MONETARY FUND (IMF). A global body that endeavors to promote stability among currencies and the worldwide economy. It was established in 1945. The IMF includes 184 members and is headquartered in Washington, D.C. It provides loans and grants to help prevent currency depreciations and to promote economic development. It has been frequently criticized for stipulations that accompany most IMF programs, including economic privatizations, financial reforms, and low-inflationary policies, since these programs often limit a government's ability to expand social spending. The IMF played a major role in resolving a series of economic catastrophes in the 1990s, including the **Mexican Economic Crisis** and the **East Asian Financial Crisis**. Successive U.S. administrations have utilized the IMF to promote free trade and **neoliberalism** in economic policies. *See also* WORLD BANK.

INTERNATIONAL TERRORISM. International terrorism emerged as a major issue for the United States during the 1990s and became the nation's main security concern after the **September 11 terrorist attacks**. During the 1980s, a number of terrorist attacks were carried out against Americans and U.S. interests around the world, including the 1983 bombing of the Marine barracks in Lebanon, a number of hijackings, and the subsequent **Lebanon Hostage Crisis**. However, the end of the **Cold War** and 1991 **Persian Gulf War** led to a brief period of decline in global patterns of terrorism. American forces did face terrorist acts during the **Somalia intervention**, but it was the 1993 **World Trade Center bombing** that initiated a new phase of international terrorism. That bombing killed six and wounded more than 1,000 and caused $600 million in damage. It marked the first significant terrorist attack on American soil and demonstrated the global reach of anti-American Islamist groups such as **Al Qaeda**. The administration of **William J. Clinton** failed to develop a comprehensive counterterrorism strategy for the United States, but the Federal Bureau of Investigation (FBI) was designated the lead antiterrorism agency and spending on counterterrorism doubled between 1993 and 2001 (to $11.1 billion). Through the decade, the FBI increased the amount of resources devoted to counterterrorism from 4 percent of total assets and personnel to 10 percent.

In 1995, two U.S. diplomats were killed and a third injured by an attack in Pakistan, but the administration's attention became focused on domestic terrorism following the 19 April 1995 Oklahoma City bombing in which the Federal Building was destroyed, killing 166 and injuring more than 400. The attack was carried out by two right-wing extremists, Terry Nichols and Timothy McVeigh. Both were tried and convicted, and McVeigh was given a death sentence.

In November 1995, Islamic terrorists detonated a bomb outside a U.S. military compound in Riyadh, Saudi Arabia. The attack killed one American and wounded more than 40. The Riyadh attack was followed on 25 June 1996 by the **Khobar Towers bombing** in which a U.S. military housing complex in Saudi Arabia was attacked with a truck bomb, killing 19 military personnel and wounding 515, including 240 Americans. U.S. officials became frustrated by the Saudi investigation into the attack. Consequently the FBI launched an initiative to develop bilateral arrangements that would allow American investigators to assist local law enforcement. The FBI increased the number of agency offices overseas from 22 to 44, with new offices opened in countries such as Egypt, Israel, Pakistan, Kazakhstan, India, and Uzbekistan. Meanwhile, throughout the 1990s, a number of U.S. citizens were killed or injured in terrorist attacks in Israel. The 7 August 1998 **embassy bombings** in Nairobi, Kenya, and Dar-es-Salaam, Tanzania, were traced to Al Qaeda and prompted retaliatory air strikes on suspected terrorist facilities in Sudan and Afghanistan. Although the attacks destroyed Al Qaeda bases, they did not kill or injure senior terrorist leaders such as **Osama bin Laden**. For the remainder of the Clinton years, 50 percent of the nation's counterterrorism budget was devoted to countering global terrorism. In 1999, Clinton signed an executive order prohibiting financial transactions with Al Qaeda and the Taliban (as well as a number of other terrorist organizations). Proposals to attempt to limit *hawala*, the informal banking system used to finance a number of terrorist groups, were rejected by the Clinton administration because of opposition by the Treasury Department, which preferred to use existing methods and channels.

Al Qaeda continued its campaign against the United States. In 1999, intelligence and law enforcement agencies disrupted a series of planned attacks on Western targets in Jordan and airports in the United States known as the **Millennium Bombing Plots**. On 12 October 2000, Al Qaeda–linked terrorists carried out the **USS *Cole* bombing**, in which a U.S. warship was struck by an explosives-laden craft, killing 17 and wounding 39. Clinton deferred reprisal action against Al Qaeda to the incoming administration of **George W. Bush**.

Bush abolished the assortment of ad hoc interagency groups working on counterterrorism and replaced it with a range of formal structures known as policy coordination committees. He also ordered a review of counterterrorism policy and directed National Security Advisor **Condoleezza Rice** to develop a series of recommendations to restructure the nation's antiterrorist policies. The 11 September 2001 terrorist attacks on the United States killed more than 3,000 Americans and led the Bush administration to initiate the global **war on terror**. The U.S.-led campaign against terrorism resulted in greater intelligence and law enforcement cooperation among countries and significantly reduced the amount of funding available to Al Qaeda and other terrorist groups. In 2001, the **United Nations** Security Council adopted Resolution 1373, which required all states to take action against terrorists and their financial networks. The United States led a multilateral military coalition that toppled the Taliban regime in Afghanistan in **Operation Enduring Freedom**.

Global terrorism decreased following the 11 September attacks, as some groups, including the Irish Republic Army, renounced their armed struggle, and as efforts to suppress terrorism achieved success. A number of senior terrorist leaders were killed or captured. The 2003 **Iraq War**, however, led to a resurgence in violence in Iraq and other areas. Like Afghanistan in the 1980s, Iraq emerged as a training area for potential Islamic terrorists. Al Qaeda and other extremist groups were able to continue operations against the United States and other Western targets, including the May 2003 bombing of a foreign workers' compound in Riyadh, the **Bali bombings**, and attacks on transport systems in Madrid and London. The United States and its allies were able to disrupt a series of terrorist plots, including 10 major planned strikes on American interests between 2001 and 2006 and more than 70 planned attacks on international targets.

IRAQ LIBERATION ACT (1998). A U.S. law that endorsed the removal of the regime of **Saddam Hussein** and the transition to democracy in Iraq. The Act listed Iraqi actions and crimes that violated international law and global norms and pledged American support—financial and military aid—of up to $97 million for Iraqi opposition groups. The measure also called on the U.S. government to provide media and broadcasting support to Iraqi opposition bodies. It did not, however, authorize military action to remove the regime without additional congressional approval. Finally, the Liberation Act called on the United States to provide assistance and support for a post-Iraqi democratic government. The Act passed the House of Representatives on a vote of 360 to 38 and received a unanimous vote in the Senate. In 1999, President **William J. Clinton** identified seven groups that qualified for aid under the program and authorized the disbursement of funds. In 2002, the Act was used as one of the bases for the congressional authorization to use military force against the Saddam regime in **Iraq War**.

IRAQ WAR (2003). A military victory for the United States that quickly overthrew the regime of **Saddam Hussein**, but led to an insurgency that killed more Americans than the initial combat and eroded public support for the ongoing U.S. occupation of Iraq. In his 29 January 2002 State of the Union address, President **George W. Bush** identified Iran, Iraq, and North Korea as part of an **axis of evil** that sought to destabilize the global order. He also promulgated a preemption doctrine (later known as the **Bush Doctrine**) and warned that states might face military strikes as a means to forestall forthcoming attacks on the United States. Bush concurrently authorized increased covert operations to destabilize the Saddam regime in accordance with the **Iraq Liberation Act**.

The Bush administration then initiated a diplomatic campaign to gather support for military action to overthrow Saddam, based on the **coalition of the willing** that it had formed in **Operation Enduring Freedom**. Two factions emerged within the administration on Iraq policy. One, led by Vice President **Richard B. Cheney** and Secretary of Defense **Donald H. Rumsfeld**, sought immediate military action even if it meant that the United States had to act unilaterally. The second group, led by Secretary of State **Colin Powell**, wanted to put together a broad coalition and argued in favor of a **United Nations (UN)** resolution authorizing the use of force to draw other nations to support American policy. Powell succeeded in convincing Bush to seek UN authorization, and Bush delivered a speech to the UN on 12 September 2002 calling for Iraqi compliance with previous UN resolutions. In November, the UN Security Council adopted Resolution 1441, which called for Iraq to comply with previous UN decisions and to readmit weapons inspectors. The resolution was unanimous and declared that Iraq would face serious consequences if it did not adhere to the UN demands (although the exact nature of the consequences was not detailed). Meanwhile, in October, Bush also obtained a congressional resolution granting the administration the authority to use force.

In November 2002, the Saddam regime allowed UN inspectors to return; however, Baghdad failed to offer full cooperation. Through January and February 2003, reports on the inspections provided support for both the pro- and antiwar camps. Hans Blix, the UN official in charge of overseeing the mission in Iraq, issued a series of reports that noted some progress in disarmament but asserted that Baghdad had failed to comply with all requirements of Resolution 1441. In the meantime, the United States increased its forces in the region and prepared for an invasion of Iraq.

As was the case in the **Afghanistan intervention**, the United States did not appeal to organizations such as the **North Atlantic Treaty Organization (NATO)** or the **Organization of American States** for direct support, but rather sought military contributions from individual countries. NATO members Belgium, France, Germany, and Luxembourg opposed military action, while other members, including Great Britain, the Netherlands, Italy, and Spain, supported the United States. In addition, the new member states (Czech Republic, Hungary, and Poland) and the candidate members from Eastern Europe (Bulgaria, Estonia, Latvia, Lithuania, Romania, Slovakia, and Slovenia) supported the United States. The division between the alliance members threatened the cohesiveness of NATO and resulted in the most public and bitter dispute since France left the alliance in 1966.

Meanwhile, Turkey, Iraq's northern neighbor, invoked Article 4 of the North Atlantic Treaty, which requires the allies to prepare assistance for any NATO member facing a threat. At the beginning of February 2003, the antiwar NATO allies blocked the effort to provide aid for Turkey. The deadlock was finally resolved, and NATO deployed surveillance aircraft and antimissile batteries to protect Turkey. American defense planners originally planned a two-front invasion, from the south through Kuwait and from the north out of Turkey. However, despite diplomatic pressure from Washington and offers of economic aid, the parliament in Ankara voted on 1 March 2003 not to allow the Americans to launch an attack from Turkish soil.

The divisions within NATO mirrored the broader divergences in the global community. Russia and the People's Republic of China opposed military action, and diplomatic efforts to gain a second UN resolution specifically authorizing the use of force failed. Opponents of military action accused the Bush administration of abusing its economic and military power and of unilateralism. Public opinion polls in Europe showed strong opposition to the invasion, while domestic sentiment in the United States favored an attack. Prior to the invasion, only Australia, Poland, and Great Britain agreed to contribute troops to the U.S.-led attack, although a number of states offered forces to a post-Saddam reconstruction or peacekeeping mission.

On 28 February 2003, with French and German support, Russia announced that it would veto any resolution authorizing the use of force against Iraq. Blocked at the UN, the Bush administration asserted that it did not need a second resolution, since Resolution 1441 already threatened action if Iraq did not come into compliance. On 16 March 2003, Bush, British prime minister Tony Blair, and Portuguese prime minister José-Manuel Durão Barroso held a press conference in the Azores in which they demanded Iraqi compliance. On 18 March, Bush issued a 48-hour ultimatum to Saddam, and the first strikes of the war occurred on 20 March.

The U.S.-led coalition had 315,000 troops, including 45,000 British, 2,000 Australian, and 200 Polish troops; in addition, Spain and Denmark fielded soldiers who provided support but did not participate in combat. The Iraqi forces numbered about 450,000, armed mainly with outdated Soviet-era weaponry. The initial military phase of the invasion went very well for the coalition forces. On 9 April, U.S. forces captured Baghdad, and on 13 April, Tikrit, the last major Iraqi stronghold, was overrun. Saddam and the regime's senior leadership went into hiding. On 1 May 2003, Bush declared that major hostilities were over.

A comparison of the 1991 **Persian Gulf War** with the 2003 Iraq War highlights the initial success of the American-led attack. In the first Gulf War, there were 500,000 American troops, compared with 250,000 in the Iraq War. The United States lost 300 killed in the first war against Saddam, in addition to 65 allied troops, but just 129 in the second (only 84 of whom died in combat), and 31 coalition soldiers. The Persian Gulf War cost $70 billion and lasted 48 days, while the Iraq War initially cost $20 billion and lasted 26 days.

However, the United States and its allies suffered growing casualties during the subsequent occupation of Iraq. An insurgency began concurrently with the invasion, fueled by Saddam loyalists and a cash incentive of $200 for each coalition soldier killed by the regime.

UN Security Council Resolution 1511 authorized the postwar deployment of a U.S.-led occupying force, and several states used the UN resolution to justify the deployments to skeptical publics. Bulgaria, Italy, Spain, Poland, and Ukraine were among the 27 states that provided troops. Iraq was divided into three zones, and Poland was given command of a multinational division in the southern zone.

The United States failed to create a stable postwar government in the immediate aftermath of the invasion. Political power was initially in the hands of Gen. Jay Garner. He was later replaced by L. Paul Bremer, who created the Coalition Provisional Authority (CPA).

Although coalition forces were able to capture many former regime figures and killed Saddam's two sons in a skirmish on 22 July 2003, the insurgency continued to expand. On 19 August, a truck bomb was detonated at the UN compound in Baghdad, killing 22, including the head of the UN mission. The world body and many other international agencies subsequently withdrew. Iraq became the main front in the **war on terror**, as **Al Qaeda** supplied weapons, funding, and fighters to Sunni factions fighting the coalition forces. Al Qaeda was responsible for a shift in strategy away from attacks on U.S. forces to suicide bombings and other strikes designed to foment sectarian strife. American prestige and credibility were undermined in the Muslim world when images of degrading and humiliating treatment of prisoners by U.S. personnel at the Abu Ghraib prison were broadcast through the world.

In September 2003, an Iraqi transitional government was formed, and on 13 December, Saddam was captured. A series of elections was held to choose an interim government, which drafted a constitution that was approved by voters. In June 2004, the CPA transferred authority to the Iraqi interim government. In May 2006, a newly elected parliament was sworn in. Saddam was convicted of crimes against humanity in 2006, sentenced to death by an Iraqi tribunal, and hanged on 30 December.

By March 2007, the Iraq War had cost the United States 3,187 dead and more than 22,000 wounded. The fiscal costs of the conflict, including military operations, the occupation, and reconstruction and economic assistance, totaled more than $350 billion by 2007.

IVORY BAN (1990). Hunting and poaching of African elephants reduced their population in the wild from 1.3 million in 1979 to 625,000 in 1989. In response to this dramatic decline, in 1990 an international convention banned the global trade of ivory. The ban was enacted by the **United Nations** Convention on International Trade in Endangered Species of Wildlife Fauna and Flora (CITES). The United States supported the ban and provided economic aid to countries such as Botswana, Kenya, and Namibia to offset the loss of income associated with it. The ban substantially slowed the rate of decline, although by 2005 the number of elephants in Africa had fallen to 580,000. Poaching remains a significant problem among countries in the region and the main cause for further reductions in the animals' population. The People's Republic of China has been the number-one destination for smuggled ivory, and it resisted calls by the United States and other CITES members for more stringent controls on illegal ivory imports. Through the 1990s, several African countries accumulated larges stockpiles of ivory from elephants that died of natural causes or had to be destroyed. The administration of President **William J. Clinton** supported a temporary lifting of the ban to allow the countries to sell their excess stocks in exchange for agreements to spend a portion of the proceeds on conservation and preservation programs. In 1999, CITES voted to allow the one-time sale of 60 tons of ivory, and in 2002, another exemption was granted.

– J –

JAPAN–UNITED STATES FRAMEWORK FOR A NEW ECONOMIC PARTNERSHIP. A 1993 agreement that served as the basis to resolve a range of outstanding trade issues between Tokyo and Washington. The accord did not solve the major economic disputes between the two countries, but it served as an umbrella for future discussions on specific issues. President **George H. W. Bush** failed in successive efforts to resolve a series of trade disputes, which centered on Tokyo's resistance to opening its markets to American products and services and U.S. domestic concerns over Japanese imports, especially automobiles and semiconductors. A series of recommendations was issued by the Structural Impediments Initiative (SII) in June 1990, but substantial progress on resolving economic tensions did not occur. In April 1993, President **William J. Clinton** and Prime Minister Kiichi Miyazawa agreed to launch a new round of negotiations, leading to completion of the framework in July 1993.

The framework consists of five broad categories, or "baskets," of issues:

1. Tokyo agreed to expand government procurement programs to foreign firms.
2. The Japanese accepted the need for regulatory reform to allow non-Japanese companies greater access to the financial services and insurance sectors of the economy.

3. The Japanese government pledged action to remove barriers to foreign firms in major industries such as automobile manufacturing.
4. Both the United States and Japan promised to harmonize domestic economic laws on a range of issues, including intellectual property rights and business law.
5. Both countries agreed to implement the SII.

The framework called for agreements to be reached on all five areas by July 1994 and for the leaders of the two countries to meet twice a year to review progress on trade relations and negotiate new accords if necessary. However, agreement on most issues did not occur until October 1994 (15 months later), and the two countries failed to achieve resolution on Japanese imports of automobiles, automobile parts, and glass. In June 1995, under the threat of American tariffs on imported Japanese luxury vehicles, Tokyo agreed to a compromise that removed some restrictions on the import of American vehicles and automobile parts.

In April 1998, Secretary of State **Madeleine Albright** finalized an agreement that expanded the service market to American companies. That year, the two countries cooperated during the **East Asian Financial Crisis**, and Washington intervened with monetary resources to protect the yen in June. In November, the two states began implementation of a joint $10 billion package to refinance or write off the debt of countries impacted by the region's economic crisis. However, the following year, the Clinton administration became increasingly critical of Japanese steel imports (which were not covered under the framework agreement). American trade officials argued that Japanese steel producers were unfairly subsidized, giving them an unfair price advantage in U.S. markets. Clinton threatened retaliatory measures.

In June 2001, at a summit in Washington, President **George W. Bush** and Prime Minister **Junichiro Koizumi** announced the formation of the Regulatory Reform and Competition Policy Initiative, an important but previously neglected component of the second basket of the framework. In spite of the implementation of most areas of the framework agreement, trade frictions continued. In 2002, Bush imposed tariffs, ranging from 8 to 30 percent on imported steel. The duties were lifted in 2003 under pressure from Japan and the **European Union**, both of which threatened retaliatory tariffs (the **World Trade**

Organization also declared the tariffs unnecessary and ruled that the volume of imported steel that was unfairly subsidized did not significantly impact the American market). In 2003, Japan banned the import of U.S. beef after mad cow disease was discovered in the United States. The ban was partially lifted in 2004 and completely eliminated in 2006. *See also* TRADE POLICY.

JIANG ZEMIN (1926–). President of the People's Republic of China (PRC) from 1993 to 2003 who oversaw a period of rapid economic growth and expanding global influence. Jiang developed a close relationship with U.S. president **William J. Clinton**. Jiang Zemin was born in Yangzhou and trained as a mechanical engineer, although he entered government service and rose to become minister of electronic industries in 1983. He later became mayor of Shanghai. Following the 1989 **Tiananmen Square Protests**, Jiang emerged as a compromise candidate to be general secretary of the Communist Party who was seen as neither too liberal nor too reactionary. Jiang initially adopted a policy of cautious political and economic reforms. In 1992, he accelerated the pace of economic restructuring and embraced a model that combined free-market principles and continued government control of some sectors of the economy. Under Jiang, the PRC's economy grew by an average of 8 percent per year.

Jiang endeavored to improve relations with the United States and other Western powers after the Tiananmen Square incident. Clinton decoupled American **trade policy** toward the PRC from that country's **human rights** record. In 1996, relations between Washington and Beijing were again strained by the **Taiwan Strait Crisis**; Jiang was also criticized in the United States for his unwillingness to allow democratization in Tibet. Nevertheless, in 1997 Jiang helped improve Sino-American relations when he became the first PRC leader to visit the United States since 1985. The presidents of the two countries agreed to implement the 1985 accord on the Peaceful Uses of Nuclear Energy. Clinton reciprocated with a state visit to the PRC the following year. The PRC president also prevented an escalation in tensions between Washington and Beijing over the U.S. bombing of the Chinese embassy during the 1999 **Kosovo War**. One of his greatest foreign policy successes was PRC entry into the **World Trade Organization** in 2001. Jiang offered diplomatic support to the United States in the aftermath of the **September 11 terrorist attacks**, but opposed U.S. military action in the 2003 **Iraq War**. In 2003, he was succeeded by **Hu Jintao** as president, although Jiang retained other party posts until 2005.

– K –

KANTOR, MICHAEL (1939–). U.S. trade representative and commerce secretary in the administration of President **William J. Clinton** known for his aggressive promotion of free trade. Michael "Mickey" Kantor was born in Nashville, Tennessee, and earned a law degree from Georgetown University. In 1992, Kantor was the campaign chair of the Clinton presidential campaign. After Clinton's inauguration, Kantor was appointed the administration's trade representative (1993–1996). He negotiated more than 200 trade agreements for the United States and was a staunch advocate for opening markets to American products. Kantor led the U.S. team during negotiations over the formation of the **World Trade Organization** and successive meetings of the **Asia-Pacific Economic Cooperation** forum. Kantor also oversaw often contentious discussions with the European Community. He was criticized for promoting exports of American products such as tobacco and weapons. In 1996, he was made secretary of commerce. Kantor resigned in 1997 and returned to private business. *See also* EUROPEAN UNION; FREE TRADE AREA OF THE AMERICAS; TRADE POLICY.

KARZAI, HAMID (1957–). A moderate Pashtun who became Afghanistan's first post-Taliban leader. Karzai was born in Kandahar to a prominent Pashtun family with ties to the Afghan monarchy. Karzai attended Himachal University in India from 1979 to 1983, before he moved to Pakistan where he was active in Afghan opposition groups as a fundraiser and spokesman. In 1992, Karzai was appointed deputy foreign minister. He initially supported the Taliban and was even asked to serve as the group's **United Nations (UN)** ambassador after the Taliban gained control of Kabul in 1996. However, he came to oppose the harsh restrictions on personal freedom and fled to the United States. His father was assassinated in 1999 by the Taliban. Karzai subsequently emerged as one of the leading anti-Taliban Pashtuns.

After the **September 11 terrorist attacks**, Washington identified Karzai was a potential figure in a post-Taliban government. In December 2001, after the fall of the regime, anti-Taliban Afghans met in Bonn, Germany, to create an interim government. Karzai was appointed chairman of the transitional government. In 2002, a Loya Jirga (a traditional Afghan council of ethnic, clan, and religious leaders) chose Karzai as interim president. Karzai pursued moderate policies in an effort to promote national unity among the country's disparate ethnic groups. He also sought to increase international aid and investment, with limited success. Karzai survived two assassination attempts and was elected president in 2004 in the country's first open presidential elections, with 55.4 percent of the vote. Karzai became increasingly critical of the international community for its failure to provide promised development assistance during his term, but remained dependent on coalition security forces to maintain stability throughout Afghanistan. *See also* AFGHANISTAN INTERVENTION; AL QAEDA; OPERATION ENDURING FREEDOM.

KERRY, JOHN F. (1943–). U.S. senator and 2004 Democratic presidential candidate. John Forbes Kerry earned a degree in political science from Yale University in 1966 and served in Vietnam in 1968–1969, where he was wounded and decorated for bravery. Upon his return from Vietnam, Kerry became a leader of the antiwar movement. In 1984, he was elected to the Senate. Kerry developed a reputation as one of the more liberal members of the Senate and opposed many of the foreign policy actions of the administration of President **Ronald W. Reagan**. Kerry supported the 1989 invasion of Panama in **Operation Just Cause**, but opposed military action in the 1991 **Persian Gulf War**. He also supported free trade initiatives such as the **North American Free Trade Agreement**.

Kerry initially supported the security policies of the administration of **George W. Bush**, including the 2001 **Patriot Act**, **Operation Enduring Freedom**, and the 2003 **Iraq War**. Later, however, he came to question the administration's justification for, and management of, the Iraq conflict. Kerry won the Democratic nomination for the presidency in 2004 and adopted a nuanced policy about the Iraq conflict in an effort to appeal to moderate voters. Kerry argued that since the invasion had occurred, the commitment in Iraq became a strategic interest. However, he criticized the Bush administration's management of the postinvasion insurgency.

Bush won the 2004 election 51 percent to 48 percent. Following the balloting, Kerry increased his criticism of the Bush administration's foreign and security policy. In 2006, Kerry worked with moderate senators to force the administration to adjust its treatment of detainees in the **war on terror**. He declined to seek the Democratic nomination in the 2008 presidential election.

KHOBAR TOWERS BOMBING. A 1996 attack on a Western housing complex by Saudi Hezbollah. The bombing was part of a larger campaign against the Saudi government because of its close ties to the United States. Prior to the Khobar Towers attack, the U.S. military in the Persian Gulf had been placed on high alert because of a terrorist attack in Bahrain that had left three dead. In the Khobar Towers attack, the terrorists used a heavy truck that was packed with more than 10,000 pounds of high explosives. The vehicle attempted to enter a compound that housed American military personnel, but was turned away by security forces. The terrorists then parked in a lot that was about 90 feet from Building 131, an eight-story structure that housed hundreds of military personnel. A security guard on station on top of the building noticed the truck and sounded an alert, and an evacuation was under way when the bomb was detonated at 9:50 P.M. by remote control. A series of concrete barriers deflected the force of the blast upward and probably prevented the collapse of the building. Nineteen American service personnel were killed, along with one Saudi national, and more than 370 were injured. Nineteen people were indicted in absentia and there was speculation of **Al Qaeda** involvement. However, intelligence sources also implicated Iranian logistical support, but without clear evidence of responsibility. The administration of President **William J. Clinton** did not take action beyond its criminal investigation. The failure of Washington to undertake strong measures in response to the attack prompted an escalation of terrorist strikes against American interests, including the 1998 **embassy bombings** in Kenya and Tanzania. *See also* INTERNATIONAL TERRORISM.

KOHL, HELMUT (1930–). The longest-serving German chancellor since Otto von Bismarck (1815–1898). Kohl was the leader who presided over **German reunification** at the end of the **Cold War** and was also instrumental in the transformation of the European Community into the **European Union.** Kohl was born in Ludwigshafen am Rhein, Germany. As a college student, he joined the Christian Democratic Union (Christlich Demokratische Union, CDU). In 1958, he received a doctorate in politics from the University of Heidelberg. Kohl was elected chair of the local CDU, a position he held until 1969. Meanwhile, in 1960, he was elected to the city council of Ludwigshafen. Three years later, he became a deputy in the state legislature. In 1969, Kohl was chosen as the deputy for the national CDU, and four years later, he became chairman of the national party.

Although the CDU did well in successive elections at the national level, the party was unable to win an outright majority, and a series of coalition governments initially kept Kohl from becoming chancellor. Following a vote of no confidence in 1982, however, Kohl became chancellor of a new coalition government. He arranged for new elections in an effort to gain a majority. In the subsequent balloting in 1983, Kohl and the CDU won 48.8 percent of the vote, while their coalition partner, the Free Democratic Party (Freie Demokratische Partei, FDP) received 7 percent.

Kohl worked to improve Franco-German relations and developed a close relationship with French president **Francois Mitterrand**. He was also a staunch supporter of the **North Atlantic Treaty Organization (NATO)** and approved a controversial plan to station intermediate-range ballistic missiles in West Germany. The CDU-FDP coalition won the 1987 elections, and Kohl remained chancellor.

In 1989, the **Berlin Wall** was torn down and the borders between East and West Germany largely opened. In 1990, in the waning days of the Cold War, Kohl met with Soviet leader **Mikhail Gorbachev** and secured a pledge that Moscow would not oppose German reunification. Kohl finalized an agreement with the leaders of East Germany for economic and political union. The plan called for a single currency and the conversion of wages, costs, and rents at an equal rate. The chancellor also entered into negotiations with Germany's western Allies, including France, Great Britain, and the United States, to ensure there were no obstacles to reunification and that the territory of the former East Germany would come under the auspices of NATO. Kohl further renounced any territorial claims still extant from World War II. On 3 October 1990, East and West Germany were reunified.

National elections in 1990 again returned Kohl as chancellor. He supported military action against the Iraqi regime of **Saddam Hussein** during the **Persian Gulf War**. Since Germany's constitution forbade the deployment of forces overseas except as part of a NATO mission, Kohl provided $5.5 billion in monetary support to the allies during the conflict. Germany was the first country to recognize Slovenia and Croatia when they seceded from Yugoslavia in 1991. Kohl also supported the anti-Communist revolutions throughout Europe. The chancellor worked with other European leaders to establish the principles behind the **Maastricht Treaty**, including agreement on a single European currency and the location of the planned European Central Bank in Frankfurt am Main. Most significantly, Kohl gained approval for strict requirements on monetary policy for states to adopt the single currency, the **euro**. Signed in 1992, the Maastricht Treaty came into force in 1993.

During the **Bosnian Conflict**, Kohl supported NATO intervention. In 1996, the Bundestag approved the deployment of 3,000 troops in the Bosnia mission (under NATO command). The vote was 499 to 93 and reflected the high level of support for Kohl's foreign policy. The mission also marked the largest deployment of troops outside of Germany since World War II.

Domestically, Kohl was forced to increase taxes in order to cover the costs of reunification and to stimulate economic growth in the territory of the former East Germany. Germany also emerged as one of the main sources of foreign aid for Russia and the states of the former Soviet Union. In the 1994 elections, Kohl's coalition was significantly reduced. He was unable to implement a series of planned economic reforms. Meanwhile, unemployment rose to more than 10 percent.

In elections in 1998, the CDU and FDP lost to a Social Democrat–led coalition. The leader of the Social Democrats, **Gerhard F. Schröder**, became chancellor. Kohl resigned as CDU leader after the election but remained in the Bundestag until 2002. After he left office, Kohl faced a variety of corruption charges, although he was never formally charged. Kohl retired from politics in 2002.

KOIZUMI, JUNICHIRO (1942–). Prime minister of Japan from 2001 to 2006 and a staunch ally of the United States in the **war on terror.** Koizumi was born in Yokosuka. In 1970, he became a staffer to the minister of finance, and two years later he was elected to the Diet. After a variety of posts in the Diet, Koizumi was appointed health and welfare minister in 1988. In the 1990s, he became one of the leaders of the reformist faction of the Liberal Democratic Party (LDP). In 1995 and 1999, he unsuccessfully campaigned for the presidency of the LDP, but in April 2001, he was elected LDP leader and subsequently became prime minister. Koizumi undertook a series of domestic initiatives to enhance the Japanese economy, including reductions in subsidies for industries, banking reforms, and the privatization of state entities such as Japan Post. He was able to attract urban voters to the LDP, but alienated some of the party's traditional rural base.

Koizumi developed a close relationship with U.S. president **George W. Bush.** He supported Bush's decision to develop a **ballistic missile defense** system and announced that Japan would participate in the future deployment of such a system. In the aftermath of the **September 11 terrorist attacks,** Koizumi offered a range of support to the United States. He visited the United States, and on 25 September 2001, he and Bush issued a joint statement in which the two leaders pledged to fight **international terrorism.** Tokyo thereafter provided both economic and security assistance to Washington. Japan spent almost $40 billion to support the U.S. dollar after the American stock market declined precipitously following the terrorist strikes. Japan also bolstered its counterterrorism cooperation with the United States and deployed assets of the nation's military, the Self-Defense Force (SDF), to provide noncombat assistance during **Operation Enduring Freedom.** The deployment of the SDF led to a constitutional debate, since the country's defense forces were legally limited to defense of the homeland. The Diet enacted a special antiterrorism law that allowed the SDF to provide transportation and logistical support for allied forces in Afghanistan. During the **Afghanistan intervention,** Japan provided $300 million in aid to Pakistan and $40 million to other neighboring states, including Tajikistan and Uzbekistan. Tokyo also gave $500 million in assistance to the fledging Afghan government after the fall of the Taliban.

Koizumi endorsed the U.S.-led invasion during the **Iraq War** and dispatched SDF troops to Iraq to participate in noncombat operations. In return, the Bush administration maintained its support for Koizumi after the prime minister made a series of controversial visits to a World War II shrine that honored Japanese military forces, including some who were convicted of war crimes and executed. The visits were condemned by the People's Republic of China and both North and South Korea. Koizumi and Bush cooperated closely during the **North Korean Nuclear Crises**, and both nations implemented stringent sanctions on Pyongyang after the regime's nuclear tests in October 2006.

Overwhelmingly reelected in 2003, Koizumi instituted reductions to the country's pension system as part of a larger program of fiscal restructuring. The reforms were highly unpopular, and Koizumi was forced to call new elections in 2005. He increased his majority in the balloting, but announced that he would step down in 2006 in line with LDP rules regarding the length of tenure for prime ministers. Before leaving office in September 2006, Koizumi, an Elvis Presley fan, was given a private tour of Graceland by Bush. *See also* JAPAN–UNITED STATES FRAMEWORK FOR A NEW ECONOMIC PARTNERSHIP; TRADE POLICY.

KOSOVO WAR. A **North Atlantic Treaty Organization (NATO)** air campaign to force the Serbs to comply with **United Nations (UN)** resolutions regarding the ethnic conflict that erupted in the Serbian province of Kosovo. By 1998, ethnic conflict between Serbs and ethnic Albanians in Kosovo had produced 120,000 internal and external refugees. In March, Serb paramilitary and government units launched a broad offensive against an Albanian rebel group, the Kosovo Liberation Army. By the end of the year, an estimated 2,000 Albanians had been killed, and an additional 400,000 had become refugees. A variety of international mediation efforts by, among others, the **Organization for Security and Cooperation in Europe (OSCE)** and the UN, failed, and the UN Security Council passed Resolution 1199, which threatened military action unless the Serbs accepted a negotiated settlement.

On 13 October 1998, under U.S. pressure, NATO authorized air strikes to support international mediation efforts. Secretary of State **Madeleine Albright** emerged as the foremost U.S. proponent of military action to end the ethnic strife. Russia sought to protect its traditional Balkan ally and prevented the United States and the Europeans from gaining a UN resolution to specifically authorize the use of force. But, through goading by Moscow, the Serbs agreed to talks, and the air strikes were canceled.

Negotiations at Rambouillet, France, in February and March 1999 failed to achieve a cease-fire. Following the breakdown of the Rambouillet talks, a new Serb offensive left at least 5,000 dead and produced more than 1.5 million refugees (more than 90 percent of the Albanian population). NATO again authorized air strikes if a last-ditch peace effort failed, which it did. The **William J. Clinton** administration tried to gain Russian support for military action, but Moscow refused. Although Russia did eventually agree to participate in the peacekeeping mission after the campaign, it initially refused to operate under NATO command.

On 24 March 1999, NATO air units launched strikes on Serb targets in Kosovo. NATO also initiated a humanitarian operation to aid the refugees. The alliance provided resources and material to build refugee camps in Albania and Macedonia, and its forces in Macedonia provided medical assistance to Kosovar refugees. NATO planners were prepared for only a brief campaign and assumed that the Serbs would capitulate after three to four days of attacks, as had been the case in the **Bosnian Conflict**. The allied commander, Gen. **Wesley Clark**, assured Clinton and Albright that the Serbs would surrender after a brief campaign.

Divisions emerged within the alliance over the use of ground forces to prompt Serb compliance. Clinton refused to consider the use of ground troops, much to the chagrin of British prime minister **Tony Blair** and French president **Jacques Chirac**, who hoped to use the threat of ground forces as a bargaining tool. With NATO employing only an aerial campaign, the Serbs were able to continue the **ethnic cleansing**. Only after NATO air units began to strike Serb targets outside of Kosovo, including Belgrade, did Serbian leader **Slobodan Milošević** agree to a cease-fire. The 77-day air campaign ended on 3 June 1999. Negotiations led to an agreement on a Serb withdrawal, and a NATO-led peace force was deployed.

During the Kosovo War, NATO air units flew more than 38,000 sorties. The military campaign was highlighted by the use of sophisticated

U.S. military technology, including precision-guided weaponry and smart bombs. Only Great Britain and France had similar capabilities to the United States. One of the central lessons from Kosovo was the stark gap between U.S. and allied military capabilities. The inability of the allies to match U.S. capabilities would lead to a number of postwar initiatives to close the technology gap within NATO.

After the campaign, a NATO-led, 50,000-troop mission known as Kosovo Force (KFOR) was deployed. KFOR included American, NATO, and **Partnership for Peace** forces and was tasked to facilitate the return and resettlement of refugees and prevent future conflict in the region. KFOR aided in the resettlement of 900,000 refugees and provided almost 10,000 tons of food and other aid for the refugees. KFOR also helped supervise and provide security for local elections, and NATO-led forces cleared some 1.1 million square meters (270 acres) of land mines. By 2005, all of the NATO members except Iceland, Latvia, and the Netherlands had contributed ground troops to KFOR at one time or another. In addition, a number of non-NATO states contributed forces, including Argentina, Armenia, Austria, Azerbaijan, Finland, Georgia, Ireland, Morocco, Sweden, Switzerland, Ukraine, and the United Arab Emirates.

Prior to the air war in Kosovo, NATO forces had been deployed in Macedonia as a staging area. Once KFOR was deployed, NATO launched Operation Essential Harvest with 2,500 troops in Macedonia. During the mission, NATO-led forces helped monitor a ceasefire between separatists and the government. Coalition forces also collected 3,300 small arms and 70,000 rounds of ammunition and arrested more than 300 rebels. In 2001, NATO followed Operation Essential Harvest with Operation Amber Fox to protect OSCE monitors engaged in an effort to end renewed strife in the country. *See also* BALKAN WARS.

KREMLIN ACCORDS. A series of agreements signed by U.S. president **William J. Clinton** and Russian president **Boris Yeltsin** in Moscow on 14 January 1994. Among the terms of the agreements, the United States and Russia agreed to not target sites in other countries with nuclear weapons during peacetime. In addition, the two leaders finalized arrangements to dismantle or transfer the remaining Soviet-era nuclear weapons in the countries of the former Union of

Soviet Socialist Republics. The two nations also agreed to share information on missile launches and to reduce their stockpiles of fissile materials. Clinton sought to persuade Yeltsin to exert pressure on the Duma to ratify the **Strategic Arms Reductions Treaty (START II)**. However, tensions over the **Kosovo War** precluded further agreement on this and other issues. *See also* ARMS CONTROL.

KYOTO PROTOCOL. One in a series of further codifications of the **United Nations (UN)** Framework Convention on Climate Change (UNFCCC). Signed at the 1992 **Earth Summit**, the UNFCCC aimed to reduce **global warming** by cutting emissions of greenhouse gases. The convention set broad goals for its signatories, but left specific targets to future protocols. It also divided the world into developed and developing countries. Wealthy and advanced developed nations, including the United States, were obligated to provide funding for economic development among poorer countries. The UNFCCC was signed by the administration of President **George H. W. Bush** and ratified by the Senate in October 1992.

Parties to the UNFCCC met in Kyoto, Japan, in 1997 to negotiate a protocol that would establish specific targets for greenhouse gas reductions. The Kyoto Protocol mandated reductions of greenhouse gas emissions to 5.2 percent below 1990 levels by 2012 (a projected reduction of almost 30 percent from 1997 levels). The protocol set specific reduction targets for industrialized states, but excluded large developing countries such as Brazil, India, and the People's Republic of China (PRC). If the developed states did not meet their goals, they would be allowed to "buy" certified credits from other states, or they could earn credits by implementing environmentally beneficial programs such as planting forests or investing in greenhouse gas reduction programs in developing countries. The implementation conditions for the protocol were met in 2004, and it entered into force in February 2005.

The Kyoto Protocol was signed by Vice President **Albert A. Gore**, but was not submitted to the Senate by President **William J. Clinton**. Senate leaders opposed the provisions of the protocol that exempted developing countries from pollution reductions. In 1997, on a unanimous vote, the Senate adopted a resolution that declared it would not enact any international environmental agreements on greenhouse gas emissions that did not also include mandatory decreases for developing states such as India or the PRC. Business groups in the United States also criticized the measure as creating an unfair economic advantage for fast-developing nations.

The administration of President **George W. Bush** refused to support the Kyoto Protocol as well. Bush did not submit the protocol to the Senate and instead lent his support to a range of alternative measures. Washington encouraged American companies and firms to adopt voluntary reductions through the use of alternative technologies. The United States also sponsored the creation of the Asia-Pacific Partnership for Clean Development and Climate in 2005. The new accord was negotiated at a meeting of the **Association of Southeast Asian Nations**. Under the agreement, the United States, Australia, India, Japan, South Korea, and the PRC would cooperate on efforts to cut greenhouse gas emissions and other forms of pollution. The Bush administration argued that such regional agreements could be more effective than the Kyoto Protocol. However, unlike Kyoto, the American-backed proposal did not establish mandatory reduction targets.

On average, the United States produces about 25 percent of the world's greenhouse gases. It also accounts for approximately 25 percent of the global economy. Without American participation in the Kyoto Protocol, the agreement's long-term success remains questionable.

– L –

LAKE, ANTHONY (1939–). National security advisor under President **William J. Clinton** who formulated the administration's policy toward the **Bosnian Conflict**. Lake was born in New York City and graduated from Harvard University in 1961. He went to work for the State Department in 1962. In 1969, Lake was appointed as a special assistant to National Security Advisor Henry Kissinger. He earned a doctorate from Princeton University in 1974. From 1977 to 1981, Lake was the director of policy planning in the State Department. After the election of **Ronald W. Reagan**, Lake became a professor at Amherst College and later at Mount Holyoke.

During the 1992 presidential campaign, Lake was a foreign policy advisor to Clinton. He was then appointed national security advisor to Clinton in 1993. Lake had a close relationship with Clinton and withstood criticism over the administration's management of the **Somalia intervention** and the U.S. policy during the **Haiti intervention**. He was instrumental in the formation of the 1994 **Framework Agreement with North Korea**, in which the United States agreed to provide food and energy aid to Pyongyang in exchange for the regime's continuing participation in the Nuclear Nonproliferation Treaty and the suspension of the country's atomic weapons program (the agreement was scrapped in 2002 following revelations that North Korea had secretly continued its pursuit of nuclear weapons). Lake developed the multilateral approach to Bosnia that resulted in the 1995 **Dayton Accords** and the subsequent deployment of a peace enforcement mission led by the **North Atlantic Treaty Organization**. In 1996, Clinton nominated Lake to replace outgoing Central Intelligence Agency director **John M. Deutch**. However, Lake withdrew his appointment due to opposition by Republicans in the Senate. He then left government service in 1997 and accepted a teaching position at Georgetown University.

LAW OF THE SEA TREATY. The **United Nations (UN)** Convention on the Law of the Sea was originally signed in 1982 by 117 countries. It entered into force in November 1994. The Law of the Sea Treaty extended the territorial limits of a country's sovereignty from three nautical miles (3.4 standard miles or 5.5 kilometers) to 12 nautical miles (13.6 standard miles or 21.9 kilometers). In addition, countries were granted exclusive fishing rights for 200 nautical miles from shore (227 standard miles or 365 kilometers) and the rights to mineral, oil, and gas deposits within that area. This 200-mile national limit became known as a country's exclusive economic zone (EEZ). Foreign companies had to negotiate agreements with each state to conduct business within its EEZ. Mineral and other resources beyond the 200-mile zone were declared common property of all people, and mining, fishing, or other extraction was to be governed by international agreements that developed quotas for individual nations and overall ceilings on annual takes. Revenues from seabed mining outside of the EEZs would be taxed, with royalties paid to the International Seabed Authority (ISA), comprised of representatives from signature states. The ISA would disperse the royalties to other international agencies and individual countries for environmental and development purposes. The Law of the Sea also guarantees legal commercial vessels the right of safe passage through a country's 12-mile territorial zone.

The United States and Great Britain initially refused to sign the convention, arguing that the prohibitions on seabed mining would constrain economic development. They also criticized the proposed ISA for its lack of oversight and control over revenues. In 1994, an agreement was reached to amend the Law of the Sea to address American concerns. The size and budget of the ISA was reduced, and the United States and other states were given veto power over ISA spending. The treaty was signed by the United States, but the Senate has not yet ratified the agreement. Nonetheless, the United States has declared that it views most of the treaty as a codification of customary international law, and it abides by the majority of the convention's provisions.

LEBANON HOSTAGE CRISIS. Beginning in 1985, Americans and other Westerners were routinely kidnapped in Lebanon by Islamic extremist groups, including Hezbollah and Islamic Jihad. Many of the groups had ties to Iran, and the administration of President **Ronald W. Reagan** arranged the release of a number of hostages by secretly providing arms to Iran (the weapons were flown into Iran in August and September 1985). The covert program was an integral component of the Iran-Contra Scandal of 1987. After the scandal, a new round of kidnappings took place in and around Beirut. Meanwhile, several foreign hostages were killed in captivity. Lt. Col. William F. Buckley, an American intelligence agent, was kidnapped in 1984 and tortured to death. Lt. Col. William Higgins, an American serving with the **United Nations** monitoring group in southern Lebanon, was kidnapped in February 1988 and later killed. The remains of Buckley and Higgins were turned over to the United States in 1991. In September 1991, under U.S. diplomatic pressure, Israel released 51 prisoners with ties to Islamic fundamentalist groups. The release, coupled with pressure from Syria and the Lebanese government, resulted in freedom for the Western hostages. Through the rest of the year, all remaining Western hostages were released. Many, including Americans Joseph Cicippio, Allann Steen, and Jesse Turner, had been in captivity for more than five years. On 4 December, Terry Anderson, the longest-held Western hostage and the last American, was released after seven years in captivity. *See also* ARAB-ISRAELI CONFLICT; INTERNATIONAL TERRORISM.

LIBERIAN CIVIL WAR. Since the end of the **Cold War**, successive U.S. administrations have endeavored to end the violence and ethnic conflict in Liberia. Liberia was founded in 1822 as a haven for freed slaves by the American Colonization Society. It declared its independence in 1847, but was not recognized by Washington until 1862. The country experienced continued ethnic conflict and strife between the descendents of the former American slaves (the Americo-Liberians) and indigenous peoples, who faced various forms of discrimination. For instance, all native peoples did not gain the right to vote until 1946. In 1980, a military coup overthrew the Americo-Liberian government and installed a regime dominated by indigenous peoples. In 1989, Charles Taylor, an Americo-Liberian, led a rebellion that overthrew the native-dominated government and initiated a civil war.

Although an international peacekeeping force was deployed in 1990, unrest continued. Through the 1990s, the administration of President **William J. Clinton** deferred to the Economic Community of West African States (ECOWAS) to lead the efforts to resolve the Liberian civil war. In 1995, ECOWAS sponsored a peace agreement that called for new elections and a transition to civilian rule. In 1997, Taylor was elected president. He supported rebel forces in Sierra Leone's ongoing civil war and launched attacks against Liberian rebels in neighboring states such as Guinea. Taylor's actions increased regional destabilization. His regime served as a conduit for the smuggling of conflict diamonds from Sierra Leone. In 1998, an opponent of Taylor took refuge in the U.S. embassy, and government forces fired on the facility. The Clinton administration ordered the embassy closed and American citizens evacuated. In 2001, the **United Nations (UN)** imposed an arms and diamond embargo on Liberia.

An anti-Taylor group, Liberians United for Reconciliation and Democracy (LURD), launched attacks on government facilities in the north of the country in 1999, and the rebellion quickly spread throughout the country. In 2003, Taylor was indicted by a UN tribunal for war crimes for his role in the conflict in Sierra Leone. Meanwhile, LURD forces advanced to the outskirts of the capital, Monrovia. President **George W. Bush** called on Taylor to step down in July 2003 and ordered the deployment of U.S. troops in August to maintain order in Monrovia. Taylor resigned and went into exile in Nigeria. American forces withdrew in September, following the deployment of a UN peacekeeping force, the UN Mission in Liberia, along with troops from neighboring states. Washington led an international effort to raise reconstruction funds, and the initiative garnered $500 million. In 2006, Ellen Johnson-Sirleaf became Liberia's president, the first female to be elected a head of state in Africa. Taylor became one of the first people to be tried before the **International Criminal Court**.

LIEBERMAN, JOSEPH I. (1942–). Centrist Democratic senator and vice presidential candidate. Joseph Isadore "Joe" Lieberman was born in Stamford, Connecticut, and received a law degree from Yale University in 1967. He was elected to the U.S. Senate in 1988 after lengthy service in the Connecticut legislature. Lieberman supported the invasion of Panama in 1989 (**Operation Just Cause**) and military action in the **Persian Gulf War**. He also supported trade liberalization initiatives, including the **North American Free Trade Agreement**.

In 2000, Lieberman became the first Jewish American to be chosen as the vice presidential candidate for a major political party. Democratic presidential candidate **Albert A. Gore** and Lieberman won the popular vote, but lost the Electoral College vote. However, Lieberman was concurrently reelected to the Senate. He supported President **George W. Bush**'s security policies, including the **Afghanistan intervention**, **Operation Enduring Freedom**, the **Patriot Act**, and the 2003 **Iraq War**. Lieberman campaigned unsuccessfully for the Democratic presidential nomination in 2004, but withdrew after failing to win any of the early primaries or caucuses. In 2006, he was defeated in the Democratic primary for his Senate seat, with many leading Democrats backing his opponent because of Lieberman's pro-Iraq War stance. After his loss, Lieberman decided to seek reelection as an independent. Gore, former President **William J.**

Clinton, and other prominent Democrats urged Lieberman to withdraw, but he easily defeated both his Democratic and Republican rivals in the balloting.

– M –

MAASTRICHT TREATY (1992). The Treaty on European Union, commonly known as the Maastricht Treaty, was the means through which the European Community (EC) became the **European Union (EU).** While the EC had made significant progress in monetary terms, there was momentum for deeper economic integration and an expansion of political cooperation. The Maastricht Treaty was an effort to create a balance between the rights and powers of individual governments while transferring some authority to the new EU. The EU itself was envisioned as an intergovernmental organization, as opposed to a supranational entity.

The Maastricht Treaty created three "pillars" within the EU: The first pillar was economic and social policy, the existing areas of the EC. The second pillar was the development of a **Common Foreign and Security Policy.** Finally, the third pillar was law enforcement and judicial. It was designed to serve as the mechanism to harmonize civil and criminal law, judicial procedures, and immigration policy. The agreement also brought a number of heretofore independent agencies under the auspices of the EU, including the **Western European Union (WEU)** and the European Court of Justice.

The Maastricht Treaty introduced the concept of EU citizenship based on the notion that there were universal rights for all citizens of EU members. In order to assuage concerns that the EU would have too much power, the treaty introduced "subsidiarity." Under this concept, the EU called for issues or policy problems to be dealt with at the lowest possible level of government. The principle was similar to the British policy of "devolution," in which power and authority were returned to local governments, and it also mirrored the broader values of American federalism. Theoretically, subsidiarity means that central governments oversee only those issues that cannot be handled at the local level.

Under the Maastricht Treaty, the EU's political institutions included the European Commission, the Council of Ministers, the European Council, and the European Parliament. The Court of Justice was the cornerstone of the judiciary, and the WEU was the main security forum. Finally, the EU's financial bodies were the European Central Bank and the European Investment Bank. One of the most important components of the treaty was the creation of a single European currency, the **euro**, through European Monetary Union (EMU). The provisions on EMU were the most specific and detailed of the Maastricht Treaty. EMU was to be achieved in a three-stage process, finalized with the introduction of the euro in 1999. In order to achieve EMU, the treaty called for the creation of the European Monetary Institute (EMI), which was tasked to serve as a coordinating body for central banks prior to the introduction of the euro. The EMI was the forerunner of the European Central Bank.

Although it signed and ratified the treaty, Great Britain negotiated an exemption that allowed it to "opt out" of later social policies. In addition, in a separate protocol, Britain was granted the ability to opt out of EMU. Sweden later also opted out of EMU. The treaty was initially rejected by Danish voters in a national referendum, but was subsequently approved after Denmark, too, was granted the ability to opt out of EMU. The agreement was only narrowly approved by voters in France.

The Maastricht Treaty entered into force in November 1993. Subsequent agreements, including the Petersburg Declaration, the Treaty of Amsterdam, the Treaty of Nice, and the proposed EU Constitution, bolstered the authority of the EU and more clearly defined its powers.

MANDELA, NELSON R. (1918–). A leader in the antiapartheid struggle in South Africa who served as the country's president from 1994 to 1999. Nelson Rolihlahla Mandela joined the African National Congress (ANC) in 1944 and was subsequently imprisoned for 27 years for his resistance to the regime. While incarcerated, Mandela's stature grew, and he became the symbolic leader of the ANC. He repeatedly refused offers of amnesty in return for renunciation of the ANC's armed struggle. Mandela was also offered freedom if he would publicly recognize the apartheid regime's four black homelands and settle in one, the Transkei; he refused the deal. He was released from prison on 11 February 1990.

As part of the dismantling of the apartheid regime, Mandela agreed to suspend the armed resistance against Pretoria. A year later, he was elected president of the ANC at the organization's first open meeting in South Africa since it was banned in 1960. Mandela worked with South African president F. W. de Klerk to create a transitional national government that would draft a new constitution and oversee the country's first postapartheid elections. In 1994, Mandela was elected president of South Africa and the ANC gained a majority of seats in the parliament.

Once in office, Mandela criticized the administration of President **William J. Clinton** for not providing more economic aid to South Africa during its transition from apartheid (Washington provided $200 million per year over a three-year period). He was also a frequent critic of U.S. military action, but denounced the United States for not taking more action to end the **Rwandan genocide.** Washington unsuccessfully urged Mandela to adopt more progressive policies toward the treatment and prevention of **HIV/AIDS.**

Mandela played a major role in improving relations between the United States and Libya. He forged close relations with Libyan leader **Muammar Gaddafi** because of Libya's support for the ANC during the apartheid era. In 1994, Mandela offered South Africa as a neutral venue to try two suspects in Libyan custody for their role in the 1988 **Pan Am Flight 103 bombing.** The offer was initially rejected by British prime minister John Major, but in 1997 Mandela was able to convince Gaddafi to turn the two suspects over for trial at The Hague and to pay reparations to the families of the victims of the attack. The resolution of the crisis helped pave the way for normalized relations between Libya and the West.

After he left office, Mandela continued to be a vocal critic of U.S. foreign policy, especially the 2003 **Iraq War**, condemning the administration of President **George W. Bush** for not gaining **United Nations** support prior to military action. In 2004, the former president announced his formal retirement from public life.

McCAIN, JOHN S. (1936–). U.S. senator from Arizona and presidential candidate who was a leader of the moderate wing of the Republican

Party. John Sidney McCain was born on American territory in the Panama Canal Zone. He graduated from the U.S. Naval Academy in 1958 and became a pilot. During the Vietnam War, McCain was a prisoner of war (POW) from 1967 to 1973. He retired from the navy in 1981 and was elected to the U.S. House of Representatives from Arizona the next year. In 1986, he was elected to the Senate, following the retirement of conservative icon Barry Goldwater (1909–1998). McCain quickly established a reputation as a maverick who voted on principle rather than following the party line. He was a staunch supporter of the military and a moderate on social issues.

McCain ran for the Republican nomination for the presidency in 2000. He won the New Hampshire primary, but lost in the more conservative Southern primaries to **George W. Bush**. He then withdrew from the race and subsequently campaigned on behalf of Bush. McCain supported a range of national security initiatives and missions after the **September 11 terrorist attacks**, including **Operation Enduring Freedom**, the **Patriot Act**, and the 2003 **Iraq War**. Meanwhile, in 2002 McCain joined with Democratic senator Russ Feingold of Wisconsin to sponsor a broad bipartisan campaign finance reform initiative (the Bipartisan Campaign Reform Act of 2003, commonly known as the McCain-Feingold Act). The senator also played a major role in the 2004 formation of the "Gang of Fourteen," a moderate group of seven Republican and seven Democratic senators who agreed to compromise on Bush's judicial appointments.

During the 2004 presidential election, Democratic candidate **John F. Kerry** approached McCain about serving as his vice presidential candidate. McCain declined and instead campaigned vigorously on behalf of Bush.

McCain's time as a POW led him to oppose the Bush administration's policies toward detainees in the **war on terror**. The administration opposed constraints on the treatment of detainees, interrogation methods, and length of detention. McCain helped craft a compromise in 2005 that prohibited cruel or degrading treatment of detainees but also retroactively protected U.S. military and intelligence from prosecution or civil suit for past involvement in interrogations. The law, the Detainee Treatment Act (commonly known as the McCain Detainee Amendment), requires interrogations to be held in compliance with existing military regulations. The next year,

McCain arranged another deal over detainee rights and the use of military tribunals in prosecuting **unlawful combatants**. McCain argued that unless the United States adopted more humane policies toward detainees, American POWs were more likely to face torture and mistreatment.

MEXICAN ECONOMIC CRISIS (1994). A brief period of intense currency instability in 1994 (also known as the Peso Crisis) that led to the worst year in the Mexican economy in modern history. In the late 1980s and early 1990s, the Mexican economy experienced a period of dramatic growth fueled by increased exports and the initial impact of the **North American Free Trade Agreement**. Mexico became the first Latin American country to be granted membership in the Organization for Economic Cooperation and Development, a body previously dominated by the United States, Europe, and Japan. However, there were several significant flaws in the Mexican economy. The country's currency was overvalued by about 20 percent, because successive governments had pursued policies to maintain an artificially strong peso by spending the central bank's reserves to support the currency. In addition, an acceleration in public spending had created a government deficit that was 7 percent of the nation's gross domestic product (GDP). Finally, corruption and graft were rampant within the government and private sector.

The incoming administration of President Ernesto Zedillo sought to loosen currency controls to allow the peso to float within a fixed band in order to preserve the country's depleted reserves, which had fallen to less than $9 billion. However, the relaxation of controls led the peso to lose half of its value, as international financiers withdrew investments or converted them into dollars. The result was a recession that caused the GDP to contract by 7 percent through 1995.

In order to help stabilize the Mexican economy and prevent a wave of illegal **immigration**, the administration of President **William J. Clinton** launched a broad effort to support the peso. The administration arranged a $50 billion package of loans and credits to bolster the Mexican currency and economy. Clinton bypassed Congress, which rejected a bill to provide monetary relief to Mexico, and used the Treasury Department's Exchange Stabilization Fund (designed to protect the U.S. dollar) to grant the

Zedillo government $20 billion in loans and credit. The **International Monetary Fund** provided an additional $18 billion, while $10 billion came from the Bank for International Settlements and Canada offered $1 billion. The stabilization effort worked, and the nation's economy began growing in 1995 and recorded GDP expansion of 5 percent in 1996, rising to 7 percent growth by 1999. In addition, the peso was stabilized. Mexico repaid the American loans by 1997. *See also* TRADE POLICY.

MICROSOFT CORPORATION. A multinational company that dominated the world's computer and software industries through the 1990s and early 2000s. In 2006, Microsoft had revenues of more than $44 billion and employed more than 71,000 people in more than 100 countries. Microsoft was founded in 1975 by Bill Gates and a small number of computer experts. The company developed DOS (Disk Operating System), a popular operating system for computers. Microsoft's development of successive operating systems, including Windows, and office management software such as Word and Excel caused the corporation to grow dramatically in the 1990s. Microsoft also created MSN (Microsoft Network) in an effort to enter the online provider market. Microsoft Explorer was introduced in 1997 as a rival to Netscape, which dominated the Internet browser market at the time. The popularity of Microsoft products helped expand Internet services and the Worldwide Web throughout the world. However, the corporation's domination of the software market led to antitrust lawsuits by various governments.

In 1990, the federal government launched a probe of Microsoft that resulted in a 1994 agreement in which the corporation agreed to make changes in its operating system to allow other Internet browsers to more easily be used in Windows. In 1997, Microsoft was taken back to court for violating the 1994 accord, and the next year, the Justice Department and 20 states filed a new antitrust suit against the company. In 2000, a judge ruled that Microsoft should be broken into two companies to end its monopoly, but the decision was reversed on appeal. A new settlement was ultimately reached, in which the company had to reveal elements of its software to competitors so they could design systems that were compatible with Microsoft's operating system. Meanwhile, the **European Union** launched its own probe of Microsoft's business practices. The corporation has become a frequent target of anti**globalization** activists for its domination of markets and its aggressive efforts to undermine competition. *See also* TRADE POLICY.

MILITARY-INDUSTRIAL COMPLEX. A term for the integrated entity formed by the close relationship that exists between the Department of Defense and the civilian companies and contractors that build or supply equipment and weapons for the U.S. military. It also includes politicians with ties to large defense firms and even labor unions whose workers' jobs are dependent on military contracts. In his 1961 farewell address, President Dwight D. Eisenhower warned of the increasing influence of a "military-industrial complex" that created unwarranted ties between the military and major defense firms. The need for ever more sophisticated weaponry and technology created deep connections between the military and private industry. Critics assert that the phenomenon has led to an iron triangle, consisting of the Defense Department, Congress, and corporations, in which the interests of the three legs have become inseparable. Congressmen and government officials support procurement programs that provide jobs or support industry in their home states or districts. Meanwhile, defense companies provide significant financial support for reelection campaigns and even outright bribes. For instance, Congressman Randy "Duke" Cunningham of California resigned and pled guilty to accepting $2.4 million in bribes and $1.9 million in gifts from defense contractors.

Sensational stories of cost overruns led to a series of procurement reforms in the 1990s and early 21st century. The 1995 decision by President **William J. Clinton** to make increased **arms sales** a national security objective reenergized the debate over the influence of large defense firms on American policy. During the presidency of **George W. Bush**, Halliburton Energy Services was cited as an example of the dangers of the military-industrial complex. The company, which had revenues of more than $20 billion in 2006 with more than 100,000 employees, gained a range of contracts with the Department of Defense—from putting out oil well fires set by Iraqi forces during the **Persian Gulf War** to providing food and logistical support for U.S. peacekeeping forces in the Balkans. During the

1990s, Halliburton was fined more than \$3.8 million for supplying Libya and Iraq with banned dual-use nuclear technology that could be used for weapons programs. However, the firm was led by former secretary of defense, and future vice president, **Richard B. Cheney.** Between 2003 and 2006, Halliburton received contracts for work in Iraq worth more than \$18 billion. The company was also contracted to provide emergency support and debris removal at military facilities impacted by Hurricane Katrina in 2005. Companies such as Halliburton reinforce the public perceptions of the military-industrial complex. *See also* DEFENSE SPENDING AND ALLIANCE BURDEN SHARING; IRAQ WAR; PEACE DIVIDEND.

MILLENNIUM BOMBING PLOTS. A series of attacks unsuccessfully attempted by terrorists against targets in the Middle East and the United States on the eve of the 21st century. The planned strikes were organized by **Al Qaeda**–linked groups, which wanted to capitalize on the symbolism of the new millennium.

The most significant plot originated in Jordan, where members of a joint Algerian-Jordanian terrorist group sought to launch a bombing campaign against Western targets. Two Palestinians, Raed Hijazi and Abu Hoshar, developed the initial plans, which were approved by Abu Zubaydah, an ally of **Osama bin Laden.** The targets included the Radisson Hotel in Amman, the border crossing between Jordan and Israel, a Christian site at Mount Nebo, and the area on the Jordan River where tradition holds that John the Baptist baptized Jesus. All of the sites were chosen because they were expected to be filled with Christian tourists. The attackers planned to detonate bombs and spread poison gas and acid to increase the number of casualties. After the attacks on these four areas, the plotters planned a subsequent round of attacks at airports and other religious shrines. The plan unraveled when Jordanian intelligence agencies intercepted communications about the attacks in November 1999. On 12 December, police arrested Hoshar and 15 others. Eventually 28 were arrested and tried, and 22 were found guilty. Several Al Qaeda leaders, including Abu Musab al-Zarqawi, were convicted in absentia.

The second failed plot involved an effort to bomb Los Angeles International Airport. In 1998, Ahmed Ressam, an Algerian living in Canada under political asylum, was recruited and trained in

Afghanistan by Al Qaeda. In 1999, he returned to Canada with smuggled bomb-making materials and $12,000 to finance the attack. Three other Algerians were supposed to help Ressam conduct the attack, but they were unable to obtain travel documents to enter Canada. Through the remainder of 1999, Ressam bought or stole additional bomb-making materials. On 14 December, he tried to enter the United States through Port Angeles, Washington. When customs officials questioned him, Ressam became nervous and tried to flee. His car was inspected, and explosives and four timing devices were discovered in his spare-tire wheel well. Ressam and four others were tried and convicted of the plot, although Ressam began cooperating with American intelligence officials in 2001.

Following the failure of the original two plots, Al Qaeda tried a third attack involving a suicide strike on a U.S. warship in Yemen. Al Qaeda planned to detonate an explosives-packed boat alongside the USS *The Sullivans*. On 3 January 2000, terrorists began moving the boat in preparation for the attack, but the overloaded vessel sank. Although the attack failed, it was a forerunner to the **USS *Cole* bombing**.

MILOŠEVIĆ, SLOBODAN (1941–2006). President of Yugoslavia during the **Balkan Wars**. He was indicted for crimes against humanity for his role in the genocide in Bosnia and Kosovo, but died during his trial at The Hague. Milošević was born in Serbia during World War II. He attended the University of Belgrade, where he was the leader of the ideology committee of the student Communist Party. In 1960, he became an advisor to the mayor of Belgrade. He went to work for a local company in 1968, before becoming the head of Yugoslavia's largest bank in 1978. In this position, he traveled frequently to Europe and the United States and developed numerous contacts with Western leaders. In 1986, he was elected to lead the Communist Party in Belgrade. Within a year, Milošević was one of the most important figures in Serbian politics. In 1988, he was able to force the Serbian president to resign and take his place. As president, Milošević used nationalism to enhance public support and, in 1989, rescinded the autonomy of provinces such as Kosovo, which was populated mainly by ethnic Albanians.

In 1990, in the waning days of the **Cold War**, Milošević oversaw the transition of the Communist Party to the new Socialist Party of

Serbia. He also supervised revisions to the Serbian constitution that bolstered the authority of the presidency. Milošević was elected president of Serbia in 1990 and reelected in 1992 in balloting marred by fraud and voter intimidation.

By 1991, the Yugoslav federal government had become increasingly ineffective and paralyzed by factionalism. That year, Slovenia, Croatia, Bosnia-Herzegovina, and Macedonia declared independence. The federal government attempted to suppress the independence movements, but the Slovenes quickly defeated the federal forces in a 10-day war. Milošević responded to the breakup of Yugoslavia by calling for the creation of a Greater Serbia that would include all ethnic Serbs. Through 1995, ethnic Serbs and Yugoslav federal troops fought against Croatian forces. During the conflict, both sides committed atrocities and **ethnic cleansing**, but Croatia eventually won. Milošević coordinated a more extensive ethnic-cleansing campaign in the **Bosnian Conflict**, during which Serbs took control of more than 70 percent of the territory and killed or displaced hundreds of thousands of ethnic Bosnians and Croats. The civil war attracted international condemnation. Milošević tried to position himself as a moderate and blamed the worst excesses on the Bosnian Serb leadership. In 1995, at the end of the Croat civil war, Croatian forces joined with the Bosnians to recapture areas gained by the Serbs. The failure of various international initiatives to end the Bosnian conflict led the **North Atlantic Treaty Organization (NATO)** to oversee peace enforcement. NATO air strikes and the Bosnian-Croat offensive prompted Milošević to seek a negotiated settlement through the 1995 **Dayton Accords**.

Milošević was limited to two terms as Serbian president, but was elected president of Yugoslavia and took office in 1997. A rebellion in Kosovo commenced that year, and Milošević authorized its brutal repression. By 1998, hundreds of ethnic Albanians had been killed and thousands displaced. Western leaders, including **William J. Clinton** of the United States, **Tony Blair** of Great Britain, and **Jacques Chirac** of France, threatened further military action. Negotiations were undertaken at Rambouillet, France, in February and March 1999, but Milošević refused to accept successive plans offered by the Western allies and the talks ended without an agreement. Milošević hoped that Russia, Serbia's traditional ally in the region, would prevent military action, but Moscow refused to intervene. NATO subsequently launched the **Kosovo War**, a 77-day aerial campaign that forced Milošević to accept a **United Nations**–sponsored cease-fire placing Kosovo under the protection of a NATO-led peacekeeping force. Meanwhile, in May 1999, Milošević was indicted by the International Criminal Tribunal for the Former Yugoslavia (ICTY).

In 2000, Milošević trailed opposition leader Vojislav Koštunica in the first round of balloting for the Yugoslav presidency. Efforts by Milošević to remain in office led to widespread street protests. He was forced to concede defeat on 5 October, and Koštunica took office the next day. In 2001, Milošević was arrested by Serb security forces and turned over to the ICTY. His trial began in 2002, but Milošević became ill and requested repeated delays. He did not appear before the court until 2004. He died of a heart attack on 11 March 2006 in the midst of his trial. *See also* ALBRIGHT, MADELEINE; CHRISTOPHER, WARREN; HOLBROOKE, RICHARD C.; HUMAN RIGHTS.

MITCHELL, GEORGE J. (1933–). Democratic senator from Maine and Senate majority leader (1989–1995). George John Mitchell was born in Waterville, Maine, and earned a law degree from Georgetown University in 1961. Mitchell was appointed to the U.S. Senate in 1980 and then elected in his own right in 1982. He became majority leader and was offered a seat on the U.S. Supreme Court in 1994 (he declined so that he could concentrate on leading the Senate). However, Mitchell decided not to run for reelection in 1994. The following year, President **William J. Clinton** asked the former senator to lead a new round of negotiations in the Northern Ireland peace process as a special representative. Mitchell led a commission that established the main principles for the peace process, including a renunciation of violence by all parties. His efforts culminated in the 1998 Good Friday Accords, which served as the basis for subsequent peace efforts. During the 2004 presidential election, Mitchell was frequently cited as the most likely candidate to become secretary of state if a Democratic candidate won the balloting. In 2005, Mitchell was appointed to a congressional committee that developed recommendations for reform of the **United Nations**.

MITTERRAND, FRANÇOIS (1916–1996). President of France from 1981 to 1995 who led the country during the final days of the **Cold War**. François Maurice Adrien Marie Mitterrand was born in Jarnac, France. In 1938 he joined the French Army and fought in World War II, where he was wounded and later captured by the Nazis. He escaped and became part of the Resistance. In 1946, he was elected to the National Assembly and subsequently appointed to a number of government offices, including minister of veteran affairs and interior minister. In 1965, he was the candidate of the United Left in the presidential elections. In the 1972 balloting, Mitterrand came in a close second with 49.2 percent. He finally won the presidency in 1982.

Although leader of the Socialists, Mitterrand undertook a range of probusiness reforms, including the decentralization of government services and restructuring the industrial sector. However, he also nationalized more than 20 large firms. Mitterrand worked to enhance European integration and supported the expansion of the European Community to Spain and Portugal in 1986. He developed a close working relationship with German chancellor **Helmut Kohl**, but had a series of disagreements with U.S. president **Ronald W. Reagan**. For instance, Mitterrand offered rhetorical support for leftist movements in El Salvador and Nicaragua at a time when the United States supported regimes attempting to suppress those groups. The French president also opposed American efforts to isolate states such as Iran, Libya, and Syria that supported terrorism. Mitterrand argued that the West should engage these states and use economic incentives to entice the regimes to abandon support for terrorist groups.

Mitterrand was reelected in 1988. He supported initiatives to reduce tensions with the Soviet Union, but endorsed the democratization efforts in eastern and central Europe. Mitterrand offered military and diplomatic assistance during the **Persian Gulf War**, but opposed American global primacy. Mitterrand's relations with **George H. W. Bush** were better than had been the case with Reagan. For instance, Mitterrand supported the U.S. invasion of Panama, **Operation Just Cause**. Nonetheless, Mitterrand worked to improve the economic and political power of the European Community as a rival to the influence of the United States. In addition, Mitterrand viewed European integration as a means to constrain the economic power of the reunified Germany and prevent that country from dominating the continent. Consequently, he supported the **Maastricht Treaty** and European Monetary Union. He opposed Germany's diplomatic recognition of Slovenia and Croatia in 1991, but endorsed **United Nations** efforts to mediate the **Bosnian Conflict**. France was one of the first countries to deploy peacekeeping forces in Bosnia. Mitterrand hoped to demonstrate that crises such as the **Balkan Wars** could be managed without the involvement of the United States. Mitterrand also proposed that the **Organization for Security and Cooperation in Europe** be strengthened as an alternative to the **North Atlantic Treaty Organization (NATO)**. The French president contended that NATO provided the United States with an undue amount of influence in European security. Mitterrand's interaction with the administration of **William J. Clinton** deteriorated over his opposition to U.S. policy toward Iraq, especially the continuation of economic sanctions on the regime of **Saddam Hussein**. Mitterrand left office in 1995 and died a year later.

MOGADISHU, BATTLE OF. A clash on 3–4 October 1993 that led to the end of the **United Nations (UN)** humanitarian mission in Somalia, Operation Restore Hope. After the overthrow of dictator Muhammad Siad Barre in 1911, civil war resulted in the deaths of more than 250,000 Somalis. In response, the UN, with support of the administration of **George H. W. Bush**, launched an operation to provide food and medical supplies. The United States deployed 25,000 troops as part of the mission. However, warlords and local militia leaders continued to struggle for predominance and hijacked aid shipments to enhance their power and influence.

On 5 June 1993, militias loyal to Mohamed Farrah Aidid ambushed and killed 24 Pakistani peacekeepers. The United States subsequently launched a series of operations to capture Aidid and his senior lieutenants. American military commanders requested a variety of heavy weapons, including main battle tanks, armed vehicles, and AC-130 gunships. Secretary of Defense **Leslie Aspin Jr.** supported increased armaments for the troops, but President **William J. Clinton** refused the requests in an effort to prevent a military escalation of what was intended to be a humanitarian operation.

On 3 October 1993, American special operations forces and Army Rangers were deployed in a quick strike to the middle of Mogadishu to apprehend a group of high-ranking Aidid officers. The plan called for the special operations units to be deployed by helicopter to capture the militia leaders and then to link with a convoy of vehicles that would carry the Americans and their captives back to their main base at a UN compound. The attack force included 160 troops, 12 vehicles, and 19 helicopters and aircraft. The U.S. forces were able to capture two of Aidid's top political advisors and other clan leaders. However, before they could return to their base, the Americans came under fire from Somali militias. Two Blackhawk helicopters were shot down, and the convoy was forced to divert their withdrawal in an effort to rescue the crews of the craft. The Ranger force became bogged down after their rescue of one helicopter crew. Somali fighters overran the second crash site, killing three crew members and capturing one, pilot **Michael Durant**. In addition, two Delta Force snipers who volunteered to deploy at the second crash site in an effort to protect the wounded crew were killed (both were posthumously granted the Medal of Honor).

At the first crash site, 90 Rangers fought through the night before a relief column rescued them the following morning. The relief force was centered around Pakistani tanks and Malaysian armored personnel carriers and highlighted the lack of heavy armament among the American troops. During the battle, 18 Americans were killed and 84 wounded. In addition, one Malaysian soldier was killed, while seven Malaysians and two Pakistanis were injured. Approximately 700 Somalis died and more than 1,500 were wounded. Durant was held hostage for 11 days. Over the next few days, pictures and films of dead Americans being dragged through the streets were broadcast throughout the world, as were images of the beaten and injured Durant.

After the battle, Clinton ordered tanks and other heavy weapons to Somalia and dispatched **Robert B. Oakley** in an effort to create a cease-fire. Clinton subsequently ordered the withdrawal of American forces after diplomatic initiatives failed. By March 1994, all U.S. troops had left. The remaining UN peacekeeping forces departed the following year. The battle marked a turning point in American foreign policy during Clinton's first term. The administration thereafter refused to intervene in other substate conflicts in the **Bosnian Conflict** or the **Rwanda genocide** and relied on airpower in other military actions such as the **Kosovo War** or the repeated strikes against Iraq. *See also* HUMAN RIGHTS; SOMALIA INTERVENTION.

MUBARAK, HOSNI (1928–). President of Egypt since 1981 and a close ally of successive American administrations. Muhammad Hosni Said Mubarak was born in the Al Monufiyah Governorate, Egypt, and earned a degree in military sciences from the Egyptian Military Academy in 1949. He joined the air force and held a variety of appointments, including chief of staff and air chief marshal. In 1975, he was appointed vice president of Egypt. Following the assassination of Anwar Sadat in 1981, Mubarak became president of the country and leader of the ruling National Democratic Party (NDP). He was reelected president on four occasions in balloting that was marred by government interference.

As president, Mubarak has pursued moderate, pro-Western policies. He was able to secure increases in U.S. military and economic assistance throughout the 1980s and 1990s. During this period, Egypt received an annual average of $1.3 billion in military aid and $815 million in economic funding from the United States. American support allowed the Egyptian military to become the second most powerful in the Middle East, behind only Israel. Mubarak supported the U.S.-led coalition in the **Persian Gulf War** and contributed troops to the military force that liberated Kuwait. In return, the United States and Europe forgave $20 billion of Egypt's foreign debt. Mubarak also lent support to successive efforts to resolve the **Arab-Israeli conflict** and hosted the **Taba Summit**. In the aftermath of the **September 11 terrorist attacks**, Mubarak increased intelligence cooperation with the United States. However, he did not support the U.S.-led 2003 **Iraq War**.

Mubarak is also popular among regional leaders. In 1989, he was able to end Egypt's suspension from the Arab League (put in place because of Sadat's peace agreement with Israel). He also twice served as chairman of the Organization of African Unity (1989–1990 and 1993–1994).

Domestically, Mubarak has faced discontent, and Egypt's unemployment rate has remained above 20 percent since 1992. He survived six assassination attempts and there has been a radical Islamic insurgency since the late 1980s led by groups such as the Muslim Brotherhood. One result has been the continued imposition of emergency rule, which provides the president with extensive security powers. In response to domestic dissatisfaction and pressure from the administration of President **George W. Bush**, Mubarak enacted some democratic reforms in 2005. For the first time in modern Egyptian history, other parties besides the NDP were allowed to field candidates in the 2005 presidential elections.

MULRONEY, M. BRIAN (1939–). Prime minister of Canada from 1984 to 1993 who formed close working relationships with American presidents **Ronald W. Reagan** and **George H. W. Bush** and closely aligned Canadian foreign policy with that of the United States. Martin Brian Mulroney was born in Baie-Comeau, Quebec. He graduated with honors from St. Francis Xavier University in 1959 and then earned a law degree from Laval University in 1964. Through the 1970s, Mulroney served in a variety of commercial firms and became well known for his efforts to combat corruption.

Mulroney had joined the Conservative Party as a student and in 1976, narrowly lost a bid to become leader of the party. In 1983, he was elected head of the Conservatives and won a seat in Parliament in a by-election. The following year, the Conservatives won the general election, and Mulroney became prime minister. He pursued a domestic reform agenda that included reducing the federal deficit and privatizing state-owned corporations. He also oversaw constitutional reforms that recognized the special status of Quebec.

Mulroney supported U.S. initiatives to improve transatlantic security, and he backed Reagan's hard-line stance against the Soviet Union. Mulroney's government increased military spending during the 1980s and ushered in a series of defense reforms. He did, however, oppose U.S. intervention in Latin America, particularly, U.S. support for the Contra rebel group in Nicaragua. Reagan and Mulroney negotiated a series of agreements to improve American-Canadian relations, including the 1988 Canada-U.S. Free Trade Agreement and an accord to reduce pollution. Mulroney's close relationship with Washington continued during the Bush administration. Canada endorsed military action during the **Persian Gulf War** and provided troops to the U.S.-led multilateral coalition. Mulroney and Bush built on earlier economic accords to develop the 1992 **North American Free Trade Agreement**.

A lingering recession in 1993 cost Mulroney that year's election. After he left office, Mulroney returned to his private law practice.

MUSHARRAF, S. PERVEZ (1943–). Pakistani general who seized power in 1999 in a military coup and became the nation's president in 2001. Seyd Pervez Musharraf was born in Delhi, India, but immigrated to Pakistan with his family after partition in 1947. He was commissioned into the Pakistani military and rose rapidly, becoming the army chief of staff in 1998. He led Pakistani forces during the 1999 Kargil War following the **India and Pakistan nuclear tests.**

Musharraf took power on 12 October 1999 in a bloodless coup. In June 2001, he also became president. Following the **September 11 terrorist attacks**, Musharraf cooperated with the United States in **Operation Enduring Freedom** and the broader **war on terror**. He attempted to suppress radical Islam, at significant political and personal risk (he survived two assassination attempts in 2003). Nonetheless, **Al Qaeda** remained active in the remote northwest corner of Pakistan. In 2002, a referendum extended the length of the president's term through 2007. In 2005, Musharraf resigned as head of the army. His relationship with the administration of **George W. Bush** became increasingly complicated as Washington exerted pressure on Musharraf to suppress pro-Taliban militias in the northwest that were launching raids into neighboring Afghanistan. In addition, Musharraf faced domestic criticism for several cross-border incursions by American-led coalition forces pursuing Taliban forces that had fled into Pakistan. *See also* ARMS CONTROL; INTERNATIONAL TERRORISM; PEARL, DANIEL.

– N –

NATIONAL COMMISSION ON TERRORIST ATTACKS UPON THE UNITED STATES (9/11 COMMISSION). In 2002, following the **September 11 terrorist attacks**, the National Commission on Terrorist Attacks upon the United States, commonly known as the 9/11 Commission, was created to identify the major flaws that had allowed the attacks to occur and to recommend new strategies and tactics to prevent, or at least minimize, future strikes on America. The bipartisan commission was composed of five Republicans and five Democrats and was chaired by former New Jersey governor Thomas Keane, a Republican. The commission was chartered by Congress and approved by President **George W. Bush**. It had access to classified documents and intelligence reports and interviewed the senior security officials from both the Bush administration and the administration of President **William J. Clinton**. There were more than 1,200 individual interviews, several of which were televised.

The Commission's final report, issued on 22 July 2004, was published in book form. Among its main recommendations were increased intelligence cooperation among security agencies in the United States, the creation of a director of national intelligence (DNI) to oversee the sundry intelligence agencies, and increased U.S. efforts to forestall the growth of **international terrorist** organizations in countries such as Pakistan and Afghanistan. The report also called for a range of improvements in border, port, and transportation security. Responding to the report, the Bush administration named **John Negroponte** as the nation's first DNI in 2005.

The Bush administration had initially sought only an internal probe of the 2001 terrorist attacks, but domestic and congressional pressure led to the formation of the 9/11 Commission. During the body's investigation, the administration refused to turn over some materials and was accused by some observers of endeavoring to minimize any criticism of its management of the attacks and their aftermath. Some critics of the commission asserted that the body did not adequately explore the counterterrorism policies of the Clinton administration and the prelude to the attacks. *See also* RICE, CONDOLEEZZA; WAR ON TERROR.

NATION-BUILDING. The effort to transform weak or failed states into viable nation-states. The majority of nation-building attempts in the 20th century failed, including efforts in Africa, Latin America, and Asia. The most successful examples of nation-building were post–World War II Germany and Japan. Both countries had economies that had been ruined by the war and faced significant political and social upheavals. The successful instances of nation-building required substantial economic aid and a long-term military presence.

Post–**Cold War** nation-building efforts by the United States largely failed. The **Somalia intervention** and the **Haiti interventions** were examples of unsuccessful initiatives. In Somalia, outside powers were unable to establish stability or ensure security. Somalia remained a failed state where greater stability existed in the breakaway provinces of Somaliland and Puntland (neither of which had international diplomatic recognition because of concerns by the global community that their independence could lead to the complete collapse of Somalia). In Haiti, political instability, including successive coups, led to continued social and economic strife, despite American- and **United Nations (UN)**–led operations to restore order.

The multilateral effort at nation-building in Bosnia was more successful. Following the **Dayton Accords**, a **North Atlantic Treaty Organization (NATO)**–led (and later **European Union (EU)**–commanded) peacekeeping mission provided a secure environment for economic and political development. There were multilateral military missions in Bosnia for more than 10 years, and the country received significant economic assistance from the EU and the United States. Bosnia reinforced the lessons of Germany and Japan.

U.S.-led nation-building in Afghanistan and Iraq has had mixed results. After the **Afghanistan intervention**, the United States employed a three-pronged nation-building strategy. First, political power was concentrated in the hands of an interim government led by **Hamid Karzai** (Karzai enjoyed the support of the main political and ethnic factions in Afghanistan and subsequently won presidential elections). Second, political and economic recovery was overseen by the UN, and later by NATO. Third, American forces continued to undertake security operations. Substantial progress in Afghanistan was undermined by a continuing insurgency by the Taliban and **Al Qaeda**, as well as the limited scope of reconstruction efforts (initially, there were only 12 regional reconstruction teams deployed outside of Kabul). It was estimated that Afghanistan needed $10 billion over a five-year period to rebuild its economy and restore its civil society. The United States and other countries also failed to provide adequate financial aid. International donors provided $4.5 billion over a five-year span, with the United States providing the largest share. Countries such as Saudi Arabia, Japan, and Australia provided far less in assistance than they had initially pledged.

Following the **Iraq War**, the United States failed to put in place a post–**Saddam Hussein** government that enjoyed popular support, although subsequent balloting established a democratically elected parliament and government. In addition, the U.S.-led coalition failed to constrain an ongoing insurgency that undermined political and social stability and prevented economic development. The insurgency weakened aid efforts, as the instability caused international organizations to withdraw staff and curtail programs. Nonetheless, U.S. efforts to provide economic assistance had some notable successes. At a November 2004 conference, international donors agreed to write off 80 percent of Iraq's $120 billion foreign debt. The effort at debt reduction was led by former secretary of state **James A. Baker III** and followed the American cancellation of 100 percent of Iraq's $4 billion debt to the United States.

NATO (NORTH ATLANTIC TREATY ORGANIZATION). An alliance formed to contain Soviet expansion in Europe during the **Cold War**, which then transformed into a broad security body that undertook a range of operations outside of its traditional geographic area in western Europe. NATO was formed by Belgium, Canada, Denmark, France, Great Britain, Iceland, Italy, Luxembourg, the Netherlands, Norway, Portugal, and the United States in 1949. During the Cold War, the alliance expanded to include Greece, Turkey, the Federal Republic of Germany, and Spain.

While the superpower conflict continued, NATO preserved the American defense commitment to Europe and provided a mechanism to coordinate defense policy among the allies. Afterward, with the end of the Cold War, U.S. officials sought to maintain the centrality of NATO to transatlantic security. The administration of **George H. W. Bush** proposed a series of reforms and restructurings of the alliance to adapt NATO to the changed security environment. A group of NATO members, led by Great Britain and including Denmark, the Netherlands, Norway, Portugal, and Turkey, strongly endorsed the American initiatives in order to ensure continued U.S. participation in European security. Other states, including Belgium, France, Germany, and Italy, wanted to emphasize a **European Security and Defense Identity**. Beginning in 1991, the alliance developed new mechanisms to improve cooperation with the states of the former Warsaw Pact, including Russia, and to allow the alliance to undertake operations outside of NATO's traditional area of operations.

In October 1992, NATO created a rapid reaction force to respond to humanitarian crises. The following year, the alliance began supervision of the no-fly zone over Bosnia. At the 1994 **Brussels Summit**, NATO initiated the **Partnership for Peace (PfP)** program, which allowed non-NATO members to participate in alliance operations and exercises and provided a means to ensure interoperability among states. At the summit, NATO further announced that it would expand to include countries in central and eastern Europe. Meanwhile, in its first combat operations, NATO launched air strikes against Serb positions in the **Bosnian Conflict**. Following the 1995 **Dayton Accords**, NATO took command of the peacekeeping operation in Bosnia. In order to assuage Russian concerns prior to enlargement, in 1997 NATO and Russia signed the Founding Act, which increased cooperation with Moscow. A similar accord, the Distinctive Charter, was signed with Ukraine. The Founding Act was followed by the creation of a Permanent Joint Council, which allowed Russia to participate in NATO meetings on a non-voting basis. A round of **NATO enlargement** in 1999 added the Czech Republic, Hungary, and Poland. In 1999, NATO forces and PfP members conducted a 77-day aerial campaign, Operation Allied Force, against Serbia during the **Kosovo War**. The alliance subsequently led the international peacekeeping force in Kosovo.

In response to the **September 11 terrorist attacks**, NATO invoked its collective defense clause, which required all member states to come to the aid of a member state under attack—in this case, the United States. NATO deployed airborne early warning craft to the United States and stationed naval forces in the Mediterranean Sea and Indian Ocean to support the American-led coalition in **Operation Enduring Freedom** during the **Afghanistan intervention**. After the fall of the Taliban, NATO took command of the international peacekeeping force in Afghanistan. The alliance also adopted new counterterrorism missions and increased intelligence cooperation among the member states.

In 2002, at its Prague Summit, a new round of **NATO expansion** was announced. In 2004, NATO welcomed Bulgaria, Estonia, Latvia, Lithuania, Romania, Slovakia, and Slovenia joined the alliance.

The **Iraq War** in 2003 divided the alliance, as states such as the Czech Republic, Denmark, Hungary, the Netherlands, Italy, Poland, Portugal, Spain, and Great Britain endorsed the U.S.-led invasion, while Belgium, France, Germany, and Luxembourg opposed it. The United

States requested NATO participation in the post–**Saddam Hussein** occupation of Iraq, but the alliance could not reach agreement on deployment, although those states that supported the United States dispatched troops on an individual basis. NATO also agreed to provide training for Iraqi security personnel. *See also* BALKAN WARS; DE HOOP SCHEFFER, JAAP; EUROPEAN UNION; ORGANIZATION FOR SECURITY AND COOPERATION IN EUROPE; SOLANA, JAVIER; WAR ON TERROR; WÖRNER, MANFRED.

NATO ENLARGEMENT (1999). In 1999, three former members of the Warsaw Pact—the Czech Republic, Hungary, and Poland—became members of their former **Cold War** nemesis, the **North Atlantic Treaty Organization (NATO)**, and increased the size of the alliance from 16 to 19 members.

Several European states, led by France, advocated the creation of new, post–Cold War security structures or the strengthening of parallel bodies such as the **Organization for Security and Cooperation in Europe**. However, the **William J. Clinton** administration sought to forestall such initiatives. Successive U.S. administrations perceived NATO expansion as a means of demonstrating the continuing utility of the transatlantic alliance. At the 1994 **Brussels Summit**, the Americans emerged with a consensus on eventual expansion, but the question remained of how broad an enlargement the alliance should undertake. Domestic considerations, including a desire to maximize the **peace dividend** that resulted from the end of the Cold War, led most partner states to favor only limited expansion. The Clinton administration estimated that expansion would cost $27–35 billion over a 10-year period. However, the **Partnership for Peace** program had elevated the capabilities and the interoperability of the aspirant states so that costs were actually closer to $1.5 billion over the next decade.

At the 1997 Madrid Summit, NATO leaders decided to invite the Czech Republic, Hungary, and Poland to join the alliance. In order to assuage Russian concerns over the potential security threat from an expanded NATO, the alliance created a new joint body with its former enemy, the NATO-Russia Permanent Joint Council. NATO also pledged not to station nuclear weapons on the soil of the new members. The three countries acceded to the Washington Treaty on 12 March 1999. Within the United States, the early controversies over costs and commitments evaporated. The Senate ratified the expansion on 30 April 1998 on a vote of 80 to 19. The parliaments and governments of the other Allies endorsed enlargement by similar majorities (the United States was actually the fifth NATO member to approve the accession of the three countries).

NATO EXPANSION (2004). The biggest expansion of the **North Atlantic Treaty Organization**'s **(NATO)** membership occurred in 2004 when the alliance admitted seven states from Eastern and Central Europe. The new members were Bulgaria, Estonia, Latvia, Lithuania, Romania, Slovakia, and Slovenia. The enlargement confirmed NATO's role as the cornerstone of European security and, along with the concurrent **European Union (EU)** expansion, helped erase the artificial divide created by the **Cold War**. The 1999 **NATO enlargement** was judged by all to have been a success, but members expressed concern that another round could make the alliance, which operated on the basis of consensus, unwieldy. In order to improve their odds for membership, a group of 10 eastern and central European states formed an informal alliance in 2000 known as the Vilnius Ten (the group included Albania, Bulgaria, Croatia, Estonia, Latvia, Lithuania, Macedonia, Romania, Slovakia, and Slovenia). The 10 held consultations and worked together to promote their candidacies. Momentum for a broad round of expansion increased after the **September 11 terrorist attacks**, since NATO membership was perceived by both existing and potential members as a means to enhance counterterrorism and bolster the capabilities of the alliance for out-of-area missions such as the **Afghanistan Intervention**. At NATO's November 2002 Prague Summit, alliance leaders finalized the list of candidate countries, which was narrowed down to seven.

The prelude to the U.S.-led invasion of Iraq occurred simultaneously with the accession protocol ratifications. Within NATO, one faction, led by France and Germany, opposed the war, while a pro-U.S. faction, led by Great Britain, Italy, and Spain, supported the invasion. The Vilnius Ten wrote an open letter of support for the United States. There was a strong reaction from French president **Jacques Chirac**, but the overt support did not lead to retaliatory action in their pursuit of either EU or NATO membership. On 29 March 2004, the seven states became members of the alliance.

NEGROPONTE, JOHN D. (1939–). Career diplomat who served in a variety of posts, including ambassadorial postings and as the U.S. representative to the **United Nations (UN)**, before he became the nation's first director of national intelligence (DNI) in 2005. John Dmitri Negroponte was born in London. After earning a degree from Yale University in 1960, he entered the Foreign Service and held a variety of postings. Negroponte was ambassador to Honduras (1981–1985), Mexico (1989–1993), and the Philippines (1993–1996). In 2001, he was appointed ambassador to the UN and oversaw the diplomatic efforts at the world body during **Operation Enduring Freedom**. Negroponte secured a unanimous UN Security Council resolution that ordered the regime of **Saddam Hussein** to disarm and allow weapons inspections or face the consequences. He also led the subsequent U.S. attempt to gain endorsements from the UN on military action against Iraq. In 2004, Negroponte became ambassador to Iraq. When the post of DNI was created, Negroponte was named by President **George W. Bush** to the post and confirmed by the Senate on a vote of 98 to 2. Once in office, he worked to improve coordination among the nation's intelligence agencies. *See also* IRAQ WAR; WAR ON TERROR.

NEOCONSERVATIVES. A group of American intellectuals and policy makers who assert that the United States should utilize its military and economic power to promote the nation's interests and foreign policy goals. Neoconservatives, or "neocons," trace their roots to a group of liberal scholars in the 1960s who became disillusioned by failure of the Democratic Party to endorse robust national defense and security policies. Many of the early neoconservatives, including Irving Kristol and Norman Podhoretz, were affiliated with conservative Democrats such as Senator Henry "Scoop" Jackson (1912–1983) of Washington State, who opposed the party's growing antiwar wing in the late 1960s and 1970s.

With the election of **Ronald W. Reagan**, most neocons became Republicans because of the president's staunch anticommunism and support for increased military expenditures. After the end of the **Cold War**, neocons criticized the defense reductions under the administrations of **George H. W. Bush** and **William J. Clinton**. They also argued that the United States should use its influence to spread democracy and free trade and condemned what they described as the neo-isolationism of the 1990s. Following the 2000 election, **George W. Bush** appointed a number of prominent neocons to his administration, including **Paul D. Wolfowitz, Peter W. Rodman,** and **Richard N. Perle.** The neocons were differentiated from traditional conservatives because of their embrace of preemptive military action to forestall security threats. Preemption was codified in the **Bush Doctrine.** Within the administration, the neocons were balanced by figures such as Secretary of State **Colin Powell** and his successor **Condoleezza Rice.** The neocons were vocal proponents of the 2003 **Iraq War.** *See also* NEOLIBERALISM; TRADE POLICY.

NEOLIBERALISM. A prominent approach to economics that emphasizes free-market capitalism and the importance of open trade. Neoliberalism, or neoliberal economics, rejects state intervention in national or global economics. It calls for deregulation of national economies and the removal of trade barriers such as tariffs or subsidies. The movement, which emerged in the 1970s, was intertwined with the broader trends of **globalization.** The end of the Cold War accelerated neoliberalism. Washington pressured global bodies such as the **International Monetary Fund** and the **World Bank** to promote neoliberal policies. Both subsequently attempted to impose neoliberal economic reforms in a top-down manner that was criticized by opponents of globalization as exacerbating the gap between rich and poor within developing countries and between rich and poor nations. In the United States, neoliberalism was initially identified mainly with the administration of President **Ronald W. Reagan** and the Republican Party. However, centrist Democrats, including **William J. Clinton,** embraced many neoliberal trade principles. The philosophy guided the Clinton administration's **trade policy** through the 1990s and was continued by the administration of Republican president **George W. Bush. Alan Greenspan,** chairman of the Federal Reserve from 1987 to 2006, was a prominent proponent of neoliberal policies. Neoliberalism was formally rejected by countries in Latin America such as Venezuela and Bolivia (Venezuelan president **Hugo Chávez** emerged as one of the foremost opponents of the economic approach). *See also* NEOCONSERVATIVISM.

NORIEGA, MANUEL (1938–). Military dictator of Panama who was overthrown in 1989 by U.S. forces in **Operation Just Cause**. Manuel Antonio Noriega was a career soldier who gained a commission in the National Guard in 1967. He received specialized training in Peru and the United States in counterinsurgency tactics. In 1969, Noriega was promoted to lieutenant colonel for his role in the coup that brought Gen. Omar Torrijos to power. Torrijos also made Noriega the chief of military intelligence, where he worked closely with U.S. intelligence agencies. Noriega received direct payments from the Central Intelligence Agency (CIA) for spying on anti-American activists in Panama and surrounding countries. He also negotiated the release of a U.S. freighter crew held by Cuban authorities. President **James E. Carter** stopped the payments, but they were resumed in the 1980s. In 1981, Torrijos died in a plane crash. Many in Panama believed that Noriega was responsible for the crash. Noriega subsequently became chief of staff of the military, and the real leader of Panama. In 1983, he made himself a general.

Noriega developed close ties to the administration of **Ronald W. Reagan**. In exchange for military and economic aid from Washington, Noriega provided assistance to the anticommunist regime in El Salvador and created a network to transfer funds to the Contra rebels in Nicaragua. Noriega also allowed the CIA and other U.S. agencies to conduct operations from Panama. However, law enforcement officials in the United States discovered that Noriega was deeply involved in the drug trade (reports about Noriega's participation in narcotrafficking surfaced as early as 1971). On 5 February 1989, Noriega was indicted in the United States for **drug trafficking**. In addition, U.S. intelligence officials found that Noriega had helped Cuban leader **Fidel Castro** smuggle goods through the U.S. economic embargo.

Noriega campaigned for the presidency in 1989 and undertook a brutal campaign to suppress the opposition. American intelligence agencies provided $10 million to aid the Panamanian opposition. In the May balloting, Noriega's opponent, Guillermo Endara, was believed to have won, but the dictator annulled the results before they were made public. In response, the administration of **George H. W. Bush** imposed a range of economic sanctions on Panama. U.S. forces were ordered to the region.

In December, a U.S. serviceman was killed by Panamanian security forces. In response, Bush ordered the invasion of Panama and the overthrow of Noriega on 20 December 1989. The invading force numbered 27,000 Americans. The Panamanian military offered little resistance. Noriega went into hiding and eventually took refuge in the Vatican Embassy in Panama City. Meanwhile, Endara was inaugurated as president of Panama. On 3 January, Noriega surrendered and was transported to the United States. He was tried on eight counts of drug trafficking and money laundering in April 1992. Noriega was found guilty and sentenced to 40 years' imprisonment (the sentence was reduced to 30 years in 1999). In 1995, Noriega was found guilty of murder in Panama following a trial in absentia.

NORTH AMERICAN FREE TRADE AGREEMENT (NAFTA). An economic accord among Canada, Mexico, and the United States that was signed on 17 December 1992 and came into force on 1 January 1994. It created a regional trade bloc that in 2004 had 430 million people and a combined annual economic output of $12.9 trillion (compared with the **European Union**'s 460 million people and $11.7 trillion).

NAFTA's genesis was the 1989 U.S.-Canada Free Trade Agreement, which removed tariffs and restrictions on trade between the two countries. Negotiations on NAFTA were initiated by President **George H. W. Bush** and completed in 1992, when the treaty was signed by the leaders of the three nations. NAFTA went into effect following ratification by the three countries in 1994. The accord established timetables for the elimination of trade barriers over a 15-year period. Some tariffs and duties were immediately reduced or abolished, while others were left in place in order to allow domestic manufacturers and producers time to transition to the new competition.

In the United States, NAFTA was very controversial. Domestic critics argued that the accord would lead to the loss of American jobs as U.S. companies moved to Mexico to take advantage of cheaper labor costs. Opponents also charged that foreign goods would flood the American market and put U.S. firms out of business. In Canada and Mexico, there was less opposition. However, critics in both countries warned that U.S. corporations would dominate local markets. In

Mexico, there was also concern that U.S. and Canadian companies would attempt to take advantage of less stringent local environmental regulations and workers' rights.

In order to allay the concerns of critics, NAFTA had a number of supplemental agreements. To assuage environmental concerns, the three countries negotiated the North American Agreement for Environmental Cooperation (NAAEC), which created the North American Commission for Environmental Cooperation. The commission was tasked to oversee issues related to pollution, conservation, health, and public policy. The long-term goal of the NAAEC was to harmonize environmental policies among the three countries. To facilitate this goal, the North American Development Bank was established to provide financing for environmental initiatives; by 2006, the bank had underwritten 37 projects in Mexico. A second major supplement was the North American Agreement on Labor Competition, which was supposed to facilitate coordination among governments to maintain or expand labor standards.

NAFTA increased trade among the three countries and helped stabilize the Mexican economy. Estimates are that NAFTA increased Mexico's economy by an annual average of 4–5 percent between 1994 and 2004. NAFTA added about 1 percent per year to the economies of the United States and Canada during the same time period. NAFTA did lead to the loss of jobs in some sectors in each of the countries, but contributed to employment growth in other areas. The three countries hoped to use NAFTA as a model for future free trade accords. For instance, after NAFTA, Mexico signed more than 40 bilateral free trade agreements. NAFTA also served as the basis for proposals for a **Free Trade Area of the Americas**. *See also* TRADE POLICY.

NORTH ATLANTIC TREATY ORGANIZATION. *See* NATO (NORTH ATLANTIC TREATY ORGANIZATION).

NORTH KOREAN NUCLEAR CRISES. North Korea's nuclear weapons program almost prompted American bombing strikes in 1994 and continues to serve as one of the main security threats in the region. Pyongyang began its nuclear program in the 1980s with the construction of a nuclear reactor at Yongbyon. The spent fuel rods from the reactor were converted into weapons-grade plutonium. As a signatory to the Nuclear Nonproliferation Treaty (NPT), North Korea was supposed to allow inspections of its nuclear facilities by international monitors, but it refused access. In 1989, U.S. intelligence discovered that North Korea had an active nuclear weapons program that would be capable of producing 30 atomic bombs per year within a five- or six-year period. North Korea had also started construction on a second, larger, nuclear reactor. The administration of President **George H. W. Bush** attempted to use international channels and diplomacy to convince Pyongyang to cease its weapons program. Specifically, administration sought **United Nations (UN)** monitoring of the country's nuclear facilities in exchange for the normalization of relations with North Korea and economic aid. In May 1992, UN inspectors were granted access to the Yongbyon reactor, but reported that North Korean officials blocked their ability to conduct a full inspection; nevertheless, they discovered evidence of the weapons program.

In March 1993, North Korea announced that it intended to withdraw from the NPT and develop nuclear weapons. The administration of President **William J. Clinton** threatened air strikes and simultaneously launched a new round of diplomacy. The result was the 1994 **Framework Agreement with North Korea**. Under the accord, the United States, Japan, and South Korea agreed to provide economic aid, including food and energy supplies, as well as to construct two light-water reactors for Pyongyang. In return, North Korea promised to end its weapons program and allow full inspections. Through the 1990s, North Korea continued to interfere with international inspectors and launched a new secret nuclear program, this time based on highly enriched uranium. By the end of the decade, North Korea had produced as many as 12 nuclear bombs through its covert program.

In October 2002, in meetings with North Korean officials, the United States revealed that it was aware of Pyongyang's secret nuclear program and attempted to convince the regime to abandon its nuclear ambitions or face the cessation of international aid. Pyongyang subsequently admitted the existence of its nuclear efforts. The regime offered to stop weapons production and allow full inspections in exchange for a nonaggression pact with the United States and new economic assistance. In November, the **George W. Bush** administration threatened to stop fuel shipments to North Korea unless the government immediately stopped its weapons program. Pyongyang refused and removed UN monitoring devices and inspection seals from its reactor at Yongbyon. It also withdrew from the NPT.

Tensions in the region escalated following joint South Korean–U.S. military exercises, and a series of missile tests by Pyongyang. In 2003, Russia and the People's Republic of China agreed to use their influence in an effort to convince Pyongyang to comply with the framework agreement. The countries joined Japan, South Korea, and the United States in negotiations with North Korea in August 2003 that were dubbed the **Six-Party Talks**. Successive rounds of negotiations failed to create a new agreement.

On 3 October 2006, Pyongyang announced that it intended to conduct a nuclear test. Despite warnings from the UN and the participants in the Six-Party Talks, on 9 October North Korea carried out its nuclear test. Five days later, the UN imposed limited sanctions on Pyongyang in response to the tests, while the United States and Japan enacted a more stringent embargo. In February 2007, Pyongyang signaled a willingness to resume the Six-Party Talks. When negotiations began, North Korea pledged to begin dismantling its nuclear programs in exchange for the resumption of food and fuel aid. Under the terms of an agreement reached on 13 February 2007, Pyongyang received 50,000 tons of fuel in exchange for allowing UN inspections of its facilities and shutting down production of fissile materials. Another 950,000 tons of fuel was scheduled to be delivered in stages as North Korea ended its nuclear efforts. *See also* AXIS OF EVIL.

– O –

OAKLEY, ROBERT B. (1934–). Career diplomat who served as a special envoy for presidents **George H. W. Bush** and **William J. Clinton** during the **Somalia intervention**. Robert Bigger Oakley was born in Dallas, Texas. After earning a degree from Princeton University in 1952, he served as an intelligence officer in the navy. Oakley then joined the Foreign Service in 1957, serving in a variety of posts in Africa, Asia, and the Middle East. In 1974, he was appointed to the

National Security Council (NSC) as the senior director for the Middle East and South Asia. He became a deputy assistant secretary of state during the administration of President **James E. Carter**, who appointed Oakley as U.S. ambassador to Zaire in 1979. President **Ronald W. Reagan** chose Oakley as ambassador to Somalia in 1982, before making the veteran diplomat the director of the State Department's Office of Terrorism in 1984 and then a member of the NSC staff three years later. Oakley served as U.S. ambassador to Pakistan from 1988 to 1991 in the Bush administration.

During the Somalia intervention, Bush asked Oakley to use the personal and professional connections developed while he was ambassador in Mogadishu to negotiate an end to conflict among the warring clans prior to the deployment of 25,000 troops as part of a United Nations–sponsored humanitarian operation. Following the 1993 **Battle of Mogadishu**, Clinton asked Oakley to again serve as a presidential envoy to the war-torn country. Oakley was unable to craft a lasting peace settlement, but he was able to continue negotiations between the country's warlords. In addition, he was able to establish a truce with Mohamed Farrah Aided to allow the withdrawal of U.S. forces. Hs also worked to secure the release of captured U.S. helicopter pilot **Michael Durant**. After his stint in Somalia, Oakley retired from public service. *See also* NATION-BUILDING.

OIL-FOR-FOOD PROGRAM. An aid initiative overseen by the **United Nations (UN)** to provide food and medicine to the Iraqi people while maintaining existing economic sanctions on the regime of **Saddam Hussein**. The Oil-for-Food Program was developed as a means of addressing criticisms of the UN sanctions on Iraq put in place after the **Persian Gulf War**. Countries such as France and Russia wanted to end, or at least reduce, economic restrictions, but the United States and Great Britain sought to continue the measures to prevent the Iraqi regime from restarting its weapons program. The program was a compromise that allowed continued sanctions and limited oil sales.

In 1991, United Nations Security Council Resolution (UNSCR) 706 authorized Iraq to sell oil and use the proceeds for humanitarian purchases. However, Saddam refused to accept the initiative. He also initially rebuffed a similar effort in 1995. Nevertheless, that year,

UNSCR 986 launched the Oil-for-Food Program following an agreement negotiated between then assistant secretary-general **Kofi Annan** and Saddam. Iraq was permitted to export $8 billion in oil per year. Revenues from the oil sales were deposited in an escrow account overseen by the UN, which supervised the purchases made with the funds.

In 1997, the first shipments of wheat and other foodstuffs were delivered to Iraq. A year later, the UN increased the annual limits on oil sales to $20.8 billion. Meanwhile, the permissible import list for Iraq was expanded to more than 6,000 individual items. France proposed several rounds of further expansion, but these initiatives were rejected by the United States. From 1997 to 2002, Iraq exported approximately $67 billion in oil and purchased $38 billion in humanitarian goods and products. Iraq was also allowed to purchase $300 million in equipment to repair and upgrade its oil facilities. The UN retained 2.2 percent of total sales to fund oversight of the program and the concurrent weapons inspections.

During the late 1990s, 60 percent of Iraq's 26 million people were dependent on the program for food and sustenance. Nonetheless, the Saddam regime diverted funds from the program for a variety of illicit activities. The regime also engaged in rampant smuggling, which generated an estimated $14 billion for Saddam and his senior leadership.

In 2003, following the **Iraq War**, UNSCR 1483 ended sanctions on Iraq and ordered the Oil-for-Food Program terminated after a six-month transition period. The remaining $14 billion in the escrow account was transferred to the interim Iraqi government.

During the program, there were repeated accusations of fraud and corruption. The UN initially refused to conduct a formal investigation, but after American forces discovered documents that implicated officials at the world body, Secretary-General Annan ordered a formal probe. To conduct the investigation, Annan formed the Independent Inquiry Committee, headed by former U.S. Federal Reserve chairman Paul Volcker. The committee's final report, issued on 7 September 2005, found substantial fraud in the program, naming more than 270 individuals, companies, and journalists who had accepted bribes from the Iraqi regime. The investigation discovered that UN officials had destroyed thousands of documents in an apparent bid to cover up the corruption. In August 2005, Aleksandr Yakovlev became the first UN official found guilty of involvement in the scandal. Yakovlev headed a UN procurement department and pleaded guilty to accepting more than $1.3 million in bribes. Several senior U.S. officials and congressmen called upon Annan to resign, but the secretary-general refused.

OPEN SKIES TREATY (2002). An agreement whose purpose was to improve security confidence in other countries by allowing unarmed aerial reconnaissance flights. The treaty was signed in 1992 and entered into force on 1 January 2002 with 34 signatories. It had initially been proposed by President Dwight D. Eisenhower in 1955, but negotiations on the initiative languished until the end of the **Cold War**. In 1989, President **George H. W. Bush** proposed the relaunch of talks. The following year, a conference on the Open Skies Treaty was held in Ottawa, Canada. Negotiations were finalized in a series of conferences, and the accord was signed by Secretary of State **James A. Baker III** on 24 March 1992 in Helsinki, Finland.

The treaty permits aerial reconnaissance flights over any country, as long as there is advance notification and the information is made available to all signatories of the treaty. The surveillance aircraft may be from the country that requests the overflight, or a state may request that the state to be observed provide an aircraft. Flights are limited to quotas established by the agreement; the United States, for example, has a quota of 41 flights per year. Countries participating in the overflights must provide copies of any information or aerial photographs collected to any other signatory upon request (although the requesting state must pay for the reproductions). In 2002, the first year of the agreement, there were 67 overflights. That figure rose to 110 in 2005. The treaty serves to reduce tensions between countries by increasing the amount of information available to neighboring states. *See also* ARMS CONTROL.

OPERATION ENDURING FREEDOM (2002–2003). The code name for the military response to the **September 11 terrorist attacks**. The core of the operation was the military campaign against the Taliban regime in Afghanistan, but it also included a wide range of counterterrorism initiatives and special operations missions. With the notable exception of the capture of **Osama bin Laden**, the military operation achieved its main objectives, including the overthrow of the Taliban regime and the destruction of **Al Qaeda**'s major training facilities in Afghanistan. Operation Enduring Freedom officially began on 7 October 2001, with the launch of air strikes and cruise missile attacks on the Taliban regime, and ended on 2 May 2003.

The military reaction to the terrorist strikes of 11 September 2001 began immediately and included a variety of defensive measures, including the deployment of aircraft to prevent further flight-based attacks. In national speeches, President **George W. Bush** announced that any military operation must accomplish three broad goals: the dismantling of the terrorist infrastructure in Afghanistan; the capture or demise of the senior Al Qaeda figures resident in Afghanistan; and an end to terrorist activities in that country. Later a fourth goal was added: the delivery of humanitarian aid to the Afghan people. The president ordered the military action to commence on 7 October. Many international organizations and other countries offered assistance to the United States. The **North Atlantic Treaty Organization (NATO)** invoked its collective defense clause (Article 5), which declares that an attack on one member state is an attack on all members. In addition, the **Organization of American States** and the Australia–New Zealand–United States treaty also activated defensive clauses.

Although the Bush administration sought the broadest possible diplomatic support, it ultimately used only minimal military contributions from other states. The coalition behind Operation Enduring Freedom eventually numbered 68 countries, with 27 states providing some type of military involvement. Allied countries also provided assistance to the United States through increased intelligence sharing, enhanced law enforcement and counterterrorism cooperation with the United States, and shouldering the burden of existing missions in order to free up American assets for use in the Afghan campaign. Regional states provided a variety of assistance to U.S. forces, including basing and overflight rights. Russia even provided weaponry for anti-Taliban groups in Afghanistan.

Central to the military campaign was an effort to attack the Taliban and Al Qaeda on multiple fronts and with a variety of weapon systems. Coalition special forces served as a liaison for air support, identified targets, and facilitated communication between the anti-Taliban forces, mainly the Northern Alliance. Coalition smart weapons were fired at targets that had been predesignated by the special operations forces, allowing for an incredible degree of accuracy. Ultimately, some 70 percent of the munitions used during the campaign were precision guided. The United States also used other state-of-the-art military equipment such as unmanned aerial reconnaissance drones. By 20 October all Taliban air defenses had been destroyed. During the remainder of the campaign, American and coalition aircraft continued combat missions and also began dropping humanitarian supplies to the Afghan people. By 1 November, 2,000 combat air sorties had been flown and a million humanitarian ration packets had been delivered to Afghan civilians. In addition, air units were able to provide supplies, including small arms, ammunition, and personal gear, for the Northern Alliance.

During this period, there were few major battles and little recognizable progress by coalition forces in terms of the capture of enemy territory. This resulted in substantial criticism over the slow pace of the campaign and questions over the effectiveness of U.S. strategy. However, on 9 November, 2,000 Northern Alliance forces, supported by coalition special forces, captured the key city of Mazar-e-Sharif. The fall of this strategic town caused the Taliban and Al Qaeda forces to rapidly collapse. Within four days, Northern Alliance troops had captured the capital city, Kabul. Meanwhile, anti-Taliban tribes rose in rebellion in the southern areas of Afghanistan, and conventional forces were deployed. By December, the Taliban and Al Qaeda forces had been reduced to small pockets of resistance. The last remaining major Taliban stronghold surrendered on 6 December.

On 22 December 2001, an interim, coalition government was inaugurated. The new government was led by exiled resistance leader **Hamid Karzai**. In addition, on 20 December, the United Nations had authorized the creation and deployment of a multilateral peacekeeping force, designated as the International Security Assistance Force (ISAF). The 6,000-member ISAF force was later placed under the auspices of NATO.

While coalition forces overthrew the Taliban regime in a relatively short period of time, they failed to capture the leader of the Taliban, Mullah Omar, or bin Laden. In addition, a Taliban-led insurgency continued in Afghanistan after Secretary of Defense **Donald H. Rumsfeld** declared an end to major combat operations on 2 May 2003. Since the fall of the Taliban, the United States has maintained between 8,000 and 12,000 troops in Afghanistan and carried out several significant operations against antigovernment rebel groups. The first major campaign was against the Tora Bora cave complex in December 2001. The operation was designed to capture major Taliban and Al Qaeda leaders, although it failed to find Omar or bin Laden. The second major sweep was Operation Anaconda in the Shah-i-Kot Valley in March 2002, and the third was Operation Mongoose in 2003. There were successive operations as ISAF's geographic mandate was expanded outside of Kabul. In May 2005, ISAF doubled the amount of territory under its control, and it took control of the country's southern provinces in 2006. That year, NATO-led forces conducted major attacks against the Taliban in operations Mountain Thrust (May) and Medusa and Mountain Fury (both in September). In October 2006, U.S. forces in Afghanistan came under NATO command.

Through 2006, 352 U.S. service personnel were killed and 1,066 wounded. The Taliban lost approximately 8,300 dead (including some 1,900 Al Qaeda fighters). There were about 28,700 Taliban prisoners of war held by either the U.S. or Afghan government. Northern Alliance troops suffered approximately 600 killed, and the post-Taliban Afghan Army lost 1,600. Estimates are that 3,700 Afghan civilians were killed during the fighting. The first three months of the war (which included the major U.S. combat operations) cost the United States $3.8 billion. *See also* AFGHANISTAN INTERVENTION; WAR ON TERROR.

OPERATION JUST CAUSE (1989–1990). The code name for the U.S. invasion of Panama in 1989 and the subsequent overthrow of dictator **Manuel Noriega** in 1990. Noriega had worked with U.S. intelligence agencies in the 1970s and 1980s, but tensions between Panama and the administration of **George H. W. Bush** became acute by 1988. Noriega was involved in **drug trafficking** and money laundering for Colombian drug cartels, and he was indicted on 5 February 1989. In addition, Noriega's security forces were waging a campaign of harassment and intimidation against the 35,000 Americans living in Panama. During the 1989 elections, Noriega initiated a broad campaign to intimidate the opposition. In the May balloting, the opposition candidate, Guillermo Endara, was widely believed to have won the balloting, but Noriega nullified the results. When Panamanian security forces killed an American serviceman on 16 December, the breaking point was reached. Bush ordered U.S. forces to go on standby.

On 20 December 1989, Bush ordered American forces to overthrow and arrest Noriega. More than 27,000 U.S. troops were involved in the attack. The Panamanian Defense Forces (PDF) numbered about 16,000. The Americans quickly captured the main strategic areas in the country, including airfields and the PDF headquarters. While the majority of the PDF surrendered, certain bands of Noriega supporters, known as Dignity Battalions, continued to fight for several more days. Meanwhile, there was widespread looting and property theft. Endara was inaugurated as Panama's president on the opening day of the invasion.

Noriega went into hiding on the day of the invasion. The United States offered a $1 million reward for the capture of the Panamanian dictator, but he took refuge in the Vatican Embassy. American forces surrounded the facility and used psychological warfare techniques, including blaring rock and roll music, to prompt Noriega's surrender. There were also demonstrations by Panamanians near the embassy, with crowds demanding that the dictator turn himself over to be tried for **human rights** violations and murder. Noriega finally turned himself in to the Americans on 3 January 1990. He was immediately transported to the United States to stand trial. Noriega was convicted and sentenced on 16 September 1992 to 40 years in prison (in 1999, the sentence was reduced to 30 years).

Americans forces suffered 23 killed and 324 wounded. There were approximately 450 Panamanian soldiers killed and more than 1,000 wounded. In addition, about 300 Panamanian civilians were killed, several thousand injured, and more than 5,000 displaced by the fighting. The U.S. military provided shelter, food, and water for about 3,000 civilians. After the invasion, the Americans disbanded the PDF. U.S. military police remained deployed throughout the year to maintain order while a new police force and national guard were trained.

The Bush administration secured support from its European allies, but there was widespread criticism from developing states. A **United**

Nations (UN) Security Council resolution condemning the invasion was jointly vetoed by France, Great Britain, and the United States. However, the **Organization of American States** adopted a decree on 22 December 1989 criticizing the military action and calling for the withdrawal of U.S. forces. Many in Latin America saw the invasion as another example of Washington's hemispheric hegemony. On 29 December, the UN General Assembly approved a similar measure.

ORANGE REVOLUTION. A series of protests and mass demonstrations in response to electoral fraud during Ukraine's 2004 presidential elections. As a result of the public action, reformist candidate Viktor Yushchenko became president.

In a runoff election on 21 November 2004, there was widespread fraud and voter intimidation. It was also revealed that Yushchenko, who had become seriously ill in September during campaigning in the initial balloting, had been poisoned with dioxin, which left him permanently scarred. It was widely believed that the attempt on Yushchenko's life was committed by supporters of his rival, Viktor Yanukovych. Yushchenko was pro-Western and campaigned for closer ties to Europe and the United States. Yanukovych sought to retain close ties with Moscow and was endorsed by Russian president **Vladimir Putin**.

The first results gave Yanukovych the majority, but international observers roundly denounced the results, and Yushchenko contested the tally. His supporters wore orange ribbons and held daily protests in Kiev, with crowds in excess of 500,000 demonstrators. In addition, a series of strikes and demonstrations occurred throughout Ukraine and a number of local and regional governments, including Kiev's city council, passed symbolic resolutions refusing to recognize the results of the election. Washington and other Western capitals called for new elections. In response to the domestic and international pressure, the Ukrainian Supreme Court annulled the results and ordered a second runoff.

In the new balloting on 26 December 2004, Yushchenko received 52 percent of the vote to Yanukovych's 44 percent. Yushchenko was inaugurated on 23 January 2005 and launched a series of reforms. He also adopted a pro-Western foreign policy, including negotiations on eventual membership for Ukraine in the **North Atlantic Treaty Organization. Neoconservatives** and members of the administration of **George W. Bush** argued that the Orange Revolution signaled a new wave of democratization and was linked to similar transitions in Georgia and Lebanon (the **Cedar Revolution**). However, U.S. support for Yushchenko strained relations with Moscow and eroded the previously close ties between Putin and Bush.

ORGANIZATION FOR SECURITY AND COOPERATION IN EUROPE (OSCE). The only security entity that provides a forum for the states of Europe, the Central Asian republics, the United States, and Canada to discuss political, security, and economic matters. The OSCE evolved from the Conference on Security and Cooperation in Europe (CSCE), an **arms control** mechanism of the **Cold War.** The OSCE's primary tasks are conflict prevention and resolution, dispute management, and the promotion of democracy. Beginning in 1972, the members of the **North Atlantic Treaty Organization (NATO)**, the Warsaw Pact, and neutral European states initiated a series of arms control and confidence-building measures known as the Helsinki Process. In 1973, formal meetings began, dubbed the CSCE. The CSCE culminated in 1975 when 35 heads of state signed the Helsinki Final Act, which created guiding principles for future interaction and discussion. After the Final Act, follow-up meetings of the CSCE were conducted in Belgrade (1978), Madrid (1980–1983), and Vienna (1986–1989).

In 1990, as the Cold War ended, the CSCE signatories met in Paris to discuss adapting and enhancing the conference. The result of the meeting was the Charter of Paris, which called for the institutionalization of the CSCE by creating a formal organization. An administrative structure was created, with a Secretariat and offices in Prague, Vienna, and Warsaw. In April 1991, a Parliamentary Assembly was established. Additional meetings in 1992 led to the creation of the post of secretary-general (the first secretary-general was appointed in June 1993), a ministerial council, and further institutional growth. The CSCE also undertook a number of missions to support peace and democracy in strife-torn regions. By 1994, the CSCE had eight missions under way. At the Budapest Summit in December 1994, the decision was made to rename the body the OSCE.

The OSCE emerged as the preferred pan-European security organization of several powers, including Russia and the neutral states. Russia made several proposals to enhance the power and scope of the OSCE by creating an executive body of the major powers, similar to the **United Nations (UN)** Security Council. While speaking at the launch of the OSCE in Budapest in 1994, Russian president **Boris Yeltsin** warned that, with the Cold War over, a "cold peace" was developing in Europe in which institutions such as NATO would continue to perpetuate the divisions created by the superpower struggle. Meanwhile, both NATO and the **Western European Union** offered their military capabilities to the OSCE to undertake appropriate peace enforcement operations.

The OSCE has 55 members. The Ministerial Council meets annually at the level of foreign ministers. The OSCE's Permanent Council is composed of permanent representatives of each of the member states. Successful preventive diplomatic missions were undertaken in Albania, Moldova, and Georgia. In these instances, the OSCE was able to deploy teams that negotiated ethnic or territorial settlements before widespread conflict broke out.

The OSCE has had less success in efforts to mediate ongoing conflicts. The greatest challenge facing European security was the civil war in the former Yugoslavia. Repeated mediation attempts by the UN and the **European Union** failed to contain the strife, nor did the deployment of peacekeeping troops in the UN mission. NATO air strikes in August 1995 compelled the Serbs to accept the **Dayton Accords**. Under the terms of this agreement, both NATO and the OSCE were given roles in the peace enforcement mission. NATO oversaw the deployment of 60,000 troops, the Implementation Force. The OSCE launched one of its largest operations in Bosnia, numbering more than 200 personnel, and supervised local elections there. It assisted in financing the balloting, trained election officials, certified political parties and candidates, and oversaw the final vote tally.

The subsequent OSCE mission to Kosovo failed to prevent the outbreak of conflict in the province in 1998. The Kosovo mission was the largest yet undertaken by the OSCE, with more than 2,000 personnel. The OSCE monitors sought to verify an end to fighting and supervise free and open elections. Serb paramilitary and government forces harassed and intimidated the OSCE, and the monitors were ultimately withdrawn and the mission declared a failure. Instead, NATO launched a 77-day air campaign to end the hostilities. While successive U.S. administrations have recognized the value of the OSCE in conducting humanitarian missions, the United States has consistently worked to maintain NATO as the cornerstone of transatlantic security and to ensure that the OSCE maintained only a secondary role. *See also* BALKAN WARS; NATION-BUILDING.

ORGANIZATION OF AMERICAN STATES (OAS). A regional security forum for the Western Hemisphere. Headquartered in Washington, D.C., the OAS includes all 35 countries of the region. Cuba remains a member, but its government has been excluded from participation in the organization since 1962. The 1947 Inter-American Treaty of Reciprocal Assistance (the Rio Treaty) created a collective security arrangement for the hemisphere, and the following year, the OAS was formed to carryout the principles of the treaty. During the **Cold War**, the United States endeavored to use the OAS to counter communism and other threats to regional security. In 1962, Cuba was suspended from the organization.

In the 1990s, Washington increasingly turned to the OAS as a means to promote regional **arms control** and efforts to combat **drug trafficking**. In 1994, at a meeting of OAS officials in Buenos Aires, the body agreed to adopt a range of confidence and security-building measures to reduce regional tensions and prevent future conflicts. The following year, at Santiago, Chile, the OAS issued the Declaration on Confidence and Security-Building Measures, which called for a range of initiatives such as giving notification before undertaking military exercises and exchanging information on military spending and weapons procurement. In 1997, the OAS members signed the Inter-American Convention against the Illicit Manufacturing of and Trafficking in Firearms, Ammunition, Explosives, and Other Related Materials, which called upon states to take actions to prevent the illegal arms trade, especially to areas in conflict. The United States and Brazil cooperated to develop the Inter-American Convention on Transparency in Conventional Weapons Acquisitions; signed in 1999 after years of negotiations, this convention requires states to report arms purchases and weapons transfers within 90 days and to file an annual report on the totality of their acquisitions. Through the 1990s, the administration of **William J. Clinton** supported a series of OAS-led operations to remove land mines in countries in the Western Hemisphere and to resolve border disputes between Belize and Guatemala as well as Peru and Ecuador.

As part of the multilateral effort to curb the illicit drug trade, the Inter-American Drug Abuse Control Commission was established in 1986 to offer recommendations to individual member states and co-ordinate national policies. Successive U.S. administrations sought stronger regional measures to control the production and transport of illegal drugs. OAS states agreed on the need to cut drug production levels, but were repeatedly unable to reach agreement on specific counternarcotics programs.

Following the **September 11 terrorist attacks**, the OAS invoked its collective defense clause and offered varying degrees of military and intelligence cooperation to the United States. On 3 June 2002, the OAS also issued the Inter-American Convention against Terrorism, which condemned **international terrorism** and called on member states to cooperate on a variety of levels to prevent terrorist strikes. The convention was followed in October 2003 by the Declaration on Security in the Americas. Most OAS members supported the U.S. global **war on terror**, and several states even contributed troops to the multinational coalition in the occupation after the **Iraq War**. However, Venezuelan leader **Hugo Chávez** led a bloc of member states that opposed more direct support of the United States and de-feated a series of efforts by Washington to forge a more robust coun-terterrorism role for the OAS. Chávez was also able to block U.S. ini-tiatives to create a **Free Trade Area of the Americas** through OAS-sponsored negotiations. *See also* HAITI INTERVENTIONS; OPERATION JUST CAUSE.

ORGANIZATION OF PETROLEUM EXPORTING COUN-TRIES (OPEC). An international cartel that seeks to control the sup-ply and prices of oil and other fuel sources. OPEC was formed in 1960. It currently consists of Algeria, Angola, Indonesia, Iran, Iraq, Kuwait, Libya, Nigeria, Qatar, Saudi Arabia, the United Arab Emi-rates, and Venezuela. OPEC countries account for approximately 65 percent of the world's proven oil reserves and, in 2006, about 40 percent of global oil production. In 1973, in response to the Yom Kippur War, Arab members of OPEC imposed an oil embargo against the West. The embargo led to shortages and inflated prices, but also spurred new exploration and production facilities. By the 1980s, oil production in the Gulf of Mexico and the North Sea had eroded OPEC's market share.

During the Iran-Iraq War (1980–1988), **Saddam Hussein** made repeated but unsuccessful proposals to curb production in order to drive up fuel prices to finance the war. The **Persian Gulf War** led to disruptions in supply and divided the OPEC members. Algeria, Kuwait, Libya, Qatar, Saudi Arabia, and the United Arab Emirates supported the U.S.-led invasion, while Iran and obviously Iraq opposed the American campaign.

Throughout the 1990s, most OPEC states routinely exceeded their quotas. This drove oil prices downward to about $10 per barrel. Venezuelan president **Hugo Chávez** launched a concerted effort to convince OPEC heads of state to cut production in order to increase revenues. In 1998, OPEC lowered quotas, and the members made at least some effort to meet the new levels. Oil prices began to increase and were driven higher by increasing demand from developing states such as India and the People's Republic of China. Hurricanes in the Gulf of Mexico in 2004 and 2005 damaged facilities and created further energy inflation. By 2006, oil prices had risen to record highs above $70 per barrel.

The relevance of OPEC declined in the 2000s as Russia became the world's largest supplier of oil and new sources of petroleum were discovered in Africa and Asia. In addition, under pressure from the United States (and in an effort to boost revenues), some OPEC members, including Algeria, Kuwait, Libya, Qatar, Saudi Arabia, and the United Arab Emirates, routinely exceeded their quotas and pumped oil at their full capacities. Meanwhile, Iran and Venezuela cut production below their quotas in an effort to offset the other members, while Indonesia and Nigeria were unable to meet their limits because of declining production and internal instability. After the fall of the Saddam regime, Iraq was not given an official quota and was allowed to pump at full capacity (although the insurgency limited its production).

The rise in oil prices led the administration of **George W. Bush** to propose new domestic exploration and increase funding for alternative energy development. However, the administration failed to develop a comprehensive energy policy as had been done in the 1970s during the previous major oil crisis. The U.S. government also undertook a variety of initiatives to support American companies that were seeking to develop oil fields in the Central Asian republics and areas of Africa, especially as China undertook an aggressive policy of securing long-term oil contracts. In 2006, the top two oil exporters to the United States were non-OPEC states Canada and Mexico, followed by OPEC members Saudi Arabia, Venezuela, Nigeria, Angola, and Iraq.

OTTAWA TREATY (MINE BAN TREATY). The Convention on the Prohibition of the Use, Stockpiling, Production, and Transfer of Antipersonnel Mines and on their Destruction (commonly known as the "Ottawa" or "Mine Ban" Treaty) prohibits the use and stockpiling of antipersonnel land mines. Negotiations over the treaty began in 1992 after the end of the **Cold War**. Civilians in many countries have been killed or injured by mines left over from conflicts during the superpower struggle. Banning such weapons became a worldwide cause through the efforts of Princess Diana of Great Britain, who publicized the destruction and personal tragedies associated with mines. The Mine Ban Treaty was finalized during a convention in Ottawa, Canada, on 3–4 December 1997 under the auspices of the **United Nations (UN)**. While the accord banned the use of the weapons, states were allowed to retain a small number of mines for training and military research purposes (mainly to develop tactics to counter the use of mines in future conflicts). States have to declare their intention to take the exemption to use mines for research and then inform the UN of the total number of mines in their stockpile. By 2006, 64 signatory countries had utilized the exemption. The treaty did not prohibit the use of other types of mines, including antitank mines or naval mines.

The accord came into force in 1998, following ratification by the 40th signatory. By 2006, 155 countries had signed the measure and 74 states had destroyed their stockpiles of antipersonnel land mines. More than 160 million mines had been destroyed through 2006. The United States, the People's Republic of China, India, and Russia did not sign the agreement. Successive American administrations have argued that the ban undermined U.S. strategy on the Korean Peninsula, where land mines were an integral component of deterrence against an attack by Pyongyang. Both the administrations of **William J. Clinton** and **George W. Bush** affirmed a willingness to sign the treaty if the United States were granted an exemption to use mines in South Korea. The United States and other countries have also developed and deployed a new class of land mines that can be used as antipersonnel devices but which are technically allowed under the treaty. *See also* ARMS CONTROL.

– P –

PAN AM FLIGHT 103 BOMBING. On 21 December 1988, a terrorist bomb exploded aboard Pan Am Flight 103 over Lockerbie, Scotland, killing 270 people. The attack was the deadliest terrorist attack on U.S. citizens until the **September 11 terrorist attacks**. On 5 December, the U.S. Embassy in Helsinki had received a warning that terrorists would blow up a Pan Am flight within a two-week period. The State Department warned embassies and airlines throughout Europe. However, airline screeners failed to take significant additional security measures. The explosive device, hidden in the luggage, detonated at around 7:00 P.M. and tore a hole in the fuselage, which then caused the Boeing 747 to disintegrate and killed all 16 crew members and 243 passengers. The forensic investigation later determined that about one pound of Semtex, a plastic explosive, had been used. The destruction was such that debris was spread over more than 845 square miles (2,189 square kilometers). Eleven people on the ground were killed when the wings, still filled with fuel, struck the earth and exploded, destroying several houses.

A range of groups claimed responsibility for the attack, but investigators traced the bombing to Libyan intelligence agencies and discovered that the incident was probably in response to U.S. military strikes against Libya in 1986. Fragments of the bomb were traced to purchases made by Abdelbaset Ali Mohmed al Megrahi, a Libyan intelligence officer. The explosive had been placed aboard the airplane in an unaccompanied piece of luggage that had originated from Luqa International Airport in Malta. Al Amin Khalifah Fhimah, a manager for Libyan Airlines, was initially suspected of involvement and was cited as the figure who arranged for the explosives-laden suitcase to be placed on the Pan Am flight. Megrahi and Fhimah were indicted for murder and an international manhunt undertaken. Both were placed in custody in Libya, but **Muammar Gaddafi** refused to turn them over for trial by the United States or Great Britain. Gaddafi offered to try the two in Libya, but his offer was rejected.

In 1994, South African president **Nelson R. Mandela** proposed his country as a neutral site for the trial, but again British prime minister John Major rejected the proposal, and President **William J. Clinton** deferred to London. In 1997, Mandela launched a new round of diplomacy to resolve the impasse. After the election of **Tony Blair**, Clinton and the new British prime minister agreed to accept a compromise proposal through which the two suspects would be transferred and tried at The Hague, in the Netherlands, under Scottish law by a Scottish court. The suspects were turned over in 1999, and the trial began in 2000. The two were charged with murder, conspiracy to commit murder, and violations of air security laws. The trial lasted 35 weeks. Fhimah was found innocent on all charges. Megrahi was found guilty of all charges and sentenced to life imprisonment. Megrahi appealed his conviction, but the appeal was denied in 2002.

In return for turning over the two suspects, UN sanctions imposed against Libya after the bombing were suspended in 1999. As part of the resolution to the attack, Gaddafi agreed to pay $2.7 billion to the 270 families who lost loved ones in the bombing. In addition, in 2003 the Libyan government, in a letter to the UN, accepted responsibility for the terrorist strike. That year, the suspended sanctions were permanently repealed. The United States also ended trade sanctions that had been imposed in the 1980s. Libya subsequently paid the families $8 million each. However, a further $2 million per victim that had been promised was withdrawn when Washington refused to remove Libya from the State Department list of countries that were state sponsors of terrorism. In May 2006, Libya was removed from the list and the United States restored full diplomatic relations with the country. *See also* INTERNATIONAL TERRORISM.

PARTNERSHIP FOR PEACE (PfP). Created in 1994, the Partnership for Peace program was developed as a means to provide non-**North Atlantic Treaty Organization (NATO)** states the ability to undertake military training with alliance forces and to participate in the operations of the organization. It was part of the broader effort by the **William J. Clinton** administration to ensure that NATO stayed relevant after the end of the **Cold War** and remained the principal transatlantic security organization. PfP allowed non-NATO states to take part in the range of alliance activities, including training exercises, academic meetings, military exchanges, political forums, and general defense collaboration. It also provided a means for aspiring NATO members to work closely with the alliance. All of the post–Cold War new NATO members were at one time PfP participants, and this fact created the perception that the program was a first step toward NATO membership. PfP also served as a means to increase cooperation with Russia. The program has been very successful, and at its height included 26 members (10 subsequently joined NATO as full members). During the peace operations in the former Yugoslavia, more than a dozen PfP states, including Russia, provided troops and assets to support the NATO-led missions. *See also* BALKAN WARS; NATO ENLARGEMENT; NATO EXPANSION.

PATRIOT ACT (2001). U.S. law enacted in the aftermath of the **September 11 terrorist attacks** in order to improve **homeland security** in the United States. The Uniting and Strengthening America by Providing Appropriate Tools Required to Intercept and Obstruct Terrorists Act, commonly known by its acronym the USA PATRIOT Act or simply the Patriot Act, contained a series of provisions to enhance the authority of law enforcement and security agencies in the United States to investigate, detain, and prosecute suspected terrorists. The Act was modeled on existent laws designed for use against organized crime. Specifically, the Patriot Act

- increased and expanded the penalties for terrorism
- eliminated some civil liberties protections for those under investigation
- authorized the government to obtain warrants from a special court, the Foreign Intelligence Surveillance Court, instead of common criminal bodies
- expanded the surveillance ability of law enforcement
- mandated greater information sharing and cooperation between law enforcement agencies and the nation's intelligence services

- strengthened the ability of the government to freeze terrorist assets and investigate money laundering
- called for improvements to border security

The legislation was passed by the House of Representatives on a vote of 357 to 66, and by the Senate 98 to 1. President **George W. Bush** signed the bill on 26 October 2001.

The Act's infringements on civil liberties were seen as necessary in a period of conflict, but Congress set time limits on some of its more controversial aspects (these sections expired in 2005). In addition, several parts of the law were declared unconstitutional, including provisions that required Internet service providers and libraries to turn over records without a warrant. The Patriot Act was strongly opposed by civil libertarian groups such as the American Civil Liberties Union. State and local governments also opposed some of the requirements of the Act under which they were forced to increase surveillance and reporting to the federal government. Opponents contended that the stipulations created an undue burden on state and local law enforcement agencies. The effort to renew those provisions of the Act set to expire in 2005 was contentious. Congress was unable to renew the measures within the time frame and instead enacted an extension in March on votes of 280–138 in the House and 89–11 in the Senate. *See also* INTERNATIONAL TERRORISM; WAR ON TERROR.

PEACE DIVIDEND. Following the end of the **Cold War**, most nations dramatically reduced their military expenditures, which allowed governments to redirect resources into social and economic spending in what was commonly referred to as the "peace dividend." The peace dividend did not impact all countries equally or in the same manner. Many nations, including the United States, experienced an economic recession as defense industries downsized and merged in an increasingly competitive market. In addition, reductions in military personnel put large numbers of new workers into the economy. American defense spending declined during the administrations of **George H. W. Bush** and **William J. Clinton**, from $376.2 billion in 1989 to $316.5 billion in 1991 and $272.1 billion in 1995. Meanwhile, there were increases in social programs, led by entitlements such as Social Security, Medicare, and Medicaid. However, by the late 1990s, the peace dividend had largely dissipated. The Clinton administration increased defense spending to $305 billion in 1998 and continued to expand expenditures thereafter (it was $396 billion for fiscal year 2001). **Operation Enduring Freedom** and the **war on terror** led the administration of President **George W. Bush** to dramatically increase defense spending to $470 billion per year by 2006. *See also* ARMS SALES AND WEAPONS TRANSFERS; DEFENSE SPENDING AND ALLIANCE BURDEN SHARING; MILITARY-INDUSTRIAL COMPLEX; QUADRENNIAL DEFENSE REVIEW.

PEARL, DANIEL (1963–2002). American journalist who was kidnapped and killed in Pakistan while investigating **Al Qaeda**. Pearl began working for the *Wall Street Journal* in 1990 and was in Pakistan in 2002 working on a story about the "shoe bomber," Richard Reid. On 23 January 2002, while on his way to interview a terrorist figure, Pearl was kidnapped by a group calling itself the National Movement for the Restoration of Pakistani Sovereignty. The kidnappers alleged that Pearl was a Central Intelligence Agency agent and made a range of demands, including the release of jailed terrorists and the cessation of U.S. military aid to Pakistan. On 21 February, a video was released showing his captors decapitating Pearl. His mutilated body was subsequently discovered on 16 May, outside of Karachi. The Federal Bureau of Investigation worked with Pakistani authorities to find Pearl's kidnappers and was able to trace the email addresses used by three of his captors to release information. Four suspects were caught in March by Pakistani law enforcement. On 15 July, all four were convicted of kidnapping and murder. Ahmed Omar Saeed Sheikh, the leader of the group, was sentenced to death. *See also* INTERNATIONAL TERRORISM; WAR ON TERROR.

PELOSI, NANCY P. (1940–). The first woman to lead a major U.S. political party in Congress and the first female Speaker of the House of Representatives. Born Nancy Patricia D'Alesandro in Baltimore, Maryland, she moved to San Francisco after she married. Pelosi was elected to the House of Representatives in 1987. Two year later, she sponsored the Pelosi Amendment, which required that international financial organizations, including the **World Bank** and the **International Monetary Fund**, carry out environmental studies to assess the impact of their programs on local ecologies or lose U.S. funding. In the 1990s, Pelosi became known as a staunch critic of the **human rights** record of the People's Republic of China. She opposed the policy of the administration of President **William J. Clinton** that decoupled **trade policy** from human rights. Pelosi was also a vocal proponent of Tibetan independence. Pelosi supported **Operation Enduring Freedom** and voted for the 2001 **Patriot Act**. However, she opposed the 2003 **Iraq War**.

Democrat Pelosi was elected minority whip in 2001 and minority leader in 2004. As leader of her party in Congress, Pelosi reversed the strategy of cooperation with the administration of President **George W. Bush** and was increasingly critical of Bush's **homeland security** policies and management of the war in Iraq. In 2006, Pelosi endeavored to force the administration to establish a timetable for withdrawal of U.S. forces from Iraq. During the 2006 midterm elections, the Democrats regained control of the House of Representatives, and Pelosi was elected Speaker. *See also* HASTERT, J. DENNIS.

PERLE, RICHARD N. (1941–). Prominent **neoconservative** intellectual and public official. Richard Norman Perle was born in New York City. He obtained a master's degree in political science from Princeton University in 1967 and then worked as an advisor to Democratic senator Henry "Scoop" Jackson, a staunch anticommunist and proponent of a large military budget, from 1969 to 1980. Perle became noted for his opposition to **arms control**. In 1981, he was appointed assistant secretary of defense for international security in the administration of President **Ronald W. Reagan**, a post he held until 1987. For the next seven years, Perle served on the Defense Policy Board Advisory Committee (DPBAC), a federal body charged to make recommendations on defense and security policy. Through the 1990s, Perle advocated regime change in Iraq, and he was one of the most vocal proponents of the 2003 **Iraq War**. He opposed the Army's requests for a larger troop contingent prior to the invasion and asserted that **Saddam Hussein** could be toppled with 40,000 soldiers (as opposed to the 250,000 requested by the military). Perle subsequently criticized the management of the Iraq insurgency and left the DPBAC in 2004. *See also* INTERNATIONAL TERROR-ISM; WAR ON TERROR.

PERRY, WILLIAM J. (1927–). Second secretary of defense in the administration of **William J. Clinton**. William James Perry was born in Vandergrift, Pennsylvania, and received a doctorate in mathematics from Pennsylvania State University in 1957. Perry had a successful career in business before he was appointed as undersecretary of defense in the administration of President **James E. Carter**. In 1993, he was again appointed undersecretary of defense, this time in the Clinton administration. When Secretary of Defense **Leslie Aspin Jr.** resigned in 1994, Clinton appointed Perry to replace him. Perry emphasized counterproliferation as one of his main priorities and worked to maintain the centrality of the **North Atlantic Treaty Organization (NATO)** to transatlantic security. He sparred with Clinton over defense cuts, but oversaw the reduction of the military by 85,000 troops, bringing the force total down to 1.52 million, the lowest level since the 1940s. Perry also implemented a number of reforms to the Pentagon's procurement system to streamline purchases and reduce redundancy and waste.

Unlike his predecessor, Perry supported U.S. military intervention in the **Bosnian Conflict**. In 1995, American troops began deployment as apart of a NATO-led peacekeeping mission. In 1996, a U.S. military facility in Saudi Arabia was attacked by terrorists in the **Khobar Towers bombing**. The attack, which left 19 dead and more than 500 wounded, forced the Pentagon to revise base security procedures and emphasized the growing threat of **international terrorism** to U.S. interests. Perry opposed military intervention during the **Rwandan genocide**, but supported stern measures against Pyongyang during the **North Korean nuclear crisis**. Perry announced his resignation in 1996, declaring he was uncomfortable putting U.S. forces in harm's way. He was succeeded by **William S. Cohen**. After leaving office, Perry returned to private life, joining the faculty of Stanford University and serving on a variety of advisory boards.

PERSIAN GULF WAR (1991). The Persian Gulf War was fought between Iraq and a coalition of nations led by the United States. The conflict began with the 2 August 1990 invasion of Kuwait by approximately 120,000 Iraqi troops and 2,000 tanks. Before the end of the week, the Kuwaiti armed forces were overrun, with the exception of a substantial portion of the air force that managed to escape to Saudi Arabia, and **Saddam Hussein** had declared Kuwait the 19th province of Iraq.

Throughout the 1980s, Iraq had accumulated a substantial debt from its 1980–1988 war with Iran and the continuing policy of the regime to maintain a substantial military infrastructure, the largest in the region. In an effort to relieve this debt, Iraq attempted to negotiate production limitations in the **Organization of Petroleum Exporting Countries** and debt rescheduling schedules. However, the Gulf States began to increase production rates beyond agreed-upon limits and Iraq drifted deeper into financial difficulties. The annexation of Kuwait was seen as a way to provide Saddam with control of a substantial portion of the world's oil reserves and the means to pay down Iraq's debt while still maintaining its military.

President **George H. W. Bush** understood that control of Kuwait represented a vital interest to the United States. Furthermore, Iraqi expansion threatened the key U.S. ally in the region, Saudi Arabia. With Kuwait conquered, Baghdad massed troops along the Kuwaiti-Saudi border, prompting fears of further Iraqi attacks. Bush set about organizing a multinational coalition of nations to oppose Saddam. Bush and Secretary of State **James A. Baker III** conducted a furious round of diplomacy to garner international support. Bush and Baker were able to secure the support of Russia, the former Cold War nemesis of the United States, as well as a range of Middle East states, including Egypt and Syria, and the Persian Gulf states, which provided troops. America's main European allies provided troops and logistical support, and on 10 August, the **North Atlantic Treaty Organization** offered support to the coalition and stationed troops to cover forces deployed to the Persian Gulf. The **coalition of the willing** eventually included Afghanistan, Argentina, Australia, Bahrain, Bangladesh, Canada, Czechoslovakia, Denmark, Egypt, France, Germany, Greece, Honduras, Hungary, Italy, Kuwait, Morocco, the Netherlands, Niger, Norway, Oman, Pakistan, Poland, Portugal, Qatar, Saudi Arabia, Senegal, South Korea, Spain, Syria, Turkey, the United Arab Emirates, and the United Kingdom, along with the United States. In addition, India allowed the United States to use refueling stations in the Indian Ocean. Bush ordered U.S. forces into the region in Operation Desert Shield, in which some 230,000 American and coalition troops deployed to defend Saudi Arabia.

The **United Nations (UN)** Security Council adopted a number of measures repudiating Saddam's invasion and implementing a range of punitive actions designed to force the withdrawal of Iraqi forces. UN Security Council Resolution (UNSCR) 660, passed on 2 August 1990, condemned the invasion and demanded the withdrawal of Iraqi forces. UNSCR 661 imposed economic sanctions upon Iraq, while nine subsequent resolutions also addressed Iraq. Finally, on 29 November 1990, UNSCR 668 set a deadline of 15 January 1991 for Iraqi withdrawal, after which the Saddam regime would face military action.

By January, coalition troops from 34 states, including approximately 540,000 U.S. troops (70 percent of the total force), were positioned for the liberation of Kuwait. The allied strategy was coordinated by Gen. **Colin Powell**, the chairman of the U.S. Joint Chiefs of Staff, and Secretary of Defense **Richard B. Cheney**.

On 17 January, Operation Desert Storm commenced with an air campaign. The allies quickly established air superiority, which they maintained throughout the conflict. By the end of the war, coalition air units would fly more than 116,000 sorties in a campaign that highlighted American precision-guided weapons and demonstrated the superiority of U.S. weaponry.

Iraqi forces intentionally released more than a million tons of crude oil into the Persian Gulf to prevent a naval landing. They also set hundreds of oil wells on fire. On 24 February, coalition forces launched a ground offensive. Iraq launched Scud missiles at coalition bases and at Israel in an effort to broaden the conflict and create divisions among the allies. Nevertheless, Allied forces quickly liberated Kuwait and drove Iraqi forces back across the border. Coalition air units continued to attack retreating Iraqi forces. Thousands of Iraqi soldiers where killed on the so-called Highway of Death when they packed a roadway during their retreat and allied aircraft were easily able to target them. The allied ground units pursued the retreating Iraqis across the border and came within 150 miles of Baghdad before withdrawing. President Bush ordered a cease-fire on 27 February, and Iraqi leaders accepted the terms of the cease-fire on 3 March 1991.

During the fighting, coalition forces lost 345 dead and more than 1,000 wounded, while Iraqi casualties were estimated to be approximately 20,000 dead and between 70,000 and 80,000 wounded. There were about 2,300 Iraqi civilian casualties and an estimated 5,000–8,000 Kuwaiti casualties during the original invasion. In addition, coalition forces captured some 71,000 Iraqis. The war cost the allies about $71 billion. The Gulf states provided $36 billion to cover the costs of the conflict, while Germany and Japan, both constitutionally forbidden from deploying military forces except for defensive operations, contributed $16 billion. In the aftermath of the conflict, a large number of veterans on both sides suffered from a range of debilitating illnesses that came to be known collectively as Gulf War Syndrome.

Under the terms of the cease-fire, Iraq had to allow UN-supervised weapons inspections, but Saddam remained in power. Kurds in northern Iraq and Shiites in southern Iraq rose in rebellion against the regime, supported by Western intelligence agencies, but the rebellions were brutally suppressed. In April 1991, the UN Security Council adopted UNSCR 688, which was used to justify the creation of no-fly zones over northern and southern Iraq. In 1992, France and the United States launched air strikes to end Iraqi offensives against the Kurds. The no-fly zones were subsequently enforced by the Americans and the British. *See also* IRAQ WAR.

PHILIPPINES HOSTAGE CRISIS. On 27 May 2001, terrorists of the **Al Qaeda**–linked Abu Sayyaf Group took 13 tourists and three workers hostage from a resort on the island of Palawan in the Philippines. Among those seized were three Americans: Guillermo Sobero and a missionary couple, Martin and Gracia Burnham. The captives were taken to Basilan Island.

Abu Sayyaf was formed in 1990 after its founder, Abdurajik Abubakar Janjalani, was given $6 million by **Osama bin Laden** to create an Islamic terrorist group among the Muslim population of the Philippines. The kidnappings were part of a broader campaign undertaken by the group to gain financial resources through ransoming captives. More than 30 foreigners and 50 Filipinos had been taken by the group over a two-year period prior to the 2001 incident. Although the Philippine government refused to pay ransom, Abu Sayyaf received approximately $5.5 million from foreign governments, business firms, and families for the release of foreign hostages. In addition, Libyan leader **Muammar Gaddafi** agreed to pay $25 million in 2000 for the release of hostages in an effort to improve his international standing, although the administration of **William J. Clinton** charged that the Libyan payment was made not for altruistic reasons but simply as a means to fund the terrorist group.

On 1–3 June 2001, Philippine security forces attacked the main Abu Sayyaf base on Basilan. During the fighting, nine of the hostages escaped, but two were killed by their captors. Abu Sayyaf subsequently captured additional 15 hostages, including children, at a hospital in the town of Lamitan. On 12 June, the terrorists killed Sobero. He was tortured and beheaded. In July, Philippine security forces captured one of Abu Sayyaf's top leaders and three other terrorists.

To support Manila's counterterrorism campaign, the United States undertook a major joint military exercise with the Philippine armed forces in December. In January 2002, 660 American special operations troops and military advisors were deployed in the Philippines to train and assist the country's security forces. The Americans were not allowed to engage in combat, but with U.S. support, Philippine security forces launched a six-month campaign to suppress the terrorists and free the remaining hostages. On 25 March 2002, Abu Sayyaf offered to release some of the hostages in exchange for a cease-fire and medical supplies. On 7 June 2002, Martin Burnham and another hostage were killed during a rescue attempt. His wife, Gracia, was injured but freed. *See also* INTERNATIONAL TERRORISM; WAR ON TERROR.

PLAN COLOMBIA. An initiative of the administration of **William J. Clinton** that aimed to improve Colombia's ability to curtail **drug trafficking** through military aid and training, as well as to diversify the country's economy. By the late 1990s, Colombia had become the main exporter of cocaine and other drugs to the United States. The Clinton administration sought to develop a program for Colombia mirroring the post–World War II Marshall Plan, albeit on a smaller scale, that would improve the country's security forces and reduce its drug economy. The initiative had its roots in an August 1998 meeting between Clinton and President Andres Pastrana, at which Clinton pledged a significant increase in U.S. aid. A central goal of Plan Colombia was to bolster the nation's military so that it could defeat the main rebel group, the Revolutionary Armed Forces of Columbia (Fuerzas Armadas Revolucionarias de Colombia, FARC), which controlled about 25 percent of the country.

The initial plan called for $1.3 billion in economic and military aid in 2000, with additional expenditures in subsequent years. Colombia became the third largest recipient of American foreign aid. Initially, 55 percent was to be designated in security assistance and the remainder in development aid. However, military assistance quickly grew as a proportion of the total funding, reaching 78 percent of expenditures in 2000. In addition to weaponry, Washington also deployed 500 soldiers to train the Colombian forces. Backed by U.S. funding, the Colombian government launched a coca eradication initiative that included aerial spraying. More than 1,000 square miles (2,600 square kilometers) of the crops were destroyed. In addition, FARC fighters were pushed back in several areas, although both FARC and right-wing militias committed a range of atrocities against local populations.

Following the inauguration of **George W. Bush**, Plan Colombia was superseded by the **Andean Counterdrug Initiative**. However, Colombia continued to receive the majority of antidrug funding ($380 million in 2001, rising to $463 million in 2004).

POWELL, COLIN (1937–). America's senior military officer during the 1991 **Persian Gulf War** and secretary of state in the first administration of **George W. Bush**. Powell was born in New York to Jamaican immigrant parents. He earned a degree in geology from the City College of New York in 1958 and was commissioned in the U.S. Army. Powell served two tours in Vietnam and was wounded and decorated for bravery. He subsequently served in a variety of military and politico-military posts. In 1987, Powell, then a lieutenant general, was appointed national security advisor to President **Ronald W. Reagan**. Promoted to general, Powell was named chairman of the Joint Chiefs of Staff by President **George H. W. Bush**. As chairman, he continued the transformation of the U.S. military from its **Cold War** strategy and posture. Powell oversaw the 1989 invasion of Panama, designated **Operation Just Cause**, and the Persian Gulf

War. The general deftly managed a broad-based military coalition of states with differing capabilities and goals. Powell refined the Weinberger Doctrine to create the Weinberger-Powell Doctrine (commonly known as the **Powell Doctrine**), which emphasized the use of overwhelming force and a clearly defined exit strategy.

Powell left government service in 1993 and became active as a philanthropist. In 1994, he undertook a mission to **Haiti** to restore democracy. In 1996, moderate Republicans endeavored to draft Powell for a presidential bid, but the former general declined to campaign after conservatives within the party vocally opposed the general's stance on issues such as abortion and affirmative action. In 2000, Powell served as a foreign policy advisor to candidate **George W. Bush**. Bush subsequently appointed Powell as the nation's first African-American secretary of state. Powell emerged as the leader of the moderate faction within the Bush administration's foreign and security policy officials. He generally advocated diplomacy and negotiation, with military action as a last resort. Powell's ideological opposites in the administration were Vice President **Richard B. Cheney** and Secretary of State **Donald H. Rumsfeld**. In the aftermath of the **September 11 terrorist attacks**, Powell was instrumental in creating the multinational **coalition of the willing** and garnering international support for **Operation Enduring Freedom**. The former general was particularly important in convincing the **North Atlantic Treaty Organization** to invoke its collective defense clause, which required all allies to come to the aid of the United States. The secretary of state also managed the effort at the **United Nations (UN)** to secure the deployment of a post-Taliban peacekeeping force in **Afghanistan**. Meanwhile, Powell worked to modernize the State Department by updating equipment and technology and refurbishing embassies and consulates.

In 2002, Powell was tasked to build a new coalition of the willing to support a U.S.-led invasion of Iraq. This time, he was able to develop only a reduced coalition that included America's main traditional allies, including Australia, Great Britain, Japan, and the Netherlands, and the newly democratized states of Eastern Europe such as Bulgaria, the Czech Republic, and Poland. The secretary was able to counter the hawks in the administration and convince Bush to endeavor to gain a UN resolution to support military action. However, the inability to secure a resolution marked a diplomatic defeat for Powell, whose influence waned following the 2003 **Iraq War**. His efforts to gather support to rebuild Iraq and deploy an international post-conflict peacekeeping force were only partially successful.

Powell supported intelligence reform initiatives, including the creation of a single office to oversee the country's intelligence agencies, the director of national intelligence. He clashed with Cheney and Rumsfeld over the treatment of detainees captured during the **war on terror**. Differences over Iraq policy and Powell's reduced influence within the administration after Iraq led to his resignation in 2004. After leaving office, Powell retired from public life, although he opposed the nomination of **John R. Bolton** as the nation's ambassador to the UN in 2005. *See also* INTERNATIONAL TERRORISM; NEOCONSERVATIVES; TRADE POLICY.

POWELL DOCTRINE. The Powell Doctrine was a series of policy guidelines developed by then chairman of the Joint Chiefs of Staff **Colin Powell** in 1990 to guide the use of military action. The origins of the doctrine were based in an earlier set of informal rules developed by Secretary of Defense Caspar Weinberger during the administration of President **Ronald W. Reagan**. The Powell Doctrine asserted that military action should be undertaken only when several conditions have been met:

1. A vital national interest must be threatened.
2. All other means to resolve the crisis have to be exhausted.
3. The costs and benefits must have been fully explored and the benefits have to clearly outweigh the costs of inaction.
4. Planners should have a clear objective that delineates victory and a well-defined exit strategy.
5. There needs to be public support for the military option. U.S. domestic approval is critical, but international endorsement should also be gained whenever possible.
6. The United States has to be able to bring overwhelming force to bear against the enemy to minimize American casualties.

The first application of the Powell Doctrine was in the 1991 **Persian Gulf War**. In contrast, the military debacle during the 1993 **Somalia intervention** was seen as a lesson of the potential for failure when the Powell Doctrine was not utilized. The doctrine was criticized for constraining U.S. policy in the 1994 **Rwandan genocide**. Although Powell was secretary of state at the time, the **George W. Bush** administration did not apply the doctrine to the 2003 **Iraq War**, since it did not identify a clear exit strategy that would facilitate the withdrawal of U.S. forces.

PUTIN, VLADIMIR (1952–). President of Russia since 1999 who strengthened the powers of the presidency and endeavored to use the country's energy wealth to maintain Russia's global influence. Vladimir Vladimirovich Putin was born in St. Petersburg (then Leningrad). He graduated from Leningrad State University in 1975 and joined the Soviet secret police, the KGB. He was stationed in East Germany for five years, beginning in 1985, and was exposed to the lifestyle and culture of the West through his activities. The experience undermined his faith in the Soviet government, especially during the collapse of East Germany. In 1990, Putin returned to Russia and was appointed dean for international affairs at Leningrad State University. He resigned from the KGB during the abortive **Soviet coup** of 1991.

In 1994, Putin was appointed first deputy mayor of Saint Petersburg. Two years later, he moved to Moscow to accept a position in the State Property Administration. Putin attracted the attention of President **Boris N. Yeltsin,** who made Putin his chief of staff and in 1998 appointed him to be director of the Federal Security Service (the successor organization to the KGB). In 1999, Yeltsin named Putin prime minister. In this role, Putin helped convince Yeltsin of the importance of deploying Russian troops as part of the peacekeeping mission in Kosovo in order to maintain Moscow's influence in the region.

Putin subsequently emerged as Yeltsin's handpicked successor. Yeltsin resigned on 31 December 1999, and Putin became president. Putin granted the former president immunity from prosecution, leading many to suggest that Yeltsin's actions were motivated by his desire to avoid criminal charges. Putin called for elections in 2000 and won the March polling with the support of the Unity (*Edinstvo*) political grouping, the largest political faction in the Duma (parliament). While most of Yeltsin's inner circle remained in power under the new president, Putin increasingly demonstrated his independence from his predecessor by appointing his own people to senior positions and implementing new policies.

Putin initially concentrated on suppressing the rebellion in Chechnya. His approach was domestically popular, but a series of high-profile terrorist acts undermined the government. In 2002, Chechen separatists seized a Moscow theater and 800 hostages; at least 117 hostages died when security forces stormed the building. In 2004, rebels took control of a school and 1,500 schoolchildren in Beslan. More than 340 civilians, including 186 children, were killed during that incident.

Domestically, Putin endeavored to implement economic reforms and strengthen the authority of the president. He relied on a group of prominent economic reformers and demonstrated an openness toward reform that his predecessor lacked. Putin revised the nation's inefficient tax code by creating a flat 13 percent income tax and introducing a value-added tax and excise duties. Putin also brought the three large utility monopolies back under state control. The government takeover of Gazprom, the giant gas and oil company, led to charges of corruption and claims that Putin authorized the action solely to gain access to the enormous cash reserves of the company. State ownership of the railroads and national electric utility were less controversial. Putin also introduced reforms to the judiciary and the Duma. Regional governments were granted broad new autonomy.

Putin increased Russia's security budget and strengthened the power and authority of the state security agencies. He also continued to emphasize nuclear weapons as deterrence from conventional attack. Initially perceived as more nationalistic and less pro-Western than Yeltsin, Putin's foreign policy was actually based on pragmatism. He worked to maintain Russia's role as a major power. After the **September 11 terrorist attacks**, Putin offered support to the United States. Russia shared intelligence with the United States about Afghanistan and transferred weapons to the anti-Taliban Northern Alliance. Putin further accepted the establishment of U.S. military bases in the Central Asian republics in a move that surprised many senior Russian officials. He also subsequently accepted the U.S. withdrawal from the Antiballistic Missile Treaty.

Despite public opposition, Putin accepted the **NATO expansion** in 2004 and negotiated a closer working relationship between Russia and its **Cold War** nemesis. Putin opposed the 2003 **Iraq War**, but was less public in his criticism than the leaders of traditional American allies France and Germany. However, Putin supported the lifting of economic sanctions on Iraq after the fall of the regime of **Saddam Hussein**. He also worked with the United States and the **European Union** on disarmament, including the reduction of Russia's arsenal of weapons of mass destruction.

Putin sought to maintain and even bolster Russian influence in Ukraine and Belarus. In the 2004 Ukrainian elections, he openly supported the losing pro-Russian candidate during what became known as the **Orange Revolution**. Meanwhile, Putin used his control of the state media to great impact during Russia's own presidential elections. Higher energy prices had increased revenues for the Russian government (and confirmed the utility of the Gazprom takeover for many Russians), which allowed Putin to increase social spending. His hard-line policy toward Chechnya remained popular, as well. Nonetheless, the president was criticized for the increasing violence in Russian society. There were several high-profile murders of journalists and repression of the press. In addition, Putin failed to take strong action to combat organized crime, which had become widespread and entrenched. Yet, most Russians approved of his first-term performance. Putin won the balloting with 71 percent of the vote in generally free and open elections.

During his second term, Putin concentrated on improving relations with Europe. In 2005, he negotiated an agreement to build an oil pipeline from Russia to Germany across the Baltic Sea. Putin also sought membership for Russia in the **World Trade Organization**. The most significant area of tension between Europe and Russia continued to be Putin's management of the Chechen crisis. European leaders condemned Putin's **human rights** record in the separatist republic and urged the president to negotiate an end to the conflict. The president was also criticized following the deaths of several prominent critics of his regime, including Alexander Litvinenko, a former military officer who died in London in 2006 from exposure to radioactive materials in his food. Meanwhile, Putin became increasingly critical of U.S. foreign policy. In February 2007, the president condemned U.S. unilateralism and NATO expansion in a major policy speech in Munich. Putin also warned of a new

Cold War in response to Washington's closer security ties with the states of central and eastern Europe.

– Q –

QUADRENNIAL DEFENSE REVIEW (QDR). A reevaluation of U.S. defense policy undertaken every four years. The QDR was mandated by Congress in 1996 as a means to ensure that the country's military will have the capabilities and resources to protect and defend America and its interests abroad. The first QDR, published in 1997 under Secretary of Defense **William S. Cohen**, called for a reallocation of defense resources and recognized that military expenditures were likely to be reduced in the near-term future. Force structures were to be reduced and more funds devoted to weapons research and procurement. Specifically, the QDR called for the development of re-action forces that could be rapidly deployed anywhere in the world to deal with the growing range of security missions, including humanitarian and crisis response operations. It also called for improvements in technology and information capabilities so that the U.S. military would achieve "full spectrum dominance"—the ability to deploy overwhelming force in any engagement while maintaining advantages in intelligence, communications, and information delivery. The QDR maintained the **Cold War** objective of winning two major theater engagements simultaneously, anywhere in the world.

The next QDR was published in the aftermath of the **September 11 terrorist attacks**. Under the direction of Secretary of Defense **Donald H. Rumsfeld**, the 2001 QDR retained the goal of successfully fighting two concurrent major theater campaigns while conducting a number of minor operations as necessary. The report called for new investments in technology and embraced **ballistic missile defense**. It further called for greater cooperation and integration between the branches of the military to improve joint operations. At the core of the 2001 QDR was the call for a transition away from Cold War weapons systems, including long-range bombers and missile systems, toward more capabilities for special operations and a renewed emphasis on protecting the American homeland.

The next QDR was not published until 2006. The 2006 report emphasized increases in special operations capabilities in order to conduct counterterrorism operations. In doing so, it endeavored to apply the lessons of counterinsurgency operations in Afghanistan and Iraq (one of the goals of the new report). It identified the nation's most likely threats, including radical Islamists, nuclear proliferation, and the potential for increased rivalry with the People's Republic of China. The QDR also endorsed the expansion of major weapons systems, including the F-22 fighter and the next-generation DD-X destroyer. In order to meet the nation's security goals, the QDR calls for a significant modernization effort over the next two decades, including increases in expenditures. *See also* DEFENSE SPENDING AND ALLIANCE BURDEN SHARING; MILITARY-INDUSTRIAL COMPLEX; PEACE DIVIDEND.

– R –

RABIN, YITZHAK (1922–1995). Prime minister of Israel, 1974–1977 and 1992–1995, under whose leadership significant progress was made in developing a framework for peace in the **Arab-Israeli conflict**. Rabin was born in Jerusalem and became a soldier in the Haganah paramilitary group on the eve of Israeli independence. He was promoted rapidly and became chief of staff in 1964. Rabin commanded the Israeli military in its dramatic victory in the 1967 Six-Day War. After the conflict, he retired from the Army and in 1968 became ambassador to the United States. Rabin returned to Israel in 1973 and was elected to the Knesset as a member of the Labor Party. From 1984 to 1990, Rabin was minister of defense in successive governments. He redeployed the Israeli troops occupying southern Lebanon to a more compact defensive perimeter and oversaw the response to the Palestinian *intifada*, or rebellion.

In 1992, Rabin was elected leader of the Labor Party. That year, the party won the largest number of seats in the Knesset and formed the first Labor government in 15 years. Rabin endorsed the Oslo Accords and accepted the principle of "land for peace," in which Israel would turn over territory in exchange for the renunciation of violence by the Palestinians and recognition of the Jewish state. In September 1993, Rabin and Palestinian leader **Yasser Arafat** exchanged recognitions. Arafat was allowed to return to Gaza and establish a Palestinian government. Some contentious issues, such as the status of Jerusalem, were bypassed for resolution in future negotiations. The prime minister and Arafat shared the Nobel Peace Prize for their peace efforts. In 1994, Rabin signed a peace agreement with Jordan. On 4 November 1995, he was assassinated during a rally in Tel Aviv by a right-wing Jewish extremist who opposed the Oslo Accords.

REAGAN, RONALD W. (1911–2004). Fortieth president of the United States, 1981–1989, who implemented a series of policies that led to the end of the **Cold War**. Ronald Wilson Reagan was born in Tampico, Illinois, and graduated from Eureka College in 1932. He had a film career that spanned nearly 30 years and 50 movies. In 1962, Reagan joined the Republican Party because of opposition to the social programs and national security policies of the Democratic Party. Elected governor of California in 1966, he was dubbed the "Great Communicator" due to his speaking proficiency and ability to elucidate grand themes in a way that resonated with the American people.

In 1980, Reagan was elected president of the United States, based on a campaign that emphasized stronger national defense, as well as tax cuts and economic reforms. Following an assassination attempt in 1981, Reagan was able to get most of his tax and economic proposals ratified by Congress. His domestic economic program, known as "Reaganomics," was based on supply-side theories, which emphasized the need to increase capital among the wealthy in order to spur investment and job creation. Reagan's tax cuts and reform of the tax system prompted a sustained period of economic growth in the United States. However, the national debt increased dramatically as Reagan substantially bolstered defense spending. He was reelected by a large margin in 1984.

Reagan was a staunch anticommunist who sought to reinvigorate the Cold War struggle. The Reagan Doctrine emphasized the need to compete with the Soviet Union on all levels and to not only contain the Soviets but also attempt to reverse their gains from the 1970s. The United States launched new covert programs to undermine pro-Soviet regimes around the globe. U.S. aid was increased to anti-Soviet forces in struggles such as the **Angolan Conflict** and the Afghan insurgency, as well as to anti-Soviet governments such as **Manuel Noriega**'s in Panama. Washington also initiated new weapons programs, notably the Strategic Defense Initiative (SDI), a space-based antimissile system. SDI spurred Soviet efforts to develop a similar system. Reagan deployed U.S. forces to overthrow a Marxist regime in Grenada following a coup, in the first major U.S. combat operation since the Vietnam War.

The president maintained a bipartisan consensus on foreign and security policy, despite controversy over American aid to the anticommunist Contra rebel group in Nicaragua. The administration secretly funneled aid to the Contras in a scheme that would become known as the Iran-Contra Scandal: The United States supplied weapons to Iran in exchange for the release of American hostages (the **Lebanon Hostage Crisis**) and used the funds from those sales to arm the Contras. Nonetheless, Congress remained generally supportive of Reagan's defense policies, especially the military buildup, although after his selection as house Speaker in 1987, Democrat **James C. Wright** clashed with Reagan over foreign policy in Latin America.

Reagan formed a close partnership with allied leaders such as **Margaret Thatcher** of Great Britain, **M. Brian Mulroney** of Canada, and **Helmut Kohl** of the Federal Republic of Germany. The president's renewed aggressiveness forced successive leaders in Moscow to increase Soviet defense spending. In 1985, Soviet premier **Mikhail Gorbachev** realized that his country could no longer keep pace with the United States and proposed a series of **arms control** agreements. That year, negotiations were restarted on the first of the **Strategic Arms Reduction Treaties (START I and II)**. Although tensions between the two superpowers were reduced in the remaining years of Reagan's presidency, U.S. military competition with the Soviet Union prompted Gorbachev to attempt to accelerate reforms. The Cold War would formally end under Reagan's vice president and successor, **George H. W. Bush**. Reagan left office as one of the most popular American presidents in the 20th century. He died on 5 June 2004.

RICE, CONDOLEEZZA (1954–). The first female national security advisor and second female secretary of state of the United States. Rice was born in Birmingham, Alabama, in the still-segregated South. She received a master's degree from Notre Dame University in 1975 and worked for the State Department during the **James E.**

Carter administration. Rice returned to academia, earned a doctorate from the University of Denver, and had a distinguished career at Stanford University. She served on the National Security Council during the administration of **George H. W. Bush** and became the foreign policy advisor for **George W. Bush** during his presidential campaign in 2000. Once in office, Bush appointed Rice as his national security advisor.

Rice emerged as a central figure in crafting the U.S. military and diplomatic strategy in wake of the **September 11 terrorist attacks**. She advocated the use of **coalitions of the willing** that would capitalize on utilizing those assets and capabilities that allied states were willing to contribute to the U.S. response, but which would retain policy control and operational command for the Bush administration. Rice helped coordinate the military campaign **Operation Enduring Freedom** (as part of the **Afghanistan intervention**) with the U.S. and allied militaries. She also worked with Secretary of State **Colin Powell** to ensure that the U.S. response to the attacks included nonmilitary actions such as increased international law enforcement cooperation and the development of a comprehensive **homeland security** policy.

Rice helped develop the 2002 *National Security Strategy of the United States*, commonly referred to as the **Bush Doctrine**, which emphasized the use of preemptive military strikes to prevent the use of weapons of mass destruction. She was also instrumental in the administration's hard-line policy toward the Iraqi regime of **Saddam Hussein**, including the effort to isolate Iraq and formulate an international coalition, and was one of the main proponents of the 2003 **Iraq War**. In March 2004, Rice became the first national security advisor to publicly testify on policy issues when she appeared before the **National Commission on Terrorist Attacks upon the United States** (9/11 Commission). During the 2004 presidential campaign, Rice became the first national security advisor to openly campaign on behalf of a candidate. She faced domestic criticism by Democrats for her hawkish security policies and for her advocacy against domestic affirmative action policies. After the election, Rice was appointed secretary of state, becoming the second female and second African American to occupy the post. She handpicked her successor as national security advisor, **Stephen J. Hadley**, her former deputy.

Once in office in 2005, Rice worked to repair relations with major allies such as France and Germany that were opposed to the U.S.-led invasion of Iraq. She also endeavored to increase international support for the continuing U.S. efforts in Iraq. The sound working relationship between Rice and Hadley ensured that the State Department and the security establishment had a high degree of cooperation. Her closeness with Bush provided her with greater access, and therefore more influence, than her predecessor Powell. One result was that in the second George W. Bush administration, Secretary of Defense **Donald H. Rumsfeld** had less influence on broad security policy, while Rice increased, or restored, the role of the State Department in formulating foreign and security policy. *See also* WAR ON TERROR.

RICHARDSON, WILLIAM B. (1947–). Member of the U.S. House of Representatives, U.S. ambassador to the **United Nations (UN)**, and energy secretary. William Blaine "Bill" Richardson was born in Pasadena, California, but lived in Mexico City until he was 13. He was elected to the House in 1982 and served until 1997, when he was appointed the nation's UN ambassador. Richardson worked to maintain international support in the UN for sanctions against Iraq at a time when both France and Russia were working to repeal the measures. He also had to manage the diplomatic response to those countries' official condemnation of U.S. air strikes on Iraq in 1998. Richardson was appointed secretary of the Department of Energy in 1998.

In 2002, he was elected governor of New Mexico, becoming the only Hispanic governor in the United States. As governor, Richardson attempted to improve the state's trade relations with Asian countries, particularly the People's Republic of China. The governor has also engaged in unofficial diplomacy. In 2003, Richardson received a delegation from North Korea and held talks over that country's nuclear program. In 2006, he led an effort to release journalists held in Sudan. *See also* DARFUR CRISIS; NORTH KOREAN NUCLEAR CRISES.

RIDGE, THOMAS J. (1945–). Member of the House of Representatives, governor of Pennsylvania, and the first secretary of **homeland**

security. Thomas Joseph "Tom" Ridge was born in Munhall, Pennsylvania, and graduated with honors from Harvard University in 1967 (he also earned a law degree in 1972 from Dickinson University). He served in Vietnam and was decorated for bravery. Ridge was elected to the House of Representatives in 1982 and governor of Pennsylvania in 1994 (he was reelected in 1998).

In 2001, Ridge was appointed director of the Office of Homeland Security and became secretary when the office was elevated to department status in 2003. Ridge oversaw the most comprehensive reorganization of the federal bureaucracy since the early **Cold War**. The new department consolidated 22 federal agencies and bureaus and more than 180,000 employees. Ridge developed a strong working relationship with both the **George W. Bush** administration and Congress. He was considered one of the moderate members of the Bush administration on security matters and civil liberties. However, he was criticized for the failure of the Homeland Security Department to implement stricter border control measures and more thorough port security. Following the 2004 presidential election, Ridge resigned in order to spend more time with his family. In 2006, he was appointed an advisor by the government of Albania. *See also* IMMIGRATION POLICY.

ROBERTSON, LORD (1946–). Tenth secretary-general of the **North Atlantic Treaty Organization (NATO)**, 1999–2003, who oversaw the first invocation of Article 5 (the collective security clause of NATO) in response to the **September 11 terrorist attacks**. George Islay MacNeill Robertson was born in Port Ellen, Scotland, and received a master's degree in economics from the University of Dundee in 1968. He became a union official. In 1978, Robertson was elected to the House of Commons as a member of the Labour Party. He was appointed to several senior posts within the party, including Labour chair for Scotland and opposition spokesman on defense. When Labour won the 1997 general election, Robertson was chosen as defense minister. He proposed a new long-range plan for the British military, including deep cuts in expenditure and the development of more flexible, rapid reaction forces. Robertson also strengthened defense-industrial cooperation with Great Britain's European allies and oversaw the continuing deployment of British troops in the NATO-led peacekeeping mission during the **Bosnian Conflict**.

Robertson was a vocal critic of the Serbian regime of **Slobodan Milošević** and was a proponent of the use of force to counter Serb aggression in the **Kosovo War**. Robertson worked with his NATO counterparts to coordinate allied operations in the 77-day bombing campaign. His public role in the Kosovo crisis made him a natural replacement for NATO secretary-general **Javier Solana** when the latter resigned to become the first coordinator for foreign policy in the **European Union**. Robertson was elevated to the peerage in August 1999, prior to his appointment as the alliance's leader on 14 October.

As NATO's senior civilian official, Lord Robertson worked diligently to improve relations with Russia, especially in light of the tensions that arose during the Kosovo campaign and the desire for Moscow's compliance in any future NATO enlargement. Robertson initiated the planning for a second post–Cold War round of **NATO expansion**.

The 11 September 2001 terrorist attacks forced Lord Robertson to make terrorism the alliance's immediate priority. Article 5 was invoked for the first time in alliance history, and all NATO members were therefore required to come to the aid of the United States. NATO deployed airborne early warning craft to the United States and stationed naval forces in the Mediterranean to interdict potential terrorists. NATO forces did not participate in **Operation Enduring Freedom**, but individual alliance countries contributed troops and aircraft to the U.S.-led **Afghanistan intervention**. Meanwhile, NATO developed a new comprehensive counterterrorism strategy. Following the fall of the Taliban, NATO also agreed to lead the peace enforcement mission in Afghanistan.

In May 2002, Robertson signed a new agreement with Russia to enhance cooperation between the alliance and Moscow. In addition, in November 2002, at the Prague Summit, NATO invited Bulgaria, Estonia, Latvia, Lithuania, Romania, Slovakia, and Slovenia to become members. The seven former members of the Warsaw Pact formally acceded to NATO in 2004 in the alliance's largest-ever expansion.

Lord Robertson oversaw one of the more contentious periods in alliance history during the 2003 **Iraq War**. The U.S.-led invasion of Iraq divided NATO. Some allies, including Belgium, France, and Germany, bitterly opposed American efforts to develop an anti-Iraqi coalition and took steps to prevent the use of NATO resources prior to the invasion. They also initially refused to allow overflight rights to aircraft involved in the invasion. Matters were further complicated in February 2003 when Turkey asked the alliance to invoke Article 4, which called upon the allies to take steps whenever the territorial integrity of a member was threatened. The anti-invasion bloc also initially obstructed efforts to provide aid to Turkey, but a compromise was reached that allowed the deployment of NATO assets, including aircraft and missile defense systems. Robertson managed to craft a series of compromises that maintained the integrity of NATO. For instance, the alliance did not deploy troops to Iraq, but NATO forces were rearranged to allow members to send troops to Iraq if they chose to do so. In addition, NATO agreed to train Iraqi security forces.

Lord Robertson announced his decision to resign as NATO chief in late 2003. In January 2004, he was replaced by **Jaap de Hoop Scheffer** of the Netherlands.

RODMAN, PETER W. (1943–). National security analyst and author who has served in a variety of government posts. Peter Warren Rodman was born in Boston and earned a law degree from Harvard University in 1969. He became a protégé of Secretary of State Henry Kissinger. Rodman was a member of the staff of the National Security Council (1969–1977) and worked for the policy planning staff at the State Department (1983–1986), before becoming an assistant to the national security advisor (1986–1990). From 1991 to 1999, Rodman was a senior editor for the conservative journal *The National Review*. He also served as director of national security programs at the Nixon Center from 1995 to 2001. Rodman wrote a series of books and articles that argued the United States would be increasingly forced to take unilateral action to safeguard its interests. In 2001, he was appointed assistant secretary of defense for international security. Rodman is identified with the **neoconservative** movement and was a proponent of military action against the regime of **Saddam Hussein**.

RUMSFELD, DONALD H. (1932–). Secretary of defense under President **George W. Bush**, 2001–2006, who played a major, and often controversial, role in shaping U.S. security policy in the aftermath of the **September 11 terrorist attacks**. Donald Henry Rumsfeld was born in Chicago. He graduated from Princeton University in 1954 and then entered the navy, serving as a pilot and flight instructor. He was discharged from active duty in 1957, but remained in the Naval Reserve until 1989, when he retired with the rank of captain.

After leaving the active navy, Rumsfeld launched a political career, taking a job as a congressional aide. In 1962, Rumsfeld successfully campaigned for a seat from Illinois in the U.S. House of Representatives. He served in the House until 1969 and developed a reputation as a moderate Republican with an interest in defense issues and a supporter of civil rights legislation. After Richard M. Nixon was elected president, he made Rumsfeld the director of the Office of Economic Opportunity; as his deputy, Rumsfeld chose future vice president **Richard B. Cheney**. In 1974, Rumsfeld was appointed as the U.S. ambassador to the **North Atlantic Treaty Organization**. After Nixon's resignation, President Gerald R. Ford asked Rumsfeld to chair his transition team. He then became White House chief of staff in 1974 and secretary of defense in 1975. As secretary, Rumsfeld sought to shift spending to the development of new weapons systems such as the B-1 bomber and the MX missile. Following Ford's defeat in the 1976 election, Rumsfeld left office and taught at Princeton University and then Northwestern University. He later had a successful business career. During the administration of **Ronald W. Reagan**, Rumsfeld was appointed to a number of advisory posts and served as an envoy to the Middle East in 1983.

In January 2001, on Cheney's advice, Bush appointed Rumsfeld secretary of defense. Rumsfeld thus became both the youngest and oldest person appointed to head the Department of Defense. Rumsfeld entered office with plans to transform the military to leaner, more flexible force structures that would allow for rapid deployments in response to regional crises. To accomplish this objective, he worked to cancel several **Cold War**–era weapons systems, including the Comanche helicopter and the Crusader self-propelled artillery piece. He also initiated the redeployment of American forces from bases created during the Cold War in a policy that mirrored the consolidation of defense facilities in the United States. Bush's decision to withdraw from the 1972 Antiballistic Missile Treaty led Rumsfeld to reorient U.S. strategic forces and emphasize **ballistic missile defense**.

Rumsfeld was in the Pentagon during the 11 September 2001 terrorist attack on the building. He played a major role in formulating the military response to the attacks. Rumsfeld oversaw the deployment of U.S. and coalition forces and the planning for the **Afghanistan intervention** and overthrow of the Taliban regime. The U.S. strategy emphasized the use of special operations troops and the anti-Taliban Northern Alliance, along with strategic and tactical air strikes. Coalition military action began in October 2001, and by December the Taliban and their **Al Qaeda** allies had been defeated. Rumsfeld was praised for the overall conduct of the war, but faced criticism for the failure to capture Al Qaeda leader **Osama bin Laden** and Taliban leader Mullah Omar. The secretary's strategy, which came to be informally known as the Rumsfeld Doctrine, called for the use of the smallest force possible, accompanied by massive air power and the use of precision-guided weaponry. Central to the success of Rumsfeld's strategy was the use of sophisticated technology and network-centric warfare.

The secretary was a staunch supporter of military action against Iraq. He believed that the removal of the regime of **Saddam Hussein** was the next logical step in the administration's global **war on terror**. In planning for the **Iraq War**, Rumsfeld envisioned a two-front campaign with a southern front from bases in Kuwait and a northern front from Turkey. However, domestic opposition in Turkey ruled out the northern front, forcing Rumsfeld to rapidly alter his plans and launch the invasion with a smaller force (some 140,000 troops, instead of the planned 230,000). Nonetheless, the U.S.-led coalition quickly overran Iraq and toppled Saddam. Within a month of the start of hostilities, American troops occupied Baghdad. In December 2003, Saddam was captured by the Americans.

Rumsfeld again received accolades for the rapid victory. However, he was criticized for the lack of postwar planning and the subsequent rise of the Iraqi insurgency. The inability of the U.S.-led coalition to contain the insurgency added to questions over the secretary's management of the conflict. During the 2004 presidential election, there were calls among senior Republicans for Rumsfeld to resign. Bush rejected these calls and kept Rumsfeld as defense chief at the start of his second term. However, following the 2006 midterm elections in which the Republican Party lost control of both chambers of Congress, Rumsfeld announced his resignation and left office in December 2006.

RWANDAN GENOCIDE (1994). The massacre of an estimated 800,000 ethnic Tutsis and moderate Hutus over a 100-day period in 1994. The genocide was an example of **ethnic cleansing**, as two Hutu groups attempted to kill or displace Rwanda's Tutsi minority. During the atrocities, the United States, other world powers, and the **United Nations (UN)** did little or nothing to stop the killing.

In 1993, the United States and France had sponsored peace negotiations between the Hutus and Tutsis, who were engaged in a civil war. The accords were unpopular with Hutu extremists, and they used the 6 April 1994 assassination of Rwandan president Juvénal Habyarimana as an excuse to launch an ethnic-cleansing campaign against their enemies. Western governments, including the administration of **William J. Clinton**, were aware of preparations by the Hutus, including an increase in the delivery of weapons from companies in France and Great Britain.

There was already a UN peacekeeping mission in the country, the UN Assistance Mission for Rwanda (UNAMIR). UNAMIR consisted of about 2,500 troops (the Clinton administration rejected a 1993 request to increase the size of the mission to 5,000 out of concern that the United States might be obligated to financially contribute to the deployment). On 7 April 1994, 15 UNAMIR troops, 10 Belgians and 5 Ghanaians, were dispatched to protect the moderate Hutu prime minister, Agathe Uwilingiyimana. However, she was killed, along with her family and the UNAMIR troops (who had been tortured). The militias simultaneously targeted other moderate Hutu leaders and began attacking Tutsis. The UNAMIR commander, Canadian general Roméo Dallaire, requested more troops and equipment, but there was little support for an expanded mission within the UN Security Council. Dallaire requested permission for UNAMIR troops to use force to defend Tutsis, but his request was denied by then assistant secretary-general **Kofi**

Annan, who feared that the militias might launch a broad campaign against the UN. Meanwhile, Belgium withdrew its 420 troops from UNAMIR once Belgian citizens had been evacuated, and on 21 April, the Security Council voted to reduce the size of UNAMIR to 250 troops and to limit its mandate in an effort to prevent the loss of additional peacekeepers.

On 29 April 1994, UN secretary-general **Boutros Boutros-Ghali** requested the Security Council to reconsider its decision and dispatch troops to stop the genocide. The Clinton administration offered to fund a peacekeeping force from the Organization of African Unity (OAU). However, the OAU heads of state requested the inclusion of American troops—which the Clinton administration rejected outright.

During this period, U.S. policy was guided by Presidential Decision Directive 25 (PDD-25), which had been developed after the failed **Somali intervention**. Written under the direction of National Security Advisor **Anthony Lake**, PDD-25 listed 16 specific criteria that had to be met before the United States would participate in peacekeeping missions. Central to the directive was an emphasis on the avoidance of American casualties unless important national interests were at stake. Meanwhile, the administration never discussed Rwanda at the cabinet level or during a formal meeting of the National Security Council (NSC). U.S. policy was overseen by an interagency group with staffers from the State Department, the Defense Department, the NSC, and the Central Intelligence Agency. The administration was even divided over whether to label the ethnic cleansing as "genocide." Concerns were raised over the domestic reaction in the United States if the administration labeled the crisis in Rwanda as a genocide and then did nothing. Consequently, it was not until 21 May—by which point more than 400,000 had been killed—that Secretary of State **Warren Christopher** authorized the use of the term *genocide* (there would be another three weeks before the administration publicly used the term).

On 17 May 1994, the Security Council adopted a compromise plan. The UN mission was recast as UNAMIR II, which would include an additional 800 troops with a limited mandate to keep the nation's main airport open and oversee the distribution of humanitarian aid from that facility. Vice President **Albert A. Gore** offered Boutros-

Ghali transport for the new force, but negotiations between the United States and the UN stalled over the delivery of the promised 50 armored personnel carriers that were not ready until after the Hutu regime had been overthrown.

On 22 June, the Security Council authorized the deployment of French forces in southwest Rwanda. The troops rapidly deployed through the region, but massacres continued and Tutsis charged that some French troops collaborated with the Hutus. The genocide was stopped by the defeat of the militias by the main Tutsi rebel group, the Rwandan Patriotic Front (RPF). By July, the RPF was in control of Rwanda, but its advance prompted a mass exodus of Hutus. More than two million Hutus fled into neighboring countries. The refugees expanded the conflict. Hutu militias among the refugees conducted raids into Rwanda, sparking an invasion of the Democratic Republic of the Congo. The UN created the International Criminal Tribunal for Rwanda to bring those involved in the genocide to justice. In addition, Rwandans used a traditional form of tribal courts, known as Gacaca, to try cases.

In 1998, during a visit to the country, Clinton issued an apology to the Rwandan people for the failure of the United States to take action to stop the genocide. Public reaction to the Clinton administration's management of the crisis added additional imperatives for action in the **Bosnian Conflict**.

– S –

SADDAM HUSSEIN (1937–2006). President of Iraq from 1979 until he was deposed in 2003 by American-led forces during the **Iraq War**. Saddam Hussein Abd al-Majidida al-Tikriti was born in Al-Awja, near Tikrit, Iraq. In 1957, he joined the opposition Ba'ath Party. Following the overthrow of the monarchy, Saddam was part of a U.S.-backed plot to overthrow the revolutionary regime. In 1963, after the Ba'athists took control of the government, Saddam returned to Iraq, but was imprisoned for three years. In 1969, he became a deputy to the president and was appointed a general in the Iraqi military. Saddam promoted economic modernization and expanded social services, funded by oil revenues. His staunch anticommunism and opposition to fundamentalist Islam resulted in American support for Saddam when he seized power in 1979.

Saddam continued his modernization and secularization programs, but ruthlessly suppressed dissent. He also sought to develop weapons of mass destruction (WMDs) and later used chemical weapons against ethnic Kurds and other opponents of the government. With U.S. backing, the regime went to war with Iran in 1980. The conflict ended in a stalemate in 1988, but resulted in more than 1 million dead on both sides and left Iraq with a war debt of $75 billion. In an effort to gain new resources to repay his debts, Saddam invaded Kuwait in August 1990, provoking the 1991 **Persian Gulf War**.

After Saddam's defeat by the American-led coalition, the **United Nations (UN)** imposed a range of economic and military sanctions on Iraq and established no-fly zones over northern and southern Iraq. Throughout the 1990s, Saddam endeavored to have the sanctions removed or reduced. He sponsored a complicated smuggling system to partially evade the sanctions in the **Oil-for-Food Program**. The Iraqi leader also provoked a series of air strikes by the United States following the discovery of an Iraqi plot to assassinate former president **George H. W. Bush** in 1993, Iraqi military action against the Kurds in 1996, and the regime's noncompliance with UN-mandated inspections for WMDs, including the ejection of UN weapons inspectors. On 31 October 1998, President **William J. Clinton** signed the **Iraq Liberation Act**, which made the removal of Saddam, or regime change, the official policy of the United States and committed the country to provide support for antiregime groups.

During the prelude to the 2003 U.S.-led invasion, Saddam offered limited cooperation with a new round of UN inspections, but the administration of **George W. Bush** asserted that the regime continued to hide WMDs, while also supporting Islamic terrorist groups. On 20 March 2003, American-led coalition forces invaded Iraq and by 9 April, allied troops had captured Baghdad. Saddam went into hiding, but was captured on 13 December.

In June 2004, Saddam and other senior officials from his regime were transferred to the custody of the Iraqi interim government. After a contentious trial, on 5 November 2006 Saddam was convicted of crimes against humanity for ordering the executions of Shiites and sentenced to death. He was executed by hanging on 30 December 2006.

SATELLITE AND CABLE NEWS. The proliferation of satellite and cable news outlets and the advent of the 24-hour news cycle has dramatically altered contemporary journalism. Through the **Cold War**, international agencies such as the BBC World Service and the Voice of America broadcast news via radio and initiated the round-the-clock news service. In 1980, the Turner Broadcasting Corporation launched CNN (Cable News Network), which provided live, 24-hour news to American cable television subscribers. CNN revolutionized the news industry. The daylong cycle of programming meant that stories and news items could be reported as they were happening. This greatly accelerated the pace of news. Critics complained that real-time news delivery led to errors, since editors could not check source materials or background content. However, the format was very popular, especially during periods of breaking news. Traditional network broadcast news lost audience share through the 1990; by 2006, CNN had a global audience of 1.5 billion people and was broadcast to 212 countries. Other rival cable news networks emerged in the 1990s.

Although foreign viewers often accuse CNN of having an American bias, within the United States, the network has frequently been accused of taking a liberal, anti-American slant. In 1996, Fox News, a conservative news service, was launched as part of the global News Corporation. By 2001, it had eclipsed CNN as the number-one-rated cable news network. CNN, Fox, and other networks such as MSNBC were criticized during the 2003 **Iraq War** when they embedded their reporters with military units. The reporters were accused of lacking objectivity.

The proliferation of Western cable and satellite news led to the creation of Al Jazeera, an Arabic- and English-language satellite network, in 1996. Al Jazeera broadcasts from Qatar. The station was created through a $150 million grant from the emir of Qatar and receives an annual subsidy from him of $30 million. The station gained fame for broadcasting statements and videos from **Al Qaeda** and other terrorist groups.

SCHRÖDER, GERHARD F. (1944–). Chancellor of Germany, 1998–2005, whose opposition to the **Iraq War** led to the most significant period of tensions in post–World War II relations between Germany and the United States. Gerhard Fritz Kurt Schröder was born in Mossenberg, Lower Saxony. He graduated from the University of Göttingen with a law degree in 1971. While a youth, Schröder joined the Social Democratic Party (Sozialdemokratische Partei Deutschlands, SPD) and rose through the ranks to become the leader of the SPD's youth organization. He was elected to the Bundestag in 1980 and to the state legislature of Lower Saxony in 1986. After the 1990 elections, he became the state's leader through a coalition between the SPD and the Green Party. Schröder's position made him a member of the executive board of the SPD. In 1998, he was chosen as the party's candidate to be chancellor. Following the balloting, the SPD and the Greens formed a coalition government, and Schröder became the leader of Germany. In 1999, he also was appointed party chief of the SPD.

Once in office, Schröder endeavored to implement a number of domestic reforms to lower the country's high unemployment rate and bolster economic growth. However, many members of the SPD opposed his economic agenda. Throughout his chancellorship, unemployment remained at or above 10 percent. Schröder supported the **North Atlantic Treaty Organization (NATO)** intervention in Kosovo and deployed German troops as part of the multilateral peacekeeping mission. German forces also participated in the NATO operation in Macedonia. He worked with French president **Jacques Chirac** and British prime minister **Tony Blair** to further European integration and was a supporter of European Monetary Union and the adoption of the **euro**.

Schröder initially supported the administration of **George W. Bush** following the **September 11 terrorist attacks**. Germany and the United States enhanced intelligence sharing and law enforcement collaboration. In addition, Germany deployed troops as part of a NATO-led force in the **Afghanistan intervention** after the fall of the Taliban. However, Schröder opposed the detainment of suspected terrorists at Guantanamo Bay and other aspects of Bush's management of the **war on terror**. Facing a difficult reelection bid in 2002, Schröder seized on public opposition to military action against Iraq as the cornerstone of his campaign. Schröder's use of Iraq as a campaign theme heightened tensions with the United States, especially after the minister of labor, Herta Däuber-Gmelin, compared Bush's policies to those of Adolf Hitler. Schröder won the election with a reduced majority. With the traditionally strong relationship between Berlin and Washington in decline, Schröder endeavored to enhance ties with Russian president **Vladimir Putin**. In 2005, the two leaders signed an agreement to construct a gas pipeline from Russia to Germany across the Baltic Sea.

SPD losses in regional balloting led Schröder to call for early elections. In the 2005 polling, no party or coalition won an outright majority. The conservative Christian Democratic Party (Christlich Demokratische Union, CDU) won the largest number of votes and formed a grand coalition with the SPD, with CDU leader Angela Merkel as chancellor. Schröder refused to participate in the new government and subsequently resigned his seat in the Bundestag on 23 November 2005.

SCHWARZENEGGER, ARNOLD A. (1947–).

Former bodybuilder and actor who was elected governor of California in a special recall election in 2003. Arnold Alois Schwarzenegger was born in Thal, Austria, and rose to international fame as a body builder. He moved to the United States in 1968 and won four Mr. Universe and seven Mr. Olympia titles. Schwarzenegger used his imposing physique and renown to become a popular and wealthy film star. He became an American citizen in 1983 and married Maria Shriver, the niece of former president John F. Kennedy, in 1986. Schwarzenegger endorsed **Ronald W. Reagan** in the 1980 and 1984 presidential elections and **George H. W. Bush** in 1988. Bush appointed the actor to chair the President's Council on Physical Fitness. In 2002, Schwarzenegger led a successful statewide ballot initiative that provided for additional funding for after-school programs. In 2003, voters forced a recall election of California governor Gray Davis. Schwarzenegger joined the campaign to replace Davis and was elected governor. As governor, he has sought to increase trade relations with the Asia-Pacific rim. Schwarzenegger also emerged as a leading proponent of moderate **immigration policy**. He favors increased border enforcement, but also a guest worker program. He was reelected in 2006. *See also* TRADE POLICY.

SCHWARZKOPF, H. NORMAN (1934–).

Popular U.S. career military officer who led the coalition forces during the **Persian Gulf**

War. Schwarzkopf was born in Trenton, New Jersey. He graduated from the U.S. Military Academy at West Point in 1956 and was commissioned in the army (he later earned a master's degree in mechanical engineering from the University of Southern California in 1964). Schwarzkopf served in the Vietnam War and held a variety of commands in the military. In 1983, he commanded the ground forces during the invasion of Grenada.

In 1988, Schwarzkopf was promoted to general and appointed commander of U.S. Central Command, with responsibility for the Middle East, South Asia, and the East Africa. Schwarzkopf developed a plan to defend the oil fields of Kuwait and Saudi Arabia that became the basis for the liberation of Kuwait following the 1990 invasion by Iraq. The general oversaw Operation Desert Shield, which included the buildup of coalition forces prior to the start of hostilities between the coalition and Iraq. Schwarzkopf's command included forces from more than 20 countries and presented numerous problems related to the interoperability of forces and the chain of command.

In January 1991, Desert Shield transitioned to Desert Storm as the coalition forces launched massive air strikes against Iraqi forces, followed by a ground campaign. Schwarzkopf's troops quickly drove Iraqi forces out of Kuwait with minimal allied casualties. During the campaign, Schwarzkopf held numerous press conferences and was a visible presence in international media coverage of the conflict. The speed and overwhelming nature of the attack led Schwarzkopf to acquire the nickname "Stormin' Norman."

Schwarzkopf retired from the military in August 1991. He wrote a best-selling autobiography in 1992. The former general's popularity was such that there was speculation that he would seek the presidency. However, Schwarzkopf chose to remain in private life. He was diagnosed with prostate cancer in 1993, but underwent successful medical treatment. *See also* POWELL DOCTRINE.

SCOWCROFT, BRENT (1925–). National security advisor for presidents Gerald R. Ford and **George H. W. Bush**. Scowcroft, a Mormon, was born in Ogden, Utah. He graduated from the U.S. Military Academy at West Point in 1947 and had a distinguished career in the U.S. Air Force. He earned a Ph.D. from Columbia University in 1967, rose to the rank of lieutenant general, and retired from active service in 1975. He was appointed national security advisor by Ford in 1975 and served until 1977. Scowcroft served in the same role under Bush from 1989 to 1993. Bush and Scowcroft had a close relationship, and the president came to rely on the former general as an integral part of his foreign and security team, which also included Secretary of State **James A. Baker III**. Scowcroft advocated an interest-based foreign policy designed to prevent U.S. military resources from becoming overstretched. He subsequently served on a number of advisory boards and emerged as a vocal opponent of the 2003 **Iraq War**.

SEPTEMBER 11 TERRORIST ATTACKS (9/11). The most devastating terrorist strikes in American history, causing more casualties and greater economic damage than any other. The campaign was planned by senior **Al Qaeda** figure Khalid Sheikh Mohammed and authorized by **Osama bin Laden**. The Al Qaeda leaders sought to complete the failed 1993 **World Trade Center bombing** and to retaliate against American support for Israel. The strikes also marked the continuation of the escalation in attacks against the United States that occurred through the 1990s, including the 1996 **Khobar Towers bombing**, the failed **Millennium Bombing Plots**, and the 2000 **USS Cole bombing**.

The 11 September 2001 strikes were carried out by 19 hijackers who took control of four passenger aircraft. At least eight other terrorists who may have been part of the plot were prevented from entering the United States because of visa or security issues. Another potential hijacker, Zacarias Moussaoui, was arrested a month before the attacks on immigration violations.

Each of the terrorist groups had at least one trained pilot. In some cases, the terrorists had entered the United States years earlier (and even attended flight school in the United States). Once in the air, the terrorists took control of the four planes using box cutters, chemical sprays, and bomb threats. In the process, they killed several crew members and passengers. The terrorists planned to fly the hijacked craft into buildings that were symbols of American economic and political power, in effect creating piloted missiles.

At 8:45 A.M. Eastern Standard Time, hijacked American Airlines Flight 11 flew into the north tower of the World Trade Center (WTC) complex in New York City. The airplane exploded on impact, killing all of the passengers and a large number of workers in the building. The explosion created an enormous fire. Approximately 18 minutes later, United Flight 175 crashed into the south tower. At 9:43 A.M., American Flight 77 flew into the Pentagon, in Arlington, Virginia, outside of Washington, D.C.

Within half an hour, the south tower of the WTC collapsed, followed shortly by the north tower. The collapse of the twin towers destroyed or damaged other buildings in the WTC complex. The design of the Pentagon, with multiple layers, contained most of the damage.

Meanwhile, passengers on the fourth aircraft, United Flight 93, became aware of the intentions of the hijackers through air and cell phone conversations. They attempted to retake control of the airplane. During the ensuing struggle, the plane crashed near Shanksville, Pennsylvania, well short of its intended target, believed to be the Capitol Building in Washington, D.C.

The attacks killed 2,973 and injured thousands (24 people remain listed as missing). Onboard the four aircraft, all 246 passengers and crew were killed. At the WTC, 2,602 were killed, including more than 400 first responders. In the Pentagon strike, 125 died. Nonetheless, at the WTC, improvements in emergency response and evacuation procedures since the 1993 attack allowed between 16,000 and 18,000 persons to escape from the buildings.

New York mayor Rudolf Giuliani became a national hero for his leadership during the attacks and their aftermath. The attacks also had a dramatic impact on the U.S. economy. The stock market suffered it largest one-week decline, more than 14.3 percent, and lost $1.2 trillion in value. The direct economic losses associated with the attacks were estimated to be between $800 billion and $1 trillion.

The attacks dramatically changed the security priorities of the United States and other developed nations. Terrorism became recognized as the main threat to international peace and stability. The United States received more than 100 bilateral declarations of support from more than 40 endorsements from international organizations. The **North Atlantic Treaty Organization**, **Organization of American States**, and Australia–New Zealand–United States Treaty all invoked their collective defense mechanisms to support the United States. In addition, the **United Nations** passed resolutions condemning the attacks and calling on all member states to aid America. Countries such as Pakistan, which had been under U.S. sanctions, and Russia, which had strained relations with America at the time, were transformed into vital partners in the **war on terror** launched by President **George W. Bush**. Bush sought to develop a broad international coalition to suppress global terrorist networks through military, financial, and law enforcement efforts.

The first phase of the war on terror was **Operation Enduring Freedom**, in which an American-led coalition overthrew the Taliban regime in Afghanistan (the regime had provided a safe haven for Al Qaeda and allowed the organization to operate a series of training camps). Although coalition forces were unable to capture bin Laden and most of the senior Al Qaeda and Taliban leadership, the terrorist network lost about a third of its personnel either killed or captured. Khalid Sheikh Mohammed was captured by Pakistani security forces and turned over to the United States for extensive questioning. Moussaoui was convicted for his role in the hijacking plot and sentenced to six life sentences. The United States provided economic and financial aid to a range of countries to bolster their ability to suppress terrorist groups.

Bush's presidency was transformed. His approval ratings rose to close to 90 percent as a result of widespread public endorsement of his leadership. Congress enacted a series of legislation to support the administration, including the authorization to use force in the **Afghanistan intervention**, the 2001 **Patriot Act**, and the 2001 **Homeland Security** Act. However, Bush was unable to maintain a bipartisan consensus on the war on terror. Following losses in Congress, as well as in state and local races, in the 2002 midterm elections, the Democratic Party adopted a more critical approach to Bush's management of homeland security and the war on terror.

The 2003 **Iraq War**, although initially supported by Congress and the American public, grew increasingly divisive as the conflict claimed more than 3,000 U.S. soldiers. Bush's popular approval declined significantly and the Republican Party lost control of both houses of Congress in the 2006 midterm elections.

In the aftermath of the attacks, Congress created a bipartisan panel to investigate the possible intelligence failures and to recommend steps to prevent future catastrophic terrorist strikes. The **National**

Commission on Terrorist Attacks upon the United States (the 9/11 Commission) conducted extensive hearings and issued a series of recommendations. The commission concluded that the nation's intelligence agencies did not cooperate or share information effectively and that the United States needed to improve homeland security, including border, port, and airline security. *See also* INTERNATIONAL TERRORISM.

SHARON, ARIEL (1928–). Prominent Israeli military leader and prime minister from 2001 to 2006. Born Ariel Scheinermann in Kfar Malal, while Palestine was still a British Colony, at age 14 he joined a Hebrew paramilitary organization, becoming an officer in the Israeli Defense Forces after independence in 1948. Sharon had a distinguished military career, rising to the rank of general. He was wounded on several occasions and was decorated for bravery. He commanded troops during the 1956 Suez Canal invasion, the 1967 Six-Day War, and the 1973 Yom Kippur War.

Sharon helped form the nationalist Likud Party in 1973 and was elected to the Knesset, but resigned from parliament a year later over differences with the Likud leadership. Prior to the 1977 elections, Sharon established a new political party, Shlomtzion. The party won only two seats in the Knesset, and Sharon merged Shlomtzion with Likud. He was appointed minister of agriculture and oversaw an expansion of Jewish settlements in the West Bank and Gaza Strip. In 1981, he became minister of defense. The former general directed Israeli strategy during the 1982 Lebanon War. He successfully prosecuted the war, but was removed from office in 1983 following revelations that Israeli forces had supported Lebanese Maronite militia fighters during the massacre of Palestinian refugees at Sabra. Sharon continued to serve in successive governments, however, as minister of trade and industry and later minister of construction, foreign minister, and again defense minister. In 1999, Sharon became leader of the Likud Party and emphasized a hard-line approach to the **Arab-Israeli conflict**. His visit to the Temple Mount in September 2000 was cited by Palestinians as the cause of the Second, or al-Aqsa, Intifada.

Sharon was elected prime minister in 2001. His stance on Palestinian issues was criticized by officials in the administration of

William J. Clinton, and his election caused an end to the **Taba Summit**. In the aftermath of the **September 11 terrorist attacks** on the United States later that year, Sharon urged the administration of **George W. Bush** to increase pressure on the Palestinian National Authority to do more to end terrorism. He also endeavored to convince the United States to help to suppress pro-Palestinian groups such as Hamas and Hezbollah. In response, Washington adopted more stringent prohibitions on terrorism financing as part of the broader **war on terror**. Meanwhile, with American and European support, Sharon initiated a policy of unilateral withdrawal from some of the occupied territories, including Gaza. The prime minister even forcibly removed 8,500 Jewish settlers from 21 areas in Gaza. The last Israeli soldiers left Gaza on 11 September 2005. The decision to withdraw led to a leadership challenge within Likud, and on 21 November 2005, Sharon resigned as chief of the party to form a new political grouping, Kadima ("Forward"). Many moderate Likud members joined the new party.

On 18 December 2005, Sharon was hospitalized following a stroke. Then on 4 January 2006, Sharon suffered a massive stroke that left him on life support. Deputy Prime Minister Ehud Olmert became acting prime minister and then succeeded Sharon following elections in March 2006 in which Kadima won the largest number of seats in the Knesset and formed a coalition government.

SIX-PARTY TALKS. A series of negotiations that began in 2003 between North Korea and Japan, the People's Republic of China, Russia, South Korea, and the United States in an effort to persuade Pyongyang to remain part of the Nuclear Nonproliferation Treaty (NPT). The talks began after the discovery that North Korea had violated the 1994 **Framework Agreement with North Korea** in which Pyongyang pledged to end its pursuit of nuclear weapons in exchange for food and energy aid from Japan, South Korea, and the United States and the potential for normalized relations with Washington.

The first meeting was held in August 2003, but the parties were able to reach agreement only on the need to meet again. At this session, a range of divisions became apparent. First, North Korean officials demanded security guarantees from the United States that Washington would not attempt regime change. In addition, Pyongyang wanted normalized relations with Washington and the concurrent removal of existing economic sanctions. However, the administration of **George W. Bush** refused to remove sanctions until it could verify that the North Korean regime had ended its pursuit of nuclear weapons and its proliferation of ballistic missile technology. Second, Japan and the United States wanted North Korea to abandon its weapons program and allow international monitors to verify disarmament before steps could be taken to normalize relations or new aid was given to Pyongyang. The People's Republic of China, Russia, and South Korea endorsed a measured approach that would reward North Korea for each step it took toward compliance with the NPT. Third, North Korea wanted to continue its civilian nuclear energy program. As part of the Framework Agreement, Japan, South Korea, and the United States had agreed to construct two light-water reactors to produce energy, in return for North Korea halting construction on nuclear plants that produced radioactive materials which could be used to develop an atomic weapon. However, both Washington and Tokyo asserted that Pyongyang used the guise of a civilian nuclear program as a cover for its military program.

During the second and third rounds of negotiations in 2004, the countries developed a statement of principles that included an agreement to denuclearize the Korean Peninsula and to develop a series of confidence-building measures to forestall future crises.

In the fourth round of talks, South Korea and the United States declared that they did not have any nuclear weapons stationed on the Korean Peninsula. The Americans and Japanese agreed to normalize relations with North Korea and provide economic aid, following the agreement on separate peace treaties and compliance with the NPT. South Korea pledged to provide the North with two million kilowatts of power per year. Pyongyang agreed in principle to abandon its weapons program and resume compliance with the NPT as well as to allow monitoring of its nuclear facilities. All parties also agreed to accept Pyongyang's civilian atomic energy program.

In April 2006, negotiations broke down after the United States froze North Korean assets in a Macau bank (the Bush administration alleged the monies were the result of illicit North Korean missile sales). North Korean officials argued that economic sanctions, the freezing of assets, and other punitive diplomatic measures had to be addressed before progress could be made on nuclear issues, while Japan, South Korea, and the United States contended that the issues were separate and distinct. On 3 October, Pyongyang announced it would test a nuclear weapon, and on 9 October, the regime announced that the test had been successful. In response, the **United Nations** Security Council unanimously adopted Resolution 1718, which condemned the nuclear test and imposed economic and military sanctions on Pyongyang. The resolution was endorsed by all of the participants of the Six-Party Talks (except North Korea). North Korea refused to participate in a sixth round of negotiations until the United States and Japan ended economic sanctions. *See also* NORTH KOREAN NUCLEAR CRISES.

SOLANA, JAVIER (1942–). Ninth secretary-general of the **North Atlantic Treaty Organization (NATO)**, the first Spaniard to serve in that capacity, who oversaw a series of dramatic changes and growth in the alliance. Francisco Javier Solana Madariaga was born in Madrid to a prominent family. He studied in Spain and then earned a doctorate in physics at the University of Virginia in 1968. Solana's early career was in academia, and he taught at institutions in the United States and Europe.

As a student, Solana had joined the banned Spanish Socialist Worker's Party (Partido Socialista Obrero Español, PSOE). He went on to hold a variety of posts in the party. Solana was elected to parliament in 1977 and appointed minister of culture in 1982. He also served as the government's spokesman. Solana initially opposed NATO and argued that the alliance created unnecessary tension with the Soviet Union. However, in 1986, he publicly campaigned on behalf of the alliance during a national referendum on Spain's continued membership in NATO. In 1988, Solana became minister of education and science. Four years later, he was appointed foreign minister. In 1995, Solana initiated a program to improve relations between the **European Union (EU)** and countries in the Mediterranean region.

In December 1995, Solana was chosen as NATO secretary-general after his predecessor, Willy Claes (1938–), was forced to resign. Solana quickly earned a reputation as a skilled negotiator and consensus builder. Two issues dominated Solana's tenure as NATO chief: the civil war in the former Yugoslavia, including the **Bosnian Conflict**, and alliance expansion. In Bosnia, plans were already in place for NATO to deploy peacekeeping forces. In January 1996, NATO deployed a 60,000-member peacekeeping mission in Bosnia, the Implementation Force—the mission was subsequently transitioned to the Stabilization Force. This deployment marked the first significant deployment of NATO forces outside of the alliance's territory. Solana endorsed the continued union between Serbia and Montenegro as a means to prevent the further disintegration of the former Yugoslavia, including the potential independence of Kosovo. Solana warned Montenegrin leaders against independence, but a referendum led to the end of the union with Serbia and complete autonomy for Montenegro, which became Europe's newest nation in 2006.

Member nations agreed on **NATO enlargement**, but there was considerable debate over the size and scope of the expansion. One faction favored a wide expansion to include as many as 10 countries. Another argued that expansion should be limited to one or two states. At the 1997 Madrid Summit, Solana crafted a compromise in which the Czech Republic, Hungary, and Poland were invited to become members of the alliance (the countries formally joined NATO in 1999). The Madrid Summit underscored the continuing utility of NATO through the alliance's willingness to include the countries of the former Soviet bloc. To assuage Moscow's concerns, in 1997 Solana negotiated the Founding Act between Russia and NATO. The accord led to the creation of the NATO-Russia Permanent Joint Council, which granted Moscow a nonvoting seat during alliance meetings. Solana also completed the NATO-Ukraine Charter on a Distinctive Partnership in 1997.

In 1999, Solana endeavored to negotiate a peaceful resolution between Serbs and ethnic Albanians in the **Kosovo War**. International efforts to mediate the conflict failed, and Solana subsequently oversaw the political components of the alliance's 77-day air campaign against Belgrade to protect the Kosovar Albanians. After Serbia agreed to terms, NATO led an international peace enforcement mission, Kosovo Force.

Solana resigned as secretary-general of NATO in October 1999 to accept a position as the EU high representative for **Common**

Foreign and Security Policy (CFSP). The next month, Solana was also appointed as secretary-general of the **Western European Union.** In these posts, Solana was able to secure agreement on the creation of a European Rapid Reaction Force to undertake humanitarian and security operations. Solana also secured consensus on CFSP among competing factions in the EU, led by Great Britain and France, who disagreed on the scale of foreign and security cooperation. Solana opposed the U.S.-led invasion in the **Iraq War** in 2003 and was a vocal critic of American treatment of detainees in the **war on terror.** He attempted to forge a common EU policy on Iraq, but was unable to bridge the divide between countries that supported the United States, including Britain, the Netherlands, and Italy, and those opposed to military force, including France, Germany, and Belgium. Nonetheless, in spite of differences, in 2004 the EU expanded to include 10 countries in eastern and central Europe that had supported the United States, such as the Czech Republic, Hungary, and Poland.

Solana's careful diplomacy led to his reappointment as the EU's first foreign minister in 2004 (Solona's position absorbed the existing post of EU commissioner for foreign relations). Solana helped arrange the 2004 "Roadmap for Peace" plan, which endorsed the creation of a Palestinian state in exchange for recognition of Israel and democratic elections in Palestine. In 2005, Solana launched accession negotiations with Ukraine on possible EU membership. Solana campaigned unsuccessfully in France for ratification of the proposed EU constitution. The May 2005 French rejection of the founding document undermined Solana's role as the coordinator for European foreign policy and called into question the future of CFSP.

SOMALIA INTERVENTION (1992–1994). The Somalia intervention began as a humanitarian operation to aid the famine-stricken country, but evolved into a **nation-building** mission that the United States abandoned in 1994 after a failed attempt to capture Somali warlord Mohamed Farrah Aidid. The Somalia intervention involved two presidencies, that of **George H. W. Bush** and **William J. Clinton.** The crisis also marked a transition in America's post–**Cold War** diplomacy away from broad efforts to reshape the global system into Bush's "new world order" to Clinton's initial neoisolationist foreign policy.

In July 1991, Somali dictator Muhammad Siad Barre was overthrown in a civil war that left the country fractured. The northern areas of Somalia declared their independence as the self-proclaimed Republic of Somaliland. The remainder of the country became divided among more than 20 warlords and clan factions. The disintegration of civil order exacerbated a regional drought and created a devastating famine. Between 1991 and 1992, more than 250,000 Somalis died from disease, starvation, or armed strife. In response, in August 1992 Bush authorized an emergency humanitarian mission to bring food and medical supplies to the Somalis in Operation Provide Relief. The effort was part of the broader **United Nations (UN)** mission known as UN Operation in Somalia (UNOSOM) I.

Emergency relief supplies began arriving on 28 August, but forces loyal to local warlords interfered with distribution of the materials by UNOSOM I. The UN appealed for military assistance to protect the humanitarian mission, and in October, Bush authorized the deployment of a small number of U.S. forces. This mission was expanded after the UN on 3 December authorized the creation of a multinational peacekeeping force, the United Task Force (UNITAF), led by the United States. In November, Bush appointed veteran diplomat **Robert B. Oakley** to represent the administration in Somalia (Oakley had previously served as U.S. ambassador there). Oakley carried out the initial negotiations over the American deployment and arranged a truce among the leading warlords. On 9 December, the first of an eventual 25,000 U.S. troops arrived in Somalia. Throughout December, UNITAF expanded its area of operations and began delivering the first assistance that many areas had received since the onset of hostilities. On 28 December, the main warlords, including Aidid, agreed to cease fighting. Bush visited Somalia to cheering crowds outside of the capital of Mogadishu, while UN secretary-general **Boutros Boutros-Ghali** had to be rescued from rioting mobs within the city.

In January 1993, violence escalated in Mogadishu. U.S. forces conducted a series of strikes against snipers' outposts and camps that had launched attacks on UN personnel and depots. The attacks marked an increase in UNITAF operations to protect humanitarian operations. Meanwhile, Clinton was inaugurated. His administration sought to reduce the American troop presence and to transition both the relief and security mission to the UN. In March, with pressure from Washington and under the auspices of the UN, the Conference on National Reconciliation in Somalia was launched in Addis Ababa, Ethiopia. The gathering produced an agreement to end violence and stop interference with food and medical distribution. Subsequently, the UN authorized UNOSOM II to supersede the Washington-led UNITAF. UNOSOM II's goals went beyond humanitarian response. The new UN objective was nation-building, the attempt to transform Somalia from a failed state back into a viable country. By May, 28 countries had contributed forces to UNOSOM II. On 4 May, Washington handed over command of military operations in Somalia to the UN.

On 5 June, militia fighters loyal to Aidid massacred 24 Pakistani peacekeepers. The following week, UN forces launched a series of missions to capture Aidid, including an air attack on an Aidid compound that killed a number of clan leaders. Four Western journalists were beaten to death when they arrived to report on the strike. Through the summer, there were dramatic increases in attacks on foreign journalists, aid workers, and UN forces. In August four U.S. soldiers were killed, and seven Nigerian peacekeepers died in September during clashes with local militias. Clinton ordered the deployment of special operations forces to find and capture Aidid. On 9 September, American and Pakistani troops killed more than 100 militia fighters and an unknown number of civilians during an attack on UNOSOM II forces. Meanwhile, Clinton asked former president **James E. Carter** to undertake negotiations with Aidid without notifying the military commanders in Somali of the new diplomatic offensive. In September, Muhammad Atef and six **Al Qaeda** terrorists traveled to Somalia to conduct anti-UN and anti-American operations and train Islamic militia fighters. Al Qaeda also provided arms and cash to the militias.

On 3–4 October, U.S. special operations forces and Army Rangers undertook a failed mission to capture Aidid in the Battle of **Mogadishu**. During the fighting, 18 Americans were killed and 84 wounded. Approximately 700 Somalis died and more than 1,500 were wounded. In addition, a U.S. helicopter pilot, **Michael Durant**, was taken prisoner, while the bodies of the dead Americans were videotaped being dragged through the streets amid cheering Somalis.

Clinton ordered additional heavy weapons and more troops to Somalia, but also dispatched Oakley as part of an initiative to revive the peace deal from the Conference on National Reconciliation in Somalia. Oakley made little progress on a broader peace settlement, but was able to gain support from warlords for the creation of a temporary cease-fire. He also worked to gain the release of Durant. On 14 October, Durant was freed.

Clinton ordered the withdrawal of American forces. In March 1994, the last U.S. troops left Somalia. Some 20,000 UN peacekeeping forces remained in the country, but they withdrew less than a year later. Clinton redeployed American soldiers to cover the UN departure. The intervention cost the United States more than $1.7 billion. In August 1995, Aidid died in interclan fighting.

The Somalia intervention was the first major foreign policy setback of the Clinton administration. Following the withdrawal, the administration initially avoided military intervention and participation in multinational peacekeeping missions in the **Balkan Wars** and various conflicts in Africa. Various senior Al Qaeda figures, including **Osama bin Laden**, subsequently asserted that the withdrawal of American forces prompted the terrorist groups to refocus their attention on U.S. targets to induce Washington to leave other countries, such as Saudi Arabia.

In the late 1990s, a transitional national government was created in Somalia that was loosely supported by the clans. The government was supported by both Clinton and President **George W. Bush**. Washington viewed the warlord government as the best means to prevent the rise of an Islamic extremist government similar to the Taliban. In the autumn of 2006, an Islamic militia group, the Islamic Courts, took control of most of Somalia, including Mogadishu, but it was driven back by militias loyal to the civil government with support from Ethiopian troops in December. In January 2007, U.S. forces launched air strikes on the retreating Islamic Courts forces based on intelligence that Al Qaeda fighters were among the fleeing militias.

SOVIET COUP (1991). In 1991, hard-line Communists attempted to overthrow **Mikhail Gorbachev** in order to stop his democratic and economic reforms and prevent the breakup of the Soviet Union. Gorbachev was scheduled to sign a new treaty granting more power and autonomy to the constituent republics within the Soviet Union. On 18 August 1991, leading conservatives in the Politburo and senior security officials seized control of the government and placed Gorbachev under arrest at his vacation dacha in the Crimea. They installed an eight-member committee to act as a transitional government. Soviet vice president Gennady Yanayev was named acting president.

Russian president **Boris N. Yeltsin** led popular opposition to the coup. He gathered liberal politicians and civilians at the Duma building and was able to convince military forces sent to arrest him to join the anticoup resistance. While the coup was supported by higher-ranking officers, most enlisted personnel and junior officers sided with Yeltsin. Meanwhile, many of the republics declared independence, and there were large opposition demonstrations throughout the Soviet Union. President **George H. W. Bush** condemned the coup, and the United States restored diplomatic relations with states such as Estonia, Latvia, and Lithuania following their declarations of independence.

Once it became clear that security forces would not support the new government, the coup collapsed on 21 August. Gorbachev was flown back to Moscow, where he resumed nominal control over the collapsing Soviet government. The coup leaders were arrested and eventually tried for treason. Yeltsin emerged as the leading political figure in the country. He banned the Communist Party in Russia and initiated a series of further economic and political reforms. By December, all 15 republics had declared independence, and Yeltsin formed the **Commonwealth of Independent States** among the former Soviet states. Gorbachev resigned and the Soviet Union ceased to exist at the end of 1991. Yeltsin was seen as more reformist and pro-Western, and Bush developed a close working relationship with the Russian leader, ushering in a new phase in American-Russian relations.

STRATEGIC ARMS REDUCTION TREATIES (START I AND II). Two treaties that reduced the nuclear weapons stockpiles of the United States and the Soviet Union (and its successor, the Russian Federation). Negotiations for START I began in 1982. Washington and Moscow set a preliminary goal of reducing nuclear warhead stockpiles to 5,000 each. The deployment of U.S. intermediate-range nuclear weapons in Europe led the Soviets to withdraw from the discussions in 1983, but the talks were resumed in 1985 with a new proposed ceiling of 6,000 warheads for each of the superpowers. Negotiations continued over the next several years as the Soviets attempted to link prohibitions on space-based weapons and defense systems, such as the American Strategic Defense Initiative (SDI), to the nuclear reductions. In 1989, Moscow abandoned the SDI linkage during negotiations between U.S. secretary of state **James A. Baker III** and his Soviet counterpart. Final agreement between the two superpowers occurred at the Washington Summit in 1990, and START I was signed on 31 July 1991 by U.S. president **George H. W. Bush** and Soviet premier **Mikhail Gorbachev**.

START I limited the United States and the USSR to a maximum of 6,000 nuclear warheads apiece, of which no more than 4,900 could be ballistic missile warheads. In addition, each country was limited to 1,600 delivery systems, including submarine launchers, bombers, and intercontinental ballistic missiles (ICBMs). The treaty reduced the total number of nuclear weapons among the two superpowers by 35 percent. START I also contained one of the most thorough inspection regimes of any **arms control** agreement and provided for 12 separate means to monitor the arsenals of **Cold War** foes. The agreement was to last for 15 years following ratification and could be extended for five-year periods thereafter.

START I was signed five months before the demise of the Soviet Union. On 23 May 1992, Belarus, Kazakhstan, Russia, and Ukraine signed the Lisbon Protocol in which they pledged to abide by the terms of START I as the successor states to the Soviet Union. Belarus, Kazakhstan, and Ukraine subsequently disarmed, or transferred to Russia, all their remaining nuclear weapons. The U.S. Senate ratified START I on 1 October 1992. By December 1994, the parliaments of the four Soviet successor states had ratified the agreement and it entered into force. Meanwhile, in December 1993, President **William J. Clinton** had ordered the United States to accelerate its reductions under START I. In March 1995, the first START I verification inspections begin. By 2001, more than 450 missile silos in the United States had been destroyed. On 5 December 2001, Washington and Moscow issued a joint statement that all obligations under START I had been met.

Bush initiated the negotiations over START II with Russian president **Boris Yeltsin** in 1992, when the two leaders agreed to reduce the total number of nuclear warheads to no more than 3,500 in each country. On 3 January 1993, Bush and Yeltsin signed the START II accord. START II called for each country to reduce its total warheads in two phases, eventually reaching a target of 3,000–3,500 warheads each. The Senate ratified the agreement on 26 January 1996, but the Duma refused to approve the treaty until the United States agreed to an additional protocol that would pledge both states not to pursue **ballistic missile defense**. The Senate would not approve the protocol, however, and the Duma then delayed ratification on several occasions to protest American military strikes on Iraq in 1998 and against Kosovo in 1999. The Duma finally approved START II on 14 April 2000. In 1997, Clinton and Yeltsin agreed to begin negotiations on a potential START III accord. However, no progress was made.

Although START II was ratified by both states, it was never implemented. Instead, it was superseded by the 2002 **Strategic Offensive Reductions Treaty**.

STRATEGIC OFFENSIVE REDUCTIONS TREATY (SORT). The Treaty on Strategic Offensive Reductions, also known as the Moscow Treaty, was designed to reduce the nuclear arsenals of the United States and Russia by two-thirds of their contemporary levels. SORT superseded the second **Strategic Arms Reduction Treaty (START II)**. In November 2001, U.S. president **George W. Bush** and Russian president **Vladimir Putin** agreed on the basic components of SORT. The treaty was signed in Moscow on 24 May 2002.

SORT limits the number of deployed warheads in each country to a maximum of 2,200. However, unlike previous U.S.-Russian **arms control** treaties, there are no verification procedures. Instead, American and Russian officials are to meet twice each year to oversee progress on the agreement. Furthermore, the reductions in warheads can be temporary (i.e., the warheads can be taken out of service and placed in storage). SORT was ratified by the Senate on 6 March 2003 and by the Duma on 14 May 2003. The Treaty entered into force on 1 June 2003 and is scheduled to remain in effect until 2012.

SUHARTO, HAJI MOHAMMAD (1921–). President of Indonesia, 1967–1998. Suharto was born in Godean, in the Dutch colony of Java. He joined the colonial army in 1940, but fought against the Dutch after World War II. He became an officer in the national military following independence and rose to the rank of major general in 1962. In 1967, Suharto became president. Through the **Cold War**, Suharto remained a close ally of the United States. However, with the end of the superpower conflict, the administration of **George H. W. Bush** became increasingly critical of Suharto's **human rights** policies and pressed for democratic reforms, as well as more autonomy for **East Timor** (which Indonesia had annexed in 1975). In 1992, Congress enacted limitations on U.S. military aid to Indonesia. The following year, Washington supported a **United Nations** Security Council resolution condemning Indonesia's brutal suppression in East Timor. In 1997, the **East Asian Financial Crisis** led to a significant economic downturn. Suharto was granted a relief package, including debt forgiveness, from the **International Monetary Fund (IMF)**. However, the IMF insisted on an austerity program that was domestically unpopular. Indonesians were also tired of the corruption and graft common in the regime. Suharto personally embezzled more than $12 billion during his tenure. In 1998, protests and the loss of military support led Suharto to resign. Repeated efforts by successive governments to prosecute him for corruption were unsuccessful.

– T –

TABA SUMMIT (2001). The last effort by the administration of **William J. Clinton** to achieve a major diplomatic breakthrough in the **Arab-Israeli conflict**. Following the failure of the 2000 **Camp David Summit**, Clinton brought Israeli prime minister **Ehud Barak** and Palestinian leader **Yasser Arafat** together at Taba, Egypt. After the Camp David Summit, the Palestinians launched a new *intifada*, or series of attacks, on Israel following a provocative visit to the Temple Mount by **Ariel Sharon**, the leader of the Likud Party and a candidate in the upcoming Israeli elections.

U.S. negotiators met with Israeli and Palestinian representatives in Washington, D.C., in December in an effort to make sure that an agreement could be reached at the proposed summit among the leaders of the three states. Unlike at the Camp David talks, the Palestinians and Israelis agreed on the broad outlines of an accord. The 1967 borders would serve as the basis for the negotiations with Israel, which was willing to turn over 100 percent of the Gaza Strip and up to 97 percent of the West Bank. The discussions also produced an agreement that Jerusalem would serve as the capital of both Israel and a Palestinian state and that the city would be under joint control of both countries. There was no specific agreement on the status of refugees and the right of return for displaced persons, but both parties pledged to develop a future settlement based on recommendations from the **United Nations**.

At Taba, Barak and Arafat endorsed the recommendations from the Washington negotiations and pledged to draft a final document. The few differences between the two sides were addressed in a compromise proposal by Clinton that offered a range of proposals, including territorial exchanges and solutions to the right-of-return issues. However, Barak did not want to finalize an agreement until after the Israeli elections, and he returned to campaigning without a final settlement. Barak lost the elections to Sharon, and the provisions of the Taba Summit were not implemented.

TAIWAN STRAIT CRISIS (1996). In 1996, military exercises by the People's Republic of China (PRC) led President **William J. Clinton** to deploy American military forces as a reaffirmation of U.S. support for Taiwan. Tensions in the Taiwan Strait began to escalate in 1994 when a Chinese submarine shadowed an American aircraft carrier battle group over a three-day period. Then in June 1995, the Taiwanese president made an unofficial visit to the United States, which was seen as a provocation by Beijing. The PRC responded by conducting a series of missile tests in July, some 37 miles (60 kilometers) from Taiwanese territory. The PRC also deployed troops, ships, and aircraft into the region and held more missile tests in August. The PRC military actions caused the Taiwanese stock market to crash and the currency to depreciate.

Ahead of the March 1996 presidential elections in Taiwan, the PRC launched a new series of military exercises in the strait. Under the 1979 Taiwan Relations Act, the United States was required to defend

Taipei from PRC aggression. Clinton thus ordered the deployment of U.S. naval forces to the strait, marking the first time since 1976 that the Americans had stationed ships in the waterway.

Tensions were ameliorated in 1997 during a state visit to the United States by PRC president **Jiang Zemin**. In addition, in 1998, the two countries signed the Agreement on Establishing a Consultation Mechanism to Strengthen Military Maritime Safety, which implemented a range of mechanisms to reduce the potential for unintended conflict between U.S. and PRC naval forces. Under the accord, military representatives from both countries would meet annually to inform each other of exercises in the region and to discuss confidence-building measures among the respective military establishments.

TALBOT, STROBE (1946–). American diplomat who served as deputy secretary of state from 1994 to 2001. Nelson Strobridge "Strobe" Talbot III was born in Dayton, Ohio, and earned a master's degree in literature from Oxford University in 1971. He met future president **William J. Clinton** while both were Rhodes Scholars, and the two became lifelong friends. Talbot had a successful career as a journalist and rose to become an editor at *Time* magazine. He was appointed to the State Department in 1993 to help manage relations with Russia and the **Commonwealth of Independent States** and became deputy secretary the following year. Through his service in the Clinton administration, Talbot promoted multilateralism and encouraged deeper American integration with international institutions such as the **North Atlantic Treaty Organization** and the **Organization for Security and Cooperation in Europe**. In 2002, Talbot became president of the Washington-based Brookings Institution think tank.

TENET, GEORGE J. (1953–). Director of the Central Intelligence Agency (CIA) from 1997 to 2005, who shared the blame for the intelligence failures that led to the **September 11 terrorist attacks** and subsequently oversaw reforms in the CIA as part of the broader reorganization of the U.S. intelligence community. George John Tenet was born to Greek immigrant parents in Flushing, Queens, in New York City. He earned a bachelor's degree from Georgetown University in

1976 and a master's degree from Columbia University two years later. Tenet worked briefly for a Greek-American lobbying firm and then served as an aid to Republican senator John Heinz of Pennsylvania. He subsequently held positions as a staffer for various Democratic senators until 1993. That year he was appointed to the presidential transition team of **William J. Clinton**. Clinton then appointed Tenet to the staff of the National Security Council. In 1995, Tenet became the deputy director of the CIA, and the following year, he was made acting CIA chief after the resignation of **John M. Deutch**.

Clinton nominated Tenet to replace Deutch, and he was unanimously confirmed by the Senate. He formally became director on 11 July 1997. Throughout his years in the Clinton administration, Tenet warned of the growing dangers of terrorism. When **George W. Bush** was elected president in 2000, he asked Tenet to remain in office. He became the first CIA director in 28 years to stay in office following the election of a new president.

As CIA director, Tenet sought to refocus intelligence resources on groups such as **Al Qaeda**, especially after the 1998 **embassy bombings** in Kenya and Tanzania. His efforts to establish reliable intelligence networks among terrorist groups were constrained by restrictions on human intelligence put in place in 1995. These restrictions were designed to prevent the United States from cooperating with individuals who may have been involved in **human rights** violations (and thereby end the long-standing practice whereby Washington had used the CIA to support totalitarian regimes in countries such as Guatemala or El Salvador). However, they prevented intelligence units from developing contacts within terrorist groups. In addition, there was a series of restrictions that prevented the CIA and the Federal Bureau of Investigation (FBI) from sharing intelligence. These prohibitions dated from the 1970s and had been put in place in response to CIA domestic operations at the time. The CIA was the country's lead counterterrorism agency for external threats, while the FBI was the agency charged with domestic counterterrorism. The inability of the two bodies to work with each other contributed to the intelligence failures surrounding the 9/11 terrorist attacks.

Following these attacks, Tenet oversaw a series of reforms and new initiatives within the CIA. The restrictions on human intelligence were lifted, and the CIA devoted new resources to building networks around the world. In addition, new imperatives on intelligence sharing were put in place. CIA operatives played an important role in the U.S.-led invasion of Afghanistan, **Operation Enduring Freedom**. They also undertook a range of operations around the world to disrupt Al Qaeda and its allies.

Prior to the 2003 **Iraq War**, Tenet marshaled significant evidence that the regime of **Saddam Hussein** was actively pursuing weapons of mass destruction, and Bush used the material to try to convince both domestic and international audiences of the need for military action. After the fall of the Iraqi regime, no evidence was found to corroborate the CIA intelligence, and Tenet subsequently publicly apologized for the agency's failures. Tenet opposed the broad intelligence reforms that culminated in the creation of the director of national intelligence to oversee the country's intelligence community. He announced his resignation on 3 June 2004 and left office in July 2004. *See also* INTERNATIONAL TERRORISM; WAR ON TERROR.

THATCHER, MARGARET (1925–). British prime minister from 1979 to 1990, the first female prime minister of Great Britain and the longest-serving British government chief since the 1800s. Thatcher was born Margaret Hilda Roberts in Grantham, Lincolnshire, to a lower-middle-class family. She graduated from Oxford University in 1951 with a degree in chemistry. Thatcher was active in conservative politics while still a student. She unsuccessfully ran for Parliament twice (when she ran in 1950, she was the youngest female candidate to seek office). She later trained as a lawyer and became a barrister in 1953. In 1959, Thatcher was elected to the House of Commons and subsequently served in a variety of senior posts in the Conservative Party. From 1970 to 1974, she was secretary of state for education and science in the cabinet of Edward Heath (1916–2005). In 1975, she replaced Heath as leader of the Conservatives after their loss in national elections. When the Conservatives won the 1979 elections, Thatcher became prime minister.

Thatcher implemented a series of economic and social reforms that revolved around privatizing state-owned agencies and reducing the welfare state. She also reformed the country's tax system. Her policies improved the British economy, but were criticized for undermining the nation's social support system. The reforms came to be known as "Thatcherism." Her foreign policy was staunchly anticommunist, and she developed a close relationship with U.S. president **Ronald W. Reagan**. She supported the U.S. bombing of Libya in 1986 in response to that country's support of terrorism. In 1982, Thatcher led the country during the Falklands War, in which Great Britain defeated Argentina. She also oversaw negotiations with the People's Republic of China over the status of Hong Kong, which ultimately led to British withdrawal from the colony in 1997. Thatcher opposed proposals in the 1980s to strengthen the power of the European Community.

In the waning days of the **Cold War**, Thatcher developed a working relationship with Soviet leader **Mikhail Gorbachev**. She supported **German reunification** and efforts to speed the end of the Cold War. She also urged strong action against the Iraqi invasion of Kuwait and supported U.S. president **George H. W. Bush** in his efforts to develop a multinational coalition to oppose the regime of **Saddam Hussein**.

An economic downturn undermined her popularity in Britain. In addition, she insisted on the implementation of a poll tax that was unpopular with both the opposition and her own party (at one point, 18 million Britons refused to pay the regressive tax). Senior party members forced Thatcher from her leadership in 1990 (although her preferred successor, John Major, became prime minister). In 1992, Thatcher resigned from the House of Commons. That same year, she was granted a life peerage as Baroness Thatcher.

THEOCONSERVATIVES. American Christian conservatives who seek to base domestic and foreign policy on religious principles. Theoconservatives, or theocons, have their roots in the Christian fundamentalist movement that became prominent in U.S. politics in the 1980s. The importance of Christian evangelical voters to the Republican Party led the party to adopt many of the goals of the movement, especially during the administration of President **George W. Bush**. However, the movement also had an impact on the administration of President **William J. Clinton**. For instance, in 1998, Congress passed the International Religious Freedom Act, which made the free exercise of religion a foreign policy goal of the United States and created a special advisor on religious freedom within the National Security

Council. In addition, under Clinton, the U.S. Commission on International Religious Freedom was established to monitor religious persecution and repression around the world. In foreign policy, theocons have had their greatest impact on U.S. opposition to multinational family planning and contraceptive programs.

TIANANMEN SQUARE PROTESTS (1989). A series of prodemocracy demonstrations in the People's Republic of China in 1989. The protests were the culmination of a movement inspired by the wave of democratization that swept across Eastern Europe at the end of the **Cold War**. The Beijing government brutally suppressed the protestors, earning international condemnation and U.S. and **European Union** sanctions.

The nationwide demonstrations followed economic and political reforms under Deng Xiaoping. Chinese students, intellectuals, and a growing business class sought further freedoms and a political transition to democracy. In 1989, prodemocracy Chinese began to gather in Beijing and other major cities following the death of former Communist Party secretary-general Hu Yaobang, a champion of economic and political liberalization. Hu had been forced to resign following student protests in 1987. On 29 April 1989, 50,000 students and prodemocracy supporters took to the streets to demand further reforms. They were soon joined by workers who were concerned by the rampant corruption among party officials. In addition to the protests in Beijing, there were large demonstrations in Chongqing, Shanghai, and Urumqi and smaller gatherings in other cities.

By May, there were more than 100,000 demonstrators. Leaders of the protestors appealed for a dialogue with the government. When the government refused, students launched a hunger strike. Meanwhile, there was growing international media coverage of the demonstrations. Government leaders initially sought to avoid violence and tried to diffuse the crisis by offering some minor reforms. Hard-liners among the Chinese leadership ousted General Secretary Zhao Ziyang because of his policy of reconciliation toward the demonstrators. Martial law was declared on 20 May.

On the night of 3 June, the military and security forces launched a coordinated assault to restore order in Beijing and other cities. In the ensuing attacks, at least 800 civilians were killed and as many as

10,000 were injured (although there remains widespread disagreement about the total number of dead and wounded). Following the crackdown, authorities arrested hundreds of students and workers. An unknown number were tried and executed, and others were given prison sentences.

U.S. president **George H. W. Bush** condemned the repression and imposed economic and military sanctions on Beijing. The European Union and individual countries followed the American example. Bush also suspended contacts between high-level American and Chinese military officials. However, on 30 June 1989, Bush secretly dispatched National Security Advisor **Brent Scowcroft** to meet with Chinese officials in an effort to prevent an escalation of tensions between the two countries. Bush believed that Sino-American relations were a key component of U.S. foreign policy and that the United States would have to repair relations in order to retain some influence with the Chinese government. Bush vetoed a bill that would have allowed Chinese exchange students to remain in the United States until Beijing liberalized.

The president's response to the massacres was widely criticized within the United States and within his own party. Many Republicans argued that the United States should have done more to support the protestors and encourage democratic reforms in the PRC. Bush's policies were continued under President **William J. Clinton**, who separated **human rights** and economic policy toward China.

TRADE POLICY. U.S. trade policy is based on the twin—though sometimes competitive—goals of expansion of free trade and promotion of domestic industries and economic sectors. Trade policy is developed through the legislative and executive branches and reflects current domestic and international law, as well as American treaty obligations, such as the **North American Free Trade Agreement (NAFTA)**, and membership in multilateral economic institutions, including the **World Trade Organization (WTO)**. U.S. trade policy historically has been based on the assumption that the American economy is highly flexible and can quickly react to changes in international markets. Economic sectors in the United States that are not competitive with foreign goods and services diminish as consumers are allowed access to less-expensive foreign products, while labor and capital are shifted to those areas where the United States has a competitive advantage.

External economic policy is developed for the president by three main groups: the trade policy staff committee; the trade policy review group; and the National Economic Council, in coordination with the National Security Council. By the end of the **Cold War**, the U.S. trade representative emerged as the main negotiator and diplomat for economic issues. The Office of the Trade Representative was created in 1962 and given greater power through a series of legislation, most notably the 1988 Omnibus Trade and Competitiveness Act that granted the office primary responsibility for creating and coordinating trade policy. In 2000, the Office of the Trade Representative was expanded through the Trade and Development Act, which created a range of new positions, including chief agricultural negotiator and the assistant U.S. trade representative for African affairs.

The growing economic power and cohesion of the European Community (later **European Union**) led the administration of **George H. W. Bush** to seek to create a free trade bloc in the Western Hemisphere. Bush sought to remove tariffs, subsidies, and other restrictions on trade as a means to expand markets for American products and ensure that U.S. consumers had access to cheaper foreign products. Building on the successful U.S-Canada Free Trade Agreement of 1988, the Bush administration negotiated NAFTA to remove trade barriers among Canada, Mexico, and the United States.

Successive administrations sought to expand NAFTA into the **Free Trade Area of the Americas (FTAA)**, which would create a regional economic bloc among all of the states of the Western Hemisphere. However, repeated rounds of negotiations over FTAA failed to overcome differences between the United States and Latin American countries led by Brazil and Venezuela. Brazil and other states sought greater access for their agricultural exports to the United States, but domestic farm groups were able to limit the ability of Washington to open these markets. Other Latin American and Caribbean states, led by Venezuela, feared American domination of their domestic markets and endeavored to bolster regional trade blocs as a means to counter U.S. economic hegemony in the hemisphere. As a result, the administrations of **William J. Clinton** and **George W. Bush** turned to bilateral free trade accords and limited regional agreements. In 2003, the Central American Free Trade Agreement (CAFTA) was signed between the United States and the countries of El Salvador, Guatemala, Honduras, and Nicaragua. In 2004, the Dominican Republic joined CAFTA, which was renamed the Dominican Republic–CAFTA (DR-CAFTA). By 2006, the United States had 114 bilateral or regional trade agreements in place and 15 free trade agreements.

In order to facilitate trade agreements, successive administrations used "fast-track" authority, which allowed Washington to negotiate economic agreements and then have Congress vote directly on the accord without the ability to add amendments. Fast-track authority also removed the requirement for the Senate to ratify agreements with a two-thirds majority. Fast-track authority was superseded by the Trade Promotion Authority (TPA) Act in 2002, which expanded the authority of the administration to start and conclude agreements. However, TPA must be regularly extended by Congress. The United States also implemented a number of programs that granted preferential trade concessions to developing states. For instance, the 2000 African Growth and Opportunity Act (AGOA) reduced or eliminated tariffs on more than 7,000 products from 37 African countries. AGOA was originally in effect until 2008, but has been extended until 2015.

In 1995, the Clinton administration supported the creation of the WTO from the General Agreement on Tariffs and Trade (GATT). The WTO institutionalized the rules and agreements of the GATT and provided a means to resolve economic disputes and disagreements among member states. The United States endeavored to use institutions such as the **International Monetary Fund (IMF)**, WTO, and **World Bank** to promote trade liberalization and open markets. Washington also sought to utilize these organizations to ensure economic stability. In addition to the U.S. financial assistance, the IMF and World Bank provided funds and aid during the **Mexican Economic Crisis** and the **East Asian Financial Crisis**.

The Clinton and Bush administrations pursued economic policies to maintain a weak dollar in order to make U.S. exports less expensive and foreign products less appealing to American consumers. The United States also maintained a variety of restrictions and tariffs on some imports. Domestic political pressure resulted in the maintenance of agricultural tariffs (which averaged 9.7 percent in 2006) and steel tariffs. In addition, American environmental and health legislation prevents the importation of some food products. *See also* GLOBALIZATION; JAPAN–UNITED STATES FRAMEWORK FOR A NEW ECONOMIC PARTNERSHIP; UNITED STATES–AUSTRALIA FREE TRADE AGREEMENT.

TRILATERAL COMMISSION. A private, nonprofit group established in 1973 to facilitate discussion and cooperation on international issues. The group's name is derived from its organization, which includes members from three geographic areas: Europe, North America, and Pacific Asia. Membership in the Trilateral Commission is limited by continent. In 2006, Europe had 150 members, all from **European Union** states, and Pacific Asia had 117, including representatives from Australia, Indonesia, Japan, Malaysia, New Zealand, the People's Republic of China, the Philippines, Singapore, South Korea, and Thailand. North America had 107 members, including 85 from the United States, 15 Canadians, and 7 Mexicans. Representatives are chosen by invitation and may not be a member of government (members of the commission who become government officials take a temporary leave of absence from the organization). Past or current U.S. members of the Trilateral Commission include former presidents **James E. Carter**, **George H. W. Bush**, and **William J. Clinton**; Vice President **Richard B. Cheney**, former secretary of defense **William S. Cohen**, and Senator Diane Feinstein of California. The secretive nature of the selection process and the meetings of the group have made the Trilateral Commission a favorite target for conspiracy theorists and anti**globalization** activists, who assert that the organization serves as a forum to undermine national sovereignty and promote the interests of multinational corporations.

– U –

UNITED NATIONS (UN). In the aftermath of the **Cold War**, the United States has had a mixed relationship with the UN, marked by both cooperation and controversy. The world body was founded in 1945, mainly through the efforts of the United States. The five major wartime allies—France, the Republic of China, the Soviet Union,

Great Britain, and the United States—were all granted permanent seats on the UN Security Council with veto power over any actions of the organization (the People's Republic of China replaced the Republic of China on the Security Council in 1972). By 2006, the membership of the UN included 192 countries, while entities such as the Vatican, the Palestinian National Authority, and the Republic of China (Taiwan) have observer status. During the Cold War, the Soviet Union regularly vetoed UN resolutions (it blocked twice as many UN actions as any of the other permanent members). Meanwhile, the United States was criticized for its repeated veto of resolutions condemning Israel during the bipolar conflict and beyond.

After the end of the superpower conflict, it appeared that a new era of cooperation would be initiated. The number of resolutions adopted by the Security Council rose dramatically (on average three times as many per year as was the case during the Cold War). In August 1990, in response to the Iraqi invasion of Kuwait, the United States secured United Nations Security Council Resolution (UNSCR) 660, which condemned the occupancy of Kuwait and ordered the regime of **Saddam Hussein** to withdraw its forces. A series of other measures followed, culminating in UNSCR 668, which set 15 January as a deadline for Iraqi withdrawal or Baghdad would face military action. The resultant **Persian Gulf War** liberated Kuwait and forced Saddam to agree to terms codified by the world body, including the end of the regime's programs to develop weapons of mass destruction. The unanimity shown by the Security Council in the face of the Iraqi aggression became the benchmark by which future international action would be measured.

Following the Gulf War, friction between the United States and the UN emerged over the **Somalia intervention**. Washington sought to turn the UN-led operation into a **nation-building** mission, while the world body endeavored to prevent the withdrawal of U.S. forces from the peacekeeping operation in the aftermath of the 1993 Battle of **Mogadishu**. The administration of **William J. Clinton** supported the UN-led peacekeeping mission in the **Balkan Wars**, but refused to deploy American troops as part of it. The inability of the UN or the **Organization for Security and Cooperation in Europe** to prevent the **Bosnian Conflict** prompted Clinton to turn to the **North Atlantic Treaty Organization** to lead the peace enforcement efforts following the **Dayton Accords**. His administration also refused to participate in the UN attempts to intervene in the **Rwandan genocide** (but then criticized the world body for not taking stronger action to stop the bloodshed).

In the 1990s, Congress blocked payment of a portion of the nation's annual payments to the world body in the **United Nations Dues Controversy**. The United States sought a reduction in its annual dues from 25 percent of the UN's total budget to 22 percent. Legislation also called for the U.S. share of the peacekeeping budget to have a ceiling of 25 percent (it had ranged as high as 31 percent). Tensions between the Clinton administration and the United Nations led Washington to oppose the reelection of **Boutros Boutros-Ghali** as UN secretary-general. The United States contended that Boutros-Ghali was unwilling to undertake necessary reforms at the world body. Instead, the Clinton administration supported the candidacy of **Kofi Annan** of Ghana, who was elected in December 1996.

Annan initiated a series of reforms and restructuring. He also negotiated a settlement with American UN ambassador **Richard Holbrooke** whereby the United States paid a portion of its arrears in exchange for the recalculation of its annual payments down to 22 percent and a series of reforms at the world body. The U.S. share of peacekeeping dues was subsequently cut to 27 percent in 2000, but this was still above the 25 percent mandated by Congress and consequently the United States continued to accrue arrears. Annan emerged as a vocal critic of U.S. policy toward Iraq. In 1998, the secretary-general condemned American air strikes because they were not authorized by the world body. The controversy over the **Oil-for-Food Program** contributed to strained relations, as charges surfaced of corruption. U.S. pressure resulted in an inquiry that discovered the fact that more than 270 UN and national officials, journalists, and individual companies had taken bribes from Iraq. In addition, UN officials destroyed documents and engaged in other activities to cover up the corruption. Annan's son was implicated in the scandal, but the secretary-general refused calls to resign.

Washington regularly criticized the UN Commission on Human Rights, which included several countries, such as Cuba, Syria, and the People's Republic of China, that had poor **human rights** records. The commission was replaced in 2006 by the UN Human Rights

Council in response to pressure from the United States and other states. The United States provided diplomatic and economic support for a range of UN operations through the 1990s and 2000s, such as the intervention in **East Timor**, as well as oversight of a range of elections.

In 2002, the United States endeavored to gain international support through the United Nations for an invasion of Iraq because of the regime's noncompliance with previous UN measures. In November 2002, the Security Council adopted UNSCR 1441, which called on Iraq to allow a new round of international inspections and disclose any weapons programs or else face serious consequences (although the consequences were not specifically detailed). France, Germany, Russia, and other countries opposed to an invasion of Iraq contended that a second resolution was required before military action could be undertaken. After failing to gain a second resolution in February 2003, however, the United States and its allies asserted that such a resolution was actually not needed because of the language of 1441. In March 2003, the United States led an invasion of Iraq that overthrew the Saddam regime. Opponents of the attack charged that the United States and its coalition bypassed the UN, while many proponents of military strikes argued that the UN's inability to endorse the invasion undermined the inherent weaknesses of the world body.

In 2005, the administration of President **George W. Bush** named **John Bolton** as UN ambassador. The appointment of the conservative Bolton was perceived as an indication of Washington's continued disfavor with the world organization. The following year, a UN panel recommended that the U.S. detention facilities for **unlawful combatants** at Guantanamo Bay be closed and that America revise its treatment of suspected terrorists captured in the **war on terror**.

In October 2006, Ban Ki-moon was elected to replace Annan as secretary-general with U.S. support. Washington hoped that the former South Korean foreign minister would be more supportive of American preferences at the UN. *See also* AFGHANISTAN INTERVENTION; INTERNATIONAL MONETARY FUND; IRAQ WAR; LIBERIAN CIVIL WAR; NORTH KOREAN NUCLEAR CRISES; WORLD BANK; WORLD CONFERENCE ON WOMEN; WORLD TRADE ORGANIZATION.

UNITED NATIONS DUES CONTROVERSY. With the end of the **Cold War**, there were calls by successive U.S. administrations for the **United Nations (UN)** to reassess the level of dues paid by America to support the organization. Throughout the superpower struggle, the United States had paid 25 percent of the overall budget of the UN and provided as much as 31 percent of the budget for peacekeeping operations. American officials argued that the fee structure had been determined at a time when the United States accounted for a much greater share of the world economy and that Washington's payments should now be reduced. In addition, senior congressmen, notably North Carolina Republican senator Jesse Helms, argued that the UN was corrupt and inefficient and, therefore, continued payments to the UN were unfair to American taxpayers. Helms wanted to link U.S. payments to reforms in the world body, and he used his power as chairman of the Senate Foreign Relations Committee to block the payment of UN dues. By 1996, the United States owed $1.2 billion in arrears. That year, faced with $3.7 billion in total arrears, the UN suspended the voting rights of 29 countries for not paying their dues. Furthermore, UN secretary-general **Boutros Boutros-Ghali** threatened to launch efforts to suspend the United States and Russia (which owed $590 million) as well. However, Washington and Moscow never took the secretary-general's threat seriously because of their veto power on the UN Security Council.

The administration of **William J. Clinton** tried to arrange a compromise whereby the United States would pay its arrears in exchange for the reduction of future dues and a series of reforms. The proposal was defeated by Republicans in Congress who wanted assurances that payments would be tied to reforms in the UN. In 1997, a second administration-backed initiative was again defeated in Congress. In 1999, Congress enacted the Helms-Biden Act, which linked the payment of $612 million in arrears to specific reforms and changes in the UN and the reduction of the American peacekeeping dues to 25 percent of the total budget. Under the measure, the United States would pay its back dues in increments as restructuring thresholds were met. In December 1999, the United States paid $100 million of its debt. However, Helms-Biden did not apply to more than $700 million that Congress had withheld to protest specific policies or programs. For instance, from 1984 to 2003, the United States refused to fund, or participate in, the United Nations Educational, Scientific, and Cultural Organization (UNESCO).

Meanwhile, the Clinton administration launched negotiations to reduce U.S. payments. In December 2000, American UN ambassador **Richard Holbrooke** reached a deal to reduce the American assessments to 22 percent of the total 2001 UN budget (one of the requirements of the Helms-Burton Act). The 3 percent reduction equaled $34 million. To compensate for the shortfall in the 2001 budget, U.S. media magnate Ted Turner volunteered to pay the difference. In addition, the American share of the peacekeeping budget was reduced to 27 percent. However, since that was still above the ceiling of 25 percent mandated by Helms-Biden, the remaining arrears (which had risen to $1.3 billion by 2001) were not paid.

In 2005, **John Bolton**, the UN ambassador appointed by the **George W. Bush** administration, proposed that member states be required to pay only for programs they supported. The following year, Bush threatened to withhold all American funding if the UN did not appoint a chief operating officer to oversee financial operations. The Bush administration also blocked a $100 million renovation plan for the UN building in New York. A compromise was reached, but the episode was demonstrative of the continuing tendency of the United States to use its financial contributions as a means to prompt preferred actions or policies.

UNITED STATES–AUSTRALIA FREE TRADE AGREEMENT. A free trade agreement (FTA) signed in 2004 that marked the culmination of a long series of efforts to remove trade barriers between the United States and Australia. The accord was also seen as a potential model for other bilateral trade deals and the manifestation of a shift in American **trade policy** away from efforts to seek broad, regional free trade areas. The first U.S.-Australia FTA was proposed in 1946. Attempts to secure an agreement broke down over U.S. agricultural subsidies and protectionist measures and concerns by successive Australian governments over the impact of American manufactured products on the domestic market. In the 1980s, negotiations over an FTA were stalled by the United States, while a 1992 initiative by President **George H. W. Bush** was rejected by Australia. In 2001, talks were relaunched. Five rounds of negotiations, led by U.S. Trade

Representative **Robert Zoellick** and his Australian counterpart, resulted in a 23-part agreement in May 2004. The FTA was approved by Congress in July 2004 and went into force on 1 January 2005. It covered all aspects of goods and services and allowed both countries to phase out some tariffs over time. For instance, the duties on Australian beef, cotton, dairy, peanut, and tobacco exports were reduced over a multiyear period. In 2005, as a result of the agreement, U.S. exports to Australia increased by $5.25 billion, while Australian exports to the United States rose by $2.97 billion. The success of the FTA led Washington to accelerate, or start new, negotiations with other countries.

UNITED STATES–JAPAN BASE CONTROVERSY. Under the terms of Japan's surrender in World War II and subsequent treaties, Tokyo provides territory to the United States for military bases. The number of American troops in Japan declined after the end of the **Cold War** from 150,000 to 100,000, including naval forces. In 1995, the two countries reached an accord on sharing the costs of the bases in which the United States accepted a larger share of the costs of maintaining the facilities, concurrent with the downsizing of some bases. Many bases were located in areas that were once remote, but had become heavily populated by the 1990s. In addition, training and other military activities posed both health and environmental concerns for local Japanese. Tensions between the two allies flared dramatically in September 1995 when three U.S. servicemen raped a 12-year-old girl on Okinawa. The three were convicted in March 1996.

In response to the rape and other concerns, Washington and Tokyo created the Special Action Committee on Okinawa (SACO) and launched a series of discussions on measures to lessen local opposition to American bases in Okinawa. Business and community leaders on the island wanted the bases to remain because of the economic impact of the facilities on the local economy (Okinawa was the poorest prefect in Japan). The SACO talks were accelerated in April 1996 during a visit to Japan by President **William J. Clinton**. As part of a package of broader security initiatives in the Japan-U.S. Joint Declaration on Security Alliance for the 21st Century, Clinton pledged to implement any recommendations by SACO.

In December 1996, the final SACO report was endorsed by the United States and Japan. In it, SACO developed 27 recommendations, which were implemented by the American military. Some bases were consolidated and the land turned over to local communities after extensive cleanup and environmental rehabilitation. In addition, training exercises were modified and the use of live ammunition reduced, while greater efforts were made to contain noise pollution.

In 2001, a U.S. submarine surfaced under a Japanese fishing vessel, killing nine. The sinking of the *Ehime Maru* led the governors of the 14 prefects that housed U.S. military facilities to urge further negotiations over the operations and management of the bases. In October 2005, Washington agreed to Tokyo's proposal to relocate one of the largest air bases on Okinawa to mainland Japan. In April 2006, the United States announced the redeployment of 8,000 Marines from Okinawa to Guam.

UNLAWFUL COMBATANTS. A category of detainees in the **war on terror**. The status was created by the administration of President **George W. Bush** to include those engaged in terrorism or who had taken up arms against the United States but were not uniformed soldiers as recognized by the Geneva Conventions. Unlawful combatants were also deemed not to be subject to the civil liberties or criminal justice system of the United States.

After the **September 11 terrorist attacks**, the Bush administration sought to define the legal status of those captured in the **Afghanistan intervention** or turned over to U.S. custody by allies such as Pakistan. Washington wanted the authority to hold these detainees, also known as enemy combatants, for lengthy periods for interrogation. International law, as codified in the Fourth Geneva Convention (1950), mandates that after capture, a tribunal must determine whether a detainee should be treated as a prisoner of war (POW) or placed in another category. The Bush administration sought to use military tribunals to determine the status of detainees. Meanwhile, the United States expanded its detention facility at Guantanamo Bay, Cuba. More than 750 detainees were held at the facility (some 340 of that total have since been released or transferred to other countries).

The Bush administration's treatment of unlawful detainees aroused both domestic and international criticism. Some opponents called for the unlawful combatants to be granted POW status, while others argued that terrorists and insurgents should be granted civil trials under American law. In addition, the Supreme Court ruled in 2006 in *Hamdan v. Rumsfeld* that the ongoing American military tribunals were unlawful. In response, Congress enacted the Military Commissions Act, which authorized the creation of military commissions to determine the status of unlawful combatants. Meanwhile, the Detainee Treatment Act of 2005 required that interrogations and detainee treatment be undertaken in accordance with U.S. military regulations on the treatment of prisoners.

USS *COLE* BOMBING. On 12 October 2000, **Al Qaeda** terrorists detonated an explosives-laden boat next to an American naval vessel, the *Cole*, in the Yemeni port of Aden. The attack killed 17 sailors and wounded 39 others. The *Cole* was a guided-missile destroyer that had stopped in Aden to refuel. Arrangements to refuel were made 12 days in advance through the port and a commercial company, and the terrorists were able to obtain advance information about the ship's arrival. About 40 minutes into the five-hour refueling process, an inflatable boat with 600–700 pounds of explosives, driven by Ibrahim al-Thawr and Abdullah al-Misawa, came alongside the *Cole*. Sailors on board the *Cole* saw the suspicious boat, but under the rules of engagement at the time, American military personnel were forbidden from firing unless they were fired upon first. The terrorists detonated the explosives, creating a 40-foot-diameter hole in the side of the vessel.

The British frigate HMS *Marlborough* was the first vessel to come to the aid of the stricken *Cole*. The destroyer was returned to the United States by a repair ship and underwent 14 months of repair and renovation before it returned to active service in April 2002.

Although there was considerable evidence that Al Qaeda was involved in the attack, the administration of **William J. Clinton** declined to undertake any action against the terrorist group outside of ongoing counterterrorist operations. With presidential elections the following month, Clinton decided to leave any action on the *Cole* attack to the succeeding administration.

In November 2002, the Central Intelligence Agency carried out an air strike by a drone on a car in Yemen carrying Abu Ali al-Harithi, one of the planners of the attack. Al-Harithi and an accomplice were killed in the strike, which took place with the tacit compliance of the Yemeni government. Meanwhile, teams from the Federal Bureau of Investigation were dispatched to aid in the investigation of the bombing. Yemeni authorities ultimately detained more than 100 people suspected of involvement in the attack. Two terrorists were tried and sentenced to death, and 15 others were given prison sentences of varying lengths. In February 2006, 23 Al Qaeda prisoners escaped from a Yemeni prison, including 13 who had been convicted of involvement in the attack.

– W –

WAR ON TERROR. The post-2001 U.S.-led economic, law enforcement, and military campaign against **international terrorism** (the American military effort against terrorism was officially designated by the Defense Department as the Global War on Terrorism or GWOT). Following the **September 11 terrorist attacks**, the administration of **George W. Bush** endeavored to create a global coalition to combat international terrorism. Bush attempted to frame the campaign as a struggle similar in nature to the **Cold War**, and he did so in ideological terms: The United States and its allies symbolized democracy and freedom, while the terrorists represented repression and brutality. Bush and other American leaders were generally careful not to characterize the conflict as an anti-Islamic campaign, although the majority of groups identified as enemies of the United States were Muslim extremist groups. The president and administration contended that terrorist groups such as **Al Qaeda** had created global networks that presented threats to international security and stability. Therefore, countries of the world should unite to suppress the terrorist networks.

U.S. annual spending directly related to the war on terror increased to $72.4 billion by 2006. The majority of the funding, $65.3 billion, went to Defense Department operations in Afghanistan, Iraq, and other areas, while $4.2 billion was allocated to the State Department and various international programs (including the promotion of democracy and economic development) and $2.9 billion was for increased intelligence capabilities.

The Bush administration developed a six-prong strategy in the war on terror. First, the United States conducted direct military action against terrorists or countries that harbored the groups. The **Afghanistan intervention, Operation Enduring Freedom**, was the initial step in the military campaign, followed by the 2003 **Iraq War**. Second, the Bush administration attempted to isolate and undermine states that were supporters of international terrorist groups, including Iran and Syria. Third, the United States undertook reforms and restructuring of its military and intelligence capabilities to develop better counterterrorism capabilities. The creation of the Department of **Homeland Security** and better coordination among the nation's intelligence agencies were the centerpiece of the enhanced antiterrorism program. Fourth, Washington provided military and economic assistance to other countries to support domestic counterterrorism programs. In a program similar to those of the Cold War, the United States deployed special operations forces to train and assist national troops in counterterrorism. American units were deployed to countries ranging from the Central Asian republics to the Philippines to states in West Africa. Fifth, the United States increased its intelligence and law enforcement cooperation with other countries and international organizations. For instance, Washington signed new bilateral agreements with nations in Europe and Asia and increased counterterrorism collaboration with the **North Atlantic Treaty Organization, Organization of American States**, and **European Union**. A component of this phase of the strategy was greater collaboration in freezing terrorist assets and eliminating funding sources. Sixth and finally, the United States initiated a series of diplomatic and financial programs to support democracy and economic development in countries on the front line of terrorist struggles.

The United States received significant international support in Operation Enduring Freedom, and the military campaign in Afghanistan achieved its main objective, the overthrow of the Taliban regime, although coalition forces failed to capture the senior leadership of Al Qaeda and the Taliban. However, the invasion of Iraq, while initially supported by the American public, met with widespread international opposition; as the insurgency in Iraq grew, U.S. domestic approval declined. Iraq became the main front in the war on terror as Al Qaeda and other foreign fighters infiltrated the country to launch attacks on American and coalition targets. By 2004, however, counterinsurgency tactics by coalition forces led to a shift in strategy by the insurgents, who increasingly attacked Iraqi government and civilian targets. In 2006, the Bush administration began to seek new strategies and tactics in Iraq following that year's midterm elections when the Democrats regained control of both houses of Congress.

The effort to increase international cooperation against terrorism was generally successful. Within a year of the 2001 attacks, there were more than 300 arrests of suspected Al Qaeda operatives around the world and 30 countries offered the United States cooperation in investigations related to the Al Qaeda strikes. In addition, the Bush administration undertook counterterrorism operations with more than 200 foreign intelligence and law enforcement organizations and developed new or enhanced cooperation agreements with more than 100 countries. The United States and its allies were able to stop a series of terrorist attacks aimed at the United States, or American interests, including 10 major plots between 2001 and 2006.

Several factors inhibited the Bush administration in the war on terror. The United States was unable to sustain the degree of international support that it had enjoyed during the Cold War. Many states continued to view terrorism more as a law enforcement issue than as a matter of national security. The Bush administration was also the target of international criticism over its treatment of those captured in the war on terror. There were frequent charges that the United States violated international law through its detainment of suspect terrorists, designated **unlawful combatants**, and even the nation's closest allies in the war on terror endeavored to change policy and secure the release of their nationals held by the United States.

American attempts to end state support for terrorism had its greatest success in Libyan leader **Muammar Gaddafi**'s renunciation of terrorism, while U.S. efforts to promote democracy were manifested in American support for the **Cedar Revolution**. However, Washington also expanded support for undemocratic regimes, such as Pakistan's. The Bush administration failed to achieve a diplomatic breakthrough in the **Arab-Israeli conflict**, one of the major contributing factors to Islamic terrorism. In addition, the administration's management of the war on terror was the subject of frequent criticism by the Democratic Party and civil libertarians. The bipartisan consensus on the war on terror, similar to that which guided U.S. foreign and security policy during the Cold War, broke down quickly after the invasion of Iraq.

WESTERN EUROPEAN UNION (WEU). The WEU was created in 1955 as a means to allow German rearmament within the auspices of a European collective security organization. At the end of the **Cold War**, it emerged as the means to propel **European Security and Defense Identity (ESDI)**, which later led to the endorsement of a **Common Foreign and Security Policy (CFSP)** within the **European Union (EU)**.

The organization's roots were in the 1948 Brussels Treaty, which created a collective defense alliance among the states of Western Europe. The original members were Belgium, France, Great Britain, Luxembourg, and the Netherlands. The creation of the **North Atlantic Treaty Organization (NATO)** in 1949 superseded the Brussels Treaty, but the framework was revived in 1955 when the WEU was formally launched to allow German rearmament (and NATO membership). By the 1970s, many of the functions of the WEU had been absorbed by other entities.

In 1984, the WEU was relaunched. Members began meeting twice a year, and the WEU was named by the European Community (EC) as the means to create ESDI. In 1990, Portugal and Spain joined the WEU; Turkey became a member in 1988, and Greece in 1995. The WEU deployed minesweepers to the Persian Gulf in 1987 to protect shipping during the Iran-Iraq War. During the **Persian Gulf War**, the WEU coordinated European naval units, since NATO could not operate out of area at that time.

During the 1991 negotiations over the **Maastricht Treaty** (which transformed the EC into the EU), the European Council called for the WEU to become the military arm of the future EU. The WEU was also tasked to become the European military pillar within NATO. In 1992, the Petersburg Declaration identified the WEU as the organization to conduct humanitarian and civil emergency operations for the EU. The Amsterdam Treaty further reinforced and enhanced the role of the WEU as the EU's security body.

The WEU undertook coordinated operations with NATO to enforce the arms embargo against the states of the former Yugoslavia (in Operation Sharp Guard). In 1993, the WEU assisted Bulgaria, Hungary, and Romania in enforcement of the embargo along the Danube River. From 1997 to 2001, the WEU undertook a crisis management role in Albania and peace enforcement missions in Croatia and the **Kosovo War**.

In 1999, **Javier Solana** was appointed the high representative for the CFSP of the EU and was concurrently appointed secretary-general of the WEU. In these twin roles, Solana was tasked with the integration of the WEU into the EU and began to transfer some functions of the former into the latter. The WEU ministerial council has not met since 2000, and the last permanent council met in 2002. The 2001 Treaty of Nice deleted the references to the WEU as Europe's defense arm as the EU endeavored to develop its own European Security and Defense Policy. In 2002, the WEU's main operational capabilities were transferred to the EU (including the satellite center). Some administrative bodies remain active, but the WEU's core security functions have now been absorbed by the EU.

WHALING. Since the 1980s, the United States has supported a ban on commercial whaling and sought to protect whale populations throughout the world's oceans. The United States was a signatory to the 1946 International Convention for the Regulation of Whaling and has been a member of the International Whaling Commission (IWC) since its inception in 1948. Overhunting significantly depleted whale populations throughout the 20th century, and in 1982 the IWC agreed to impose a moratorium on commercial whaling, which took affect in 1986. (Limited aboriginal subsistence whaling continued to be permitted by indigenous populations in America, Greenland, Russia, and St. Vincent and the Grenadines.) The restrictions resulted in the lowest annual recorded number of whales caught, just 326, in 1989. In 1994, Washington supported the creation of the Southern Ocean Whale Sanctuary, a 19.3-million-square-mile (50-million-square-kilometer) haven.

Whales were allowed to be hunted for scientific research, and countries such as Japan exploited this loophole to catch whales whose meat was subsequently sold in commercial markets. By 2006, Japanese whalers were taking more than 1,000 whales per year, including endangered species. Other states such as Norway also engaged in scientific whaling. Washington has consistently opposed scientific whaling.

Membership in the IWC was open to all states, and Japan launched a campaign in the late 1980s to convince other countries to join the body and vote with it in supporting a relaxation of the moratorium on commercial whaling, in exchange for foreign aid. In 2006, there were even eight landlocked members of the IWC. Japan provided more than $300 million to IWC members Antigua and Barbuda, Dominica, Grenada, Guinea, Morocco, Panama, St. Lucia, St. Vincent and the Grenadines, St. Kitts and Nevis, and the Solomon Islands—all countries with little or no history of whaling. In return, the states have repeatedly voted along with Japan and other prowhaling states to curtail the ban on hunting. Meanwhile, the United States and other antiwhaling nations, including Australia, New Zealand, and the **European Union** states (with the exception of Denmark) have sought to bring in members who would oppose commercial whaling. The United States has led the international effort to prevent relaxation of the ban on commercial hunts.

WOLFOWITZ, PAUL D. (1943–). President of the **World Bank** since 2005, after serving in a variety of government and academic posts. Wolfowitz was instrumental in formulating the **Bush Doctrine** and was a staunch proponent of military action against the regime of **Saddam Hussein**.

Paul Dundes Wolfowitz was born in 1943 in Ithaca, New York. He graduated in 1965 with a degree in mathematics. In 1972, he earned a doctorate in political science from the University of Chicago. Wolfowitz initially pursued an academic career and taught at Yale University. However, in 1973 he was appointed to the U.S. Arms Control and Disarmament Agency. During his service, Wolfowitz's work attracted the attention of then secretary of defense **Donald H. Rumsfeld**. In 1977, Wolfowitz became the deputy assistant secretary of defense for regional programs. He produced several important studies for the Pentagon, including a recommendation for the creation of a new military command that would be able to respond to threats in the Middle East. He resigned in 1980 and accepted a teaching position at Johns Hopkins University.

Following the election of **Ronald W. Reagan**, Wolfowitz was appointed chief of the State Department's Policy Planning Staff. In 1982, he was promoted to the assistant secretary of state for East Asian and Pacific affairs. Wolfowitz subsequently served as U.S. ambassador to Indonesia from 1986 to 1989. In 1989, **George H. W. Bush** recalled Wolfowitz and made him the undersecretary of defense for policy under Secretary of Defense **Richard B. Cheney**. Wolfowitz oversaw the Pentagon's 700-person planning cell and worked to revise U.S. military strategy in the wake of the end of the **Cold War**. He then coordinated strategy among the branches of the U.S. military and coalition forces during the 1991 **Persian Gulf War**. In 1992, Wolfowitz authored a report, *Defense Planning Guidance*, which later served as the basis for the Bush Doctrine.

After Bush's defeat in the 1992 election, Wolfowitz left government service and returned to academia. He was a professor at the Naval War College and then accepted a post as the dean of the School of Advanced and International Studies at Johns Hopkins University. He served as a foreign policy advisor to Republican presidential candidate Robert Dole in the 1996 election. During this period, Wolfowitz became increasingly noted as a proponent of **neoconservatism**.

During the 2000 presidential campaign, Wolfowitz was a foreign policy consultant, along with future national security advisor **Condoleezza Rice**, to **George W. Bush**. In the aftermath of the **September 11 terrorist attacks**, Wolfowitz pressed for the development of a broad offensive against **international terrorism**. Wolfowitz and Rumsfeld argued that the Taliban and **Al Qaeda** could be defeated with only minimal assistance from allies. This contrasted with recommendations from Rice and Secretary of State **Colin Powell**, who wanted to utilize the widespread support offered to the United States as a way to promote future cooperation in counterterrorism efforts. After the defeat of the Taliban, Wolfowitz joined other senior officials in advocating an attack on Iraq as the next step in the **war on terror**. He was instrumental in the development and implementation of the Bush Doctrine, which was codified in the 2002 *National Security Strategy of the United States.*

Wolfowitz was a strong proponent of the use of force against Iraq. During the planning for the **Iraq War**, he resisted calls by military commanders for a large deployment and contended that the defeat of Iraq could be accomplished with 100,000 troops (140,000 were actually used). The subsequent insurgency undermined public confidence in Rumsfeld and Wolfowitz. Critics argued that Iraq demonstrated the limits of neoconservatism.

After the 2004 presidential election, Bush nominated Wolfowitz to be president of the **World Bank**. Although there was opposition to his appointment because of Wolfowitz's conservative reputation, he was confirmed and assumed office on 1 June 2005. As head of the World Bank, Wolfowitz adopted a moderate reform policy designed to increase the efficiency of the organization. He also increased the bank's emphasis on democracy and began a long-term shift away from loans to developing countries toward grants. He resigned in 2007.

WOOLSEY, R. JAMES, JR. (1941–). Director of the Central Intelligence Agency (CIA), 1993–1995. Robert James Woolsey Jr. was born in Tulsa, Oklahoma, and became a Rhodes Scholar, earning a master's degree from Oxford in 1965 and a law degree from Yale University three years later. Woolsey was in the Army from 1968 to 1970 and then served in a variety of government posts in his early career, rising to be undersecretary of the navy from 1977 to 1979. Although a Democrat, Woolsey was appointed as a delegate to the **Strategic Arms Reduction Treaty (START)** talks during the administration of President **Ronald W. Reagan**. In 1991, he was named the U.S. ambassador during the negotiations on the **Conventional Forces in Europe Treaty**. Woolsey was named to head the CIA in 1993 by President **William J. Clinton**. He and Clinton had a difficult relationship. Clinton sought to concentrate on domestic issues and resisted planning initiatives by Woolsey. During his tenure as head of the CIA, Woolsey never had an individual meeting with Clinton. He resigned in 1995. Woolsey supported **Operation Enduring Freedom** and the 2003 **Iraq War**.

WORLD BANK. The World Bank Group (commonly referred to as simply the World Bank), founded in 1945, consists of five international financial institutions that provide grants, loans, and technical assistance to countries in an effort to promote economic development and alleviate poverty: the International Bank for Reconstruction and Development, the International Finance Corporation, the International Development Association, the Multilateral Investment Guarantee Agency, and the International Center for Settlement of Investment Disputes. The World Bank's services are generally focused on the developing world and cover issues such as economic development in general, strengthening financial networks, improvements in health care and education, environmental protection, and infrastructure improvements in areas such as transport, power, and water systems, as well as anticorruption programs. The World Bank generally reflects the policy preferences of the developed countries. The United States controls 16.4 percent of the total votes of the body, and since major changes to the World Bank's institutions require a majority of 85 percent, the United States has an effective veto over policy. The World Bank has been one of the main targets of anti**globalization** activists around the world, and its meetings frequently provoke large protests. However, many of the bank's programs have funded substantial improvements in regions of Africa, Latin America, and Asia. Traditionally, an American is chosen as president of the World Bank, a post held by Lewis T. Preston (1991–1995), James D. Wolfensohn (1995–2005), and **Paul Wolfowitz** (2005–2007). *See also* INTERNATIONAL MONETARY FUND.

WORLD CONFERENCE ON WOMEN (1995). The Fourth World Conference on Women was held in Beijing 5–15 September 1995. The conference was subtitled "Action for Equality, Development, and Peace." More than 5,000 delegates from 189 nations and 2,100 nongovernmental organizations attended the meeting. The delegates adopted a Platform for Action that called for the removal of impediments to women's full participation in the economic, social, and political sectors. There was considerable criticism by **human rights** groups over the location of the conference because of the People's Republic of China's history of repression and past policies toward women. Included in the Platform for Action was a call for gender evaluation studies to be included in all legislation and policies so that the impact of governmental action on women could be assessed before programs were implemented. The **United Nations (UN)** and individual governments pledged to adopt the Platform for Action. Progress on the implementation of the conference's goals was assessed in 2000 under the auspices of the UN. The review found that progress had been made in several areas, but that the overall goals of the conference had yet to be met and that most governments had failed to undertake significant commitments to improve gender equality.

WORLD TRADE CENTER BOMBING (1993). On 26 February 1993, Islamic terrorists exploded a car bomb in the parking garage of the North Tower (Tower 1) of the World Trade Center (WTC) in New York City in an unsuccessful effort to make the building collapse into the South Tower (Tower 2), therefore destroying both buildings. The attack was conducted by a network of terrorists affiliated with **Al Qaeda**. The bombing was planned by Ramzi Yousef with support and financial assistance from Khalid Sheikh Mohammed, who later orchestrated the **September 11 terrorist attacks**. At least 12 other terrorists assisted with the making of the bomb or provided other logistical support.

The bomb consisted of approximately 1,300 pounds (600 kg) of nitrogen-based fertilizers and other volatile chemicals. In addition, it was loaded with poisonous sodium cyanide tablets whose fumes were meant to be dispersed through the building's ventilation system to cause greater casualties. The explosives were packed into a large Ford van that had been rented from a Ryder Rental Corporation outlet in Jersey City, New Jersey. The van was parked in a lot underneath Tower 1, and the bomb detonated at 12:18 pm via a timed fuse. The resultant explosion scattered more than 6,800 tons of steel and concrete and left a crater more than 150 feet (46 meters) in diameter. It destroyed five levels of the parking lot, but did not bring down the building. The explosion killed six people and injured more than 1,000. Approximately 50,000 people had to be evacuated from the WTC. The bomb also destroyed two main sewer lines and multiple water mains and it cut off electricity and phone service for much of the area. More than 2 million gallons of water and sewage had to be pumped from the building. The cyanide was consumed by the blast and did not affect anyone.

Investigators were able to identify the van used in the attack and then discover the identities of the main plotters. Yousef was captured in Pakistan in 1996 in a joint operation between Pakistani and American security forces. He was tried and convicted for his role in the attack, as were nine others; all received prison sentences of 240 years. The bombing led to dramatic improvements in emergency response in New York City, including better coordination among first responders. The administration of **William J. Clinton** increased the counterterrorism capabilities of the Federal Bureau of Investigation (FBI) but continued to view terrorism as a law enforcement issue rather than a matter of national security. One consequence was the continuation of policies that prevented the FBI and the nation's intelligence agencies, including the Central Intelligence Agency, from sharing information or conducting joint operations. *See also* WAR ON TERROR.

WORLD TRADE ORGANIZATION (WTO). The WTO was created in 1995 from the General Agreement on Tariffs and Trade (GATT) as a body to lower tariffs and, therefore, enhance trade and oversee economic disputes between nations. GATT had been created in 1948, and the body achieved notable gains in eliminating tariffs. However, it was less successful in overcoming nontariff barriers to trade such as subsidies and commercial practices. Consequently, during the Uruguay Round of GATT (1986–1995), a range of reform proposals were considered. Participant countries in GATT agreed that further economic progress could be accomplished only through the development of dispute resolution mechanism and trade review mechanisms. To accomplish these tasks, there were calls for the creation of an institutional framework. The result was the launch in 1995 of the WTO, which has since endeavored to promote free trade and prevent trade wars between regional economic blocs such as the **European Union (EU)** and the **North American Free Trade Agreement**.

The new body initially had 73 members (that number had grown to 150 by 2007). The members of the EU are represented by a joint delegation. Members of the WTO were required to sign and adhere to some 30 separate economic agreements. These accords cover areas such as agricultural policy, market access, export subsidies, and tariffs and trade. The institutional framework of the WTO consists of the

Ministerial Conference, which includes the trade or finance ministers of member states and meets every two years. The day-to-day operations of the WTO are undertaken by the General Council, headquartered in Geneva; the Dispute Settlement Body; and the Trade Policy Review Body. There are also several area-specific bodies and subsidiary agencies. The WTO operates on a consensus basis rather than by majority voting.

The WTO has been the focus of intense internal and external criticism. WTO members have often divided between developed and developing states on issues related to **globalization** and development. These disagreements have repeatedly resulted in the failure to gain consensus on controversial issues such as agricultural subsidies and tariffs on manufactured goods. For instance, efforts to resolve use of agricultural subsidies by the United States and the EU began in 1996, but a series of plans to resolve the dispute were defeated until August 2004 when discussions in Geneva resulted in an accord whereby the subsidies were lowered in developed countries while developing countries agreed to lower barriers to manufactured products. Final approval of the Geneva agreement could not be reached, and in 2006 these agenda items were suspended.

The WTO has been a target of antiglobalization forces. In 1999, at the Third Ministerial in Seattle, there was widespread rioting and looting by anti-WTO protestors. Subsequent meetings have also faced large demonstrations. Critics of the WTO assert that the organization forces developing countries to open their markets to developed states and thereby perpetuates the existing inequities in the global economy, while critics in developing countries complain about losses of production facilities and jobs.

WÖRNER, MANFRED (1934–1994). Secretary-general of the **North Atlantic Treaty Organization (NATO)** during the final days of the **Cold War** and the uncertain period immediately following the end of the superpower struggle. A former defense minister, Wörner was the first German to serve as NATO leader. Wörner was born in Stuttgart, Germany. In 1958, he earned a doctorate in international law from the University of Munich and joined the German Air Force Reserve as a fighter pilot. Wörner became an advisor to the state government of

Baden-Württemberg in 1962. He was elected to the Bundestag at the age of 30 as a member of the Christian Democratic Union (Christlich Demokratische Union, CDU). He developed a reputation as West Germany's foremost expert on international security. In 1982, Wörner was appointed minister of defense. In that position, he sought to balance the often competing demands inherent in the Germany's security relationships with France and the United States. Wörner also endeavored to bolster relations with East Germany in the final days of the Cold War.

Wörner became NATO secretary-general on 1 July 1988. He faced a range of challenges during his tenure, including overseeing the end of the Cold War, **German reunification**, and changes in the alliance's missions and scope. Wörner preserved consensus over contentious issues such as the German reunification. He also worked closely with the United States to maintain the centrality of NATO in European security. Wörner helped manage the negotiations that culminated in the 1990 **Conventional Forces in Europe Treaty**, and he also forged a consensus on NATO support for peace efforts in the former Yugoslavia. Meanwhile, the alliance reached out to the states of the former Eastern Europe through the **Partnership for Peace** initiative and the initial talks over **NATO enlargement**. Wörner oversaw the promulgation of a new Strategic Concept of NATO in 1991. He endured a lengthy battle with intestinal cancer and died in office on 13 August 1994. He was temporarily replaced by Sergio Balanzino (1934–), who served as acting secretary-general, until Belgium's Willy Claes was sworn in on 17 October 1994.

WRIGHT, JAMES C. (1922–). Speaker of the U.S. House of Representatives, 1987–1989. James Claude "Jim" Wright was born in Fort Worth, Texas. He was a bombardier in the Army Air Forces during World War II. After the war, Wright served in the Texas legislature and was mayor of Weatherford, Texas, before being elected to the House in 1954. The Texas congressman was elected majority leader in 1979 and became Speaker of the House in 1987. Wright clashed repeatedly with the administration of President **Ronald W. Reagan** on foreign and security policy, eroding a general bipartisan consensus on national security that existed under his predecessor, Thomas

"Tip" O'Neill. Wright sought greater congressional oversight of the nation's intelligence agencies, and he endeavored to reduce tensions between Washington and Managua through personal diplomacy with Nicaraguan president Daniel Ortega. Administration officials accused Wright of usurping the executive branch's constitutional role in formulating foreign policy. In 1989, the House Ethics Committee found that the Speaker had violated congressional rules on gifts and limitations on speaking fees. He resigned as Speaker on 31 May 1989 and then from Congress on 30 June. Wright was succeeded as Speaker by **Thomas S. Foley**.

– Y –

YELTSIN, BORIS N. (1931–2007). Russia's first post-Communist leader, serving as president from 1991 to 1999. Boris Nikolayevich Yeltsin was born in Butka, Sverdlovsk, in 1931. An athletic youth, Yeltsin graduated from Ural Polytechnic Institute in 1955 with a degree in construction. He joined the Communist Party in 1961 and became the head of construction and engineering for the regional party committee in 1968. In 1976, Yeltsin became first secretary of the party's regional committee for Sverdlovsk. He developed a reputation as a reformer and caught the attention of **Mikhail Gorbachev**. When Gorbachev became premier in 1986, he believed Yeltsin could serve as an important ally in his efforts to modernize the Soviet Union and appointed him to the Politburo. However, Yeltsin not only attacked the hard-liners in the Kremlin but also criticized Gorbachev for not being more aggressive in his reform program. Yeltsin's behavior led to his dismissal from the Politburo in 1987.

Yeltsin became increasingly nationalistic and publicly advocated that Russia should break away from the Soviet Union. In 1989, Yeltsin was elected to the Soviet Parliament in the first semi-open elections in Soviet history. He was appointed to the Supreme Soviet and, in 1990, was elected chairman of the Presidium of the Supreme Soviet of the Russian Soviet Federated Socialist Republic, commonly known as the parliament or Duma. Yeltsin grew enormously popular because he appealed to both reformers who were seeking to liberalize the Soviet Union and conservatives who supported Russian nationalism. In 1990, Yeltsin quit the Communist Party, while the Duma declared itself the sovereign political authority in Russia (although the declaration had little practical impact at the time).

Yeltsin became Gorbachev's main political rival. His power was bolstered in June 1991 when he was elected president of Russia with 57 percent of the vote (easily defeating Gorbachev's handpicked candidate). The election confirmed that Yeltsin had eclipsed Gorbachev as the leading force for reform. During the **Soviet coup** of 1991, Yeltsin led the anticoup elements, including the army, which suppressed the Communists. Within four months of the aborted coup, all 15 republics of the Union of Soviet Socialist Republics (USSR) had declared independence. In December 1991, Yeltsin and the leaders of Ukraine and Belarus announced the formation of the **Commonwealth of Independent States**, a voluntary economic and political confederation of the former Soviet states. Russia took the seat of the USSR in the **United Nations (UN)**, and Gorbachev resigned as Soviet premier, marking the official end of the USSR.

The administration of **George H. W. Bush** supported Yeltsin, who was perceived as more pro-Western and more interested in democratic and economic reforms than was Gorbachev. Bush and Yeltsin had a good working relationship, although Yeltsin was critical of the United States for not providing more assistance to help Russia transition to a market economy. Yeltsin and Bush cooperated on most security matters, including counterproliferation programs and **arms control**.

By 1991, Yeltsin was the recognized leader of the Russian Federation. However, Russia faced a number of internal problems, including a deteriorating economy and separatist movements. In 1992, Yeltsin initiated a broad reform program that resulted in high inflation. Meanwhile, former party officials were able to take control of state industries and property that was supposed to be privatized. Yeltsin's popularity rapidly eroded, and opponents in the Duma tried to impeach him. Yeltsin won a referendum in April 1993 and subsequently used the army to disband the Duma. He then introduced constitutional changes that bolstered the authority of the presidency. Subsequent elections gave Yeltsin a majority in the

Duma, and he continued a moderate reform program. Russia received significant foreign aid during Yeltsin's tenure, including $40 billion from the **International Monetary Fund**. Nonetheless, Yeltsin faulted the West for not investing more in Russia and blamed many of the country's economic woes on the lack of aid and assistance from the West.

In 1994, he ordered Russian federal forces into Chechnya to quell a separatist rebellion. Russian forces initially suffered a series of defeats and responded with a brutal campaign against the rebels. A cease-fire was reached in 1996, but renewed fighting and terrorism continued. Yeltsin's relationship with President **William J. Clinton** was more uneasy than had been the case with Bush. Tensions with the United States and Western Europe accelerated over **North Atlantic Treaty Organization (NATO)** involvement in the peacekeeping operation in the former Yugoslavia (a role opposed by Russia). Yeltsin also contested **NATO enlargement** in 1997, but agreed to the inclusion of the Czech Republic, Hungary, and Poland in exchange for an alliance pledge to not station nuclear weapons on the soil of the former Soviet bloc states.

Yeltsin was reelected in a runoff in 1996 after failing to gain an absolute majority in the first round of voting. Relations between the United States and Russia deteriorated during Yeltsin's second term. The Clinton administration opposed a series of Russo-Iranian nuclear and military agreements, while Yeltsin protested U.S. strikes against Iraq following that country's refusal to allow UN weapons inspectors to resume inspections (Yeltsin even recalled Russia's ambassador to the United States). Yeltsin also endeavored unsuccessfully to block NATO military action during the **Kosovo War** in 1999.

Renewed fighting in Chechnya and health problems related to alcoholism undermined Yeltsin's domestic standing toward the end of his second term. He repeatedly dismissed cabinet members, including four prime ministers and in 1999 his entire cabinet. In May 1999, the Duma again tried to impeach Yeltsin. He appointed **Vladimir Putin** as prime minister and worked to ensure that Putin would succeed him. Yeltsin resigned in December 1999 after Putin granted him immunity. After leaving office, Yeltsin suffered from a variety of health problems.

– Z –

ZOELLICK, ROBERT B. (1953–). U.S. trade representative, 2001–2005, and deputy secretary of state, 2005–2006. Robert Bruce Zoellick earned a law degree from Harvard University in 1981 and entered government service. He worked in the Treasury Department from 1985 to 1988 and then served as undersecretary of state for economic agricultural affairs. Zoellick represented the United States at the Group of Seven meetings in 1991 and 1992. During the remainder of the 1990s, he held several academic posts. In 2000, Zoellick was an advisor to **George W. Bush** during the latter's presidential campaign. Zoellick was subsequently named the country's trade representative. He successfully negotiated the final agreement that allowed the People's Republic of China to join the **World Trade Organization**. He also oversaw talks on other trade agreements with countries such as the Dominican Republic, Jordan, and Vietnam, as well as the **Central American Free Trade Agreement**. Zoellick worked with Republicans in Congress to pass the 2002 Trade Act, which renewed and expanded the president's ability to negotiate and implement commercial agreements. In February 2005, Zoellick was appointed deputy secretary of state. He was a staunch advocate of American intervention in the **Darfur Crisis**. Zoellick resigned in June 2006. *See also* TRADE POLICY.

Appendix A
Presidents and Terms of Office, 1989–2007

George H. W. Bush, 1989–1993
William J. Clinton, 1993–2001
George W. Bush, 2001–

Appendix B
Secretaries of State, 1989–2007

GEORGE H. W. BUSH ADMINISTRATION

James A. Baker III, 1989–1992
Lawrence Eagleburger, 1992–1993

WILLIAM J. CLINTON ADMINISTRATION

Warren Christopher, 1993–1997
Madeleine Albright, 1997–2001

GEORGE W. BUSH ADMINISTRATION

Colin Powell, 2001–2005
Condoleezza Rice, 2005–

Appendix C
Major Speeches and Documents

GEORGE H. W. BUSH INAUGURAL ADDRESS, 1989

[Washington, D.C., 20 January 1989]

I come before you and assume the Presidency at a moment rich with promise. We live in a peaceful, prosperous time, but we can make it better. For a new breeze is blowing, and a world refreshed by freedom seems reborn; for in man's heart, if not in fact, the day of the dictator is over. The totalitarian era is passing, its old ideas blown away like leaves from an ancient, lifeless tree. A new breeze is blowing, and a nation refreshed by freedom stands ready to push on. There is new ground to be broken, and new action to be taken. There are times when the future seems thick as a fog; you sit and wait, hoping the mists will lift and reveal the right path. But this is a time when the future seems a door you can walk right through into a room called tomorrow.

Great nations of the world are moving toward democracy through the door to freedom. Men and women of the world move toward free markets through the door to prosperity. The people of the world agitate for free expression and free thought through the door to the moral and intellectual satisfactions that only liberty allows.

We know what works: Freedom works. We know what's right: Freedom is right. We know how to secure a more just and prosperous life for man on Earth: through free markets, free speech, free elections, and the exercise of free will unhampered by the state.

For the first time in this century, for the first time in perhaps all history, man does not have to invent a system by which to live. We don't have to talk late into the night about which form of government is better. We don't have to wrest justice from the kings. We only have to summon it from within ourselves. We must act on what we know. I take as my guide the hope of a saint: In crucial things, unity; in important things, diversity; in all things, generosity.

Source: http://www.bartleby.com/124/pres63.html

THE CLINTON DOCTRINE

[Speech by William J. Clinton, San Francisco, 26 February 1999]
The world we want to leave our children and grandchildren requires us to make the right choices, and some of them will be difficult. America has always risen to great causes, yet we have a tendency, still, to believe that we can go back to minding our own business when we're done. To-day we must embrace the inexorable logic of globalization—that every-thing, from the strength of our economy to the safety of our cities, to the health of our people, depends on events not only within our borders, but half a world away. We must see the opportunities and the dangers of the interdependent world in which we are clearly fated to live.

There is still the potential for major regional wars that would threaten our security. The arms race between India and Pakistan reminds us that the next big war could still be nuclear. There is a risk that our former adversaries will not succeed in their transitions to freedom and free markets. There is a danger that deadly weapons will fall into the hands of a terrorist group or an outlaw nation, and that those weapons could be chemical or biological. There is a danger of deadly alliances among terrorists, narco-traffickers, and organized criminal groups. There is a danger of global environmental crises and the spread of deadly diseases. There is a danger that global financial turmoil will undermine open markets, overwhelm open societies, and undercut our own prosperity.

We must avoid both the temptation to minimize these dangers, and the illusion that the proper response to them is to batten down the hatches and protect America against the world. The promise of our fu-ture lies in the world. Therefore, we must work hard with the world—to defeat the dangers we face together and to build this hopeful moment together, into a generation of peace, prosperity, and freedom. Because of our unique position, America must lead with confidence in our strengths and with a clear vision of what we seek to avoid and what we seek to advance.

Our first challenge is to build a more peaceful 21st century world. To that end, we're renewing alliances that extend the area where wars do not happen, and working to stop the conflicts that are claiming lives and threatening our interests right now.

The century's bloodiest wars began in Europe. That's why I've worked hard to build a Europe that finally is undivided, democratic and at peace. We want all of Europe to have what America helped build in Western Europe—a community that upholds common standards of human rights, where people have the confidence and security to invest in the future, where nations cooperate to make war unthinkable.

That is why I have pushed hard for NATO's enlargement and why we must keep NATO's doors open to new democratic members, so that other nations will have an incentive to deepen their democracies. That is why we must forge a partnership between NATO and Russia, between NATO and Ukraine; why we are building a NATO capable not only of deterring aggression against its own territory, but of meeting challenges to our security beyond its territory—the kind of NATO we must advance at the 50th Anniversary Summit in Washington this April.

We are building a stronger alliance with Japan, and renewing our commitment to deter aggression in Korea and intensifying our efforts for a genuine peace there. I thank Secretary Perry for his efforts in that regard. We also create a more peaceful world by building new partnerships in Asia, Africa, and Latin America. Ten years ago we were shouting at each other across a North-South chasm defined by our differences. Today, we are engaged in a new dialogue that speaks the language of common interests—of trade and investment; of education and health; of democracies that deliver not corruption and despair, but progress and hope; of a common desire that children in all our countries will be free of the scourge of drugs. Through these efforts to strengthen old alliances and build new partnerships, we advance the prospects for peace. However, the work of actually making peace is harder and often far more contentious.

It's easy, for example, to say that we really have no interests in who lives in this or that valley in Bosnia, or who owns a strip of brushland in the Horn of Africa, or some piece of parched earth by the Jordan River. But the true measure of our interests lies not in how small or distant these places are, or in whether we have trouble pronouncing their names. The question we must ask is, what are the consequences to our security of letting conflicts fester and spread. We cannot, indeed, we should not, do everything or be everywhere. But where are values and our interests are at stake, and where we can make a difference, we must be prepared to do so. And we must remember that the real challenge of foreign policy is to deal with problems before they harm our national interests.

Source: http://www.mtholyoke.edu/acad/intrel/clintfps.htm

GEORGE W. BUSH, STATE OF THE UNION ADDRESS, 2002

[Axis of Evil Speech, Washington, D.C., 29 January 2002]
Our nation will continue to be steadfast and patient and persistent in the pursuit of two great objectives. First, we will shut down terrorist camps, disrupt terrorist plans, and bring terrorists to justice. And, second, we must prevent the terrorists and regimes who seek chemical, biological or nuclear weapons from threatening the United States and the world.

Our military has put the terror training camps of Afghanistan out of business, yet camps still exist in at least a dozen countries. A terrorist underworld—including groups like Hamas, Hezbollah, Islamic Jihad, Jaish-i-Mohammed—operates in remote jungles and deserts, and hides in the centers of large cities.

While the most visible military action is in Afghanistan, America is acting elsewhere. We now have troops in the Philippines, helping to train that country's armed forces to go after terrorist cells that have executed an American, and still hold hostages. Our soldiers, working with the Bosnian government, seized terrorists who were plotting to bomb our embassy. Our Navy is patrolling the coast of Africa to block the shipment of weapons and the establishment of terrorist camps in Somalia.

My hope is that all nations will heed our call, and eliminate the terrorist parasites who threaten their countries and our own. Many nations are acting forcefully. Pakistan is now cracking down on terror, and I admire the strong leadership of President Musharraf. But some governments will be timid in the face of terror. And make no mistake about it: If they do not act, America will.

Our second goal is to prevent regimes that sponsor terror from threatening America or our friends and allies with weapons of mass destruction. Some of these regimes have been pretty quiet since September the 11th. But we know their true nature. North Korea is a regime arming with missiles and weapons of mass destruction, while starving its citizens.

Iran aggressively pursues these weapons and exports terror, while an unelected few repress the Iranian people's hope for freedom.

Iraq continues to flaunt its hostility toward America and to support terror. The Iraqi regime has plotted to develop anthrax, and nerve gas, and nuclear weapons for over a decade. This is a regime that has already used poison gas to murder thousands of its own citizens—leaving the bodies of mothers huddled over their dead children. This is a regime that agreed to international inspections—then kicked out the inspectors. This is a regime that has something to hide from the civilized world.

States like these, and their terrorist allies, constitute an axis of evil, arming to threaten the peace of the world. By seeking weapons of mass destruction, these regimes pose a grave and growing danger. They could provide these arms to terrorists, giving them the means to match their hatred. They could attack our allies or attempt to blackmail the United States. In any of these cases, the price of indifference would be catastrophic.

We will work closely with our coalition to deny terrorists and their state sponsors the materials, technology, and expertise to make and deliver weapons of mass destruction. We will develop and deploy effective missile defenses to protect America and our allies from sudden attack. And all nations should know: America will do what is necessary to ensure our nation's security.

We'll be deliberate, yet time is not on our side. I will not wait on events, while dangers gather. I will not stand by, as peril draws closer and closer. The United States of America will not permit the world's most dangerous regimes to threaten us with the world's most destructive weapons. Our war on terror is well begun, but it is only begun. This campaign may not be finished on our watch—yet it must be and it will be waged on our watch.

We can't stop short. If we stop now—leaving terror camps intact and terror states unchecked—our sense of security would be false and temporary. History has called America and our allies to action, and it is both our responsibility and our privilege to fight freedom's fight.

Source: http://www.whitehouse.gov/news/releases/2002/01/20020129 11.html

UNITED NATIONS SECURITY COUNCIL RESOLUTION 678

[Authorization to use force prior to the Persian Gulf War, 1990]
The Security Council . . .

Noting that, despite all efforts by the United Nations, Iraq refuses to comply with its obligation to implement resolution 660 (1990) and the above-mentioned subsequent relevant resolutions, in flagrant contempt of the Security Council,

Mindful of its duties and responsibilities under the Charter of the United Nations for the maintenance and preservation of international peace and security,

Determined to secure full compliance with its decisions,

Acting under Chapter VII of the Charter,

1. Demands that Iraq comply fully with resolution 660 (1990) and all subsequent relevant resolutions, and decides, while maintaining all its decisions, to allow Iraq one final opportunity, as a pause of goodwill, to do so;
2. Authorizes Member States co-operating with the Government of Kuwait, unless Iraq on or before 15 January 1991 fully implements, as set forth in paragraph 1 above, the above-mentioned resolutions, to use all necessary means to uphold and implement resolution 660 (1990) and all subsequent relevant resolutions and to restore international peace and security in the area;
3. Requests all States to provide appropriate support for the actions undertaken in pursuance of paragraph 2 of the present resolution;
4. Requests the States concerned to keep the Security Council regularly informed on the progress of actions undertaken pursuant to paragraphs 2 and 3 of the present resolution;
5. Decides to remain seized of the matter.

Source: http://daccessdds.un.org/doc/RESOLUTION/GEN/NR0/575/28/ IMG/NR057528.pdf?OpenElement

NORTH AMERICAN FREE TRADE AGREEMENT, 1992

[Preamble]

The Government of Canada, the Government of the United Mexican States and the Government of the United States of America, resolved to:

STRENGTHEN the special bonds of friendship and cooperation among their nations; CONTRIBUTE to the harmonious development and expansion of world trade and provide a catalyst to broader international cooperation;

CREATE an expanded and secure market for the goods and services produced in their territories;

REDUCE distortions to trade;

ESTABLISH clear and mutually advantageous rules governing their trade;

ENSURE a predictable commercial framework for business planning and investment;

BUILD on their respective rights and obligations under the General Agreement on Tariffs and Trade and other multilateral and bilateral instruments of cooperation;

ENHANCE the competitiveness of their firms in global markets;

FOSTER creativity and innovation, and promote trade in goods and services that are the subject of intellectual property rights;

CREATE new employment opportunities and improve working conditions and living standards in their respective territories;

UNDERTAKE each of the preceding in a manner consistent with environmental protection and conservation

PRESERVE their flexibility to safeguard the public welfare;

PROMOTE sustainable development;

STRENGTHEN the development and enforcement of environmental laws and regulations; and

PROTECT, enhance and enforce basic workers' rights. . . .

Source: http://www.nafta-sec-alena.org/defaultsite/index_e.aspx?detailid =79

THE BUSH DOCTRINE

At the time of the Gulf War, we acquired irrefutable proof that Iraq's designs were not limited to the chemical weapons it had used against Iran and its own people, but also extended to the acquisition of nuclear weapons and biological agents. In the past decade North Korea has become the world's principal purveyor of ballistic missiles, and has tested increasingly capable missiles while developing its own WMD arsenal. Other rogue regimes seek nuclear, biological, and chemical weapons as well. These states' pursuit of, and global trade in, such weapons has become a looming threat to all nations.

We must be prepared to stop rogue states and their terrorist clients before they are able to threaten or use weapons of mass destruction against the United States and our allies and friends. Our response must take full advantage of strengthened alliances, the establishment of new partnerships with former adversaries, innovation in the use of military forces, modern technologies, including the development of an effective missile defense system, and increased emphasis on intelligence collection and analysis.

Our comprehensive strategy to combat WMD includes:

Proactive counterproliferation efforts. We must deter and defend against the threat before it is unleashed. We must ensure that key capabilities—detection, active and passive defenses, and counterforce capabilities—are integrated into our defense transformation and our homeland security systems. Counterproliferation must also be integrated into the doctrine, training, and equipping of our forces and those of our allies to ensure that we can prevail in any conflict with WMD-armed adversaries.

Strengthened nonproliferation efforts to prevent rogue states and terrorists from acquiring the materials, technologies, and expertise necessary for weapons of mass destruction. We will enhance diplomacy, arms control, multilateral export controls, and threat reduction assistance that impede states and terrorists seeking WMD, and when necessary, interdict enabling technologies and materials. We will continue to build coalitions to support these efforts, encouraging their increased political and financial support for nonproliferation and threat reduction programs. The recent G-8 agreement to commit up to $20 billion to a global partnership against proliferation marks a major step forward.

Effective consequence management to respond to the effects of WMD use, whether by terrorists or hostile states. Minimizing the effects of WMD use against our people will help deter those who possess such weapons and dissuade those who seek to acquire them by persuading enemies that they cannot attain their desired ends. The United States must also be prepared to respond to the effects of WMD use against our forces abroad, and to help friends and allies if they are attacked.

It has taken almost a decade for us to comprehend the true nature of this new threat. Given the goals of rogue states and terrorists, the United States can no longer solely rely on a reactive posture as we have in the past. The inability to deter a potential attacker, the immediacy of today's threats, and the magnitude of potential harm that could be caused by our adversaries' choice of weapons, do not permit that option. We cannot let our enemies strike first.

In the Cold War, especially following the Cuban missile crisis, we faced a generally status quo, risk-averse adversary. Deterrence was an effective defense. But deterrence based only upon the threat of retaliation is less likely to work against leaders of rogue states more willing to take risks, gambling with the lives of their people, and the wealth of their nations.

In the Cold War, weapons of mass destruction were considered weapons of last resort whose use risked the destruction of those who used them. Today, our enemies see weapons of mass destruction as weapons of choice. For rogue states these weapons are tools of intimidation and military aggression against their neighbors. These weapons may also allow these states to attempt to blackmail the United States and our allies to prevent us from deterring or repelling the aggressive behavior of rogue states. Such states also see these weapons as their best means of overcoming the conventional superiority of the United States.

Traditional concepts of deterrence will not work against a terrorist enemy whose avowed tactics are wanton destruction and the targeting of innocents; whose so-called soldiers seek martyrdom in death and whose most potent protection is statelessness. The overlap between states that sponsor terror and those that pursue WMD compels us to action.

For centuries, international law recognized that nations need not suffer an attack before they can lawfully take action to defend themselves against forces that present an imminent danger of attack. Legal scholars and international jurists often conditioned the legitimacy of preemption on the existence of an imminent threat—most often a visible mobilization of armies, navies, and air forces preparing to attack.

We must adapt the concept of imminent threat to the capabilities and objectives of today's adversaries. Rogue states and terrorists do not seek to attack us using conventional means. They know such attacks would fail. Instead, they rely on acts of terror and, potentially, the use of weapons of mass destruction—weapons that can be easily concealed, delivered covertly, and used without warning.

The targets of these attacks are our military forces and our civilian population, in direct violation of one of the principal norms of the law of warfare. As was demonstrated by the losses on September 11, 2001, mass civilian casualties is the specific objective of terrorists and these losses would be exponentially more severe if terrorists acquired and used weapons of mass destruction.

The United States has long maintained the option of preemptive actions to counter a sufficient threat to our national security. The greater the threat, the greater is the risk of inaction— and the more compelling the case for taking anticipatory action to defend ourselves, even if uncertainty remains as to the time and place of the enemy's attack. To forestall or prevent such hostile acts by our adversaries, the United States will, if necessary, act preemptively.

Source: United States, Office of the White House, *National Security Strategy of the United States* (Washington, D.C.: GPO, 2002), online at http://www.whitehouse.gov/nsc/nss5.html

Bibliography

CONTENTS

I. INTRODUCTION

The scholarly literature on post–Cold War American diplomacy can be divided into three broad areas. The first revolves around the transition from the Cold War into the evolving global system of the 1990s. These works generally concentrate on the presidency of George H. W. Bush, although many books, particularly those on U.S.-Russian and U.S.-European relations, tend to extend into William J. Clinton's tenure. The second general category of books examines the Clinton years and the struggle to define new foreign policy goals and prioritize national interests. The third and final literature group analyzes George W. Bush and his foreign policy. While the books of the first two categories cover many subjects, including trade, security, and environmental policy, the works on the second Bush presidency tend to focus on the war on terror and the Iraq War. There are also a number of very good books that cover all or most parts of post–Cold War U.S. diplomacy.

Broad, comprehensive works on U.S. foreign policy include Patrick Callahan's *Logics of American Foreign Policy: Theories of America's World Role*, Stanley A. Renshon and Deborah Welch Larson's edited book *Good Judgment in Foreign Policy: Theory and Application*, William H. Meyer's *Security, Economics and Morality in American Foreign Policy: Contemporary Issues in Historical Context*, Arthur Cyr's *After the Cold War: American Foreign Policy, Europe and Asia*, and Jürgen Rüland, Theodor Hanf, and Eva Manske's collection of essays, *U.S. Foreign Policy toward the Third World: A Post–Cold War Assessment*. Expansive works that offer critical analyses of American foreign policy range from *Bait and Switch: Human Rights and U.S. Foreign Policy* by Julie Mertus to *The Age of War: The United States Confronts the World* by Gabriel Kolko.

The post–Cold War role of the United States is the subject of Joseph Nye's excellent 1991 work *Bound to Lead: The Changing Nature of American Power* and historian H. W. Brands's *The United States in the World* from 1994. However, the best work is likely Jonathan Clarke and James Chad's *After the Crusade: American Foreign Policy for the Post-Superpower Age*. A thorough examination of the challenges facing presidents in the aftermath of the bipolar conflict is the edited work by Anthony J. Eksterowicz and Glenn P. Hastedt, *The Post–Cold War Presidency*.

Among the better works on American diplomacy during the Clinton years are Lea Brilmayer's *American Hegemony: Political Morality in a One-Superpower World*, Michael J. Hogan's *The Ambiguous Legacy: U.S. Foreign Relations in the "American Century,"* and Ian Clark's *The Post–Cold War Order*. Seyom Brown's *The Faces of Power: United States Foreign Policy from Truman to Clinton* places George H. W. Bush and Clinton in a historical context, as does

Stephen Skowronek's *The Politics Presidents Make: Leadership from John Adams to Bill Clinton*. Perhaps the most influential work on America's role in the world in the 1990s is Richard N. Haass's *The Reluctant Sheriff: The United States after the Cold War*, although Samuel Huntington's *The Clash of Civilizations and the Remaking of World Order* elicited both praise and condemnation about its emphasis on the global threats to American and Western culture. The U.S. emphasis on a new world order in which democracy and free trade reign supreme were explored in Francis Fukuyama's *The End of History and the Last Man*, a book which argued that the triumph of Western politics and economics over communism marked a reversal of Marxism and the potential end of ideological challenges to the United States. Both Huntington's and Fukuyama's works were influential in the neoconservative movement that influenced many in the administration of President George W. Bush.

The Cold War has an extensive body of literature and is one of the most studied eras in American history. The presidency of George H. W. Bush likewise has a rich and diverse range of scholarship that examines the causes and consequences of the end of the bipolar struggle. Most works on the subject tend either to focus on a specific event or period or to present a broad overview of the superpower conflict. Many of the best examinations of the end of the superpower struggle were written by participants in the Bush administration. Former secretary of state James A. Baker (with Thomas M. DeFrank) in *The Politics of Diplomacy: Revolution, War, and Peace, 1989–1992* wrote an insightful and detailed account of his service during the Bush administration, while Michael Beschloss and former diplomat Strobe Talbot penned *At the Highest Levels: The Inside Story of the End of the Cold War*, based on extensive interviews and discussions with senior politicians and diplomats from a range of countries. George W. Bush's *All the Best: My Life in Letters and Other Writings* offers insight into the decision-making processes and personalities of his administration. Colin Powell's *My American Journey* deals extensively with the period, including the Persian Gulf War. Among the excellent works on the Bush presidency are Colin Campbell and Bert A. Rockman's *The Bush Presidency: First Appraisals*, Richard Rose's *The Postmodern President: George Bush Meets the World*, and the broader study by Bruce Russett, *Grasping the Democratic Peace: Principles for a Post–Cold War World*.

The literature on the foreign policy of William J. Clinton is not as robust as that of the immediate post–Cold War era, although issue-area studies are common. The period lacks a substantial number of comprehensive works that provide a broad overview of the administration's policies. In addition, many of the works on Clinton tend to be biased and overly critical or praising of American diplomacy during the era. As is the case with his predecessor, many of the more illuminating books on Clinton's foreign affairs were written by members of the administration such as Madeleine Albright's *Madam Secretary* (with Bob Woodward). Woodward also penned an interesting survey of the internal workings of the administration, based on extensive interviews, in *The Agenda: Inside the Clinton White House*. Ryan Hendrickson's *The Clinton Wars: The Constitution, Congress, and War Powers* is an excellent overview of the controversies surrounding military interventions. The most thorough examination of the military actions of the Clinton years is contained in Shirley Anne Warshaw's *The Clinton Wars*. More general studies of the Clinton presidency include Elizabeth Drew's *On the Edge: The Clinton Presidency* and John F. Harris's *The Survivor: Bill Clinton in the White House*. Noted presidential historian Colin Campbell and Bert A. Rockman wrote a masterful account of the Clinton presidency in *The Clinton Legacy*. Richard Miniter's *Losing Bin Laden: How Bill Clinton's Failures Unleashed Global Terror* is a partisan review of American policy during the period, but it presents the mainline criticisms of Clinton's diplomacy in detail.

Most of the literature on the diplomacy of George W. Bush and his administration focuses on the war on terror and the war in Iraq. Broad works on the Bush administration and its foreign policy include Alexander Moens's *The Foreign Policy of George W. Bush: Values, Strategy and Loyalty*. Noted scholar Joseph S. Nye Jr. argued in favor of a more multilateralist approach by the administration in the aftermath of the 2001 terrorist attacks in *The Paradox of American Power: Why the World's Only Superpower Can't Go It Alone*. Bill Sammon conducted extensive interviews with administration officials for *Fighting Back: The War on Terrorism—From Inside the Bush White House*, a work that is highly supportive of Bush's foreign policy. Former Bush speechwriter David Frum, who helped craft the 2002 "Axis of Evil" speech, also produced a highly complimentary view of Bush and his staff in *The Right Man: The Surprise Presidency of George W. Bush*. James Mann's *The Rise of the Vulcans: The History of Bush's War Cabinet* takes the opposite tack and is very critical of the administration. Former cabinet official Paul O'Neill (with Ron Suskind) also condemned many aspects of the administration's diplomacy and internal dynamics in *The Price of Loyalty*. Finally, there are several very good works that describe the impact of the September 2001 attacks on Bush and the revolution in his presidency. These include Frank Bruni's *Ambling into History: The Unlikely Odyssey of George W. Bush* and Bob Woodward's *Bush at War*, based on numerous interviews and interaction with administration officials, as well as Stanley A. Renshon's award-winning *In His Father's Shadow: The Transformation of George W. Bush*.

One of the most bedeviling problems to confront successive American presidents has been the Arab-Israeli conflict. Through Bush, Clinton, and the second Bush, efforts to end the fighting between Palestinians and Israelis were only partially successful, and each gain was often accompanied by corresponding failures. U.S. diplomatic efforts to resolve the Arab-Israeli conflict are examined broadly in Vaughn Shannon's *Balancing Act: U.S. Foreign Policy and the Arab-Israeli Conflict* and Dalia Dassa Kaye's *Beyond the Handshake: Multilateral Cooperation in the Arab-Israeli Peace Process, 1991–1996*. Helena Cobban, in *The Israeli-Syrian Peace Talks: 1991–1996 and Beyond*, provides a broader analysis of Washington's attempts to reduce regional tensions. American involvement in the peace process as an extension of the U.S.-Israeli alliance is covered in Herbert Druks's *The Uncertain Alliance: The U.S. and Israel from Kennedy to the Peace Process* and Melman Yossi's *Friends in Deed: Inside the U.S.-Israeli Alliance*. Gilead Sher details Clinton's final unsuccessful push for a resolution to the conflict in *The Israeli-Palestinian Peace Negotiations, 1999–2001: Within Reach*. Noam Chomsky's *Fateful Triangle: The United States, Israel, and the Palestinians* offers a leftist critique of U.S. Middle East policy through 1999, while Naseer Hasan Aruri roundly condemns the intervention of the United States in the conflict in *Dishonest Broker: The U.S. Role in Israel and Palestine*.

   The Bush administration's 1990 invasion of Panama is covered in Kevin Buckley's *Panama: The Whole Story* and Russell Crandall's *Gunboat Democracy: U.S. Interventions in the Dominican Republic, Grenada, and Panama*. Ronald Fernandez explores Operation Just Cause in the broader context of U.S. intervention in the region in *Cruising the Caribbean: U.S. Influence and Intervention in the Twentieth Century*. Other prominent books on the invasion include *Operation Just Cause: The Storming of Panama* by Thomas Donnelly, Margaret Roth, and Caleb Baker, and the edited work *Operation Just Cause: The U.S. Intervention in Panama* by Bruce W. Watson and Peter G. Tsouras. Manuel Noriega (with Peter Eisner) wrote an interesting account form his perspective, in which he challenges the main contentions for the invasion, in *America's Prisoner: The Memoirs of Manuel Noriega*.

   The U.S. intervention in the Balkans is examined in the historical and political analysis of Lester H. Brune's *The United States and the Balkan Crisis, 1990–2005: Conflict in Bosnia and Kosovo*. Other broad analyses include *Armed Humanitarians: U.S. Interventions from Northern Iraq to Kosovo* by Robert C. DiPrizio; Peter Siani-Davies's edited volume of essays, *International Intervention in the Balkans since 1995*; *NATO's Balkan Interventions* by Dana H. Allin; and Joyce Kaufman's *NATO and the Former Yugoslavia: Crisis, Conflict, and the Atlantic Alliance*. The latter two works examine the American role against the backdrop of NATO and European interplay. Kosovo is the subject of Andrew J. Bacevich and Eliot A. Cohen's edited collection *War over Kosovo: Politics and Strategy in a Global Age*. Former general Wesley Clark, the U.S. commander during the intervention, assembled his perspectives in *Waging*

Modern War: Bosnia, Kosovo, and the Future of Combat. Jonathan Dean's *Ending Europe's War's: The Continuing Search for Peace and Security* is probably the best comprehensive work on the Balkan Wars and the interplay of U.S. and European diplomacy.

The Persian Gulf War also generated an extensive body of literature. Good, utilitarian surveys of the war include Anthony A. Evans, *The Gulf War: Desert Shield and Desert Storm, 1990–1991*; Lawrence Freedman and Efraim Karsh, *The Gulf Conflict, 1990–1991: Diplomacy and War in the New World Order*; and Dilip Hiro, *Desert Shield to Desert Storm: The Second Gulf War*. Informative studies on the diplomacy, military strategy, and weaponry used in the conflict are Michael R. Gordon and Bernard E. Trainor, *The Generals' War: The Inside Story of the Conflict in the Gulf*; Rick Atkinson, *Crusade: The Untold Story of the Persian Gulf War*; Mashhud H. Choudhry, *Coalition Warfare: Can the Gulf War-91 Be the Model for Future?*; James P. Dunnigan and Austin Bay, *From Shield to Storm: High-Tech Weapons, Military Strategy, and Coalition Warfare in the Persian Gulf*; and Thomas A. Keaney and Eliot A. Cohen, *Revolution in Warfare? Airpower in the Persian Gulf*. Mark Schissler offers a provocative exploration of the issues and difficulties that confronted the U.S.-led multilateral force in *Coalition Warfare: More Power or More Problems?* The seminal analysis of the decision to go to war remains Steve Yetiv's *Explaining Foreign Policy: U.S. Decision-Making and the Persian Gulf War*.

The terrorist attacks of 11 September 2001 and the subsequent war on terror have produced a wealth of literature. Among the important works on the 2001 attacks and their aftermath are Victor David Hanson's *An Autumn of War: What America Learned from September 11 and the War on Terrorism*, Brigitte L. Nacos's *Terrorism and Counterterrorism: Understanding Threats and Responses in the Post-9/11 World*, and Peter L. Bergen's *Holy War, Inc.: Inside the Secret World of Osama bin Laden*. The impact of the war on terror on global politics is the subject of Daniel Benjamin's edited volume *America and the World in the Age of Terror: A New Landscape in International Relations*, in which most of the essays assert that the September 2001 attacks and Washington's response dramatically changed the world's diplomacy. The international ramifications of the war on terror are also the subject of an edited collection by Mary Buckley and Robert Singh, *The Bush Doctrine and the War on Terrorism: Global Responses, Global Consequences*, whose theme is also the focus of noted political scientist Robert Jervis's broader work, *American Foreign Policy in a New Era*. The impact of the September 2001 terrorist strikes on U.S.-Russian relations, in the context of NATO, is explored in Jakub M. Godzimirski's *11 September 2001 and the Shift in Russia's Policy towards NATO*. A highly critical view of the Bush administration's management of the war on terror is Daniel Benjamin and Stephan Simon's *The Next Attack: The Failure of the War on Ter-*

ror and a Strategy for Getting It Right, while David Frum and Richard Perle's *An End to Evil: How to Win the War on Terror* generally praises the government, but calls for more extensive measures to combat international terrorism.

The Iraq War prompted a range of studies, most of which either broadly endorsed or roundly condemned the U.S.-led invasion. However, there were several balanced, broad surveys as well. For background on U.S.-Iraqi tensions, including the impact of the international embargo on the country in the 1990s, see Anthony S. Cordesman and Ahmed S. Hashim's *Iraq: Sanctions and Beyond*. The ramifications of the war on America's relationship with its traditional allies are analyzed in William Shawcross's *Allies: The U.S., Britain, Europe and the War in Iraq*.

Books that were generally supportive of military action against Iraq included Joseph Braude's *The New Iraq: Rebuilding the Country, Its People, the Middle East and the World*, Daniel Byman and Matthew Waxman's *Confronting Iraq: U.S. Policy and the Use of Force since the Gulf War*, Lawrence Kaplan and William Kristol's *The War over Iraq: Saddam's Tyranny and America's Mission*, and Kenneth Pollack's *The Threatening Storm: The Case for Invading Iraq*. Among the best scholarly works critical of the Iraq War or the Bush administration's handling of the conflict are *The Iraq War: Causes and Consequences*, edited by Rick Fawn and Raymond Hinnebusch; Charles W. Kegley and Gregory A. Raymond's *After Iraq: The Imperiled American Imperium*, and Bob Woodward's *Plan of Attack*. The American military strategy of "shock and awe" during the war was based on network-centric warfare and the earlier work of Harlan Ullman, with James Wade Jr., *Rapid Dominance, a Force for All Seasons: Technologies and Systems for Achieving Shock and Awe; A Real Revolution in Military Affairs*.

Arms control in the post–Cold War era is explored in a number of works. A general overview of the threats posed by weapons of mass destruction and their proliferation is Malcolm Dando's *The New Biological Weapons: Threat, Proliferation, and Control*. An interesting behind-the-scenes view of arms control efforts at the end of the Cold War and in the immediate aftermath is Maynard W. Glitman's *The Last Battle of the Cold War: An Inside Account of Negotiating the Intermediate Range Nuclear Forces Treaty*. The arms control initiatives of the Clinton administration are detailed in Joshua Lederberg's *Biological Weapons: Limiting the Threat* and Edward M. Spiers' *Chemical and Biological Weapons: A Study of Proliferation*. Two of the best studies on arms control and nonproliferation during the second Bush presidency are Thomas Graham Jr.'s *Commonsense on Weapons of Mass Destruction* and Michael Levi and Michael O'Hanlon's *The Future of Arms Control*.

David B. H. Denoon explores American antimissile policy in *Ballistic Missile Defense in the Post–Cold War Era*. Ballistic missile defense is also the subject of Richard Dean Burns and Lester H. Brune's *The Quest for Missile Defenses, 1944–2003*, Anthony H. Cordesman's *Strategic Threats and National Missile Defenses: Defending the US Homeland*, Roger Handberg's *Ballistic Missile Defense and the Future of American Security: Agendas, Perceptions, Technology, and Policy*, and James M. Lindsey and Michael O'Hanlon's *Defending America: The Case for Limited National Missile Defense*.

Defense and homeland security policy volumes abound. István Gyarmati and Theodor Winkler's edited collection *Post–Cold War Defense Reforms: Lessons Learned in Europe and the United States* examines U.S. military policy in comparison with the nation's European counterparts. The great historian John Lewis Gaddis explores defense policy in response to unforeseen attacks such as those of 11 September 2001 in *Surprise, Security and the American Experience*. The revolution in military affairs and its impact on U.S. defense policy is debated by policy makers and military officials in Stephen D. Wrage's edited book *Immaculate Warfare: Participants Reflect on the Air Campaigns over Kosovo and Afghanistan*. Military innovations and changing doctrine form the core of Michael O'Hanlan's *Defense Planning for the Late 1990s: Beyond the Desert Storm Framework*. Helen Caldicott's *The New Nuclear Danger: George W. Bush's Military-Industrial Complex* is highly critical of the administration's military buildup, especially in terms of its strategic forces.

Homeland security is analyzed by a range of authors in Ivo Daadler's edited volume *Assessing the Department of Homeland Security*, while Arthur S. Hulnick's *Keeping Us Safe: Secret Intelligence and Homeland Security* focuses on the nation's intelligence agencies and their role in protecting the country. Meanwhile, a number of works are critical of contemporary homeland security policy, including Donald Kettl's *System under Stress: Homeland Security and American Politics*.

America's domestic and international environmental policies are the focus of the edited book by Paul G. Harris, *International Environmental Cooperation: Politics and Diplomacy in Pacific Asia*; Sebastian Oberthur and Herman E. Ott's *The Kyoto Protocol: International Climate Policy for the 21st Century*; and the collection by Dennis L. Soden, *The Environmental Presidency*. American environmental policy is explored in an international context in Miranda A. Schreurs in *Environmental Politics in Japan, Germany and the United States* and by Lynton Keith Caldwell in *International Environmental Policy: Emergence and Divergence*. Environmental policy in regard to the broader issue of climate change is the subject of David G. Victor's *Climate Change: Debating America's Policy Options*. Two of the better works on the increasing importance of ecological considerations are by Terry L. Anderson: Anderson and Donald R. Leal's *Free Market Environmentalism*, and the edited volume by Anderson and Henry I. Miller, *The Greening of U.S. Foreign Policy*.

Globalization became an increasingly popular topic during the 1990s. Serge Latouche's *The Westernization of the World*, John Tomlinson's *Globalization and Culture*, and Roland Robertson's *Globalization* provide broad examinations of global cultural and trade patterns. The best broad study of globalization in the 1990s is Hans-Henrik Holm and Georg Sorensen's edited collection *Whose World Order? Uneven Globalization and the End of the Cold War*. Tony Smith argues in favor of the spread of U.S. culture and politics in *America's Mission: The United States and the Worldwide Struggle for Democracy in the Twentieth Century*, but James Watson's seminal edited volume *Golden Arches East: McDonald's in East Asia* is more critical of the impact of globalization. Joseph Stiglitz wrote a highly critical work on globalization and American trade policy in *Globalization and Its Discontents*, while Thomas Friedman's *The World Is Flat* presents the opposite perspective.

The challenges faced by the United States from terrorism and American responses to the security challenge are reviewed in Peter Caram's *The 1993 World Trade Center Bombing: Foresight and Warning*, Graham E. Fuller and Ian O. Lesser's *Sense of Siege: The Geopolitics of Islam and the West*, P. Wilkinson's *Terrorism versus Democracy: The Liberal State Response*, Bruce Hoffman's *Inside Terrorism*, and the collection of essays edited by Patrick Hayden, Tom Lansford, and Robert Watson, *America's War on Terror*. Al Qaeda and the American efforts to suppress it form the core of Simon Reeve's *The New Jackals: Ramzi Yousef, Osama Bin Laden and the Future of Terrorism*, Jason Burke's *Al-Qaeda: The True Story of Radical Islam*, and Ahmed Rashid's masterful *Taliban: Militant Islam, Oil and Fundamentalism in Central Asia*. A broad work on state response to terrorism is Adam Garfinkle's edited book, *A Practical Guide to Winning the War on Terrorism*.

The nation's trade policy has been widely studied. The North American Free Trade Agreement is examined in Bruce Ackerman and D. Golove's *Is NAFTA Constitutional?* and Maxwell A. Cameron and Brian W. Tomlin's *The Making of NAFTA: How the Deal Was Done* U.S. and regional trade issues form the core for the essays in Jeffrey Gedman's collection *European Integration and American Interests: What the New Europe Really Means for the United States*, as well as for Miles Kahler's book *Regional Futures and Transatlantic Economic Relations* and Jagdish N. Bhagwati's *Free Trade Today*. Bilateral trade issues are studied in a large number of books, such as Manuel F. Casanova's edited work *The U.S.-Singapore Free Trade Agreement* and John N. McDougall's *Drifting Together: The Political Economy of Canada-US Integration*. The increasing use of economic sanctions as a foreign policy tool is explored by Richard N. Haass in *Economic Sanctions and American Diplomacy*. Trade policy is also the subject of Stephen D. Cohen, Robert A. Blecker, and Peter D. Whitney's *Fundamentals of U.S. Foreign Trade Policy: Economics, Politics,*

Laws, and Issues and William A. Lovett, Alfred E. Eckes Jr., and Richard L. Brinkman's *U.S. Trade Policy: History, Theory, and the WTO.*

United States foreign policy toward specific regions has been the subject of a plethora of studies and analyses. America's relations with Africa are examined in Richard Sandbrook's *Closing the Circle: Democratization and Development in Africa* and F. Ugboaja Ohaegbulam's *U.S. Policy in Postcolonial Africa: Four Case Studies in Conflict Resolution.* Case studies of the U.S. and particular regions in Africa include James J. F. Forest and Matthew V. Sousa's *Oil and Terrorism in the New Gulf: U.S. Energy and Security Policies for the Gulf of Guinea* and Peter Woodward's *U.S. Foreign Policy and the Horn of Africa,* as well as the official history of military intervention in Liberia and surrounding states, James G. Antal and R. John Vanden Berghe's *On Mamba Station: U.S. Marines in West Africa, 1990–2003.* Bilateral relations are explored in Les de Villiers, *In Sight of Surrender: The U.S. Sanctions Campaign against South Africa, 1946–1993*; Princeton Nathan Lyman, *Partner to History: The U.S. Role in South Africa's Transition to Democracy*; and Daniel Spikes, *Angola and the Politics of Intervention.*

U.S. relations with Asia are the topic of books on both regional and bilateral ties. Broader works include Edward Lincoln's *East Asian Economic Regionalism,* Tae-hyo Kim and Brad Glosserman's edited book *The Future of U.S.-Korea-Japan Relations: Balancing Values and Interests,* and John Ravenhill's *APEC and the Construction of Pacific Rim Regionalism.* Comprehensive studies on bilateral relations range from Nicholas Evan Sarantakes's *Keystone: The American Occupation of Okinawa and U.S.-Japanese Relations* to the edited volume by Robert S. Ross, *After the Cold War: Domestic Factors and U.S.-China Relations.*

The long-standing economic, political, and security ties between the United States and Europe are the focus of a rich and deep body of works. Among the more significant are Adam Bronstone's *European Union–United States Security Relations: Transatlantic Tensions and the Theory of International Relations,* Helga Haftendorn and Christian Tuschhoff's edited work *America and Europe in an Era of Change,* and the provocative *Of Paradise and Power: America and Europe in the New World Order* by Robert Kagan. The better studies of bilateral relations include John Drumbell's *A Special Relationship: Anglo-American Relations in the Cold War and Beyond,* James Goodby's *Europe Undivided: The New Logic of Peace in U.S.-Russian Relations,* and Gregory Treverton's *America, Germany and the Future of Europe.*

Many of the books on U.S. relations with Latin America and the Middle East are highly critical of American actions and policies. Among the better, and more balanced, examinations of Washington's role in the region are Stewart

Brewer's *Borders and Bridges: A History of U.S.-Latin American Relations* and Kathryn Sikkink's *Mixed Signals: U.S. Human Rights Policy and Latin America*. Major studies of bilateral relations include Tony Payan's *The Three U.S.-Mexico Border Wars: Drugs, Immigration and Homeland Security* and Sara Schoonmaker's *High-Tech Trade Wars: U.S.-Brazilian Conflicts in the Global Economy*. Useful analyses of drug trafficking and interdiction is Coletta A. Youngers and Eileen Rosin's edited book *Drugs and Democracy in Latin America: The Impact of U.S. Policy*.

Notable works on U.S. foreign policy toward the Middle East include Douglas Little's *American Orientalism: The United States and the Middle East since 1945*, Barry Rubin's *The Long War for Freedom: The Arab Struggle for Democracy in the Middle East*, and Steve Yetiv's *America and the Persian Gulf: The Third Party Dimension in World Politics*. Contemporary Middle East policy, outside of the war on terrorism, is best viewed through the volume of essays edited by Ivo Daalder, Nicole Gnesotto, and Philip Gordon, *Crescent of Crisis: U.S.-European Strategy for the Greater Middle East*; or Leon Hadar's *Sandstorm: Policy Failure in the Middle East*. More narrow studies range from John Miglietta's *American Alliance Policy in the Middle East, 1945–1992: Iran, Israel, and Saudi Arabia* to William A. Rugh's *American Encounters with Arabs: The "Soft Power" of U.S. Public Diplomacy in the Middle East*.

The evolution of NATO, in the context of transatlantic security, is the subject of Alexander Moens, Lenard J. Cohen, and Allen Gregory Sens's edited volume *NATO and European Security: Alliance Politics from the End of the Cold War to the Age of Terrorism*. Books on Washington's transatlantic security policy, including topics such as NATO expansion or U.S.-Russian relations, are the focal point of Anatol Lieven and Dmitri Trenin's collected volume of essays *Ambivalent Neighbors: The EU, NATO and the Price of Membership* and Charles Barry's *Transforming NATO Command and Control for Future Missions*. One of the best extensive studies of the alliance is Lawrence Kaplan's *NATO Divided, NATO United: The Evolution of an Alliance*.

Critical studies of U.S. policy and the United Nations are presented in Yehuda Z. Blum's *Eroding the United Nations Charter* and the collected essays of Erskine Childers's *Challenges to the United Nations: Building a Safer World*. Among the better surveys of contemporary U.S.-UN interaction are Paul Kennedy's *The Parliament of Man: The Past, Present, and Future of the United Nations* and James S. Sutterlin's *The United Nations and the Maintenance of International Security: A Challenge to Be Met*. American policies toward the UN and other international bodies are compared in the edited collection by Rosemary Foot, S. Neil MacFarlane, and Michael Mastanduno, *U.S.*

Hegemony and International Organizations: The United States and Multilateral Institutions.

There are also a number of bibliographies, encyclopedic works, and historical dictionaries related to U.S. post–Cold War diplomacy. For instance, Frances Scott compiled a short bibliography on American military action in *U.S. Intervention Policy in the Post–Cold War World*. However, the grand bibliographic source on American diplomacy is Robert L. Beisner's massive, two-volume edited set, *American Foreign Relations since 1600: A Guide to the Literature*. Oxford University Press commissioned a five-volume set on U.S. diplomacy that was published in 1997: Bruce W. Jentleson and Thomas G. Patterson, *Encyclopedia of U.S. Foreign Relations*. Alexander DeConde, Richard Dean Burns, and Fredrik Logevall edited a three-volume set, *Encyclopedia of American Foreign Policy*, whose second edition came out in 2002.

Scarecrow Press has produced a range of historical dictionaries that deal with topics related to post–Cold War U.S. diplomacy. These volumes also have extensive bibliographies that may supplement the works cited herein. For instance, the Historical Dictionaries of War, Revolution, and Civil Unrest series includes Ludwig W. Adamec's *Historical Dictionary of Afghan Wars, Revolutions and Insurgencies*, Jeffrey A. Larsen and James M. Smith's *Historical Dictionary of Arms Control and Disarmament*, and P. R. Kumaraswamy's *Historical Dictionary of the Arab-Israeli Conflict*, among other titles. The Historical Dictionaries of Religions, Philosophies, and Movements series includes Sean K. Anderson and Stephan Sloan's *Historical Dictionary of Terrorism*, while the Historical Dictionaries of Intelligence and Counter-Intelligence series features country-specific volumes on prominent American allies, such as Nigel West's *Historical Dictionary of British Intelligence* and Ephraim Kahana's *Historical Dictionary of Israeli Intelligence*, besides volumes on the United States (Michael A. Turner, *Historical Dictionary of United States Intelligence*) and Russia (Robert W. Pringle, *Historical Dictionary of Russian and Soviet Intelligence*). The series on International Organizations has Terry M. Mays's *Historical Dictionary of Multinational Peacekeeping* and Jacques Fomerand's *Historical Dictionary of the United Nations*, along with a host of other volumes on major global bodies. In addition, the Historical Dictionaries of U.S. Diplomacy series includes volumes such as Robert Sutter's *Historical Dictionary of United States–China Relations*; John Van Sant, Peter Mauch, and Yoneyuki Sugita's *Historical Dictionary of United States–Japan Relations*; Joseph Smith's *Historical Dictionary of United States–Latin American Relations*; and Peter L. Hahn's *Historical Dictionary of United States–Middle East Relations*. Finally, country series covering Africa, Asia, Europe, Latin America, Oceania, and the Middle East have volumes on most countries in their specific areas.

II. FOREIGN RELATIONS

Arquilla, John. *The Reagan Imprint: Ideas in American Foreign Policy from the Collapse of Communism to the War on Terror.* Chicago: Ivan R. Dee, 2006.

Brands, H. W. *United States in the World.* Boston: Houghton Mifflin, 1994.

Brilmayer, Lea. *American Hegemony: Political Morality in a One-Superpower World.* New Haven, Conn.: Yale University Press, 1995.

Brown, Seyom. *The Faces of Power: United States Foreign Policy from Truman to Clinton.* New York: Columbia University Press, 1994.

Callahan, Patrick. *Logics of American Foreign Policy: Theories of America's World Role.* New York: Longman, 2004.

Clark, Ian. *The Post–Cold War Order.* New York: Oxford University Press, 2001.

Clarke, Jonathan, and James Chad. *After the Crusade: American Foreign Policy for the Post-Superpower Age.* Lanham, Md.: Madison Books, 1995.

Cyr, Arthur. *After the Cold War: American Foreign Policy, Europe, and Asia.* New York: New York University Press, 1997.

Eksterowicz, Anthony J., and Glenn P. Hastedt, eds. *The Post–Cold War Presidency.* New York: Rowman & Littlefield, 1999.

Fukuyama, Francis. *The End of History and the Last Man.* New York: Avon, 1993.

Haass, Richard N. *The Reluctant Sheriff: The United States after the Cold War.* New York: Council on Foreign Relations, 1997.

———, ed. *Economic Sanctions and American Diplomacy.* New York: Council on Foreign Relations, 1998.

Hogan, Michael J. *The Ambiguous Legacy: U.S. Foreign Relations in the "American Century."* Cambridge: Cambridge University Press, 1999.

Huntington, Samuel P. *The Clash of Civilizations and the Remaking of World Order.* New York: Simon & Schuster, 1996.

Kolko, Gabriel. *The Age of War: The United States Confronts the World.* Boulder, Colo.: Lynne Rienner, 2006.

Melanson, Richard A. *Reconstructing Consensus: American Foreign Policy since the Vietnam War.* New York: St. Martin's, 1991.

Mertus, Julie. *Bait and Switch: Human Rights and U.S. Foreign Policy.* New York: Routledge, 2004.

Meyer, William H. *Security, Economics and Morality in American Foreign Policy: Contemporary Issues in Historical Context.* Upper Saddle River, N.J.: Pearson Prentice Hall, 2004.

Nye, Joseph S. *Bound to Lead: The Changing Nature of American Power.* New York: Basic Books, 1991.

Patrick, Stewart, and Shepard Foreman, eds. *Multilateralism and US Foreign Policy: Ambivalent Engagement.* Boulder, Colo.: Lynne Rienner, 2002.

Renshon, Stanley A., and Deborah Welch Larson, eds. *Good Judgment in Foreign Policy: Theory and Application.* New York: Rowman & Littlefield, 2003.

Ruggie, John G., ed. *Winning the Peace: America and World Order in the New Era.* New York: Columbia University Press, 1996.

Rüland, Jürgen, Theodor Hanf, and Eva Manske, eds. *U.S. Foreign Policy toward the Third World: A Post–Cold War Assessment.* Armonk, N.Y.: M. E. Sharpe, 2006.

Skowronek, Stephen. *The Politics Presidents Make: Leadership from John Adams to Bill Clinton.* Cambridge, Mass.: Harvard University Press, 1997.

Weart, Spencer R. *Why Democracies Will Not Fight One Another.* New Haven, Conn.: Yale University Press, 1998.

III. GEORGE H. W. BUSH AND HIS ADMINISTRATION

Baker, James A., III, with Thomas M. DeFrank. *The Politics of Diplomacy: Revolution, War, and Peace, 1989–1992.* New York: Putnam, 1995.

Beschloss, Michael, and Strobe Talbot. *At the Highest Levels: The Inside Story of the End of the Cold War.* Boston: Little, Brown, 1995.

Bush, George W. *All the Best: My Life in Letters and Other Writings.* New York: Touchstone, 1999.

Campbell, Colin, and Bert A. Rockman. *The Bush Presidency: First Appraisals.* Chatham, N.J.: Chatham House, 1991.

Green, F. *George Bush: An Intimate Portrait.* New York: Hippocrene Books, 1991.

Hill, Dilys M., and Phil Williams. *The Bush Presidency: Triumphs and Adversities.* New York: St. Martin's, 1994.

Medhurst, Martin J., ed. *The Rhetorical Presidency of George H. W. Bush.* College Station: Texas A & M University Press, 2006.

Powell, Colin, with Joseph E. Persico. *My American Journey.* New York: Random House, 1995.

Rose, Richard. *The Postmodern President: George Bush Meets the World.* Chatham, N.J.: Chatham House, 1991.

Russett, Bruce M., *Grasping the Democratic Peace: Principles for a Post–Cold War World.* Princeton, N.J.: Princeton University Press, 1993.

IV. WILLIAM J. CLINTON AND HIS ADMINISTRATION

Albright, Madeleine, and Bill Woodward. *Madam Secretary.* New York: Miramax Books, 2003.

Campbell, Colin, and Bert A. Rockman. *The Clinton Legacy.* New York: Chatham House, 2000.

Drew, Elizabeth. *On the Edge: The Clinton Presidency.* New York: Simon & Schuster, 1995.

Harris, John F. *The Survivor: Bill Clinton in the White House.* New York: Random House, 2005.

Hendrickson, Ryan C. *The Clinton Wars: The Constitution, Congress, and War Powers.* Nashville, Tenn.: Vanderbilt University Press, 2002.

Lippman, Thomas W. *Madeleine Albright and the New American Century.* Boulder, Colo.: Westview Press, 2000.

Miniter, Richard. *Losing Bin Laden: How Bill Clinton's Failures Unleashed Global Terror.* Washington, D.C.: Regnery, 2003.

Warshaw, Shirley Anne. *The Clinton Wars.* New York: Facts on File, 2004.

Woodward, Bob. *The Agenda: Inside the Clinton White House.* New York: Simon & Schuster, 1994.

V. GEORGE W. BUSH AND HIS ADMINISTRATION

Bruni, Frank. *Ambling into History: The Unlikely Odyssey of George W. Bush.* New York: HarperCollins, 2002.

Daalder, Ivo H., and James M. Lindsey. *America Unbound: The Bush Revolution in Foreign Policy.* Washington, D.C.: Brookings Institution, 2003.

Frum, David. *The Right Man: The Surprise Presidency of George W. Bush.* Waterville, Maine: Thorndyke Press, 2003.

Mann, James. *The Rise of the Vulcans: The History of Bush's War Cabinet.* New York: Viking Penguin, 2004.

Minutaglio, Bill. *First Son: George W. Bush and the Bush Family Dynasty.* New York: Random House, 1999.

Moens, Alexander. *The Foreign Policy of George W. Bush: Values, Strategy and Loyalty.* Aldershot, England: Ashgate, 2004.

Nye, Joseph S., Jr. *The Paradox of American Power: Why the World's Only Superpower Can't Go It Alone.* New York: Oxford University Press, 2002.

Renshon, Stanley A. *In His Father's Shadow: The Transformation of George W. Bush.* New York: Palgrave, 2004.

Sammon, Bill. *Fighting Back: The War on Terrorism—From Inside the Bush White House.* Washington, D.C.: Regnery, 2002.

Suskind, Ron, and Paul O'Neill. *The Price of Loyalty.* New York: Simon & Schuster, 2004.

Woodward, Bob. *Bush at War.* New York: Simon & Schuster, 2002.

VI. ARAB-ISRAELI CONFLICT

Aruri, Naseer Hasan. *Dishonest Broker: The U.S. Role in Israel and Palestine.* Cambridge, Mass.: South End Press, 2003.

Ben-Zvi, Abraham. *The United States and Israel: The Limits of the Special Relationship.* New York: Columbia University Press, 1993.

Chomsky, Noam. *Fateful Triangle: The United States, Israel, and the Palestinians.* Cambridge, Mass.: South End Press, 1999.

Cobban, Helena. *The Israeli-Syrian Peace Talks: 1991–1996 and Beyond.* Washington, D.C.: United States Institute of Peace Press, 1999.

Druks, Herbert. *The Uncertain Alliance: The U.S. and Israel from Kennedy to the Peace Process.* Westport, Conn.: Greenwood Press, 2001.

Kaye, Dalia Dassa. *Beyond the Handshake: Multilateral Cooperation in the Arab-Israeli Peace Process, 1991–1996.* New York: Columbia University Press, 2001.

Melman, Yossi. *Friends in Deed: Inside the U.S.-Israeli Alliance.* New York: Hyperion Books, 1994.

Shannon, Vaughn. *Balancing Act: U.S. Foreign Policy and the Arab-Israeli Conflict.* Aldershot, England: Ashgate, 2003.

Sher, Gilead. *The Israeli-Palestinian Peace Negotiations, 1999–2001: Within Reach.* New York: Routledge, 2006.

VII. PANAMA INVASION (OPERATION JUST CAUSE)

Buckley, Kevin. *Panama: The Whole Story.* New York: Simon & Schuster, 1991.

Crandall, Russell. *Gunboat Democracy: U.S. Interventions in the Dominican Republic, Grenada, and Panama.* Lanham, Md.: Rowman & Littlefield, 2006.

Donnelly, Thomas, Margaret Roth, and Caleb Baker. *Operation Just Cause: The Storming of Panama.* Toronto: Maxwell Macmillan, 1991.

Fernandez, Ronald. *Cruising the Caribbean: U.S. Influence and Intervention in the Twentieth Century.* Monroe, Maine: Common Courage Press, 1994.

Noriega, Manuel, and Peter Eisner. *America's Prisoner: The Memoirs of Manuel Noriega.* New York: Random House, 1997.

Watson, Bruce W., and Peter G. Tsouras, eds. *Operation Just Cause: The U.S. Intervention in Panama.* Boulder, Colo.: Westview Press, 1991.

VIII. BALKAN WARS

Allin, Dana H. *NATO's Balkan Interventions*. London: Oxford University Press, 2002.

Bacevich, Andrew J., and Eliot A. Cohen, eds. *War over Kosovo: Politics and Strategy in a Global Age*. New York: Columbia University Press, 2001.

Brune, Lester H. *The United States and the Balkan Crisis, 1990–2005: Conflict in Bosnia and Kosovo*. Claremont, Calif.: Regina Books, 2005.

Clark, Wesley. *Waging Modern War: Bosnia, Kosovo, and the Future of Combat*. Washington, D.C.: Public Affairs, 2001.

Dean, Jonathon. *Ending Europe's War's: The Continuing Search for Peace and Security*. New York: Priority Books, 1995.

DiPrizio, Robert C. *Armed Humanitarians: U.S. Interventions from Northern Iraq to Kosovo*. Baltimore, Md.: Johns Hopkins University Press, 2002.

Gordy, Eric D. *The Culture of Power in Serbia: Nationalism and the Destruction of Alternatives*. University Park: Pennsylvania State University Press, 1999.

Kaufman, Joyce P. *NATO and the Former Yugoslavia: Crisis, Conflict, and the Atlantic Alliance*. Lanham, Md.: Rowman & Littlefield, 2002.

Lambeth, Benjamin S. *NATO's Air War for Kosovo: A Strategic and Operational Assessment*. Santa Monica, Calif.: Rand, 2001.

Siani-Davies, Peter, ed. *International Intervention in the Balkans since 1995*. New York: Routledge, 2003.

IX. PERSIAN GULF WAR

Atkinson, Rick. *Crusade: The Untold Story of the Persian Gulf War*. Boston: Houghton Mifflin, 1993.

Choudhry, Mashhud H. *Coalition Warfare: Can the Gulf War-91 Be the Model for Future?* Carlisle Barracks, Penn.: U.S. Army War College, 1992.

Dunnigan, James P., and Austin Bay. *From Shield to Storm: High-Tech Weapons, Military Strategy, and Coalition Warfare in the Persian Gulf*. New York: Morrow, 1992.

Evans, Anthony A. *The Gulf War: Desert Shield and Desert Storm, 1990–1991*. London: Greenhill, 2003.

Freedman, Lawrence, and Efraim Karsh. *The Gulf Conflict, 1990–1991: Diplomacy and War in the New World Order*. Princeton, N.J.: Princeton University Press, 1993.

Gordon, Michael R., and Bernard E. Trainor. *The Generals' War: The Inside Story of the Conflict in the Gulf.* Boston: Little, Brown, 1995.

Hiro, Dilip. *Desert Shield to Desert Storm: The Second Gulf War.* New York: HarperCollins, 1992.

Keaney, Thomas A., and Eliot A. Cohen. *Revolution in Warfare? Airpower in the Persian Gulf.* Annapolis, Md.: Naval Institute Press, 1995.

Mueller, John E. *Policy and Opinion in the Gulf War.* Chicago: University of Chicago Press, 1994.

Schissler, Mark. *Coalition Warfare: More Power or More Problems?* Newport, R.I.: U.S. Naval War College, 1993.

Sick, Gary S., and Lawrence G. Potter, eds. *The Persian Gulf at the Millennium: Essays in Politics, Economy, Security, and Religion.* New York: St. Martin's, 1997.

Yetiv, Steve A. *Explaining Foreign Policy: U.S. Decision-Making and the Persian Gulf War.* Baltimore, Md.: Johns Hopkins University Press, 2004.

X. SEPTEMBER 11, 2001, ATTACKS AND THE WAR ON TERROR

Benjamin, Daniel, ed. *America and the World in the Age of Terror: A New Landscape in International Relations.* Washington, D.C.: Center for Strategic and International Studies, 2005.

Benjamin, Daniel, and Stephan Simon. *The Next Attack: The Failure of the War on Terror and a Strategy for Getting It Right.* New York: Henry Holt, 2005.

Bergen, Peter L. *Holy War, Inc.: Inside the Secret World of Osama bin Laden.* New York: Free Press, 2001.

Buckley, Mary, and Robert Singh, eds. *The Bush Doctrine and the War on Terrorism: Global Responses, Global Consequences.* New York: Routledge, 2006.

Frum, David, and Richard Perle. *An End to Evil: How to Win the War on Terror.* New York: Random House, 2003.

Godzimirski, Jakub M. *11 September 2001 and the Shift in Russia's Policy towards NATO.* Oslo, Norway: Norske Atlanterhavskomite, 2002.

Jervis, Robert. *American Foreign Policy in a New Era.* New York: Routledge, 2005.

Lansford, Tom. *A Bitter Harvest: US Foreign Policy and Afghanistan.* Aldershot, England: Ashgate, 2003.

Nacos, Brigitte L. *Terrorism and Counterterrorism: Understanding Threats and Responses in the Post-9/11 World.* New York: Longman, 2006.

Tanner, Stephen. *Afghanistan: A Military History from Alexander the Great to the Fall of the Taliban.* New York: Da Capo, 2002.

XI. IRAQ WAR

Braude, Joseph. *The New Iraq: Rebuilding the Country, Its People, the Middle East and the World.* New York: Basic Books, 2003.

Byman, Daniel, and Matthew Waxman. *Confronting Iraq: U.S. Policy and the Use of Force since the Gulf War.* Santa Monica, Calif.: Rand, 2000.

Cordesman, Anthony S., and Ahmed S. Hashim. *Iraq: Sanctions and Beyond.* Boulder, Colo.: Westview Press, 1997.

Fawn, Rick, and Raymond Hinnebusch, eds. *The Iraq War: Causes and Consequences.* Boulder, Colo.: Lynne Rienner, 2006.

Kaplan, Lawrence, and William Kristol. *The War over Iraq: Saddam's Tyranny and America's Mission.* San Francisco: Encounter Books, 2003.

Kegley, Charles W., and Gregory A. Raymond. *After Iraq: The Imperiled American Imperium.* New York: Oxford University Press, 2007.

Pauly, Robert J., and Tom Lansford. *Strategic Preemption: US Foreign Policy and the Second Iraq War.* Aldershot, England: Ashgate, 2004.

Pollack, Kenneth M. *The Threatening Storm: The Case for Invading Iraq.* New York: Random House, 2002.

Shawcross, William. *Allies: The U.S., Britain, Europe and the War in Iraq.* New York: Public Affairs, 2004.

Ullman, Harlan, and James Wade Jr. *Rapid Dominance, a Force for All Seasons: Technologies and Systems for Achieving Shock and Awe; A Real Revolution in Military Affairs.* London: Royal United Services Institute for Defence Studies, 1998.

Woodward, Bob. *Plan of Attack.* New York: Simon & Schuster, 2004.

XII. ARMS CONTROL AND DISARMAMENT

Dando, Malcolm. *The New Biological Weapons: Threat, Proliferation, and Control.* Boulder, Colo.: Lynne Rienner, 2001.

Glitman, Maynard W. *The Last Battle of the Cold War: An Inside Account of Negotiating the Intermediate Range Nuclear Forces Treaty.* New York: Palgrave Macmillan, 2006.

Graham, Thomas, Jr. *Common Sense on Weapons of Mass Destruction.* Seattle: University of Washington Press, 2004.

Lederberg, Joshua. *Biological Weapons: Limiting the Threat.* Cambridge, Mass.: MIT Press, 1999.

Levi, Michael A., and Michael O'Hanlon. *The Future of Arms Control.* Washington, D.C.: Brookings Institution Press, 2005.

Spiers, Edward M. *Chemical and Biological Weapons: A Study of Proliferation.* New York: St. Martin's, 1994.

XIII. BALLISTIC MISSILE DEFENSE

Burns, Richard Dean, and Lester H. Brune. *The Quest for Missile Defenses, 1944–2003.* Claremont, Calif.: Regina Books, 2003.
Carter, Ashton B., and David N. Schwartz, eds. *Ballistic Missile Defense.* Washington, D.C.: Brookings Institution, 1984.
Causewell, Erin, ed., *National Missile Defense: Issues and Developments.* New York: Nova Science, 2002.
Cordesman, Anthony H. *Strategic Threats and National Missile Defenses: Defending the US Homeland.* Westport, Conn.: Praeger, 2001.
Denoon, David B. H. *Ballistic Missile Defense in the Post–Cold War Era.* Boulder, Colo.: Westview Press, 2000.
Handberg, Roger. *Ballistic Missile Defense and the Future of American Security: Agendas, Perceptions, Technology, and Policy.* Westport, Conn.: Praeger, 2001.
Lindsey, James M., and Michael O'Hanlon. *Defending America: The Case for Limited National Missile Defense.* Washington, D.C.: Brookings Institution Press, 2002.

XIV. DEFENSE POLICY AND HOMELAND SECURITY

Caldicott, Helen. *The New Nuclear Danger: George W. Bush's Military-Industrial Complex.* New York: W. W. Norton, 2004.
Daadler, Ivo, ed. *Assessing the Department of Homeland Security.* Washington, D.C.: Brookings Institution Press, 2002.
Gaddis, John Lewis. *Surprise, Security and the American Experience.* Cambridge, Mass.: Harvard University Press, 2004.
Gyarmati, István, and Theodor Winkler, eds. *Post–Cold War Defense Reforms: Lessons Learned in Europe and the United States.* Washington, D.C.: Brassey's, 2002.
Hillyard, Michael. *Homeland Security and the Need for Change.* San Diego: Aventine Press, 2003.
Hulnick, Arthur S. *Keeping Us Safe: Secret Intelligence and Homeland Security.* Westport, Conn.: Praeger, 2004.

Kettl, Donald. *System under Stress: Homeland Security and American Politics.* Washington, D.C.: CQ Press, 2004.

O'Hanlan, Michael. *Defense Planning for the Late 1990s: Beyond the Desert Storm Framework.* Washington, D.C.: Brookings Institution Press, 1995.

O'Hanlon, Michael, Peter R. Orszag, Ivo H. Daalder, I.M. Destler, David L. Gunter, Robert E. Litan, and James B. Steinberg. *Protecting the American Homeland: A Preliminary Analysis.* Washington, D.C.: Brookings Institution, 2002.

Wrage, Stephen D., ed. *Immaculate Warfare: Participants Reflect on the Air Campaigns over Kosovo and Afghanistan.* Westport, Conn.: Praeger, 2003.

XV. ENVIRONMENTAL POLITICS AND POLICY

Anderson, Terry L., and Donald R. Leal. *Free Market Environmentalism.* Rev. ed. New York: Palgrave Macmillan, 2001.

Anderson, Terry L., and Henry I. Miller, eds. *The Greening of U.S. Foreign Policy.* Stanford, Calif.: Hoover Institution Press, 2000.

Caldwell, Lynton Keith. *International Environmental Policy: Emergence and Divergence.* Durham, N.C.: Duke University Press, 1996.

Harris, Paul G., ed. *International Environmental Cooperation: Politics and Diplomacy in Pacific Asia.* Boulder: University Press of Colorado, 2002.

Oberthur, Sebastian, and Herman E. Ott. *The Kyoto Protocol: International Climate Policy for the 21st Century.* New York: Spring, 1999.

Schreurs, Miranda A. *Environmental Politics in Japan, Germany and the United States.* New York: Cambridge University Press, 2002.

Soden, Dennis L., ed. *The Environmental Presidency.* Albany: State University of New York Press, 1999.

Victor, David G. *Climate Change: Debating America's Policy Options.* New York: Council on Foreign Relations, 2004.

XVI. GLOBALIZATION

Berger, Peter L., and Samuel P. Huntington, eds. *Many Globalizations: Cultural Diversity in the Contemporary World.* New York: Oxford University Press, 2002.

Friedman, Thomas. *The World Is Flat: A Brief History of the Twenty-First Century.* New York: Farrar, Straus and Giroux, 2005.

Fukuyama, Francis. *State-Building: Governance and World Order in the 21st Century.* Ithaca, N.Y.: Cornell University Press, 2004.

Holm, Hans-Henrik, and Georg Sorensen, eds. *Whose World Order? Uneven Globalization and the End of the Cold War.* Boulder, Colo.: Westview Press, 1995.

Latouche, Serge. *The Westernization of the World.* Cambridge, England: Polity, 1996.

Robertson, Roland. *Globalization.* London: Sage, 1992.

Smith, Tony. *America's Mission: The United States and the Worldwide Struggle for Democracy in the Twentieth Century.* Princeton, N.J.: Princeton University Press, 1994.

Stiglitz, Joseph. *Globalization and Its Discontents.* New York: Norton, 2003.

Tomlinson, John. *Globalization and Culture.* Cambridge, England: Polity, 1999.

Watson, James L., ed. *Golden Arches East: McDonald's in East Asia.* Stanford, Calif.: Stanford University Press, 1997.

XVII. TERRORISM

Burke, Jason. *Al-Qaeda: The True Story of Radical Islam.* New York: Penguin Books, 2004.

Caram, Peter. *The 1993 World Trade Center Bombing: Foresight and Warning.* London: Janus, 2002.

Fuller, Graham E., and Ian O. Lesser. *Sense of Siege: The Geopolitics of Islam and the West.* Boulder, Colo.: Westview Press, 1995.

Garfinkle, Adam, ed. *A Practical Guide to Winning the War on Terrorism.* Stanford, Calif.: Hoover Institution Press, 2004.

Hanson, Victor David. *An Autumn of War: What America Learned from September 11 and the War on Terrorism.* New York: Anchor Books, 2002.

Hayden, Patrick, Tom Lansford, and Robert Watson, eds. *America's War on Terror.* Aldershot, England: Ashgate, 2003.

Hoffman, Bruce. *Inside Terrorism.* New York: Columbia University Press, 1998.

Rashid, Ahmed. *Taliban: Militant Islam, Oil and Fundamentalism in Central Asia.* New Haven, Conn.: Yale University Press, 2000.

Reeve, Simon. *The New Jackals: Ramzi Yousef, Osama Bin Laden and the Future of Terrorism.* Boston: Northeastern University Press, 1999.

Wilkinson, P. *Terrorism versus Democracy: The Liberal State Response.* London: Frank Cass, 2001.

XVIII. TRADE POLICY

Ackerman, Bruce, and D. Golove. *Is NAFTA Constitutional?* Cambridge, Mass.: Harvard University Press, 1995.

Bhagwati, Jagdish N. *Free Trade Today.* Princeton, N.J.: Princeton University Press, 2002.

Cameron, Maxwell A., and Brian W. Tomlin. *The Making of NAFTA: How the Deal Was Done.* Ithaca, N.Y.: Cornell University Press, 2000.

Casanova, Manuel F., ed. *The U.S.-Singapore Free Trade Agreement.* New York: Novinka Books, 2005.

Cohen, Stephen D., Robert A. Blecker, and Peter D. Whitney. *Fundamentals of U.S. Foreign Trade Policy: Economics, Politics, Laws, and Issues.* Boulder, Colo.: Westview Press, 2003.

Gedman, Jeffery, ed. *European Integration and American Interests: What the New Europe Really Means for the United States.* Washington, D.C.: American Enterprise Institute, 1997.

Haass, Richard N. *Economic Sanctions and American Diplomacy.* New York: Council on Foreign Relations, 1998.

Kahler, Miles. *Regional Futures and Transatlantic Economic Relations.* New York: Council on Foreign Relations, 1995.

Lovett, William A., Alfred E. Eckes Jr., and Richard L. Brinkman. *U.S. Trade Policy: History, Theory, and the WTO.* Armonk, N.Y.: M. E. Sharpe, 2004.

McDougall, John N. *Drifting Together: The Political Economy of Canada-US Integration.* Orchard Park, N.Y.: Broadview Press, 2006.

Meyer, William H. *Security, Economics and Morality in American Foreign Policy: Contemporary Issues in Historical Context.* Upper Saddle River, N.J.: Prentice Hall, 2004.

XIX. UNITED STATES RELATIONS WITH AFRICA

Antal, James G., and R. John Vanden Berghe. *On Mamba Station: U.S. Marines in West Africa, 1990–2003.* Washington, D.C.: History and Museums Division, 2004.

De Villiers, Les. *In Sight of Surrender: The U.S. Sanctions Campaign against South Africa, 1946–1993.* Westport, Conn.: Praeger, 1995.

Forest, James J. F., and Matthew V. Sousa. *Oil and Terrorism in the New Gulf: U.S. Energy and Security Policies for the Gulf of Guinea.* Lanham, Md.: Lexington Books, 2006.

Haass, Richard N., ed. *Transatlantic Tensions: The United States, Europe, and Problem Countries.* Washington, D.C.: Brookings Institution Press, 1999.

Lyman, Princeton Nathan. *Partner to History: The U.S. Role in South Africa's Transition to Democracy.* Washington, D.C.: United States Institute for Peace Press, 2002.

Ohaegbulam, F. Ugboaja. *U.S. Policy in Postcolonial Africa: Four Case Studies in Conflict Resolution.* New York: Peter Lang, 2004.

Rotberg, Robert I., ed. *Battling Terrorism in the Horn of Africa.* Washington, D.C.: Brookings Institution Press, 2005.

Sandbrook, Richard. *Closing the Circle: Democratization and Development in Africa.* New York: St. Martin's, 2000.

Spikes, Daniel. *Angola and the Politics of Intervention.* Jefferson, N.C.: McFarland, 1993.

Woodward, Peter. *U.S. Foreign Policy and the Horn of Africa.* Aldershot, England: Ashgate, 2006.

XX. UNITED STATES RELATIONS WITH ASIA

Cha, Victor. *Alignment Despite Antagonism: The United States-Korea-Japan Security Triangle.* Stanford, Calif.: Stanford University Press, 1999.

Gries, Peter Hays. *China's New Nationalism: Pride, Politics, and Diplomacy.* Berkeley: University of California Press, 2004.

Ikenberry, G. John, and Takashi Inoguchi, eds. *Reinventing the Alliance: U.S.-Japan Security Partnership in an Era of Change.* New York: Palgrave, 2003.

Kim, Tae-hyo, and Brad Glosserman, eds. *The Future of U.S.-Korea-Japan Relations: Balancing Values and Interests.* Washington, D.C.: Center for Strategic and International Studies, 2004.

Kirby, William C., Robert S. Ross, and Gong Li, eds. *Normalization of U.S.-China Relations: An International History.* Cambridge, Mass.: Harvard University Press, 2005.

Lincoln, Edward. *East Asian Economic Regionalism.* Washington, D.C.: Brookings Institution Press, 2004.

Mann, James. *About Face; A History of America's Curious Relationship with China from Nixon to Clinton.* New York: Random House, 1999.

Ravenhill, John. *APEC and the Construction of Pacific Rim Regionalism.* New York: Cambridge University Press, 2001.

Ross, Robert S., ed. *After the Cold War: Domestic Factors and U.S.-China Relations.* Armonk, N.Y.: M. E. Sharpe, 1998.

Sarantakes, Nicholas Evan. *Keystone: The American Occupation of Okinawa and U.S.-Japanese Relations.* College Station: Texas A&M University Press, 2000.

Selden, Mark, and Alvin Y. So, eds. *War and State Terrorism: The United States, Japan, and the Asia-Pacific in the Long Twentieth Century.* Lanham, Md.: Rowman & Littlefield, 2004.

XXI. UNITED STATES RELATIONS WITH EUROPE

Baylis, John. *Anglo-American Relations since 1939: The Enduring Alliance.* New York: St. Martin's, 1997.

Bluth, Christoph, Emil Kirchner, and James Sperling, eds. *The Future of European Security.* Aldershot, England: Dartmouth, 1995.

Brenner, Michael, ed. *Multilateralism and Western Security.* New York: St. Martin's, 1995.

Bronstone, Adam. *European Union–United States Security Relations: Transatlantic Tensions and the Theory of International Relations.* New York: St. Martin's Press, 1997.

Drumbell, John. *A Special Relationship: Anglo-American Relations in the Cold War and Beyond.* London: Palgrave, 2000.

Goodby, James. *Europe Undivided: The New Logic of Peace in U.S.-Russian Relations.* Washington, D.C.: United States Institute of Peace Press, 1998.

Gordon, Philip H. *A Certain Idea of France.* New York: St. Martin's, 1993.

Grapin, Jacqueline, ed. *Europe and the US: Partners in Defense.* Washington, D.C.: European Institute, 1998.

Haftendorn, Helga, and Christian Tuschhoff, eds. *America and Europe in an Era of Change.* Boulder, Colo.: Westview Press, 1993.

Heuser, Beatrice. *Transatlantic Relations: Sharing Ideals and Costs.* London: Royal Institute of International Affairs, 1996.

Holmes, John W., ed. *Maelstrom: The United States, Southern Europe and the Challenges of the Mediterranean.* Cambridge, England: World Peace Foundation, 1995.

Kagan, Robert. *Of Paradise and Power: America and Europe in the New World Order.* New York: Alfred A. Knopf, 2003.

LeFeber, Walter. *America, Russia and the Cold War.* New York: McGraw-Hill, 1997.

Serfaty, Simon. *Stay the Course: European Unity and Atlantic Solidarity.* Washington, D.C.: Center for Strategic and International Studies, 1997.

Smith, Michael, and Stephen Woolcock. *Redefining the U.S.-EC Relationship.* New York: Council on Foreign Affairs, 1993.

Treverton, Gregory. *America, Germany and the Future of Europe.* Princeton, N.J.: Princeton University Press, 1992.

XXII. UNITED STATES RELATIONS WITH LATIN AMERICA

Brewer, Stewart. *Borders and Bridges: A History of U.S.-Latin American relations.* Westport, Conn.: Praeger, 2006.

De la Garza, Rodolfo O., and Harry P. Pachon, eds. *Latinos and U.S. Foreign Policy: Representing the "Homeland"?* Lanham, Md.: Rowman & Littlefield, 2000.

Grandin, Greg. *Empire's Workshop: Latin America, the United States and the Rise of the New Imperialism.* New York: Metropolitan Books, 2006.

McPherson, Alan, ed. *Anti-Americanism in Latin America and the Caribbean.* New York: Berghahn Books, 2006.

Menjivar, Cecilia, and Nestor Rodrigua, eds. *When States Kill: Latin America, the U.S., and Technologies of Terror.* Austin: University of Texas Press, 2005.

Payan, Tony. *The Three U.S.-Mexico Border Wars: Drugs, Immigration and Homeland Security.* Westport, Conn.: Praeger, 2006.

Schoonmaker, Sara. *High-Tech Trade Wars: U.S. Brazilian Conflicts in the Global Economy.* Pittsburgh, Penn.: University of Pittsburgh Press, 2002.

Sikkink, Kathryn. *Mixed Signals: U.S. Human Rights Policy and Latin America.* Ithaca, N.Y.: Cornell University Press, 2004.

Wiarda, Howard J., with Esther M. Skelley. *Dilemmas of Democracy in Latin America: Crises and Opportunities.* Lanham, Md.: Rowman & Littlefield, 2005.

Youngers, Coletta A., and Eileen Rosin, eds. *Drugs and Democracy in Latin America: The Impact of U.S. Policy.* Boulder, Colo.: Lynne Rienner, 2005.

XXIII. UNITED STATES RELATIONS WITH THE MIDDLE EAST

Cordesman, Anthony S., and Ahmed S. Hashim. *Iran: Dilemmas of Dual Containment.* Boulder, Colo.: Westview, 1997.

Daalder, Ivo, Nicole Gnesotto, and Philip Gordon, eds. *Crescent of Crisis: U.S.-European Strategy for the Greater Middle East.* Washington, D.C.: Brookings Institution Press, 2006.

Friedman, Robert O., ed. *The Middle East Enters the Twenty-First Century.* Gainesville: University Press of Florida, 2002.

Fuller, Graham, and Ian Lesser. *A Sense of Siege: The Geopolitics of Islam and the West.* Boulder, Colo.: Westview Press, 1995.

Hadar, Leon. *Sandstorm: Policy Failure in the Middle East.* New York: Palgrave Macmillan, 2005.

Kemp, Geoffrey, and Robert E. Harkavy. *Strategic Geography and the Changing Middle East.* Washington, D.C.: Brookings Institution Press, 1997.

Little, Douglas. *American Orientalism: The United States and the Middle East since 1945.* Chapel Hill: University of North Carolina Press, 2002.

Miglietta, John. *American Alliance Policy in the Middle East, 1945–1992: Iran, Israel, and Saudi Arabia.* Lanham, Md.: Lexington Books, 2002.

Rabil, Robert G. *Syria, the United States, and the War on Terror in the Middle East.* Westport, Conn.: Praeger, 2006.

Rubin, Barry. *The Long War for Freedom: The Arab Struggle for Democracy in the Middle East.* Hoboken, N.J.: John Wiley, 2006.

Rugh, William A. *American Encounters with Arabs: The "Soft Power" of U.S. Public Diplomacy in the Middle East.* Westport, Conn.: Praeger, 2006.

Sick, Gary S., and Lawrence G. Potter, eds. *The Persian Gulf at the Millennium: Essays in Politics, Economy, Security, and Religion.* New York: St. Martin's, 1997.

Yetiv, Steve. *America and the Persian Gulf: The Third Party Dimension in World Politics.* Westport, Conn.: Praeger, 1995.

XXIV. NORTH ATLANTIC TREATY ORGANIZATION (NATO)

Barry, Charles. *Transforming NATO Command and Control for Future Missions.* Washington, D.C.: National Defense University, 2003.

Carpenter, Ted Galen, and Barbara Conroy, eds. *NATO Enlargement: Illusions and Reality.* Washington, D.C.: CATO Institute, 1998.

Duffield, John S. *Power Rules: The Evolution of NATO's Conventional Force Posture.* Stanford, Calif.: Stanford University, 1995.

Gardner, Hal. *Dangerous Crossroads: Europe, Russia, and the Future of NATO.* Westport, Conn.: Greenwood, 1997.

Grapin, Jacqueline, ed. *Europe and the US: Partners in Defense.* Washington, D.C.: European Institute, 1998.

Kaplan, Lawrence. *NATO Divided, NATO United: The Evolution of an Alliance.* Westport, Conn.: Praeger, 2004.

Lansford, Tom. *All for One: NATO, Terrorism and the United States.* Aldershot, England: Ashgate, 2002.

Lesser, Ian O. *NATO Looks South: New Challenges and New Strategies in the Mediterranean.* Santa Monica, Calif.: Rand, 2000.

Lieven, Anatol, and Dmitri Trenin, eds. *Ambivalent Neighbors: The EU, NATO and the Price of Membership.* Washington, D.C.: Carnegie Endowment for International Peace, 2003.

Moens, Alexander, Lenard J. Cohen, and Allen Gregory Sens, eds. *NATO and European Security: Alliance Politics from the End of the Cold War to the Age of Terrorism.* Westport, Conn.: Praeger, 2003.

Van Heuvan, Marten H. A. *Russia, the United States, and NATO: The Outlook for European Security*. Atlantic Council Occasional Papers. Washington, D.C.: Atlantic Council, 1994.

XXV. UNITED NATIONS

Aksu, Esref, and Joseph A. Camilleri, eds. *Democratizing Global Governance*. New York: Palgrave Macmillan, 2002.

Blum, Yehuda Z. *Eroding the United Nations Charter*. Boston: Marcus Nijhoff, 1993.

Childers, Erskine, ed. *Challenges to the United Nations: Building a Safer World*. New York: St. Martin's, 1995.

Foot, Rosemary, S. Neil MacFarlane, and Michael Mastanduno, eds. *U.S. Hegemony and International Organizations: The United States and Multilateral Institutions*. New York: Oxford University Press, 2003.

Kennedy, Paul. *The Parliament of Man: The Past, Present, and Future of the United Nations*. New York: Random House, 2006.

Smith, Courtney B. *Politics and Process at the United Nations: The Global Dance*. Boulder, Colo.: Lynne Rienner, 2006.

Sutterlin, James S. *The United Nations and the Maintenance of International Security: A Challenge to Be Met*. 2nd ed. Westport, Conn: Praeger, 2003.

XXVI. BIBLIOGRAPHIES, ENCYCLOPEDIAS, AND HISTORICAL DICTIONARIES

Adamec, Ludwig W. *Historical Dictionary of Afghan Wars, Revolutions and Insurgencies*. Lanham, Md.: Scarecrow Press, 2005.

Anderson, Sean K., and Stephan Sloan. *Historical Dictionary of Terrorism*. Lanham, Md.: Scarecrow Press, 2007.

Beisner, Robert L., ed. *American Foreign Relations since 1600: A Guide to the Literature*. 2 vols. Santa Barbara, Calif.: ABC-CLIO, 2003.

DeConde, Alexander, Richard Dean Burns, and Fredrik Logevall, eds. *Encyclopedia of American Foreign Policy*. 2nd ed. New York: Charles Scribner's Sons, 2002.

Fomerand, Jacques. *Historical Dictionary of the United Nations*. Lanham, Md.: Scarecrow Press, 2007.

Garrett, Benjamin C., and John Hart. *Historical Dictionary of Nuclear, Biological and Chemical Weapons*. Lanham, Md.: Scarecrow Press, 2007.

Hahn, Peter L. *Historical Dictionary of United States–Middle East Relations.* Lanham, Md.: Scarecrow Press, 2007.

Jentleson, Bruce W., and Thomas G. Patterson, eds. *Encyclopedia of U.S. Foreign Relations.* 5 vols. New York: Oxford University Press, 1997.

Kahana, Ephraim. *Historical Dictionary of Israeli Intelligence.* Lanham, Md.: Scarecrow Press, 2006.

Kumaraswamy, P. R. *Historical Dictionary of the Arab-Israeli Conflict.* Lanham, Md.: Scarecrow Press, 2006.

Larsen, Jeffrey A., and James M. Smith. *Historical Dictionary of Arms Control and Disarmament.* Lanham, Md.: Scarecrow Press, 2005.

Mays, Terry M. *Historical Dictionary of Multinational Peacekeeping.* Lanham, Md.: Scarecrow Press, 2003.

Pringle, Robert W. *Historical Dictionary of Russian and Soviet Intelligence.* Lanham, Md.: Scarecrow Press, 2006.

Scott, Frances. *U.S. Intervention Policy in the Post–Cold War World.* Colorado Springs, Colo.: United States Air Force Academy, 1994.

Smith, Joseph. *Historical Dictionary of United States–Latin American Relations.* Lanham, Md.: Scarecrow Press, 2006.

Sutter, Robert. *Historical Dictionary of United States–China Relations.* Lanham, Md.: Scarecrow Press, 2005.

Turner, Michael A. *Historical Dictionary of United States Intelligence.* Lanham, Md.: Scarecrow Press, 2005.

Van Sant, John, Peter Mauch, and Yoneyuki Sugita. *Historical Dictionary of United States–Japan Relations.* Lanham, Md.: Scarecrow Press, 2007.

West, Nigel. *Historical Dictionary of British Intelligence.* Lanham, Md.: Scarecrow Press, 2005.

About the Author

Tom Lansford is assistant dean of the College of Arts and Letters and associate professor of political science at the University of Southern Mississippi. He is a member of the governing board of the National Social Science Association, an associate editor for the journal *White House Studies*, and an associate editor for *Politics and Ethics Review*. He has published articles in journals such as *Defense Analysis*, the *Journal of Conflict Studies*, *European Security*, *International Studies*, *Security Dialogue*, and *Strategic Studies*. Lansford is the author or coauthor of a number of books, including *The Lords of Foggy Bottom: The American Secretaries of State and the World They Shaped* (2001), *All for One: NATO, Terrorism, and the United States* (2002), *A Bitter Harvest: U.S. Foreign Policy and Afghanistan* (2003), and *Strategic Preemption: U.S. Foreign Policy and the Second War in Iraq* (2004). He is also coeditor of several collections, including *America's War on Terror* (2003), *George W. Bush: A Political and Ethical Assessment at Midterm* (2004), and *Transatlantic Security Dilemmas: Old Europe, New Europe and the U.S.* (2005). He is the author of more than a hundred encyclopedic entries, book chapters, and short essays.